Sex for Life

INTERSECTIONS
Transdisciplinary Perspectives on Genders and Sexualities
General Editors: Michael Kimmel and Suzanna Walters

Sperm Counts: Overcome by Man's Most Precious Fluid
Lisa Jean Moore

The Sexuality of Migration:
Border Crossings and Mexican Immigrant Men
Lionel Cantú, Jr.
Edited by Nancy A. Naples and Salvador Vidal-Ortiz

Moral Panics, Sex Panics:
Fear and the Fight over Sexual Rights
Edited by Gilbert Herdt

Out in the Country:
Youth, Media, and Queer Visibility in Rural America
Mary L. Gray

Sapphistries: A Global History of Love between Women
Leila J. Rupp

Strip Club: Gender, Power, and Sex Work
Kim Price-Glynn

Sex for Life:
From Virginity to Viagra, How Sexuality Changes Throughout Our Lives
Edited by Laura M. Carpenter and John DeLamater

Sex for Life

From Virginity to Viagra, How Sexuality Changes Throughout Our Lives

EDITED BY

Laura M. Carpenter and John DeLamater

NEW YORK UNIVERSITY PRESS
New York and London

NEW YORK UNIVERSITY PRESS
New York and London
www.nyupress.org

References to Internet websites (URLs) were accurate at the time of writing.
Neither the editors nor New York University Press is responsible for URLs
that may have expired or changed since the manuscript was prepared.

Library of Congress Cataloging-in-Publication Data

Sex for life : from virginity to Viagra, how sexuality changes throughout
our lives / edited by Laura M. Carpenter and John DeLamater.
p. cm.
Includes bibliographical references and index.
ISBN 978-0-8147-7252-2 (cloth : alk. paper)
ISBN 978-0-8147-7253-9 (pbk. : alk. paper)
ISBN 978-0-8147-2381-4 (ebook)
ISBN 978-0-8147-2382-1 (ebook)
1. Sex. 2. Sex customs. 3. Sexual health. 4. Sex (Psychology)
I. Carpenter, Laura M. II. DeLamater, John D.
HQ12.S422   2011
306.7—dc23   2011044700

New York University Press books are printed on acid-free paper,
and their binding materials are chosen for strength and durability.
We strive to use environmentally responsible suppliers and materials
to the greatest extent possible in publishing our books.

Manufactured in the United States of America
c   10 9 8 7 6 5 4 3 2 1
p   10 9 8 7 6 5 4 3 2 1

Contents

PART VI. Conclusion

Acknowledgments

No book would ever come to fruition without the hard work and vision of many individuals, and this is especially true of edited volumes. We, the editors, would first and foremost like to thank the 19 accomplished scholars who contributed their original research to this volume. Quite simply, this book would not exist without them. Nor would it exist without the work of the women and men whose theories and empirical inquiries launched and developed the study of sexualities over the life course; many of them are named in the introduction.

Thanks also go to the scholars who participated in our panel on "Sexuality over the Life Course" at the 2007 annual meeting of the American Sociological Association but who were not able to contribute to this volume: Elisabeth P. Burgess, Denise Donnelly, Gloria Gonzáles-López, and Patricia Koch. Adina Nack, Koji Ueno, Paisley Currah, and Ritch Savin-Williams kindly alerted us to the outstanding work of other scholars in the field.

At New York University Press, we have been lucky to have Executive Editor Ilene Kalish and Editorial Assistant Aiden Amos assisting us every step of the way. The "Intersections" series editors Michael Kimmel and Suzanna Walters have also lent their support to this ambitious project. Thanks, too, to Nicolette Pawlowski at the University of Wisconsin-Madison, without whom there would be no bibliography.

Laura would additionally like to thank Constance A. Nathanson, Young J. Kim, and Emily Agree, who sparked and nourished Laura's interest in aging and the life course. Laura is deeply grateful for comments and advice from Elizabeth A. Armstrong, Dana Britton, Karen Campbell, Monica J. Casper, Diane diMauro, Judith Lorber, Amanda Nothaft, Richard Pitt, Jennifer Reich, and seminar participants at the University of Wisconsin-Madison, Columbia University Mailman School of Public Health, and Emory University. The Social Science Research Council Sexuality Research Fellowship Program and the National Institute of Aging generously funded Laura's postdoctoral fellowships. Finally, Laura is grateful for the wisdom, support, and love of her friends and family, especially Jason Philip Miller, who knows more than a little about writing, editing, and life course transitions.

John would like to thank Janet Hyde and the numerous graduate and undergraduate students who coauthored papers on the impact of various life course transitions on sexuality over the past 15 years. He has benefited greatly from comments by participants in the Social Psychology and Microsociology and Interdisciplinary Sexuality Seminars. John also thanks the American Association of Retired Persons for sharing with him the data that provided the empirical foundation for several of his publications in this area.

Studying Sexualities over the Life Course

Introduction

Sexualities over the Life Course:
The Development of a Perspective

JOHN DELAMATER AND LAURA M. CARPENTER

How do sexual and social experiences—childhood sex play, immigration, or divorce, for example—at one point in a person's life affect his or her sexual beliefs and behaviors later on? How are individuals' sexual biographies shaped by broader cultural and historical changes, such as the sexual "revolution" of the late 1960s and the early 1970s or the increasing availability of same-sex marriage? In what ways do intersections among gender, race, ethnicity, social class, and sexual orientation influence these life course processes, even as life course processes influence those intersecting social statuses in turn? We explore these questions in this book.

Introduction

As a relatively new area of inquiry, the study of human sexuality from a life course perspective is rapidly coming into its own. This burgeoning field began in earnest in 1994, with the publication of Alice Rossi's highly regarded edited volume, *Sexuality across the Life Course* (University of Chicago Press). Since then, scholars of sexuality have greatly expanded the range of topics they study as well as the theoretical approaches they deploy. Although the sexual scripting approach remains ascendant, other perspectives—from biopsychosocial models to Foucauldian genealogies to Bourdieuian fields approaches[1]—are increasingly employed. Life course theory and research have evolved as well, with researchers increasingly replacing models of linear progress—for instance, from education to work to retirement—with perspectives positing multiple and overlapping trajectories, such as work, health, and sexuality, that extend from birth to death. In addition to these theoretical and substantive developments, the past 15 years have seen a dramatic increase in the number of scholars interested in sexuality and the life course (evidenced, for example, by the growth of American Sociological Association interest sections in these areas).

The reader may wonder why we require another perspective in the study of sexuality. We have already noted one reason: the need for serious exploration of how events at one stage in life affect sexual attitudes, behavior, and relationships at other, later stages. Until recently, theory, research, and public policy discussions on sexual topics have tended to focus on childhood (e.g., childhood sexual play, child sexual abuse) or adolescence (e.g., first coitus, teen pregnancy) or young adulthood (e.g., "hooking up," transitions into committed relationships) or adulthood (e.g., marital and extramarital sexuality, aging among sexual minorities). With some reflection, however, one realizes that what happens in adulthood is not unrelated to what took place in adolescence or even childhood. If the reader considers his or her own sexual biography, the importance of such early events will probably be clear. Furthermore, discussions of adult and later-life sexuality often imply a linear, static sexual lifestyle, whether asexual, heterosexual, gay, or lesbian. But consequential events— turning points—such as meeting a new partner, dissolving a relationship, or contracting a serious illness can happen to anyone at any time.

Another contribution to be made by this perspective involves the recognition that sexuality cannot be reduced to just biological (anatomy, sexual functioning), psychological (sexual desire, emotions), social (intimate relationships, immediate social context), or cultural (sexual scripts, religious and moral beliefs) forces. Any expression of sexuality is likely to be influenced by factors within each of these disciplinary "silos." Thus, the life course perspective has encouraged the development of transdisciplinary perspectives, incorporating biological, psychological, social, and cultural dimensions; these are often referred to as biopsychosocial models.

An Example: Menopause

Consider an example of the contributions that a biopsychosocial, life course perspective can make toward understanding an important phenomenon that affects women's (and their partners') sexuality and sexual functioning: menopause.

A substantial literature examines the changes associated with menopause in women. Until recently, research in this area was dominated by a medical perspective. A variety of experiences are associated with the cessation of menstruation, including irregular menstrual periods (until they cease), hot flashes, reduced energy or fatigue, stiff or sore muscles, irritability, negative mood, and short- or long-term depression (Dennerstein, Dudley, & Burger, 2001; Lock, 1993). Several changes involve sexuality, through direct and indirect mechanisms: vaginal dryness, vaginal atrophy (shrinkage), dyspareunia (painful intercourse), loss of sexual desire, and declining frequency of intercourse (DeLamater & Sill, 2005).

Medical researchers view all of these phenomena as *symptoms* that can be attributed to the hormonal changes that occur in a woman's body or to consequences of those changes. Research in the 1960s identified a slow decline in the level of estrogen circulating in the body as characteristic of the *climacteric*—the ovaries stop releasing eggs and menstruation gradually ceases (Kingsberg, 2002). The "obvious" treatment for this gradual change, when it is viewed as problematic, is estrogen replacement therapy. Widely used, the treatment reduces the menopausal "symptoms," as well as osteoporosis and the risk of heart disease; but it also elevates the risk of breast and uterine cancer (Lund, 2008). Hormone replacement treatment therapy has been refined in an effort to reduce these risks, yet it remains controversial.

The life course perspective gives us another lens through which we can view menopause, situating the changes associated with it in a specific phase of life and with characteristics associated with that stage. The average age of menopause in the United States is between 51 and 52, with a range from 44 to 55 years of age (Lund, 2008). Think about the psychological, social, and health-related phenomena that women experience during these years.

First, let's examine *psychological phenomena*, including attitudes toward menopause, reproduction, and aging. Attitudes toward menopause are often negative. In part, this reflects the nature of the symptoms that many women experience, including both physical (hot flashes, night sweats) and psychological (depression, irritability). This pejorative view is reinforced by the "discourse of decline" that characterizes the traditional medical literature on menopause (Tomlinson, 1999). Both the occurrence of specific menopause symptoms and attitudes toward and interpretations of those symptoms as positive or negative vary by culture (Robinson, 1996). The experience of menopause is also related to attitudes toward and interest in sex (Avis et al., 2000). Analyses of data from the Massachusetts Women's Health Study found that peri- and postmenopausal women were more likely than premenopausal women to agree that growing older is related to a loss of interest in sex, and to report a decline in sexual interest since age 40.

Cessation of menstruation signals the end of the ability to have children and thus interacts with attitudes toward reproduction. Many women with male partners report relief and pleasure at no longer having to worry about birth control (Winterich, 2003). Others experience the end of their reproductive years as a serious loss. Insofar as U.S. society is pronatalist—that is, valuing reproduction highly and expecting heterosexual couples to have children—a woman who has defined herself partly in terms of motherhood may find this loss upsetting or depressing. Some postmenopausal women report a cessation of sexual activity (Thirlaway, Fallowfield, & Cuzick, 1996). When individual women (and men) cease sexual activity on the grounds that it can no longer result in reproduction, that cessation is not a consequence of hormonal changes, it is a consequence of cultural beliefs. Attitudes about reproduction depend, of course, on chronological age and birth cohort—the period of time in which one was born—and on whether a woman has had as many children as she wishes to.

Youth is highly valued in U.S. society, especially among women, and aging is not revered, in contrast to how it is viewed in some other cultures (Calasanti & Slevin, 2001; Gullette, 2004). Given these attitudes, the mere fact of aging can be depressing; depression, in turn, is associated with loss of interest in sexual activity (DeLamater & Karraker, 2009). A woman who perceives menopause as a sign of aging may fear she is no longer sexually attractive to her partner (Trudel, Turgeon, & Piché, 2000); in fact, some (but not all) partners may concur (Barbre, 1993; Winterich, 2003).

In these ways, some of the unpleasant physical and psychological experiences associated with midlife may stem from cultural values and related individual attitudes. So, too, may declining interest in and frequency of partnered sexual activity.

Social phenomena also affect how menopause is experienced. During midlife, many people experience changes in their roles as spouses or partners. In many marriages, longevity of the relationship is associated with declining marital (as well as sexual) satisfaction (VanLaningham, Johnson, & Amato, 2001). Individuals in intimate relationships typically find their partners less sexually attractive over time, whether due to "habituation"— that is, becoming increasingly accustomed to one another (Call, Sprecher, & Schwartz, 1995)—or because the partner changes physically (e.g., gets wrinkles or gains weight). Consequently, sexual activity may become less exciting and less gratifying. On the other hand, longer relationships also enable partners to learn better how to bring one another sexual pleasure (Liu, 2003).

Changes in parental status often occur at about the same time as menopause. Many women experience the "loss" of their role as an active, everyday parent during midlife; this is sometimes called "empty nest syndrome." Between 1960 and 1980, men and women married, on average, at ages 22 or

23 and 20 or 21, respectively, and they had two or three children by the time they were 35 (Fields, 2003). These parents' children reached the age of 18 and left home when the parents were 42 to 55. Losing the parental role can have important consequences, including depression and associated physical and psychological symptoms. Research with Mexican women found that the principal correlate of reports of severe "empty nest syndrome" was negative attitudes toward sexuality (Huerta, Mena, Malacara, & Diaz de Leon, 1995).

Health-related phenomena, such as the effects of medications and illness, represent additional influences on menopause. As people age, they use an increasing number of medications to combat illness and to counter other physical changes. A wide variety of medications may affect sexual desire, especially antidepressants and drugs intended to lower the heart rate or blood pressure (DeLamater & Sill, 2005). Various illnesses also affect sexual functioning. Cardiovascular conditions, diabetes, and cancer—just to name a few—all have major impacts on sexual functioning (Genazzani, Gambacciani, & Simoncini, 2007). In the case of cancer, for example, the woman undergoing chemotherapy or radiation therapy may experience a loss of sexual interest or desire, vaginal atrophy, and increased sexual anxiety (Park et al., 2007). Cancers of the male and female reproductive organs may negatively impact self-image and lead people—or their partners—to perceive themselves as no longer sexual.

The psychological, social, and health-related experiences that occur alongside menopause during the midlife years must further be viewed in the context of women's personal sexual histories; social, cultural, and geographical locations; and broader historical trends. The life course perspective understands people's sexual histories as cumulative in nature. Accordingly, a woman who had enjoyed a series of satisfying sexual relationships in her twenties and thirties, gaining physical and emotional sustenance and learning new techniques along the way, might well approach menopause quite differently—using creative means to ensure that she continues to experience her customary level of pleasure, for instance—than a woman who had moved from one disappointing (or worse) relationship to another during the same phase of life.

One must also bear in mind that experiences of, and responses to, menopause vary from culture to culture and place to place. In Japan, for example, the chief symptoms of menopause are stiff shoulders and irritability, while the hot flashes typical in North American women are rare—differences that cannot be reduced merely to dietary patterns or biomedical regimes (Lock, 1993). Even within the United States, women's responses to menopause differ significantly by racial/ethnic background and social class (Martin, 1987). These differences may affect sexuality in both direct and indirect ways.

Finally, although the physiological aspects of menopause are relatively unchanging, North Americans have approached it in distinctive ways at different historical junctures. Concern that menopause compromises, or destroys, women's femininity is far less intense today than it was in the 1950s, for example, thanks largely to the feminist and women's health movements (Lorber & Moore, 2002). However, as an increasing number of women "delay" childbearing and thus have children "late" in life, or not at all, more women will reach menopause without having as many children as they had hoped to, likely intensifying negative feelings, and fewer will experience the "empty nest" and menopause simultaneously.

In short, if we want a complete understanding of the changes that occur at midlife in a population of human beings, we need to consider social, cultural, historical, psychological, and physiological factors. In this sense, *changes at midlife present a puzzle.* Any specific change—at the individual or group level—may be caused by a variety of factors, and almost certainly by two or more factors working in concert. A transdisciplinary or biopsychosocial perspective sensitizes us to this multiplicity of potential influences.

Much of the literature on midlife sexuality has focused on women, in part because of the visibility of the cessation of menstruation. But we should also consider midlife changes in men. Life course scholarship has drawn attention to the distinctive pathways women and men typically follow through work and family life, given their different gender socialization and the cumulative opportunities and constraints that socialization brings about (Moen, 1996; O'Rand, 2003). Perhaps even more important, but less often explored, is the extent to which people's gender identities (i.e., the way they "do" gender) also evolve over the life course (see chapter 1). These general insights can be fruitfully applied to sexuality.

The one aspect of male aging that has been extensively researched is sexual functioning. Studies have shown that males are increasingly likely to experience problems in sexual functioning, particularly erectile disorders, as they age (Lindau et al., 2007). As they grow older, men experience a gradual lengthening of the time necessary to achieve an erection, some decline in the rigidity of the erect penis, and an increase in the time it takes to experience a second erection (Araujo, Mohr, & McKinlay, 2004). As with menopause in women, these processes have usually been viewed from a medical perspective. Physicians point to a decline in cardiovascular functioning with age, which slows the rate at which the penis becomes engorged with blood, the process that produces an erection. The "obvious" contemporary treatment for this "problem" is Viagra; hundreds of millions of prescriptions have been written since its introduction in 1998 (Loe, 2004; Salonia et al., 2003). Viagra is a PDE-5 inhibitor; it affects the functioning of the muscles in the penis, which in turn influences speed and quality of erection. In random controlled trials, about 50% of the men taking Viagra experienced an increase in the proportion of successful attempts at vaginal intercourse (Tharyan & Gopoalakrishanan, 2009). Again, a life course perspective broadens our view. The factors that influence women at midlife also influence men: attitudes about sex, reproduction, and aging; changes in social roles; changes in health; aspects of personal sexual history; and location in place and time.

Major Developments in the Perspective

Any recapitulation of major theoretical and empirical contributions to the life course perspective here must remain, of necessity, incomplete. Here, we briefly discuss some of the developments that we believe have shaped the life course perspective, and we review associated transdisciplinary models for studying sexuality.

Sociological Roots

Arguably the first major empirical analysis using the life course framework was Glen Elder, Jr.'s *Children of the Great Depression*, published in 1974. A longitudinal study of two birth cohorts of children, born in 1920–1921 and in 1928–1929, the book reveals the very different ways in which these children experienced the Great Depression. The former cohort were teens in the 1930s and typically gained a strong sense of independence from helping their families survive (even as their educations were cut short), whereas the latter cohort were children during those years and found it harder to achieve financial and emotional stability as they aged. Elder outlines the immediate effects of economic deprivation on children, parents/adults, and family relationships and then analyzes how these early experiences influenced the adult lives of the children in the earlier and later cohorts. His analysis considers especially deprivation's effects on gender relations in adulthood, patterns of vocational and occupational achievement, and health. His emphasis on the historical contingency of age-related patterns called into question the regularities and continuities in development, social relationships, and behavior that many psychologists and sociologists had previously documented.

In the decades since *Children of the Great Depression*, Elder has continued to contribute to the development of the perspective. In addition to numerous empirical publications, the collection he edited with Janet Giele, *Methods of Life Course Research: Qualitative and Quantitative Approaches* (Giele & Elder, 1998), provided an important codification of the methods then employed. *The Craft of Life Course Research* (Elder & Giele, 2009), a new edited volume, showcases contemporary methods.

The Scripting Approach

The roots of our perspective also can be found in the sexual scripting approach (Gagnon & Simon, 1973). A central component of the analytic framework presented in chapter 1, the scripting approach contributed three key assumptions to the study of sexuality. First, it asserts that all partnered sexual behavior occurs in and is influenced by social interaction, especially the relationship between the partners. Thus, it posits immediate social context as an important influence, in contrast to biological and evolutionary models that emphasize genetics and selection as the signal determinants of behavior. Since most partnered behavior involves two people, this leads to a couple-centered approach. Second, the scripting approach asserts that the scripts that influence people are in turn influenced by prior experience. This insight is one of the bases for our focus on how prior experience influences present behavior. Third, the scripting approach calls attention to the relevance of cultural scenarios, that is, the notions and ideals that circulate in the larger social and historical context. For example, in the mid- to late twentieth century in the United States, many men's and women's ideas about and behavior in romantic and sexual relationships revolved around the romantic-love ideal (Lantz, Keyes, & Schultz, 1975), even as recreational scenarios became increasingly destigmatized.

Sexuality across the Life Course

Nearly 20 years had passed after Elder's landmark study before scholars began to train a life course lens on sexuality. *Sexuality across the Life Course*, edited by the sociologist Alice S. Rossi, was published in 1994. This groundbreaking volume came about through the efforts of a number of MacArthur Foundation-funded life course scholars who decided to collect their sexuality-related research in an edited book.

The Rossi volume made important theoretical and empirical contributions. First, it brought together a collection of papers indicating the breadth of then-contemporary scholarship that was influenced by this emerging perspective. The papers covered a range of sexual life stages and relevant events. Topics included specific phases of the life course (adolescence, midlife, old age) and "selected health issues" (effects of chronic disease, sexual problems, offending and victimization) as well as "sexual diversity," represented by separate chapters on Black men, Black women, and homosexuality. In so doing, the book drew attention to sexuality as a legitimate and important topic for life course scholars and signaled potential contributions of the perspective to understanding sexual expression. Second, the book's chapters illustrated the broad range of methodologies, including both quantitative (survey) and qualitative (intensive interviews and focused group discussions), that could be used in research on sexuality. Third, it was one of the first publications to articulate an interdisciplinary biopsychosocial model for thinking about influences on sexuality across a person's life. Several chapters reflected aspects of the model, providing guidelines for subsequent researchers.

Although enormously influential, *Sexuality across the Life Course* is dated in several ways. First, the empirical studies it contains draw on data that are now over 17 years old. Second, theoretical and substantive work on sexualities and on the life course has undergone major changes since 1994. Using the word "sexualities" at numerous junctures in this book, thereby underscoring the diversity of possible beliefs, behaviors, and identities under consideration, is one of the ways we highlight new directions in the field. Third, Rossi's collection was written at a time when most scholars were only beginning to recognize that social statuses like gender, race, ethnicity, and social class have intersecting, rather than additive, effects (Collins, 1990). Thus, where Rossi's volume examines race, gender, and sexual identity in separate chapters, complex analyses of social location are incorporated in almost every chapter in our book. Finally, whereas Rossi's collection largely presents "snapshots" of sexuality in different life stages, our book attends more carefully to the ways that specific aspects of sexuality, such as interest in sex and favored sexual scripts, unfold across multiple stages of the life course (see especially the chapters by Carbone-Lopez, Das et al., and Green).

Expanding and Refining the Perspective

A number of major works built on, expanded, or challenged this body of early work. The discussion here is necessarily selective and limited; we beg indulgence for any glaring omissions.

Writing at the same time as Rossi, Marsiglio and Greer (1994) examined the multiple influences shaping older (age 60+) men's sexuality. They considered physiological aging, social transitions (e.g., becoming a grandfather), age- and gender-specific sexual scripts, and the social construction of gender. Thus, they illustrated the application of a biopsychosocial perspective to a particular gender-and-life stage combination, as we did with menopause above.

Three years later, Browning and Laumann (1997) explicated the impact of a relatively rare but very powerful childhood event, sexual abuse, on long-term outcomes among U.S. women. They illustrated the explanatory power of life course concepts by showing how the *turning point* of sexual abuse launched some—but not all—women who were abused in childhood along a *pathway* of interrelated negative experiences, resulting in higher rates of sexually transmitted infections (STIs), unintended pregnancies, and involuntary sexual encounters later in life.[2] More recently, Cherlin and colleagues (2004) examined the effects of childhood abuse on the formation of marital or stable cohabitation relationships. Illustrating the strengths of combining ethnographic and survey data, they compared the effects of childhood abuse with the effects of physical abuse in adulthood. Women who experienced abuse in childhood were less likely to be married or cohabiting and more likely to be in transitory unions than women who experienced abuse only in adulthood, illustrating the fact that similar experiences at different life stages can have different effects (known as the "life stage principle").

Prior to 2000, most work on minority sexual identity adopted a developmental model. This model assumes that development of identity as a lesbian or gay man basically involves changing one's self-definition; that is, one's identity is fundamentally formed through a psychological process involving several distinct stages that occur in a linear progression during adolescence and young adulthood. A widely used model, developed by Cass (1979), specifies six stages, from identity confusion to identity tolerance to identity synthesis. Drawing on the life course perspective, Savin-Williams and Diamond (2000) challenged the view that minority sexual identity develops rather quickly and in a linear fashion. They employed the concept of *trajectories*, positing four "milestones" in the development of sexual identity as gay or lesbian: same-sex attraction, self-labeling, same-sex sexual contact, and disclosure ("coming out").[3] Using interview data, Savin-Williams and Diamond found that there are gender differences in the timing, spacing, and sequencing of these developmental milestones—that is, women and men "organize" these transitions into different trajectories. In addition, the stages that Savin-Williams and Diamond posited are more interactional in nature than the

Cass stages. The four milestones involve not only changes in cognitions and self-labeling but also same-sex behavior and the reactions of others.

Diamond's (2003, 2008a) continuing work challenges another tenet of theorizing on sexual identity: the assumption that once it has been developed, identity (and corresponding attraction and behavior) is fixed for life (see also Rust, 1996). Her longitudinal study of young nonheterosexual women ages 18 to 25 found that one quarter of the women who initially claimed an identity as lesbian or bisexual relinquished it over a 5-year period; one half of them reclaimed a heterosexual identity, while the other half rejected identity labels. These changes stemmed primarily from changes in how women interpreted or acted on their sexual attraction to women and men. Women who held rigid beliefs about the connection between behavior and identity and who engaged in relatively little same-sex behavior might change their identity, whereas women who perceived that connection as fluid often maintained an identity in the absence of behavioral confirmation. Diamond's work indicates that, at least in women, sexual identity is fluid and may change in response to life events.

The life course perspective suggests that differences in the timing and sequencing of earlier life events influence later personal and social outcomes. The work of Savin-Williams and Diamond (2000) demonstrated the impact of timing and sequencing on sexual identity formation. Donnelly, Burgess, Anderson, Davis, and Dillard (2001) turned their attention to involuntary celibacy, which is when a person desires to have sex but is unable to find a partner. Using data collected on the Internet, Donnelly and colleagues identified three different groups—"virgins," "singles," and the "partnered"— within this larger category. Their analysis indicates how "off-time" (early or late) transitions into and out of dating, sexual intimacy, and long-term relationships can accumulate to produce involuntary celibacy.

In the past decade, several studies have examined the impact of specific life events on sexual scripts and relationships. These explicitly remind us that although sexual aspects of life may remain unchanged for some people for many years, other lives are dramatically affected by certain events; life course scholars call such life course–altering events "turning points." One such event, experienced by about half of the U.S. population, is the termination of a long-term, committed relationship or marriage. Wade and DeLamater (2002) conceptualized the ending of both cohabiting and marital relationships as relationship dissolution, a major life transition. Dissolution involves the loss of access to a socially legitimate sexual partner. When a person subsequently develops a new sexual relationship, she or he gains an opportunity to adopt new sexual scripts. Analyses indicated that whether a newly single person acquires a new partner is influenced by his or her income, prior relationship status, and whether the person is caring for children—that is, by the person's past trajectory and current social context.

One of the first life transitions to be recognized and studied as affecting a heterosexual couple's sexual activity and relationship was the birth of a child. Research on this topic dates to at least 1973. Early research interviewed women three times during pregnancy, and again at about 1, 12, 26, and 52 weeks postpartum (Kumar, Brant, and Robson, 1981). Recognizing that the birth of a child impacts both partners, Hyde and colleagues (1996) collected data from 570 women and 550 of their partners, from pregnancy through 12 months postpartum, including measures of several sexual behaviors and sexual satisfaction. Reports of frequency of sexual activity before the birth were significantly and substantially correlated with reported frequency after the birth, suggesting stability across the transition. However, the birth itself was associated with a marked reduction in sexual activity. Reports of behavior by husbands and wives corresponded closely. Women who did not breastfeed and their husbands reported greater sexual satisfaction following birth than women who breastfed and their husbands. Notably, across the several studies that have been published, breastfeeding is consistently negatively related to frequency of postpartum sexual activity. The most likely reason is that lactation suppresses estrogen production, which results in decreased vaginal lubrication, in turn making intercourse uncomfortable. Thus, the change in sexual behavior reflects in part a physiological consequence of breastfeeding.

DeLamater has elaborated the biopsychosocial model and systematically applied it to sexuality in later life. Using data on men and women over 45, he and his colleagues have examined the influence of biological (health, diagnosed illness, medications), psychological (attitudes about sexual behavior and relationships for older men and women), and social (relationship status, evaluation of the relationship, partner's health) phenomena on sexual desire (DeLamater & Sill, 2005). The results indicate that desire (measured by frequency of thoughts about and desire for sexual activity) was more closely related to psychological factors (the importance of sex to the person) and age than to biological factors; for women, the presence of a partner was also important. A subsequent analysis tested the same model, with the addition of desire, in explaining frequency of sexual behavior, both partnered and solo (i.e., masturbation) (DeLamater & Moorman, 2007). Again, psychological (attitudes) and social (presence of partner, partner's health) factors were more important than biological (illness, medications) ones.

Related Research

Other researchers have provided important insights into sexuality over the life course without taking an explicit life course perspective. One example is González-López's (2005) exploration, based on extended interviews, observation, and auto-ethnography, of the ways immigration from Mexico to the Los Angeles metropolitan area affects men's and women's sexual lives. Eschewing the monolithic notions of *machismo* and *marianismo* that suffuse the literature, she examined the effects of pre-immigration life experiences, including being raised in "regional patriarchies" that produce distinctive regional femininities and masculinities (for example, rural and urban). Some women and men bring with them experiences of child sexual or physical abuse. In addition, González-López examined the socioeconomic, residential, and social networking circumstances following immigration, tracing the impact of each on the person's sexual beliefs and expressions. Whether a woman works and is capable of being self-supporting profoundly influences her sexual life; women who work for pay tend to exercise much greater agency in their heterosexual relationships. Finally, like many U.S. residents from all backgrounds, Mexican immigrants confront "work, work, work," finding that the fast pace of U.S. life and the demands of paid employment affect their intimate relationships. González-López argues that a specific man or woman's sexual attitudes and behavior reflect the interaction of many of these factors. Her highly nuanced analysis reflects life course thinking without using a formal life course model.

Another example is Schlesinger's (1996) analysis of the ways that chronic pain affects women's sexual partnering and activity. Drawing on in-depth interviews with 28 heterosexual women, aged 20 to 50, who suffer from chronic back, muscle, or joint pain, Schlesinger shows how the early (off-time) onset of physical impairments represents a dramatic turning point in women's sexual trajectories. Women who were single when their chronic pain began typically wished to be (hetero)sexually active but felt that their physical conditions had made doing so less likely or more complicated. Two women had lost or ended relationships due to their partners' lack of sympathy. Conversely, the 18 women living with male partners explained how their ability to communicate and negotiate with those partners had enabled them to make adjustments that facilitated feeling and being sexual (e.g., finding new positions). However, some partnered women reported withdrawing from sex because of pain or what they saw as negative changes to their physical appearance (e.g., surgical scars), and several women decided not to have children because of their pain. Despite some positive developments (e.g., improved communication and creative responses), as a rule, the transition to chronic pain represented a disadvantage for sexual life, which seemed to set familial and other disadvantages into motion.

An Invited Panel on Sexuality over the Life Course

Inspired by our own research on turning points (Carpenter, 2005; Wade & DeLamater, 2002) and by burgeoning interest in sexuality in later life, we organized an invited panel entitled "Sexuality over the Life Course" for the 2007 annual meeting of the American Sociological Association. We had hoped to gauge the vitality of contemporary work in this area and were delighted when we had no difficulty recruiting scholars to present their research. The final program included papers by Burgess and Donnelly, Koch, González-López, and Waite, Laumann, and Das. A revised and extended version of the latter presentation is included in this volume.

A review of those presentations suggested four themes. First, all four illustrated the emphasis on partnered sex in North American societies. The United States, like other societies, has a "couples" model of sexual expression and relationships (Gagnon, Giami, Michaels, & de Colomby, 2001). This is evident in many ways, including continuing negative attitudes toward masturbation (much less polyamory, long-term romantic/sexual relationships among three or more people [Sheff, 2005]). The pressure to express sexuality in a coupled context is especially evident in Burgess and colleagues' work on involuntary celibacy. One of the barriers faced by these adults is the stigma of being unpartnered and sexually inexperienced or a virgin (however defined).

Second, all of these conference papers, like many chapters in this volume, demonstrated the importance of normative transitions and of the timing of life course transitions. Transitions involving movement into and out of coupled relationships—dating; entering a long-term, committed relationship such as cohabitation or marriage; dissolution of a long-term relationship through divorce or widowhood—are especially important. Making these transitions "on time," in accord with social norms regarding appropriate ages for the transition, is associated with more successful and satisfying sexual relationships.

Third, gender proved especially significant for the timing and sequencing of transitions. Age norms differ by gender, with men being expected to make transitions to partnered sex earlier, and to committed relationships later, than women. Men and women experience adult virginity differently, as Donnelly and colleagues (2001) and Carpenter (2005) demonstrate.

Fourth, and finally, biology matters. Koch's paper, like the larger literature on menopause, highlighted the significance of biology during midlife. Waite and colleagues explicated the impact of biology, specifically aging-related changes, in later life. We also recognize that biology is influential in adolescence (e.g., Udry & Campbell, 1994). However, neither life course scholars nor sexuality scholars have paid sufficient attention to biology as an influence during other life stages, including in childhood and in adulthood before or after the climacteric.

Sexualities over the Life Course: This Volume

In short, it is time to take stock of past research in sexuality over the life course, to foster dialogue among scholars working in this exciting area, and to chart new directions for future efforts. The life course perspective is a powerful and uniquely sociological tool for studying the social world—and it is highly fruitful when applied to the study of sexuality. The theoretical and empirical work collected in *Sex for Life* moreover speaks to important public policy issues, such as sex education, aging societies, and the increasing politicization of scientific research.

The following chapters explore the influential past, exciting present, and promising future of sexuality research from a life course perspective. Taken together, these chapters reveal the diverse research methods and disciplinary approaches being brought to bear on this all-important topic.

In addition to this introduction, part I features a chapter reviewing the broad conceptual framework guiding the book. Part II focuses on sexualities in childhood and adolescence. One of the few scholars studying sexuality in early life, the social work professor Jeffry Thigpen, examines in chapter 2 how preteens' sexual attitudes and experiences both coincide and differ across gender and racial backgrounds. In chapter 3, the psychologists Stephen T. Russell, Kali S. Van Campen, and Joel A. Muraco explore the complicated pathways along which homosexual and heterosexual identities develop during adolescence. Kristin Carbone-Lopez, a criminal justice and women's studies scholar, analyzes the long-term consequences of physical and sexual assault in childhood in chapter 4.

Sexualities from young adulthood through early midlife are addressed in part III. In chapter 5, the education scholar William Jeynes charts how parental divorce influences adolescents' sexual behaviors and attitudes. Lisa Wade, a sociologist, and Caroline Heldman, a political scientist, join forces in chapter 6 to shed light on first-year college students' experiences adapting to the "hookup" culture that pervades many campuses; gender differences are only part of the story. In chapter 7, Adam Isaiah Green shows how gay and straight men's sexual life histories are powerfully shaped by the combination of early-life expectations about marriage and social structures that make marriage differentially available.

Part IV investigates sexual turning points that may occur at any point during the life course. In chapter 8, Yen Le Espiritu, an ethnic studies professor, considers how immigration between the Philippines and the United States has altered men's and women's sexual lives across two generations. How women who become single in midlife approach dating risks and sexual health, including STIs, is the subject of Bronwen Lichtenstein's chapter 9. Working from a sociologically informed disability studies perspective, Alexis A. Bender illuminates in chapter 10 the complex ways in which men (re)construct masculinity and sexual "normalcy" following spinal cord injuries. That the effects of such turning points differ depending on the age at which they occur is but one insight of these studies.

The four chapters that compose part V all examine different aspects of sexuality in midlife and old age. In chapter 11, the sociologist Heather E. Dillaway asks how European American and African American women's relationship statuses, reproductive histories, and social locations influence their experiences of sexuality during menopause. Insights from three major surveys of sexual behavior, as they pertain to the frequency of sexual thoughts, masturbation, and subjective sexual well-being, are the focus of chapter 12 by Aniruddha Das, Linda J. Waite, and Edward O. Laumann. The sociologists Kathleen F. Slevin and Christine E. Mowery explore the intersections of bodily changes, ageism, and sexuality among old lesbians and gay men in chapter 13. Meika Loe investigates intimacy and pleasure among nonagenarians and centenarians living in upstate New York in chapter 14.

We conclude the book, in part VI, with a synthesis of this innovative empirical research and our vision for future research on sexualities from birth to death and every age in between.

The diverse disciplinary affiliations of our contributors reflect the appeal of the life course perspective to a broad range of scholars. As the editors, we have deliberately sought to highlight the multidisciplinary nature of contemporary work in sexualities over the life course. Contributors come from disability studies, education, ethnic studies, political science, psychology, social work, sociology, and women's studies. Their work, in turn, produces a multidisciplinary picture of the interrelations of life course events and sexual functioning.

Research methods vary across disciplines, so the collected chapters reflect diverse methodologies. Several are based on in-depth interviews, focus groups, and/or participant observation, and use inductive techniques, such as grounded theory, for analyzing those data. These approaches give us insight into the subjective experiences, processes, and perspectives of individual men and women, even when samples are relatively small. Depending upon the questions asked, such research can provide a retrospective longitudinal analysis, as illustrated by Dillaway's chapter. In contrast, Espiritu uses interviews with mothers and daughters as the basis for an intergenerational analysis. Yet insofar as these qualitative studies use nonrandom, nonrepresentative samples, there is no way of knowing how common or typical the reported experiences are in some larger group or population. Results that are representative of a larger group or population are a potential strength of analyses of survey data. Chapters in this volume report results of cross-sectional and longitudinal quantitative analyses (Carbone-Lopez, Thigpen), a synthetic cohort or quasi-panel study (Das et al.), and secondary analyses of quantitative data (Jeynes). Each chapter illustrates these methods' contributions to understanding sexualities.

Of course, there are limits to the breadth and coverage of every collection. At the outset, we made the decision to limit our collection to research on North American populations. Demonstrating the complex contours and capabilities of the life course perspective on sexualities from childhood to old age in the United States and Canada is such an extensive undertaking, we felt that we could not do justice to cross-national differences in the same volume.

As the United States and Canada have become more heterogeneous through immigration and intermarriage, it is imperative to study and represent the experiences of an ever-wider range of racial and ethnic groups. Given their distinctive histories, cultures, and structural circumstances—compare, for instance, fifteenth-generation descendants of Africans brought to the United States as slaves with second-generation Black migrants from Caribbean countries like the Dominican Republic—different groups are likely to follow different sexuality and life course patterns. Indeed, the extant research reveals both unique patterns as well as similarities across race and ethnicity. Likewise, there is good reason to believe that financial hardship, especially chronic hardship, will impede sexual activity and functioning insofar as hardship is associated with increased symptoms of physical illness, depression, and functional impairment in later life (Kahn & Pearlin, 2006). Given its explicit recognition of sociocultural and historical factors, the life course perspective is well positioned conceptually to illuminate the sexuality trajectories that are distinctive to people with specific combinations of racial, ethnic, and social class identities.

The picture we present here is necessarily constrained by the studies that are being done. Limited coverage of variation by race, ethnicity, and social class is, unfortunately, typical of research on sexuality. Although an increasing number of scholars are investigating sexualities among people of color, both within specific groups (e.g., collections edited by Battle and Barnes [2010] and Asencio [2009]) and comparatively (e.g., O'Sullivan & Meyer-Bahlburg, 2003), and across social class (e.g., Wilkins, 2008), very little of this work takes a life course perspective. Two exceptions include Newman's (2006) analysis of the impact of minority poverty on functioning at midlife and beyond and Laumann and colleagues' (2005) large-scale, quantitative studies of differences and similarities among entire ethnic (and socioeconomic) communities in Chicago. Conversely, participants in life course–sensitive studies have been overwhelmingly White or European American. Insofar as most of the chapters in this book address race, ethnicity, and/or class variation in some manner, *Sex for Life* represents a considerable advance over Rossi's volume. However, several chapters here are based on samples of Whites, and other authors' samples include too few racial/ethnic minorities to analyze separately. In these instances, we wonder whether the results would be the same if the research were conducted with members of other ethnic groups. Likewise, more than a few of our chapters fail to examine fully the impact of social class, including variations in education, income, power, and prestige, on sexuality. These are areas where further theoretical and empirical work is sorely needed.

In short, this volume presents the proverbial "tip of the iceberg." The chapters included here represent research that we, the editors, felt would showcase the breadth of the life course perspective on sexualities. We wanted to cover a variety of life stages, including childhood, adolescence, midlife, and old age, and transitions and widely recognized turning points such as childhood abuse, parental divorce, immigration, and traumatic injury. However, we could not include every study on sexuality that uses or is consistent with the life course perspective. Nor could we include work that has not yet been conducted (or completed). Of particular note, scholars have only recently begun to bring life course insights to the study of transgender men and women—individuals whose gender differs from their assigned (generally biological) sex. For example, DuBois's (2009) preliminary research reveals the multiple, often stressful *and* joyful, turning points (including what feels like "second puberty") and "comings out" experienced by female-to-male transsexuals. Witten (2003) explores the social and biological specificities of growing older among transgender men and women. Such inquiries have tremendous potential to expand our understanding of the intertwining of gender and sexuality over the life course.

Social science and medical scholars are commonly criticized for focusing on negative outcomes of sexual activity to the exclusion of positive aspects, like sexual pleasure and desire, as well as everyday sexuality. A great deal of literature focuses on the "problems" of teenage or "premarital" sexual activity, such as unintended pregnancy and abortion, and on STIs, HIV/AIDS, sexual dysfunction, and sex work. Far less published research considers "typical" or "everyday" sexual relationships and behavior, especially in childhood and long-term adult relationships. Vance (1993) famously called this bias the danger-pleasure dichotomy. Higgins and Hirsch bemoan "the pleasure deficit" (2007), the failure to explore the nature of optimal sexual functioning and sexual pleasure seeking, especially in research on women.

Several factors have contributed to this tendency to accentuate the negative. Some of these topics—teen pregnancy, for example—are associated with poor physical and mental health (both as cause and effect) and some, such as STIs and HIV/AIDS, have personal and social costs that many researchers, practitioners, and policy makers legitimately want to reduce. Federal funding agencies and private foundations have shown greater willingness to fund research on problems than research on normal or typical sexual development and functioning. The requirements for human subject review (although critical for protecting vulnerable populations) have made the study of some topics, such as childhood sexual development, difficult if not impossible in the United States. Fear of social and personal reprisals have prevented some researchers from studying intimacy and sexual pleasure; Alfred C. Kinsey, the author of the first widely read scholarly studies of human sexual behavior (*Sexual Behavior in the Human Male* [Kinsey, Pomeroy, & Martin, 1948] and *Sexual Behavior in the Human Female* [Kinsey, Pomeroy, & Gebhard, 1953]), continues to be vilified by some more than 50 years after his death. Sexuality researchers of a certain age remember U.S. Senator William Proxmire giving his dreaded "Golden Fleece" award to Elaine Walster (Hatfield) for receiving a federal grant to study love (Shaffer, 1977). In selecting topics to address, we tried to avoid this bias toward the "negative" while still recognizing the dangers and downsides that do exist. We hope that readers will agree that the studies collected in this volume encompass virtually every valence of sexuality, from the positive and pleasurable to the ordinary and everyday to the painful and problematic—often within the same chapter, reflecting the complexities of human life.

1. Following Foucault (1978), genealogical analyses demonstrate how given systems of thought derive from contingent turns of history. Stoler (1995), for example, charts the interdependent development of discourses of sexuality and race in nineteenth-century European colonies. Drawing on Bourdieu's concept of fields—settings with specific rules in which people are positioned socially—Green (2008) and others seek to identify the structures of collective sexual life and track the evolution of historically specific erotic worlds and schemas. Biopsychosocial models are discussed later in this chapter.

2. Turning points are events that dramatically alter an individual's anticipated progress through the life course. Pathways are the routes that individuals follow along multiple, intersecting trajectories from birth to death. See chapter 1.

3. "Trajectories" are the routes that individuals take from birth to death *in a particular realm of life*, such as in work, family, or health. See chapter 1.

Studying Gendered Sexualities over the Life Course

A Conceptual Framework

LAURA M. CARPENTER AND JOHN DELAMATER

From the moment we're born, each of us begins to accumulate a wide range of physical, emotional, and intellectual experiences. Many of these experiences—from being gently caressed by a caregiver to watching one's parents go through an acrimonious divorce to observing the depiction of same-sex and heterosexual couples on television sitcoms—contribute to the complex constellation of desires, attitudes, and behaviors that comprise our sexuality. Early events and encounters influence later ones, in sometimes straightforward and sometimes indirect ways, such that every life course is composed of an ongoing chain of interrelated experiences. Each person's sexual life course is unique, owing in part to the specific experiences she has, the choices she makes or has foisted upon her, and the sequence in which those events and choices occur. Yet sexual life courses also tend to follow recognizable patterns. For example, no two readers of this book will have engaged in precisely the same acts with precisely the same sequence of partners, evoking an identical series of emotions and physical sensations. However, readers who approve of casual sex will likely have had sexual encounters with more partners, to whom they feel less emotionally connected, than those readers who disapprove of casual sex, decisions that, in turn, enhanced or minimized their risk of contracting sexually transmitted infections (STIs) and opportunities for learning new sexual techniques. When and where people are born—be it in rural Mississippi in the 1940s, Mexico City in the 1960s, or suburban Maryland in the 2000s—further determines the opportunities and constraints that give shape to the pathways that people take, as do their gender, racial/ethnic background, social class, sexual identity, and religious beliefs.

How can we, as researchers and individuals, best make sense of the complex, particular yet patterned, ways in which sexuality unfolds over the life course? This chapter sets forth a comprehensive, general conceptual framework that can be used to investigate sexual phenomena. By providing the tools for unpacking the lifelong, cumulative chains of advantageous and disadvantageous transitions within sexual, gender, and other life trajectories, such a framework can help us make sense of the similarities and differences that coexist across individuals and groups. For example, why don't all women who have been sexually abused as children report further unwanted encounters or little enjoyment of sex? Such a framework can also shed light on processes of change and continuity in individual sexual lives, including the means through which people select and reject sexual scripts. For instance, consider the 45-year-old man who announces to his family and close friends that he plans to transition to a feminine gender identity; the seeds of this apparently dramatic change can likely be found in childhood and adolescent experiences. Perhaps most important, such a framework can illuminate fundamental but poorly understood aspects of gendered sexuality—like sexual agency, assertiveness in intimate relationships, and sexual desire—that unfold across the entire life course.

The benefits of a wide-ranging, general conceptual framework are many. Yet, although a growing number of researchers have trained a life course perspective on sexuality-related phenomena, we are the first to propose a comprehensive, transposable conceptual framework containing all the elements that are necessary for a thoroughgoing analysis of virtually any aspect of sexuality. Previous studies have typically focused on a specific event or transition (e.g., widowhood) or stage in the life course (e.g., adolescence) rather than considering paths or trajectories over life courses in their entirety. Scarcely any studies have unpacked the lifelong processes through which a person's sexual scripts develop and change, and none have posited cumulative (dis)advantages as fundamental to understanding gendered sexuality over the life course. Few researchers have explored cohort differences that might emanate from changing sociohistorical contexts. Only a handful of works in this area have conceptualized gender in terms of power relations or social structures, and none posit gender and sexuality as jointly constructed.

Our framework, which we call the gendered sexuality over the life course (GSLC) model, draws on influential approaches and recent developments from life course sociology, feminist theory, and the scripting approach to sexuality. It starts from the premise that events at different stages of life must be understood as fundamentally connected. Additionally, it conceptualizes gender and sexuality as jointly constructed within specific social-structural contexts and sexual identity as developing over, and influencing experiences across, the life course. More specifically, the GSLC framework posits that sexual beliefs and behaviors result from individuals' lifelong accumulations of advantageous and disadvantageous experiences—social, psychological, and physiological—and their adoption or rejection of sexual scripts within specific sociohistorical contexts (including social institutions that may constrain or facilitate human agency). Women and men follow distinctive sexual trajectories insofar as they accrue gender-specific experiences and scripts—and insofar as sexual identity and gender trajectories intertwine.[1]

In the following pages, we delineate the GSLC framework, beginning with its theoretical and conceptual underpinnings.[2] We then present the specific components of the GSLC model and show how they fit together. To illustrate our discussion, we draw on examples from our own and other scholars' empirical research.

Theoretical and Conceptual Underpinnings

The Life Course Perspective

Scholars conceptualize individual life courses as being composed of multiple, simultaneously occurring *trajectories* through various dimensions of life, such as family, employment, and sexuality.[3] Each trajectory extends from birth until death and can be divided into a sequence of *transitions*, or movement from one social role to another (Elder, 1985; O'Rand, 2003). Retirement, for example, marks a transition from being a worker to becoming a non-worker in the employment trajectory, while (first) childbirth and adoption mark family transitions from being a nonparent to a parent, and first genital sex with a partner marks a transition from being "inexperienced" to "active" in the sexual trajectory. Of course, the different trajectories of a single life do not unfold in isolation but intersect in significant ways. For example, the arrival of a new child usually prompts parents to change their work routines, at least temporarily; conversely, people in highly demanding occupations may choose to have fewer children because their paid work leaves little time or energy for a larger family.

Trajectories in a particular dimension of life unfold in distinctive ways to the extent that different individuals undergo different transitions. Moreover, most transitions have more than one potential outcome. For instance, not every heterosexual person marries, and lesbian, gay, bisexual, transgender, and queer (LGBTQ) people cannot marry same-sex partners in most locales. Those who do marry may, in turn, experience continued marriage or separation, divorce, or widowhood; and people who do not remain married—

for whatever reason—may or may not marry again (Sussman, Steinmetz, & Peterson, 1999). Transitions that dramatically alter the direction of a particular trajectory are called *turning points* (Clausen, 1995). For example, being diagnosed with an incurable STI—HPV or herpes—leaves many women feeling as though they have moved from being sexually "invincible" to being "damaged goods," provoking a variety of (often sequential) responses, from denial and deception to treatment seeking to reintegration of the sexual self (Nack, 2008).

The timing, order, and duration of earlier transitions influence later transitions, with the opportunities and constraints brought about by each transition promoting later rounds of opportunity and constraint (O'Rand, 1996). For example, with respect to timing, people who marry before age 20 are more likely to get divorced (Raley & Bumpass, 2003). Whether they divorce or not depends on subsequent events, such as the timing of children's arrival (the sooner after marriage that children are born, the higher the chance of divorce) and whether the couple experiences financial hardship. If they divorce, they will likely remarry, especially the men (Wu & Schimmele, 2005). Other research has suggested that the normative order of transitions in young adulthood is to finish education, find employment, and then enter a long-term relationship. Men and women whose "careers" follow this sequence tend to enjoy more economic success and have more stable marriages than those who do not (Teti, Lamb, & Elster, 1987; Teti & Lamb, 1989).

Transitions with a positive valence—those that are socially defined as positive (e.g., settling down with a long-term partner versus remaining involuntarily single) or that lead to beneficial outcomes (e.g., a cohabiting relationship that enhances the partners' happiness and financial stability versus one that leads to alcoholism and reciprocal abuse)—tend to produce advantageous transitions at later life stages. Transitions with a negative valence—those that are socially disapproved or that cause harm or disadvantage—tend to generate further disadvantages. Life course scholars conceptualize these dynamics in terms of cumulative advantages and disadvantages. To the extent that different members of a cohort accumulate different patterns of advantages and disadvantages, diversity—and inequality—among cohort members will increase over time (O'Rand, 1996). Consider a hypothetical cohort's educational trajectories. Of all the students who attend high school, only some will perform well academically and, of those, only some will go on to college (a positive transition), the completion of which is a prerequisite for enrollment in law, medical, and other professional schools. Each stage of educational attainment (positive transitions) brings about better employment opportunities—jobs with higher salaries, longer promotion ladders, and more generous benefits—which lead, in turn, to further opportunities, such as greater financial security. Other cohort members may accrue disadvantages—poor academic performance, dropping out, or working "dead-end" jobs with few benefits or room for advancement. At the group level, these cumulative processes result in considerable educational, economic, and even health inequalities as cohort members reach midlife.

Similar dynamics can be observed in sexual life. Browning and Laumann (1997) show how different trajectories after childhood sexual abuse produce diverse adult outcomes, with some survivors reporting substantially more adverse consequences than others. Women who had been sexually abused as children were significantly more likely than nonabused women to engage in consensual vaginal sex before age 16, which in turn made them more likely to bear children before age 18, more likely to contract an STI, and more likely to have sex with 11 or more partners after age 18. Their research also demonstrated that girls who had been sexually abused were more likely to experience forced sex as women; forced sex, in turn, was associated with higher levels of sexual dysfunction. Not all of the abused women followed these pathways, however; some diverged from them at every stage. In effect, Browning and Laumann infer, each negative transition reinforced the disadvantageous sexual scripts learned from past experiences; each positive transition reduced disadvantage and perhaps created advantage going forward.

Determining whether any particular sexuality-related experience is advantageous or disadvantageous should be done with care. Such assessments are, to some extent, subjective, and one must avoid moralizing or imposing one's own views. Moreover, any given encounter may include advantageous *and* disadvantageous elements. As a general rule, sexuality-related experiences can be assessed as advantageous when they bring physical or emotional pleasure, enhance health, or increase a person's self-esteem.[4] They can be assessed as disadvantageous when they are coerced, painful, or result in STIs or an unwanted pregnancy. Experiences that are consonant with an individual's moral convictions or deeply held desires are likely to be advantageous, because they reinforce those inner "gyroscopes." Such attributions should be made with caution, however. For example, a person who feels sexually "worthless" may select inconsiderate or cruel partners and risky sexual situations (e.g., unprotected sex) (Carpenter, 2005), choices that could arguably be considered to be disadvantageous in some objective sense. Optimally, researchers might base their determinations of sexual (dis)advantage on individuals' subjective interpretations, such as could be offered in life history interviews.

Especially in societies like the contemporary United States, life trajectories are diverse and diversity within cohorts tends to increase over time (O'Rand, 1996). Consider, for instance, the different sexual trajectories set into motion by the varied approaches to virginity loss that coexist in America today (Carpenter, 2005). Individuals who disdain virginity tend to initiate sexual activity at relatively early ages, thereby expanding their opportunities to accumulate skills for negotiating with sexual partners as well as increasing their chances of contracting STIs. After the loss of a long-term partner later in life, sexual negotiation skills gained in youth may prove beneficial whereas STIs may prove a hindrance. Conversely, people who venerate virginity typically delay sexual activity until later ages and have relatively few partners outside of marriage or committed relationships. Consequently, although less likely to contract STIs, they experience few opportunities to learn different ways of negotiating with partners; these factors may, in turn, affect later-life relationships in positive and negative ways (respectively).

As people accumulate life transitions—growing older in sociological terms as they acquire new social roles—they are also aging physiologically (Riley, 1987). They may, moreover, experience variations in physical and mental health, including minor and major illnesses. Biological aging and health and illness trajectories, are, therefore, integral parts of a complete analysis of gendered sexuality over the life course. Of particular relevance to sexuality, the hormonal changes that accompany puberty may intensify youths' desire for sexual activity while the maturation of the female and male reproductive organs makes it possible for vaginal intercourse to result in pregnancy (Rossi, 1994). Later in life, physiological changes such as slower, weaker erections for men and reduced lubrication after menopause for women may make it more difficult and/or painful to engage in certain sexual activities (Schiavi, 1994). Many illnesses negatively affect sexual functioning and desire, as do many treatments for those illnesses; these illnesses become more common with advancing age (Genazzani et al., 2007). The development of secondary sexual characteristics—breasts in females, deepening voices in males, body hair in both—at puberty may signal sexual "readiness" to both the youth and to potential partners (Udry & Campbell, 1994). Conversely, physical signs of aging—thinning hair, wrinkles, diminished muscle tone—may leave women and men seeing themselves, or being seen by others, as less "sexy" or less appropriate as sexual partners (Bordo, 1999; Koch, Mansfield, Thurau, & Carey, 2005). Some of the illnesses associated with aging, such as cancers of the reproductive system, are gendered, in that the conditions and their consequences are different for men and women. Following treatment for cervical cancer, one half of the survivors reported dyspareunia, and 60% reported that sex was not pleasurable (Park et al., 2007). Following a prostatectomy, men who are given sildenafil prescriptions reported significantly greater erectile function and ability to achieve intercourse (Hong et al., 2007).

Human Agency in a Sociohistorical Context

People make the choices that shape their pathways through life, but they do not make them in circumstances of their own choosing; this is a fundamental insight of the life course perspective (Elder, 1985; Mills, 1959). Life course analyses of sexuality therefore take both human agency and the sociohistorical context into account (Elder, 1994). Research shows that individuals attempt to shape their life trajectories, in both the short and the long term, in ways consistent with their sense of self (Hitlin & Elder, 2007). On an everyday basis, such decisions may be so routine as to seem involuntary, as when opting not to flirt with the grocery store clerk confirms a young wife's identity as a good spouse. Conversely, a man's identity as a successful "Don Juan" may lead him to attempt to cast everyone he meets as a sexual partner. When changes in circumstances, such as divorce or rape, disrupt habitual responses, people exercise agency in ways that are guided by their already-existing self, biography, and values (Hitlin & Elder, 2007). For instance, women who were socialized to believe that sexual intimacy should only occur within marriage often become celibate after the death of their spouse, especially if they have had limited opportunities to remain socially active (Levy, 1994; Lopata, 1973).

Of course, agency can only be exercised within the limits imposed by biology and social structures (Hitlin & Elder, 2007). For example, a woman's efforts to conceal her sexual inexperience from the first man with whom she has vaginal sex may be stymied by hymeneal bleeding (Carpenter, 2005). Most prisons feature regulations and demographics that prevent inmates from pursuing heterosexual relationships that are actively sexual (Kunzel, 2008). Laws defining marriage as a contract between one man and one woman mean that, in most U.S. states, lesbians and gay men cannot legally marry their same-sex partners.

Situating individuals' life course trajectories, transitions, and cumulative (dis)advantages in a sociohistorical context is also crucial (Elder, 1985). In the U.S. context, for example, the booming economy and cultural emphasis on traditionalism that followed World War II promoted early marriage, high fertility, and conservative sexual values among the cohort born in the 1930s (D'Emilio & Freedman, 1997). Likewise, the secure prosperity, proliferation of mass media and consumerism, and social justice movements (civil rights, antiwar, feminist) of the mid- to late 1960s—along with the development of highly effective contraceptive technologies (the Pill and the IUD)—fostered a permissive and relatively gender-egalitarian sexual culture among Baby Boomers (Seidman, 1991). For their part, members of Generation X came of age during a period of rising cohabitation and divorce rates, increasingly "delayed" first marriages, and shrinking gender differences in education and labor-force participation (Sussman et al., 1999). Gen-Xers also confronted the resurgence of moral conservatism, a backlash against second-wave feminism, behavioral and other responses to the HIV/AIDS epidemic, and increasing visibility of LGBTQ communities (Risman & Schwartz, 2002). Life course analyses must take care to distinguish the changes effected by such broad social forces from those brought about by physical, social, and psychological changes. Conversely, they must also consider how changes in life course patterns may transform social institutions, as when widespread changes in sexual morality in the 1960s and 1970s facilitated the "institution-alization" of cohabitation (Riley, 1987).

The Ongoing Mutual Construction of Gender and Sexuality

In most societies, cumulative (dis)advantage processes are gendered, insofar as women and men tend to follow different pathways through the life course (Moen, 1996). For example, the disadvantages that women historically experienced early in their educational trajectories, such as being clustered in non-academic and nonprofessional tracks in high school and college, constrained later career opportunities and resulted in minimal retirement resources. Conversely, men's early advantages—academic tracks in high school, more diverse majors in college, better paying jobs, and longer promotion ladders—enhanced their later prospects. The same is true with sexual phenomena like virginity loss. Because women are typically encouraged to "save themselves," they tend to delay sex and choose their first partners carefully (even to the point of later regretting their choosiness) (Carpenter, 2005). Familiarity with a partner makes it easier to communicate about contraception and safer sex, in turn forestalling STI transmission, but it may make it more difficult to heal emotionally if or when that first relationship ends. Men, in contrast, are urged to "get it over with," so they are more likely to initiate sex with strangers or acquaintances, which tends to inhibit communication about safer sex. Failure to practice safer sex increases the likelihood of contracting STIs, including chronic ones, like herpes, which may complicate future relationships.

But gender is not simply a social status that predisposes individuals to adopt certain beliefs and behaviors. Individuals actively construct—or "do"—gender throughout their lives, within specific institutional and socio-historical contexts (West & Zimmerman, 1987). Gender itself can be understood as a trajectory in this sense. "Doing" gender is an inherently longitudinal process. Adolescent girls experiment, practice, and resist gender in a "trying-on" process (Williams, 2002). People become, and remain, gendered through continually experimenting with gender rules—following some, disobeying others—and gauging others' reactions and revising their gender performances accordingly (Lucal, 1999; Pascoe, 2007). Moments of experimentation and revision may lead to transitions in one's gender trajectory. For example, women tend to be passive in sexual relationships not only, or simply, because childhood socialization taught them to behave in a "subdued" fashion and to defer to men, but also because of lifelong cultural and experiential lessons that teach them that nonpassivity brings undesirable consequences. Adolescent girls who openly express (much less act on) their sexual desires often find themselves taunted as "sluts" and, accordingly, they may alter their behavior to avoid further insults and ostracizing (Tolman, 1994). Taking these lessons with them into young adulthood and beyond, young women may be reluctant to ask sexual partners (especially male ones) for what they want sexually (Gomez & Marin, 1996)—though some women seem to overcome this, at least partially, by midlife (Meadows, 1997). Life course scholars have not adequately recognized the ongoing accomplishment of gender. Nor have interactionist gender theories incorporated an explicitly longitudinal dimension. Yet a life course model is ideally suited to capture the fact that gender is (re)created through accumulated transitional moments over the life course, including sexual transitions.

The relationship between gender, sexuality, and sexual identity has been the subject of much feminist theorizing (Rubin, 1975, 1984). Some scholars contend that gender relations determine sexuality (MacKinnon, 1989), while others argue that institutionalized heterosexuality is more fundamental (Ingraham, 1996). Valentine (2004) proposes approaching the relationship between gender and sexuality as an empirical question, with distinctive answers in different social and historical locations. Pascoe (2007), for example, demonstrated how high school boys simultaneously construct and negotiate sexual identity and masculinity at institutional, interactional, and individual levels. In schools that sponsor activities, like proms and homecoming assemblies, that valorize particular versions of gendered heterosexuality (e.g., the "ladies' man" athlete), boys routinely distance themselves from the specter of failed masculinity (e.g., through homophobic remarks) in public interactions, and they enact heterosexuality (e.g., by "getting" girls), thereby achieving identities as masculine individuals. Likewise, Montemurro (2006) showed how, in a context of competing notions of femininity, bridal showers and bachelorette parties permit women to construct alternate versions of gendered, heterosexual identities.

Our GSLC framework offers an empirically based tool for examining the mutual construction of sexual identity and gender in specific contexts. Throughout the life course, transitions in an individual's sexual and sexual identity trajectories will affect his gender trajectory, even as the gender-related transitions that he experiences help to construct his sexual and sexual identity trajectories. Attending to these mutually constitutive processes can provide insight into the ongoing gendering—and (hetero)sexualizing—of every aspect of human life.

Gender, sexuality, and sexual identity do not, however, coexist or interact in isolation. As feminist theorists like Collins (1990) and Weber (2001) have shown, the combination of gender and sexuality intersects with race, ethnicity, and social class to shape social experiences in powerful ways. For example, the African American male students in Pascoe's (2007) study were able to incorporate putatively "feminine" attributes, such as stylish dressing and skillful dancing, into masculine, heterosexual identities because of pre-existing racialized stereotypes of Black men as hyper(hetero)sexual and masculine. Similarly, Carpenter (2005) found that middle-class youth were more likely than their working-class counterparts to favor the relatively gender-neutral interpretation of virginity loss as a step in a process—possibly due to their college-educated parents' relative permissiveness and/or familiarity with anthropological research on rites of passage. Analyses that go beyond "controlling" for social identity and location by explicitly engaging with the complex *intersections* of gender, sexuality, social class, race, and ethnicity are essential for developing a full understanding of sexuality-related life course processes.

The Sexual Scripting Approach

Transitions in virtually every life trajectory—such as widowhood (family), promotion to a position with greater authority (work), or onset of depression (health)—represent points at which people may adopt new ways of negotiating their sexual lives. The scripting approach (Gagnon & Simon, 1973) offers a useful tool for understanding such processes. It proposes that people's sexual lives are governed by socially learned sets of sexual desires and conduct, rather than by biological imperatives.

Sexual scripts exist at three interrelated levels (Simon & Gagnon, 1986). At the societal level, *cultural scenarios*, which are created and perpetuated by social institutions like schools, religious institutions, and mass media, serve as sexual "road maps" that people can consult to guide their choices about when, how, why, and with whom to be sexual. Stereotypes about divorced men's sexual insatiability and the belief that widows should remain "faithful" to their deceased husbands are cultural scenarios. Various cultural scenarios may be simultaneously available in a single society, although some may be perceived as specific to certain social groups (as with the two just mentioned). At the level of social interaction, people "write" *interpersonal scripts* when they influence and are influenced by one another's sexual conduct and beliefs. Think, for example, of the implicit and explicit negotiations that occur on a first date or during a sexual encounter (Rose & Frieze, 1993). Interpersonal scripts often entail improvisations on existing scenarios, as when sexual partners who prefer different cultural scenarios must find ways to compromise. The individual, or *intrapsychic*, level of scripting refers to people's particular desires, fantasies, and intentions (which are influenced by cultural scenarios and interpersonal scripts).

Historically and today, in most societies, women and men are encouraged to follow different sexual scripts. To the extent that the scripts people follow in one stage of life help to determine what scripts are available and appealing to them at later stages, this is a gendered process that tends to produce different cumulative outcomes for women and men. For example, heterosexual women who have learned the "nice girls don't plan to have sex" script are more likely to engage in unprotected sex and thus to experience unintended pregnancy, which may in turn preclude certain sexual and relationship options later (Thompson, 1995).

Sexual identity, social class, race, ethnicity, and other aspects of social identity—as they intersect with gender—likewise shape life trajectories by conferring opportunities and constraints and by influencing preferences for sexual scripts. An important transition in almost everyone's life is the decision to engage in sexual intercourse for the first time. A longitudinal study of 9,525 students using data from the National Center for Education Statistics found that initiating vaginal sex between the eighth and tenth grades is related to gender (males are more likely), race (Blacks are more likely), and academic ability (high-ability youth are less likely). There was also evidence of school effects: with every 10% increase in the proportion of sexually initiated students at a specific school, the likelihood of an individual student engaging in first (hetero)sex increased by 3% (Fletcher, 2007).

Bringing the Elements Together

Optimal insight into the ways that sexuality unfolds over the life course can be gained by employing every element of the GSLC model: transitions, turning points, and their timing, sequence, and duration; cumulative (dis) advantages at individual and group levels; intersections among life trajectories; physiological processes; human agency; the sociohistorical context and the effects of generation; the dynamics of gender and sexual identity, and their intersections with other aspects of social identity; and the adoption or rejection of sexual scripts. Table 1.1 provides a checklist of features to which GSLC-based research projects should attend.

Here we consider one example: sexual desire over the life course. A central aspect of sexuality, sexual desire has rarely been studied from a social perspective, and it has not been examined to any great extent by scholars taking an explicit life course approach. Our discussion, therefore, concentrates on the steps and processes that would be undertaken for a GSLC analysis, rather than on empirical findings.[5]

Our analysis begins with the question: What transitions and turning points might affect sexual desire over the life course? Transitions that entail a move from partnered to nonpartnered status, such as from marriage/cohabitation to divorce/relationship dissolution, come immediately to mind, as do transitions between (socially constructed) life stages, such as childhood to adolescence and early adulthood to middle age. (Life-stage transitions are often associated, though not identical, with biological phenomena, such as the onset of puberty or menopause; see below.) Lest the analyst miss the effects of less "obvious" transitions, we recommend brainstorming across the entire life course, from birth to death, envisioning what events might occur at each stage and how each might shape desire. It is, moreover, imperative to consider not only transitions that are specifically sexual—first orgasm, virginity loss, rape (to name a few)—but also the full range of life trajectories that unfold alongside the sexuality trajectory, including (but not limited to) work, family, health, and residence.

As each relevant transition is identified, the researcher should interrogate its relationship to sexual desire. For example, moving in with a partner is likely to increase desire (at least in the short term), whereas losing a partner tends to diminish desire. Asexual individuals (who report no sexual attrac-

TABLE 1.1
Elements to Consider When Employing the GSLC Model

Element	Questions to Ask
Transitions	Between what social roles are people moving? How are those transitions timed (on-time, early, late) and ordered?
Turning points	Do some transitions represent major changes in life course? With what consequences?
Cumulative (dis)advantage processes	How do experiences at one life stage impact later experiences? Are these chains of experience positive, negative, mixed?
Intersections among trajectories	How does the sexuality trajectory affect other life trajectories (e.g., family, work, education), and vice versa?
Physiological processes	How might physiological changes and illness/treatment, including those related to aging, affect this aspect of sexual life?
Agency	In what ways are people exercising agency (short- and long-term)? What constraints do biology and social structure impose?
Sociohistorical context and generation	How might major historical changes affect this aspect of sexuality? To what extent do members of different generations have distinctive experiences?
"Doing" gender and sexual identity	What gender and sexual identities are being accomplished via sexual conduct? How are gender and sexuality co-constructed?
Other aspects of social identity	How do race, ethnicity, social class, religion, and other aspects of social identity—intersecting with gender and sexual identity—affect GSLC dynamics?
Sexual scripts	What sexual scripts are available? Which do people choose? Which do they reject?

tion to other people) are more likely to have never had a long-term partner, and they report fewer lifetime sexual experiences (Bogaert, 2004). Transitions that effect dramatic changes in sexual desire represent turning points.[6]

The researcher should furthermore consider the timing of each (relevant) transition, how long each stage or status lasted, and the order in which the transitions occurred. For example, a man who is widowed relatively early in life may experience less diminishment of desire—given cultural scripts for sexuality for men in their thirties and forties—than a man widowed at a later age. The longer he remains a widower, the more his desire may decline, as he becomes increasingly accustomed to his new status. Knowing the sequence in which transitions occur not only represents a crucial step in mapping life pathways and cumulative (dis)advantage processes, but it also can provide direct insight into the dynamics of desire (or other phenomena of interest). For instance, we might predict that a woman would experience greater diminishment of sexual desire over the long run if she was raped prior to her first experience of orgasm or partnered sex than if the rape occurred after she had enjoyed some (potentially) pleasurable and voluntary sexual encounters. The Life History Calendar technique may prove especially useful in mapping the timing, sequence, and duration of transitions and turning points over individuals' sexual life histories (Freedman, Thornton, Camburn, Alwin, & Young-DeMarco, 1988).

In addition to establishing the timing, sequence, and duration of key transitions that are relevant to desire, the researcher should assess whether those transitions are relatively advantageous, disadvantageous, or neutral. Such assessments make it possible to envision cumulative (dis)advantage processes at work, at both the individual and group levels. For example, a child whose early experiments with masturbation (itself both a consequence and a cause of desire) are punished by her parents may begin to feel guilty about her sexual desires, which in turn may make her feel less able, as an adolescent, to say "no" to sexual encounters she does not desire. Conversely, a child whose parents treat masturbation as an ordinary (if private) behavior may feel free to explore his sexual responses such that he is better prepared to be an expressive and creative partner when he begins to have sex with others.

Considering how different life trajectories intersect, and with what effects, is also critical. For example, stressful events in a person's work trajectory are likely to diminish sexual desire, which in turn might cause problems in an existing relationship. Unemployment is stressful and can cause depression and marital dissatisfaction (Vinokur, Price, & Caplan, 1996), which could end the relationship, constituting a transition in the family trajectory. Conversely, when an individual recovers from a long-term illness (health trajectory), she may experience a return to previous levels of sexual desire, which might inspire her to search for a new relationship.

As the foregoing example indicates, physiological processes frequently influence life course processes. Highly sexed women, defined as those who prefer sexual stimulation to orgasm six times per week or more, report that maintaining long-term sexual relationships with men and friendships with women is very difficult (Blumberg, 2003). The researcher should, therefore, explore how physiology and physiological changes, including those related to aging, as well as illnesses (physical and mental) and treatments for them, affect the sexual phenomenon of interest. Certain physiological processes, like puberty and menopause, are closely related to life-stage transitions; major illnesses and recoveries also can usefully be conceptualized as transitions in the health trajectory (which often affect education, work, family, and even residential trajectories). Other physiological processes may be more helpfully viewed as intensifying or mitigating factors. Reproductive cancer may negatively impact a man's body image and sense of masculinity, exacerbating reduced desire and sexual attraction to a long-term partner, or it may create a new awareness of the importance of sexual intimacy and could increase his desire for intimacy with a partner.

Agency—the choices that individuals make, and their beliefs about their ability to make them—and the social, structural, and biological factors that enable or constrain agency, must also be explored. People choose whether or not to act on their sexual desires, taking short- and often long-term consequences into account. (Of course, all too frequently, women and men are forced to engage in sexual acts they do not desire.) For example, a young woman may base her decision whether or not to have vaginal sex with a particular partner on the immediate likelihood of obtaining pleasure from the encounter as well as on the long-term likelihood of becoming pregnant or contracting an STI if a contraceptive or a condom is not readily available. Biology constrains such choices, however, as when a man with severe hypertension finds it difficult to achieve an erection sufficient for engaging in the penetrative sex he desires. Social structures also act as impediments; sex-segregated institutions such as boarding schools, seminaries, and prisons constrain the development or maintenance of cross-gender relationships, while facilitating the formation of same-gender ones. The exercise of agency (or lack thereof), within the boundaries set by biology and social structures, profoundly shapes the sexual life course at every stage.

All of these dynamics must be located in sociohistorical context. More-over, the researcher should not neglect the closely related effects of birth cohort (or generational) processes. We recommend reviewing major social changes, at local, national, and international levels, that took place during the entire lives of study participants. Not every event will make a meaning-ful impact on every sexual phenomenon, however; those that did make an impact may affect individuals and cohorts differently, depending on their ages at the time (i.e., the life-stage principle, discussed in the introduction). For example, some scholars suggest that young women who came of age in the 1990s—a period when highly sexualized images of male bodies prolifer-ated in the mass media—may experience more sexual desire in response to visual cues than women who came of age just a decade earlier, when fewer such images were available (Bordo, 1999). Women who were in their thir-ties and forties during the 1990s may have experienced desire when viewing such images, even as they continued to prefer verbal cues, given their early socialization.

Gender and sexual identity are thought to have powerful effects on sex-ual desire, especially as they intersect. The researcher should consider what gender and sexual identities individuals co-construct when they engage in particular sexual practices. For women, openly expressing sexual desire helps to create a "bad girl" identity (gender)—though of different valences depending on whether the object(s) of desire are male or female (sexual identity) (Carpenter, 2005; Thompson, 1995). Likewise, men who do not exhibit the high levels of desire that men are "supposed" to possess may have their masculinity—and their (hetero)sexual identity, or their status as "normally" lusty gay men—called into question (Pascoe, 2007). Race, ethnicity, social class, and (often) religious background intersect with gen-der and sexual identity to further shape desire. For example, young Black women, aware that they are stereotyped as hypersexual, often work to con-ceal, or even repress, their sexual desires (Tolman, 1994, 1996); such ste-reotypes—and efforts to counter them—may be intensified for girls from working-class and poor families (Carpenter, 2005). Similarly, embracing a conservative Christian identity enables some young men to resist express-ing their sexual desires without sacrificing their senses of masculinity (Wilkins, 2008).

As a final step in the analysis, the researcher should consider how the sexual phenomenon in question articulates with sexual scripts at the cul-tural, interactional, and individual psychological levels. Cultural scenarios for sexuality are strongly patterned by gender, sexual identity, race, ethnicity, social class, and religion. Historically, cultural scenarios for heterosexuals have cast men as the sexual desirers and women as the objects of desire. So absent is desire from mainstream scripts for adolescent women that Fine (1988) contended that young women are hindered by a "missing discourse of desire." Gendered scripts about desire play out differently in same-sex relationships, such that two men are assumed to exacerbate one another's high levels of desire (often so much so as to preclude monogamy) whereas two women are assumed to experience so little desire that they may rarely have sex. Although many people embrace mainstream sexual scripts—with varying degrees of consciousness—others reject them. For example, a woman who personally feels a great deal of desire (her intrapsychic script) may refuse to play the culturally prescribed role of sexual object and behave instead as a desirer/initiator. Such refusals can, and do, lead to negative sanctions from sexual partners, however, and may prompt complicated negotiations between partners (i.e., interpersonal scripts) (Dworkin & O'Sullivan, 2005).

Moving Forward with the GSLC Framework

This volume is premised on the conviction that the life course approach—and the GSLC framework in particular—has a great deal to offer researchers who are interested in sexuality. Each chapter in the book brings multiple elements from the GSLC model to bear on a wide range of sexuality-related phenomena.

Transitions and their timing, sequence, and duration are central factors in every study collected here. Some contributors focus on life stage transitions—such as that from childhood to adolescence (Russell et al.) or from midlife to old age (Slevin and Mowery)—while others concentrate on social and institutional transitions, such as the move from high school to college (Wade and Heldman) or from being single to being married or partnered (Green). Several chapters investigate the long-term effects of dramatic turning points, including sexual assault (Carbone-Lopez), parental divorce (Jeynes), and spinal cord injury (Bender).

Analyses of cumulative advantages and disadvantages are likewise ubiquitous. Dillaway, for example, demonstrates how the lifelong accumulation of reproductive and sexual experiences gives shape to women's feelings about sexuality and menopause. Loe highlights continuities in pleasure-seeking from youth to old age as well as the pathways along which aging adults develop new sources of pleasure. Das, Waite, and Laumann show how chains of opportunities and constraints—including the acquisition and loss of partners and the approval or disapproval of adult children—affect older men's and women's sexual conduct and thoughts.

Many chapters illuminate the ways in which intersecting life trajectories affect sexuality. Espiritu, for example, examines the complex interrelationship among immigration, family transitions, and sexual beliefs and behavior. Green charts intersections among sexual identity, family, and geographic trajectories. The impact of physical and mental health trajectories on sexuality features prominently in the work of Lichtenstein (STIs), Bender (traumatic injury), and Das and colleagues (age-related health problems). Other contributors explore physiological processes like puberty (Russell et al.) and menopause (Dillaway).

How people make choices about sexuality (i.e., agency), given the particular sociohistorical contexts in which they live, is explored in depth by Green (opportunities for same-sex marriage), Wade and Heldman (distinctive college cultures), and Espiritu (Philippines versus the United States). Thigpen, Espiritu, Loe, and Das and colleagues provide valuable insights into the ways in which generation affects sexual attitudes and conduct.

Every chapter addresses how gender and sexual identity—in combination with race, ethnicity, and social class—shape sexual pathways. Thigpen, for example, examines how gender and race differentially influence children's (presumed) heterosexual behavior in early life. Slevin and Mowery show how gender and social class contribute to distinctive experiences of bodily aging for gay men and lesbians. In Espiritu's analysis of first- and second-generation Filipino/a Americans, gender, ethnicity, and nationality play the most critical roles.

Sexual scripting processes also remain prominent throughout the book. Wade and Heldman explore how first-year college students negotiate the dramatic difference between the sexual scripts they followed in high school and the ones that prevailed on their new campus. Carbone-Lopez reveals how sexual and physical abuse can prompt young women to adopt particular (often harmful) sexual scripts.

The following chapters demonstrate how these various elements come together to illuminate the complex dynamics of sexualities over the life course. In chapter 15, we return to this conceptual framework, highlighting the contributions of the authors assembled here and pointing to ways in which the framework may be enhanced by future scholars.

NOTES

An earlier version of this framework appeared in *Sociological Perspectives*, 53, 155–178.

1. We use the term "sexual trajectory" to refer to the unfolding of a person's sexual attitudes and experiences, broadly speaking, while "sexual identity trajectory" refers more specifically to experiences and self-understandings related to sexual identity. Although analytically separable, these trajectories are clearly intertwined.

2. In chapter 12 of this volume, Das and colleagues present a distinctive framework that draws on many of the elements employed here.

3. A previous generation of life course scholars tended to think in terms of a single trajectory that encompassed shifts from education to work to retirement (for a critique, see O'Rand, 1996, 2003).

4. These guidelines are derived from the World Health Organization's definition of sexual health as "a state of physical and emotional well-being in which an individual enjoys freedom from sexuality-related disease, dysfunction, coercion, and shame, and thus the ability to enjoy and act on her or his sexual feelings" (Carpenter, 2007).

5. It should be noted that the elements of the framework are intertwined to a considerable extent, such that this outline is more discrete than most analyses would be in practice.

6. Life course scholars typically reserve the designation "turning point" for transitions that objectively cause a major change in course—as from high to low levels of desire—even as they recognize that individuals may subjectively understand events that produce relatively little change as turning points (Clausen, 1995).

PART II

Sexualities in Childhood and Adolescence

Childhood Sexuality

Exploring Culture as Context

JEFFRY W. THIGPEN

Antoinette, a 10-year-old African American girl removed from her biological parents' home a year earlier and placed in the state's foster care system for reasons related to parental neglect, has recently experienced a disruption in her placement.[1] After her foster mother discovered Antoinette glancing at graphical depictions of male and female genitalia in a health textbook belonging to an older foster child within the home, Antoinette was labeled as having a sexual behavior problem, referred for intensive therapy to address her behavior, and transferred to an alternate foster care setting where her behavior could be more closely monitored. According to the policies of the child welfare system, Antoinette's behavior departed from what is developmentally typical or normative. But what constitutes normative ranges of sexual behavior in preadolescent children? And to what extent do a child's gender and cultural background contribute to variations in normative ranges of sexual behavior?

Although a fair amount of scholarly attention has been given to sexuality in adolescence and adulthood, the literature addressing childhood sexuality is sparse and limited. Contributing to this imbalance are the cultural belief that children are not overtly interested in sex until puberty (Freud, 1905, cited in Strachey, 1962) and the cultural belief in the sexual innocence of children, which emerged alongside the reconceptualization of childhood as a distinct period of life characterized by purity, innocence, and faith during the early modern period in Europe (Bullough, 2004). In the United States, the belief that children are sexually innocent has given rise to a set of social policies and laws that promote and protect children's sexual innocence by penalizing those who would expose them to overt sexual themes and sexual contact.

Social and legal proscriptions around childhood sexuality have legitimized two interrelated lines of inquiry that accentuate protection from sexual victimization: adult-child sexual contact and sexual aggression in childhood. Adult-child sexual contact has received considerable attention in the literature because the predominant psychogenic and traumagenic frameworks have theorized this type of experience to result in long-term social and emotional problems for the victimized child (Finkelhor & Browne, 1985). Although many studies have found evidence in support of these models, Browning and Laumann (1997) cast doubt on the direct and long-term effects of adult-child sexual contact. Applying a life course perspective, these researchers contend that adult-child sex represents a life course transition that prematurely introduces the victimized child to coupled sexual activity. The transition to coupled sex, in turn, potentially alters a child's sexual trajectory or pathway insofar as the abuse experience may establish a template of sexual interaction that promotes risky sexual behavior in adolescence and adulthood. An active and risky pattern of sexual behavior following the abuse experience increases the likelihood of diminished social and emotional functioning later in life. However, those who avoid such a pattern are less likely to experience adverse outcomes in adolescence and adulthood. In this way, the long-term effects of adult-child sex are variable and indirect.

Because a substantial percentage of individuals characterized as sexual abusers are youth under the age of 18, a growing branch of study devoted to understanding children who sexually aggress toward other children has recently emerged (Friedrich, 2007). Sexual aggression is generally described as abusive behavior that has both sexual and aggressive features committed by a child upon another child who is viewed as being weaker or vulnerable (Araji, 1997). Childhood sexual aggression has been theoretically linked to dysregulation of affect and behavior as a consequence of maltreatment (Friedrich, 1997a). It is presumed that the majority of these children are reacting to their own sexual victimization (Araji, 1997) and that the propensity to sexually aggress toward others will continue into adolescence and adulthood (Burton, 2000).

Even though the literatures addressing adult-child sexual contact and sexual aggression in childhood appropriately elucidate childhood events and experiences that have implications for development and behavior over the life course, they also function to problematize childhood sexuality by drawing attention to what is assumed to be abnormal sexual behavior and expression. Sexual behavior as a probable outcome of sexual victimization in childhood has been investigated in numerous studies (Kendall-Tackett, Williams, & Finkelhor, 1993; White, Halpin, Strom, & Santilli, 1988). By comparing the sexual behaviors of sexually abused and nonabused children, these studies show elevated levels of sexual behavior among children with histories of sexual abuse. Importantly, however, these studies additionally reveal the ubiquity of sexual behavior among nonabused children. Furthermore, they illuminate the poor state of knowledge regarding normative sexual behavior and development in childhood. It is difficult to identify pathological sexual behavior without knowing what is typical. That pathological sexual behavior in childhood is clinically assessed relative to deviations from what is assumed to be *normal* behavior underscores the necessity of increasing our knowledge and understanding of typical childhood sexual behavior (Carpentier, Silovsky, & Chaffin, 2006).

Normative Sexual Behavior in Childhood

Recent studies have expanded our knowledge of normative childhood sexual behavior by showing that children between 2 and 12 years of age engage in self-stimulatory behavior, demonstrate interest in sexual topics, reveal their bodies and sexual parts to adults and children, and show interest in viewing the bodies of others (Friedrich, Fisher, Broughton, Houston, & Shafran, 1998; Thigpen, 2009).[2] Other studies suggest that children between the ages of 2 and 7 normally demonstrate knowledge of various aspects of sexuality such as sexual body parts and functions (Gordon, Schroeder, & Abrams, 1990a, 1990b; Grocke, Smith, & Graham, 1995) and that they engage in both same-gender and cross-gender sexual play (Lamb & Coakley, 1993; Leitenberg, Greenwald, & Tarran, 1989; Okami, Olmstead, & Abramson, 1997).

Genital manipulation and masturbatory behaviors are more prevalent among boys, suggesting behavioral differentiation by gender (Gagnon, 1985; Friedrich et al., 1998; Thigpen, 2009). Age as an index of physical, cognitive, and social development has similarly been found to be related to childhood sexual behavior both qualitatively and quantitatively. In a study of 2- to 7-year-olds, for example, Gordon and colleagues (1990b) found that older children were significantly more knowledgeable about aspects of sexuality such as sexual behavior, pregnancy, and sexual abuse prevention. An inverse relationship between age and observed sexual behavior has been found in some studies of 2- to 12-year-old children, suggesting that sexual behavior becomes more covert as children approach puberty (Friedrich et al., 1998).

Factors other than gender and age that influence sexual expression in childhood have been investigated in only a few studies. Liberal parental attitudes regarding sexuality have been found to be associated with specific behaviors such as increased masturbation (Gagnon, 1985), frequency of touching parents' genitals (Rosenfeld, Bailey, Siegel, & Bailey, 1986), and frequency of sexual behavior overall (Friedrich et al., 1998). Some studies have shown childhood sexual behavior to be specifically linked to permissive family practices such as parental nudity in the home and co-sleeping (Friedrich, Grambsch, Broughton, Kuiper, & Beilke, 1991; Friedrich et al., 1998; Thigpen & Fortenberry, 2010), while others have not found such effects (Lewis & Janda, 1988; Okami, Olmstead, Abramson, & Pendleton, 1998). Although the findings of these studies are preliminary, they point to the contextual nature of childhood sexual behavior and, as such, reflect a critical gap in our knowledge and understanding of sexuality in childhood.

Childhood Sexuality: Exploring Culture as Context

Human sexual behavior is at once biological, psychological, and social. Within the social dimension, attention has been given to the social-psychological meanings that underlie and produce sexual behavior (Foucault, 1978; Gagnon & Simon, 1973). Because sexual meanings vary across different cultural contexts, culture is vital in understanding human sexual behavior.

Defined as the patterns of ideas and beliefs shared by members of a group, culture is an important contextual factor shaping the sexual behavior and expression of children (Frayser, 1994). The pathway by which culture influences sexual behavior in childhood is illuminated in social constructionist perspectives on human sexuality. As a broad theoretical paradigm, social constructionism assumes that reality emerges through social interaction and common meanings and through the language with which people make sense of and order the world (Berger & Luckman, 1966; Gergen, 1985). Social constructionist approaches posit variation in human behavior as resulting from culturally determined understandings of behavior acquired through enculturation. This perspective views human sexual behavior as learned behavior that emerges from a complex psychosocial process of development beginning in childhood (Foucault, 1978; Gagnon & Simon, 1973). Very early in life, individuals begin to learn implicitly and explicitly the sexual beliefs, attitudes, and behaviors of their culture. In this way, the sexual behavior of children is both shaped by and reflective of the cultural context in which they are embedded.

Ford and Beach (1951) classify societies as restrictive, semirestrictive, or permissive in relation to sexual attitudes, beliefs, and practices. In restrictive societies such as the United States, children are not recognized as sexual beings, and the acquisition of sexual knowledge and experience during childhood is deliberately impeded (Casper & Moore, 2009; Heins, 2007). A few cross-cultural studies have demonstrated the capacity of culture to shape children's sexual behavior (Friedrich, Sandfort, Oostveen, & Cohen-Kettenis, 2000). Goldman and Goldman (1982), for example, found significant differences in the sexual knowledge of 5- to 15-year-old Australian, English, North American, and Swedish children. That Swedish children were more knowledgeable about many aspects of sexuality was attributed to compulsory sexuality education in schools as well as permissive sexual beliefs and attitudes within Swedish culture. In a comparison of the sexual behavior of Swedish and American preschoolers, Larsson, Svedin, and Friedrich (2000) similarly attributed the higher level of sexual behavior found among Swedish children to cultural differences.

Less is known about the ways in which culture shapes the sexual behavior of children of different racial/ethnic backgrounds residing within the United States. In fact, researchers have called attention to the omission of non-White children from studies of childhood sexual behavior (Gordon & Schroeder, 1995). While the existence of distinctive cultures based on race/ethnicity continues to be debated, Helms (1994) argues that subsidiary cultures identified with particular collective identity groups exist within and alongside the broader, macro-level culture of the United States. To that end, race can be viewed in cultural terms and taken to reflect the customs, traditions, products, and values of a racial group. Exploring cultural influences on the sexual behavior of children is important because sexual beliefs and attitudes have been shown to vary across different racial and ethnic groups within the United States. Research shows that African Americans, on average, begin heterosexual sex earlier, have higher rates of sex in adolescence, and have higher numbers of sexual partners in adulthood than Whites and Mexican Americans (Laumann, Gagnon, Michael, & Michael, 1994; Mahay, Laumann, & Michaels, 2001). In a study of 3- to 6-year-old children, significant differences in the average frequency of sexual behavior were observed among African American, Latino, and White American boys and girls (Shafran, 1995). Although these differences did not remain significant when family socioeconomic status was held constant, racial/ethnic differences pertaining to family sexual attitudes and family sexual behavior did. More specifically, African American and Latina mothers held more conservative attitudes than White mothers regarding sex education for young children, childhood sexual behavior, and family sexual behavior. African American and Latina mothers also reported that they intentionally structured their home environments in such a way that their children had fewer opportunities to witness nudity, to co-bathe with another child or parent, or to be exposed to sexual media. Yet, although assessing differences in the average frequency level of sexual behavior between children of different racial/ethnic backgrounds may yield useful information, an analytic strategy that relies solely upon summaries of frequencies may conceal specific behaviors or patterns of behavior within and between cultural groups.

Further exploration of culture's influence on childhood sexual behavior within the United States is critical for at least three reasons. First, such studies are likely to broaden our general knowledge of childhood sexuality by establishing similarities and dissimilarities in the sexual behavior of children from different racial/ethnic groups. Second, this research can shed light on the socio-sexual development of children, particularly the ways in which children of different racial/ethnic backgrounds are socialized toward or away from different types of behavior. Finally, exploring the influence of culture on childhood sexuality is important because assuming that childhood sexual behavior is invariant across racial/ethnic groups is potentially harmful insofar as problematic sexual behavior in childhood is formally defined and assessed relative to deviations from normal. Increasing our empirical understanding of childhood sexual behavior as it occurs within and across multiple groups will undoubtedly aid professionals in assessing the normalcy of childhood sexual behavior. This chapter explores the influence of culture on childhood sexuality by investigating similarities and differences in the sexual behaviors of 7- to 12-year-old African American and White children as reported in two studies that separately used the Child Sexual Behavior Inventory (CSBI; Friedrich, 1997b) to investigate the sexual behavior of children without known or suspected histories of sexual abuse.

Methods

Samples

Data pertaining to the sexual behavior of 7- to 12-year-old White and African American children, respectively, were drawn from published studies conducted by Friedrich and colleagues (1991) and by Thigpen (2009). Both studies were carried out in cities in the midwestern United States. The demographic information pertaining to the entire sample of both studies and to the subsample of 7- to 12-year-old children and their caregivers analyzed here is presented in tables 2.1 and 2.2.

TABLE 2.1

Demographics of the Samples

	Original Sample of 2–12 Year-Old Children		Subsample of 7–12 Year-Old Children	
	Friedrich et al.	Thigpen	Friedrich et al.	Thigpen
	(1991)	(2009)	(1991)	(2009)
	n=880	n=249	n=380	n=92
	Children			
Racial/Ethnic Background				
% African American	†	100	††	100
% White	98	0	†	
Age, mean years	6.3	5.8	9.1	9.3
Sex				
% Female	48	47	54	48
% Male	52	53	46	52
% in single-parent families	12	48	††	39.1
% in families with annual incomes <$15K	4	53.4	††	42.4
	Primary Caregivers			
Relationship to child				
% Biological/ Adoptive mother	99.6	90	††	95.7
% Stepmother	.4	0		0
% Other	0	10		4.3
Educational attainment				
Mean years (Std. deviation)	14.5 (2.2)	12.5 (2.0)	††	12.8 (2.3)

†The racial/ethnic background of the Friedrich et al. (1991) sample was reported as 98% White. Information pertaining to the racial/ethnic background of the remaining 2% is not provided.
††Full demographic data for the subsample of 7- to 12-year old children were not provided in Friedrich et al. See demographic data pertaining to the entire sample.

TABLE 2.2

Age and Sex Distribution of 7- to 12-Year-Old Children Included in the Analysis

	Age in Years						Total	Mean Age
	7	8	9	10	11	12		
Male								
Friedrich et al. (1991)	49	41	45	27	25	19	206	8.97 Years
Thigpen (2009)	9	5	7	16	8	3	48	9.37 Years
Female								
Friedrich et al. (1991)	37	37	22	28	26	24	174	9.23 Years
Thigpen (2009)	12	6	5	7	7	7	44	9.27 Years

Friedrich and Colleagues (1991)

To assess the frequency of a wide variety of sexual behaviors in children without histories of sexual abuse, Friedrich and his colleagues (1991) administered an early version of the CSBI to primary caregivers of 2- to 12-year-old children who were recruited from a primary care pediatric clinic. Primary caregivers completed the CSBI confidentially on site or returned it to the investigators via mail. Out of a total eligible pool of 1,231, 871 primary caregivers were recruited. They completed 1,091 surveys (some caregivers were allowed to report on two children). Two hundred eleven surveys were excluded for a variety of reasons, including missing data, caregiver-child pairs residing outside the county in which the study was conducted, the child having a chronic physical condition or a physical or mental disability, and the child having a suspected or confirmed history of sexual abuse. A total of 880 surveys were included in the analysis, representing an 80.6% response rate.

Ninety-eight percent of the children in the sample were White. They ranged in age from 2 to 12 years with a mean age of 6.3 years. Fifty-two percent were boys. Nearly all (99.6%) of the children were being parented primarily by their biological or adoptive mothers. Twelve percent were being reared in single-parent families, and less than 5% of their families had annual incomes less than $15,000. Mothers of children in the sample had attained 14.5 years of education, on average.

Three hundred eighty 7- to 12-year-old children from the Friedrich et al. (1991) study constitute the White subsample in the present analysis. The average age within the subsample is 9 years and the majority of children (54%) are female. Additional demographic information specific to 7- to 12-year-old children is not available because demographic information presented in the study reflects the entire sample of 2- to 12-year-olds and their caregivers. As a result, the ways in which the 7- to 12-year-old subsample might differ demographically from children and caregivers in the entire sample are unknown.

Thigpen (2009)

To enhance knowledge of childhood sexual behavior as it occurs within a specific racial/ethnic subgroup, Thigpen (2009) explored the range and frequency of sexual behavior of 2- to 12-year-old African American children without known histories of sexual abuse. Primary caregivers of these children were recruited from a public pediatric clinic and were administered the third version of the CSBI (Friedrich, 1997b) orally in a face-to-face interview format.[3] Of the 306 primary caregivers screened for inclusion in the study, four (1%) were deemed ineligible as a result of their children having known or suspected histories of sexual abuse or mental, physical, or developmental disabilities. Seventy-five primary caregivers, or 25%, refused to participate in the study due to lack of interest or time. Two hundred twenty seven primary caregivers were recruited into the sample and interviewed, representing a 74% participation rate. Sexual behavior data were collected on 249 children as 22 primary caregivers reported on two of their children.

All 249 of the children for whom CSBI data were collected were African American and 53% were male. Children in the sample ranged in age from 2 to 12 years with an average age of 5.8 years. Ninety percent of these children were being reared primarily by their biological or adoptive mothers, and 48% were being parented solely by mothers. On average, primary caregivers of these children had attained 12.5 years of education and a majority of the children's families (53%) had reported annual incomes of less than $15,000.

Ninety-two of the 249 children were 7 to 12 years of age, comprising the African American subsample in the present analysis. The average age for the 7- to 12-year-old subgroup was 9 years; 52% were male. Of these children, 39% were being reared in single-parent families and 42% in families with reported annual incomes below $15,000. Almost all of the children were being parented primarily by their biological or adoptive mothers. The average educational attainment for their caregivers was slightly above a high school education.

Child Sexual Behavior Inventory

The CSBI is a parental report measure of childhood sexual behavior developed by William Friedrich. Although the CSBI is primarily used as a tool to aid clinical practitioners in distinguishing sexually abused children from nonabused children, it has been widely used in research studies examining the sexual behavior of children with and without histories of sexual abuse. The third and current version of the instrument contains 38 items assessing a broad range of sexual behavior in nine behavioral domains: boundary problems, exhibitionism, gender role behavior, self-stimulation, sexual anxiety, sexual interest, sexual intrusiveness/sexual aggression, sexual knowledge, and voyeuristic behavior (see tables 2.3 and 2.5 for details).[4] These domains reflect content coverage only and are not intended to be used as subscales (Friedrich, 1997b). The CSBI is coded to capture the frequency of its items as observed by the primary caregiver in the 6-month period preceding the administration of the instrument (i.e., 0 = never, 1 = less than once per month, 2 = one to three times per month, 3 = once per week). A total raw score is obtained by summing the primary caregiver's responses to all 38 items. A mean frequency score is computed by dividing the raw score by the number of items, representing the average frequency of sexual behavior. The total raw and mean frequency scores are taken to reflect the overall level and average frequency of sexual behavior. These summary indices are not a part of the primary analytic strategy in the present analysis as they may veil patterns of sexual behavior that vary across children of different racial/ethnic backgrounds. However, the total raw score was used to explore the potential confounding of race and class within the African American sample as discussed below.

Analytic Approach

The overall analytic approach used in the present analysis involved comparing the proportion of children in each sample who were reported to have displayed the behaviors that compose the CSBI. Because of changes in the actual number and wording of items over time, only 22 items could be compared in the present analysis.

To assess meaningful behavioral differences between African American and White children, a two-step analytic strategy proposed by Friedrich and colleagues (2000) was modified and used. First, behaviors that differed by five percentage points or more between the two samples were identified. Second, behaviors that differed by ten percentage points or more were identified and regarded as significant.[5] To assess whether differences were statistically significant, one-tailed z-tests for difference in proportions were conducted for each item.[6] Statistical significance was set at the .05 level.

Gender and Class Considerations

Qualitative differences in the sexual behavior of boys and girls have consistently been documented (Gagnon, 1985; Friedrich et al., 1998; Thigpen, 2009). As a result, similarities and differences in the sexual behaviors of African American and White children were assessed separately by gender in the present analysis.

The potential confounding of race and social class for the African American sample was explored in two ways.[7] First, CSBI total raw scores were calculated for subgroups of 7- to 12-year-old African American children based on the primary caregiver's level of education, that is, one group that had primary caregivers with 13 years of education or less and a second group that had primary caregivers with 14 years of education or more.[8] Sixty-two percent of primary caregivers had 13 years of education or less; 38% had 14 years of education or more. The average CSBI total raw scores for children whose primary caregivers had attained 13 years of education or less and those with 14 years of education or more, respectively, were 2.66 and 1.65. An independent samples T-test revealed that this difference was not statistically significant ($t = 1.122$, $p = .265$).[9] CSBI data for African American boys and girls whose primary caregivers had different levels of education were therefore combined.

The present study also explored the confounding of race and class by assessing differences within the African American sample when CSBI items differed by ten percentage points or more between the African American and White samples. For each behavioral item, the statistical significance of differences in the proportion of African American caregivers with different levels of education having observed the behavior was assessed using z-tests for differences in proportions. The statistical significance was set at the .05 level.

Results

Boys

The subsample of male children contained 206 White boys and 48 African American boys. The average age for both groups was roughly 9 years (see table 2.2).

Table 2.3 shows the prevalence of the 22 CSBI items for boys. Behaviors reflecting self-stimulation, boundary-related difficulties, sexual interest, voy-

TABLE 2.3

Prevalence of Child Sexual Behavior Inventory (CSBI) Items
for 7- to 12-Year-Old African American and White Boys

CSBI Items by Domain of Sexual Behavior	White Boys	African American Boys
	n=206	n=48
	%	%
Gender Role-Related Behavior		
1. Dresses like the opposite sex	3.4	0.0
2. Wants to be the opposite sex	1.9	0.0
Self-Stimulation		
3. Touches his private (sex) parts in public places	15.5	8.0
4. Masturbates with hand	11.2	4.0
5. Masturbates with toy or object	0.0	0.0
6. Touches his private (sex) parts at home	36.4*	21.0*
7. Puts objects in vagina/rectum	0.0	0.0
Boundary-Related Behavior		
8. Rubs body against people or furniture	4.4	6.0
9. Touches or tries to touch mother's or women's breasts	11.7	4.0
10. Hugs adults he doesn't know well	2.4	0.0
Sexual Interest		
11. Makes sexual sounds (signs, moans, heavy breathing)	3.9	6.2
12. Talks flirtatiously	2.9	8.0
13. Is very interested in the opposite sex	19.9***	42.0***
Sexual Intrusiveness/Sexual Aggression		
14. Asks others to engage in sexual acts with him	0.0	0.0
15. When kissing, tries to put tongue in other person's mouth	2.4	0.0

TABLE 2.3 *(continued)*

CSBI Items by Domain of Sexual Behavior	%	%
Voyeuristic Behavior		
16. Tries to look when people are nude or undressing	27.7*	15.0*
17. Tries to look at pictures of nude or partially dressed people	27.2	15.0
18. Wants to watch TV or movies that show nudity or sex	6.8*	17.0*
Sexual Knowledge		
19. Pretends that dolls or stuffed animal are having sex	2.9	10.0
20. Talks about sexual acts	9.2	8.0
Exhibitionistic Behavior		
21. Shows private (sex) parts to adults	9.7	0.0
22. Shows private (sex) parts to other children	4.4	0.0

*p < .05, ** p < .01, ***p < .001

eurism, and sexual knowledge were observed in both African American and White boys. Touching of the genitals at home, trying to look when people are nude or undressing, trying to look at pictures of nude or partially dressed people, and showing a keen interest in the opposite sex were the most prevalent behaviors in both samples. Placing objects in their rectums, masturbating with a toy/object, or asking others to engage in sex were not observed for African American or White boys.

White boys displayed a broader range of behavior: 19 items were observed for them compared to 13 items for African American boys. Prevalence rates were also higher for White boys on 13 of the 19 behavioral items. A five percentage point difference between the two samples emerged for 11 behaviors. African American boys had higher prevalence rates for four behaviors: talking flirtatiously, showing interest in the opposite sex, wanting to watch television or movies that show nudity or sex, and pretending that dolls or stuffed animals are having sex. Conversely, White boys had higher prevalence rates for seven behaviors: touching private parts in public, masturbating with a hand, touching private parts at home, touching or trying to touch women's breasts, trying to look when people are nude or undressing, trying to look at pictures of nude or partially dressed people, and showing private parts to adults.

Five items differed by ten percentage points or more between African American and White boys: touching private parts at home, being very interested in the opposite sex, trying to look when people are nude or undressing, trying to look at pictures of nude or partially dressed people, and wanting to watch television or movies that show nudity or sex. Proportions of reported behaviors were statistically significantly higher for White boys for touching private parts at home ($z = 1.89$, $p = .02$) and trying to look when people are nude or undressing ($z = 1.69$, $p = .04$). For African American boys, proportions were statistically significantly higher for being very interested in the opposite sex ($z = 2.79$, $p = .00$) and wanting to watch television or movies that show nudity or sex ($z = 1.90$, $p = .02$). African American and White boys did not differ significantly in their attempts to look at pictures of nude or partially dressed people. No statistically significant differences in the prevalence of the five behaviors that differed between African American and White boys by ten percentage points or more were found between African American boys whose primary caregivers had different levels of education (see table 2.4).

Girls

The subsample of female children comprised 174 White and 44 African American girls. Girls in both groups were, on average, 9 years of age (see table 2.2).

Prevalence rates for the 22 CSBI items for African American and White girls are presented in table 2.5. Girls in both samples were reported to display behaviors reflecting self-stimulation, boundary-related difficulties, sexual interest, and voyeurism. Showing interest in the opposite sex and talking flirtatiously were the most prevalent behaviors within both samples, although observed percentages differed.

As with boys, White girls displayed a wider range of behavior as all 22 of the behavioral items were observed for them compared to only 11 items for African American girls. Prevalence rates were higher among White girls for 20 of the behavioral items; African American girls had higher prevalence rates for wanting to watch television or movies that show nudity or sex and dressing like the opposite sex.

TABLE 2.4

*Prevalence of CSBI Items for 7- to 12-Year-Old African American Boys
by Primary Caregiver Level of Education (n=48)*

CSBI Items	Primary Caregiver Educational Attainment			
	≤ 13 Years	≥ 14 Years		
	(n=32)	(n=16)	z-value	p-value
	%	%		
1. Is very interested in the opposite sex	46.8	31.2	0.725	.47
2. Touches his private (sex) parts at home	18.7	25.0	0.126	.90
3. Tries to look when people are nude or undressing	18.7	6.2	0.723	.47
4. Tries to look at pictures of nude/partially dressed people	21.8	0.0	1.591	.11
5. Wants to watch TV or movies that show nudity or sex	25.0	0.0	1.780	.07

Seven behaviors differed by at least five percentage points between African American and White girls: masturbating with a hand, touching her private parts at home, showing interest in the opposite sex, trying to look when people are nude or undressing, trying to look at pictures of nude or partially dressed people, wanting to watch television or movies that show nudity or sex, and talking about sexual acts. Wanting to watch television or movies that show nudity or sex was the only one of these seven behaviors that was more prevalent among African American girls.

Five behaviors differed by at least ten percentage points between the two subsamples: touching private parts at home, being very interested in the opposite sex, trying to look when people are nude or undressing, trying to look at pictures of nude or partially dressed people, and wanting to watch television or movies that show nudity or sex. Proportions of these five behaviors were statistically significantly higher for White girls on touching private parts at home

TABLE 2.5

Prevalence of CSBI Items for 7- to 12-Year-Old African American and White Girls

CSBI Items by Domain of Sexual Behavior	White Girls	African American Girls
	n = 174	n = 44
	%	%
Gender Role–Related Behavior		
1. Dresses like the opposite sex	2.9	4.6
2. Wants to be the opposite sex	1.1	0.0
Self-Stimulation		
3. Touches her private (sex) parts in public places	2.9	0.0
4. Masturbates with hand	8.6	0.0
5. Masturbates with toy or object	1.7	0.0
6. Touches her private (sex) parts at home	18.4***	2.3***
7. Puts objects in vagina/rectum	0.6	0.0
Boundary-Related Behavior		
8. Rubs body against people or furniture	4.6	0.0
9. Touches or tries to touch mother's or women's breasts	9.2	4.6
10. Hugs adults she doesn't know well	4.0	0.0
Sexual Interest		
11. Makes sexual sounds (signs, moans, heavy breathing)	0.6	0.0
12. Talks flirtatiously	14.9	13.7
13. Is very interested in the opposite sex	32.8	22.7
Sexual Intrusiveness/Sexual Aggression		
14. Asks others to engage in sexual acts with her	0.6	0.0
15. When kissing, tries to put tongue in other person's mouth	1.7	0.0

TABLE 2.5 *(continued)*

CSBI Items by Domain of Sexual Behavior	%	%
Voyeuristic Behavior		
16. Tries to look when people are nude or undressing	14.9	4.6
17. Tries to look at pictures of nude or partially dressed people	18.4*	4.6*
18. Wants to watch TV or movies that show nudity or sex	3.4*	13.7*
Sexual Knowledge		
19. Pretends that dolls or stuffed animals are having sex	7.5	4.6
20. Talks about sexual acts	10.3	4.6
Exhibitionistic Behavior		
21. Shows private (sex) parts to adults	6.9	2.3
22. Shows private (sex) parts to other children	2.3	0.0

*p < .05, ** p < .01, ***p < .001

($z = 2.43$, $p = .00$) and trying to look at pictures of nude or partially dressed people ($z = 2.03$, $p = .02$). The difference between proportions for wanting to watch television or movies that show nudity or sex was statistically significantly higher for African American girls ($z = 2.28$, $p = .01$). Differences between African American and White girls regarding trying to look when people are nude or undressing and being very interested in the opposite sex were not statistically significant. For the five behaviors that differed between African American and White girls by ten percentage points or more, no statistically significant differences in prevalence were observed between African American girls whose primary caregivers had different levels of education (see table 2.6).

Discussion

Similarities and differences in the sexual behaviors of 7- to 12-year-old African American and White children emerged in the present analysis. African Ameri-

TABLE 2.6

Prevalence of Select CSBI Items for 7- to 12-Year-Old African American Girls
by Primary Caregiver Level of Education (n=44)

Select CSBI Items	Primary Caregiver Educational Attainment			
	≤ 13 Years (n=25) %	≥ 14 Years (n=19) %	z-value	p-value
1. Is very interested in the opposite sex	12.0	36.8	1.584	.113
2. Touches her private (sex) parts at home	0.0	5.2	0.139	.89
3. Tries to look when people are nude or undressing	8.0	0.0	0.531	.595
4. Tries to look at pictures of nude/partially dressed people	8.0	0.0	0.531	.595
5. Wants to watch TV or movies that show nudity or sex	12.0	15.7	-0.081	1.00

can and White boys alike displayed a wide range of behaviors, with behaviors reflecting sexual interest, self-stimulation, and voyeurism being most prevalent within both groups of boys. Despite these broad similarities, African American and White boys did exhibit differential patterns of sexual behavior. White boys displayed a broader range of behaviors and the prevalence of the majority of behaviors was higher for White boys. Qualitative and quantitative behavioral differences also emerged between the two groups. Self-stimulatory behaviors inclusive of genital touching and masturbation were significantly more prevalent among White boys as were voyeuristic behaviors, specifically trying to look when people are nude or undressing and trying to look at pictures of nude or partially dressed people. Behaviors largely reflecting sexual interest such as talking flirtatiously and being very interested in the opposite sex were significantly more prevalent among African American boys.

Similar to boys, African American and White girls displayed a broad range of sexual behaviors. Within this range, behaviors reflective of sexual interest were most prevalent, specifically talking flirtatiously and being very interested in the opposite sex. The sexual behaviors of African American and White girls differed in that a much wider range of behaviors—11 compared to 22 behavioral items, respectively—was noted for White girls. In addition, the prevalence of the majority of behaviors was considerably higher for White girls. Moreover, significant qualitative and quantitative differences between the two groups were noted. Among White girls, the self-stimulatory behaviors of masturbation and genital touching were more prevalent, as was the voyeuristic behavior of trying to look at pictures of nude or partially dressed people. The voyeuristic behavior of wanting to watch television or movies that show nudity or sex was more prevalent among African American girls.

That sexual interest and voyeurism, a specific aspect of sexual interest characterized by a child's efforts to view the sexual parts of others, emerged as the most prominent types of sexual behaviors across racial/ethnic and gender categories may suggest that these behaviors are normative for 7- to 12-year-old children. Recent research has shown that sexual interest is more prevalent among older (i.e., 6- to 12-year-old) children (Thigpen, 2009). Several studies additionally connect the onset of sexual attraction, fantasy, and behavior with the maturation of the adrenal glands at about the age of 10 (Herdt & McClintock, 2000). In the present analysis, the average age across the four subgroups of children was approximately 9 years; substantial percentages of these children were between 10 and 12 years old. Although it is plausible that biological factors account for the sexual interest of children around the age of 10, it is likely that social factors also contribute to their increased interest in sexual matters insofar as other people increasingly recognize children's sexual capacity as they approach puberty. Some of the children in the present analysis may have been pubertal, particularly within the African American sample, as African American children are known to begin sexual maturation earlier than children of other racial groups (Sun et al., 2002).

Gender Differences in Sexual Behavior

Behavioral differentiation by gender was also observed across racial/ethnic groups. Two patterns were noted. First, genital touching and masturbatory behaviors were less prevalent among girls. Taking into account the findings of several published research studies, Rutter (1971) discusses the higher prevalence of genital manipulation and masturbatory behaviors among boys and points to thigh rubbing as an alternative source of stimulation for girls. Although it is not clear what underlies these differences, Hyde and DeLamater (2011) theorize that they stem from the greater visibility of the penis and the likelihood that boys experience pleasure when the penis comes in contact with external objects such as clothing. It is worth noting that pronounced gender differences in masturbation are observed in adulthood (Laumann et al., 1994), suggesting that early differences may be reinforced and exaggerated over the life course via cumulative experiences.

The lower prevalence of the majority of sexual behaviors for girls is a second gender-related behavioral pattern that emerged in the analysis. It is conceivable that different behavioral patterns appeared among boys and girls because they are socialized differently. Money and Ehrhardt (1996) contend that children learn what it means to be male and female very early in life through a socialization process that involves being consistently treated as masculine or feminine. Through this process, children acquire the attitudes, behaviors, and values consistent with their gender assignment (Amaro, Navarro, Conron, & Raj, 2002), which they must continually accomplish, or "do," throughout the life course in order to be seen as properly gendered beings (see chapter 1, this volume). Recent research by Martin and Luke (2010) illuminates how gender influences children's sexual socialization. In their study, mothers of 3- to 6-year-old children were significantly more likely to discuss issues pertaining to sexual morality with their daughters than with their sons. An alternate explanation for the lower prevalence of sexual behaviors among girls in the present analysis involves the possibility that primary caregivers are biased to report behavior that is consistent with cultural ideas regarding appropriate gendered behavior. Female sexuality has historically been regarded as inherently passive and considered only in terms of reproduction. Long-standing and constraining cultural notions of the sexually demure female and the sexually aggressive male persist today (Amaro et al., 2002). It follows that primary caregivers may have reported behaviors consistent with these cultural ideas, and perhaps they underreported the sexual behavior of girls. Studies have shown that adults experience more anxiety over girls' displays of sexual behavior than over boys' behavior (Borneman, 1990; Goldman & Goldman, 1982). Research also suggests that parents may more frequently admonish the sexual behaviors of girls than those of boys, thus potentially inhibiting girls' sexual expression (Boat & Everson, 1992).

Cultural Influences on Childhood Sexuality

Analysis revealed two behavioral patterns for which cultural explanations are plausible. First, the different prevalence of genital touching and masturbation reported for African American and White boys and girls may stem from cultural differences. Studies have shown that White adults are more likely than African American adults to engage in sexual practices such as masturbation and oral and anal sex (Laumann et al., 1994; Weinberg & Williams, 1988). To the extent that these behaviors are regarded as inappropriate by African Americans (Staples, 1973; Sterk-Elifson, 1994), it may be that African American primary caregivers socialize their children away from such behaviors.

A second behavioral pattern for which a cultural explanation is conceivable pertains to the differential breadth of sexual behaviors reported for African American and White children. The range of reported sexual behaviors was narrower for African American boys and girls. The prevalence rates for the majority of behaviors were considerably lower as well. The different attitudes and beliefs known to exist among African American and White adults may underlie these patterns insofar as they influence the way African American and White parents socialize their children. Holding social class constant, Mahay, Laumann, and Michaels (2001) found that race/ethnicity had an independent effect on the sexual beliefs, attitudes, and practices of U.S. adults. Based in conservative Protestant religious ideologies, the belief systems of African Americans were more traditional in that African Americans were more likely than Whites to regard reproduction as the sole purpose of sex and more likely to disapprove of premarital sex, homosexuality, and teenage sex.[10] Whites held more liberal attitudes regarding premarital sex, homosexuality, and the influence of religion on sexual beliefs. It is possible that a traditional belief system, holding that procreation is the sole purpose of sex and that teenage sex is wrong, would also influence parents' beliefs about the sexual behavior of children and, importantly, influence parents' reactions to children's displays of sexual behavior. Children reared in a more traditional environment are potentially more likely to be admonished for behaving in a way that parents perceive as sexual. This type of parental reaction, in turn, is likely to diminish the likelihood that the behavior will occur in the future, at least in the presence of the parent. As Gagnon and Simon (1973) discuss, parental reactions have the potential to communicate a sense of judgment that morally conditions the child around sexual matters, including sexual behavior.

Several competing explanations for the patterns of behavior linked to culture in the present analysis should be noted. First, the observed differences may be a function of social class rather than of race/ethnicity. The role of social class in mediating sexual beliefs and behaviors has been well documented (Laumann et al., 1994; Mahay et al., 2001; Weinberg & Williams, 1988). However, if the behavioral differences observed in the present analysis were due to social class, different patterns should have been found for children of African American primary caregivers with varying levels of education and similar behavioral patterns should have emerged for children of African American and White primary caregivers with comparable levels of education. Social class did not have an effect in the present analysis; patterns of behavior were not significantly different for African American primary caregivers with different levels of education. Further, differential behavioral patterns were reported by African American and White primary caregivers who had similar levels of education. That said, subgrouping the African American sample based on the primary caregiver's level of education reduced the size of each subgroup, potentially affecting the accuracy of the statistical analyses. The influence of social class on the sexual behavior of children warrants further investigation.

Differences in family structure may also be a reason for the differential patterns of behavior observed for African American and White children. Forty-eight percent of African American primary caregivers characterized their family structure as single-parent compared to 12% of White primary caregivers. It is possible that opportunities to observe child behavior differ between single-parent and two-parent family structures.

That African American primary caregivers may have underreported the sexual behaviors of their children is a final alternative explanation for the patterns of behavior theorized to be associated with culture in the present analysis. West (2001) contends that long-standing and widely held perceptions about the uncontrollable sexual appetites of African American men and women have created a legacy of sexual silence within the African American community. African Americans remain reluctant to discuss sexuality openly out of fear that doing so will confirm such long-standing stereotypes. As a result, African American primary caregivers may have represented their children in such a way as to avoid reinforcing racialized notions of hypersexuality (Roberts, 1997; Collins, 2005).

Cultural explanations for the differences in the behavioral patterns of African American and White children in the present study are tenable; the findings suggest that culture is an important contextual factor to consider in understanding the sexual behavior of children within a multicultural society such as the United States. The recent trend toward identifying children with sexual behavior problems underscores the importance of understanding the cultural context insofar as problematic sexual behavior in childhood is assessed relative to deviations from what is assumed to be normal (Carpentier et al., 2006). Because what is known about normative sexual behavior and development in childhood is limited, all children are at risk for having their behavior pathologized and labeled. African American children are at an increased risk for labeling given that they have been largely absent from the few studies that have been conducted (Thigpen, Pinkston, & Mayefsky, 2003). Pervasive societal stereotypes of African American hypersexuality as well as the traditional sexual views of African American primary caregivers may also place these children at risk.

Several limitations of this exploratory analysis should be noted. First, measures of childhood sexual behavior that rely upon parental reports are not likely to yield a complete picture of the sexual behavior of children, especially as the children grow older. However, our societal commitment to the idea of sexual innocence in childhood is likely to impede researchers who seek to talk to children about their sexual behaviors. Second, administration of the CSBI in a face-to-face interview format may have influenced the reports of African American primary caregivers. None of the primary caregivers refused to answer any of the items, and none indicated that the nature of the questions made them uncomfortable (Thigpen & Fortenberry, 2010). A third limitation also pertains to the CSBI, particularly the heteronormative nature of its items. The instrument does not assess sexual behavior that occurs between children of the same sex. This is an important omission insofar as the occurrence of both same-gender and cross-gender sexual play has been documented (Lamb & Coakley, 1993; Leitenberg et al., 1989), suggesting that sexual play between children of the same sex is common. Fourth, regional differences may have had an effect on the findings. Both studies were carried out in midwestern cities. However, the cities differ demographically and economically. A final limitation pertains to the 18-year time lapse between the two studies. Although there are no known broad structural changes that occurred during this time period that would directly affect sexual behavior in these two samples, it is conceivable that there might be a cohort effect, given the increasing pervasiveness of sexual themes and messages in mass media over time. This may reflect—or create—changes in societal attitudes regarding sexuality.

The study of childhood sexuality is in its infancy. More research is needed to understand sexuality more fully in this distinct developmental period. Future research using more rigorous designs and methodologies should be undertaken to confirm (or disconfirm) the role of culture in shaping children's sexual behavior and expression. Emphasis should also be given to other aspects of socio-sexual development insofar as the unique sexual learning and experiences that take place in childhood do not occur within a vacuum. Rather, sexual learning and experiences occur in the broader social context in which families and other prominent figures in children's lives exist. It is important to understand how different contexts influence sexual development and behavior. The role of parents should receive particular attention because parents' beliefs and attitudes about sexuality are likely to be conveyed to their children implicitly and explicitly, including messages that potentially reproduce and normalize heterosexuality (Martin, 2009). Parental beliefs and attitudes about childhood sexual behavior should be explored as these meaning systems are likely to prompt reactions that will mediate the sexual expression of children in significant ways. An additional line of inquiry should address how sexual learning and experience in childhood affect sexual development in adolescence and adulthood; the continuities and discontinuities of sexuality over the life course are, as yet, unclear.

NOTES

1. Antoinette is a pseudonym.

2. Normative here refers to the typical range of sexual behaviors observed in children, particularly those children without histories of sexual abuse or sexual aggression.

3. Concerns about literacy, interpretation of items, and the overall response rate motivated this mode of administration. All interviews were conducted in private exam rooms by trained research assistants. Primary caregivers were informed of their right to refuse to answer any questions. Although this mode of administration differs from that used by Friedrich et al. (1991), the instrument's creator states that no research suggests that reading the items to the caregiver or using the CSBI in a structured interview format invalidates the responses (Friedrich, 1997b).

4. Analyses of the CSBI's psychometric properties suggest that it is a reliable and valid measure of childhood sexual behavior for children from families of diverse social and economic backgrounds (Friedrich, 1997b). Reliability means that a measurement procedure yields consistent results. Validity exists when a measurement procedure measures what it is purported to measure. The reliability and validity of the CSBI were assessed using data from samples of primary caregivers of sexually abused and nonabused children. Thigpen (2009) assessed the reliability of the CSBI for African American children; his analysis yielded an Alpha coefficient of .72, indicating reasonable internal consistency. For the present analysis, a separate reliability analysis was conducted specifically for 7- to 12-year-old African American children. This analysis yielded a similar result ($\alpha = .87$). An Alpha coefficient of .82 was reported for the earlier version of the CSBI used in the Friedrich et al. (1991) study. Separate reliability analyses were not reported for children of different ages, however.

5. Friedrich and colleagues' (2000) analytic strategy regarded behaviors that differed by 20 percentage points or more as significant. Because only one behavior in the present analysis differed by 20 percentage points or more across children's race, the cut-off point was lowered to ten percentage points or more.

6. The two-sample z-test compares proportions from two independent samples to determine if the observed difference is real or due to chance variation (Freedman, Pisani, & Purves, 1998).

7. Confounding refers to the potential to attribute behavioral differences to race when, in fact, they are attributable to social class (or vice versa).

8. The primary caregiver's level of education was selected as an indicator of social class in the present analysis. The educational break specified above was an attempt to divide the African American sample along class lines consistent with the average level of maternal/primary caregiver education reported in the Friedrich et al. (1991) sample (i.e., 14.5 years).

9. An independent samples T-test is a statistical test that compares the average scores of two groups on a given variable.

10. Beliefs among African Americans were patterned by gender, with women holding more traditional beliefs (as noted above) and men taking a more recreational stance (i.e., not regarding reproduction or relational intimacy as the chief purpose of sex).

3

Sexuality Development in Adolescence

STEPHEN T. RUSSELL, KALI S. VAN CAMPEN,
AND JOEL A. MURACO

"Abstinence" has been a focal point in policy and public debates about adolescent sexuality for over 30 years. As a candidate, President Barack Obama made news when he promised to end federal funding for "abstinence-only" sexuality education in public schools, programs that emphasize chastity until marriage and disallow education about contraception. Instead, the Obama administration has returned to an earlier framework for adolescent sexuality policy, focusing on teenage pregnancy prevention (for a history of such policies through the Reagan era, see Nathanson, 1991). Both policy frames reveal deeply held views of adolescent sexuality as something to be contained or something (inherently) risky to be prevented. Beyond policy debates, these tropes of containment or prevention feed concerns about a wide range of issues related to teens and sexuality, such as gay youth suicide, oral sex orgies, and "girls gone wild." Yet many scholars argue for a holistic, developmental view, one that includes the possibility of a positive framework for understanding adolescent sexuality (Russell, 2005).

Adolescence is a crucial stage of the life course for the development of sexuality. It is characterized by dramatic developmental changes entailing not only the physical changes of puberty but also the cognitive capacities that enable young people to understand and analyze interpersonal relations and social institutions, including cultural meanings of sexuality. Most societies view sexual activity prior to adolescence as either innocent childhood exploration or as pathologically precocious and deviant. As they approach puberty, children become markedly more interested in sexuality (Thigpen, 2009). However, little research has addressed childhood sexuality before puberty, so we know little about how children develop interest in sexuality or about what they do sexually (see Thigpen, this volume). Most researchers agree that the possibilities for developing a sexual self are chiefly constructed and integrated into one's identity beginning in adolescence. During this life stage, the ways that societies view sexuality in general—and adolescent sexuality in particular—enable and constrain young people's sexual development (that is, their sexual identities, experiences, and agency). These opportunities and constraints are further contingent on social statuses, including gender, race, ethnicity, social class, and sexual orientation. Given the sexual trajectories available during this life stage, sexuality development in adolescence sets the stage for expressions of sexuality throughout the rest of the life course.

This chapter frames its discussion of adolescent sexuality around the need to shift from a historical discourse of risk and restriction to the possibility for positive development of sexual agency. This shift will, in turn, promote opportunities for sexual health. Our focus is primarily on Western societies, for that is our location and the vantage point from which most research and theory has come. We briefly review the developmental changes of adolescent sexuality that have importance for sexuality trajectories at the individual, social, and cultural levels. Next, we turn to the roles that culture and sexual socialization play in individuals' adoption or rejection of cultural-level sexual scripts. We link this discussion of social context to the current realities and possibilities for adolescents' sexual agency, particularly with respect to gender, race and ethnicity, social class, and sexual identity statuses within U.S. society (and perhaps in other Western societies). Throughout, we argue for reconceptualizing adolescent sexuality development from a positive perspective. Doing so will maximize opportunities for adolescents to make healthy sexual choices and ensure their sexual well-being.

Sexual Risk, Developmental Change, and Positive Sexuality

For more than 100 years, the scientific study of adolescence has focused predominantly on the problems that teenagers may experience. Some theorists argue that this problem focus derives from the way adolescence itself has been historically conceptualized, as a period of life that needs to be tightly regulated by society, with sexual regulation at its core (Lehr, 2008). This strict regulation of adolescent sexuality has occurred in the context of a broader Western societal ambivalence regarding youth, sexuality, and youthful sexualities. Especially in the United States, we glamorize youthful sexuality even as we construct adolescent sexuality as a social problem and endorse public policy that largely restricts adolescent sexual activity (Russell, 2005). Because of this ambivalence, the field of adolescent sexuality research as a whole has been unable to shake the "problem and disease" framework. Research and health interventions largely focus on problems associated with sexuality, such as violence, disease, or pregnancy. Lack of integrated, interdisciplinary dialogue makes it difficult to situate normative adolescent sexuality development in the broader context of sexuality across the life course.

Large-scale historical changes have made the reframing of adolescent sexuality a societal imperative. Contemporary youth reach sexual maturity at much earlier ages than they did a century ago, due in part to advances in hygiene and nutrition (Karlberg, 2002). This trend has altered both the individual life course and previous patterns of human variation in health and development. For example, in the early 1900s, the changes associated with puberty marked the shift to adult roles and responsibilities with little transition between childhood and adulthood (Modell, 1989). As adolescence emerged as a life stage during the postindustrial period, it came to be viewed as a time of physical maturation, advancing education, and the learning of trades. Once adolescence became an institutionalized phase of the life course, long-held religious and cultural proscriptions on nonmarital sexual activity became specific prohibitions against adolescent sexual expression outside the marital context (Lehr, 2008). The result has been a widening gap between the age at which young people become physically and sexually mature and the age at which they earn the social statuses of adulthood. Learning to negotiate this gap has become a fundamental developmental challenge for young people today, as well as for the adult caretakers and institutions that guide them.

At a basic level, clearer understanding is needed of the multidimensionality of adolescent development as it relates to sexuality. Although families and schools often focus on the physical changes of puberty and expectations for sexual behavior, they typically pay less attention to the dramatic psychological and social changes that are triggered by puberty. Relationships with parents, peers, and the wider adult community notably shift as adolescents' physical appearance transforms from that of children to sexually mature adults. These interpersonal changes prompt young people to consider new meanings and attributions of their changing bodies and social relationships. By mid-adolescence, individuals demonstrate the cognitive capacity to understand, interpret, adopt, and at times challenge the sexual scripts that shape sexualities in their communities and cultures (DeLamater & Hasday, 2007). Yet typical sexual socialization practices in the family consist merely of parents' communication of their goals for adolescents' individual sexual values and behaviors (Fisher, 2004); sex education in schools, at least in the United States, often provides little more (Schalet, 2004). Thus, almost no publicly sanctioned discourse on adolescent sexuality includes critical analysis of dominant understandings of sexuality, or the possibilities of positive sexuality development in which young people can explore sexuality responsibly and safely.

The risk framework limits the possible pathways for healthy development across adolescence because it largely defines sexual trajectories in terms of uncompromising, dichotomous, negative sexual scripts: a teen is "abstinent" or loses her or his virginity; a teen is healthy or gets a sexually transmitted infection (STI); young women are either "good girls" or "sluts," while young men are "losers" or "players." As a result, sexual possibilities have narrowed dramatically, such that losing one's virginity is understood as a major life marker (Carpenter, 2005), and few pathways for gradual sexual awakening and development exist during the teenage years.

Yet new discourses have come from marginalized groups, those who have not shared the prevailing adolescent sexual scripts. Beginning with the civil rights movement in the 1950s, multiple social movements in the United States and elsewhere in the West have challenged social norms and boundaries pertaining to adolescence and to sexualities (Herdt, Russell, Sweat, & Marzullo, 2007). Sexual liberation and the youth counterculture in the 1960s, followed by the women's movement and gay and lesbian liberation movements of the 1970s, fundamentally transformed cultural understandings of adolescence and sexuality. These movements created possibilities for affirmative discourse about sexuality and desire among people of color, women, sexual minorities, and even youth, and opportunities to expand or challenge dominant sexual scripts for adolescents.

A small but growing body of work has conceptualized *positive sexuality development* (sometimes called "healthy sexuality development") in adolescence (Russell, 2005). In Germany, healthcare and family planning services are available to all people regardless of age and income, and young people can obtain contraceptives at little or no cost (Carpenter, 2001). Compared to German adolescents, American teens use contraceptives much less frequently, and their birth, pregnancy, and abortion rates are four times higher. In her comparative studies of parents and adolescents in the United States and the Netherlands, Schalet (2004) found that, as part of a cultural transition since the mid-1960s, Dutch society has reconceptualized adolescent sexuality as something that can be discussed openly among family members. Dutch parents normalize talk about sex with their children so that sexuality does not produce anxiety or emotional disruptions in the family. They teach their children to recognize and regulate their sexuality and to understand sex in the context of relationships. As a result, Dutch teenagers exhibit safer and more protective sexual behaviors (e.g., significantly lower pregnancy, birth, abortion, and STI rates) than their U.S. counterparts. In contrast, adolescent sexuality in the United States is dramatized as "raging hormones" (Schalet, 2004, p. 2) that lead to out-of-control, dangerous, and immoral behavior, prompting the belief that U.S. teens must be tightly regulated.

Other empirical work has shown the potentially positive roles of romance and sexual intimacy in young people's lives. For example, a study of college students found that a positive first sexual experience was predicted by body satisfaction, exposure to parental messages about sexual freedom, the degree to which the experience was intentional (versus spontaneous), and the extent to which students endorsed "nontraditional" gender roles (Smiler, Ward, Caruthers, & Merriwether, 2005). As societies seriously consider romantic and sexual experiences among youth as potentially affirmative, they become open to considering other positive implications of adolescent sexual expression. A study of Australian adolescent women showed that those who had more sexual experience reported more awareness of sexual feelings and sexual agency (Horne & Zimmer-Gembeck, 2005). Another study of U.S. adolescent couples found that kissing and desire were strongly linked to relationship satisfaction and commitment (Welsh, Haugen, Widman, Darling, & Grello, 2005). However, for younger adolescent couples, sexual intercourse was negatively associated with relationship quality, whereas for older couples, intercourse was positively associated with commitment. By moving beyond assumptions that the "outcomes" of sexual behavior will be negative for all youth, these studies highlight what has long been known about adult sexual relationships: sexual expression can promote close relationships and commitment. Yet we need to better understand developmental differences.

Sexual Agency and the Opportunities and Constraints of Social Statuses

Central to models of positive sexuality development is sexual agency, or feelings of empowerment in the sexual domain. Sexual agency can be understood as individuals' beliefs in their ability to act upon sexual needs in a relationship, such as enjoying sex, refusing unwanted sex, or insisting on the use of protection (Impett, Schooler, & Tolman, 2006). Sexual agency is one dimension of the larger construct of human agency, which evolves throughout the life course in tandem with human development. Agency as a general construct refers to the beliefs that people hold about their efficacy to produce results by their actions; these beliefs influence how individuals negotiate pathways throughout life (Bandura, 2006). Not only are efficacy beliefs the foundation for motivations, well-being, and accomplishments, but they are also a key personal resource in self-development, adaptation, and change.

Historically, leading theorists asserted that adolescents lack agency due to incomplete individual development of cognition and self-determination, as well as structural conditions that constrain individual autonomy, such as the lengthening period of economic and social dependency that now characterizes adolescence and young adulthood (Lehr, 2008). Hence social control is frequently used to direct young people along developmental pathways. Yet evidence shows that adolescents are active agents who must regularly make choices about their behaviors and select their environments and relationships (Human Rights Watch, 2001). The cultivation of sexual agency is critical during adolescence. As young people negotiate their emerging sexuality in changing relationships, they increasingly need to rely on social self-regulative skills and personal efficacy to exercise control over sexual situations (Bandura, 2006). However, most societies foster ignorance and fail to prepare young people to manage their sexuality for themselves and in relations with others. Instead, adolescent sexuality is socially regulated and, for individual youth, personally un(der)examined. High rates of unintended pregnancy, STIs, and sexual coercion and assault among U.S. adolescents can be understood as evidence of the large-scale absence of sexual agency (Fine & McClelland, 2006).

In important ways, possibilities for and constraints on sexual agency depend on an individual's social statuses such as gender, sexual orientation, race/ethnicity, and social class. These statuses should not be understood as individual properties but as markers for structural or institutional opportunities and barriers that operate in young people's lives. Adolescents can transcend or reframe their social statuses by rejecting or transforming the meanings and sexual scripts related to these statuses; as we will describe below, many do. However, at least in the United States, people under 18 have few rights to act independently in the face of conflict with their parents, and even fewer rights to acquire the information they need to develop sexual identities and sexual agency. Further, many young people experience substantial harm from lack of societal acceptance of their sexual choices. Young women must navigate cultures of sexism as they come into an understanding of their sexual selves. Queer youth may be challenged because they navigate marginalized sexual identities and gender nonconformity. Racial and ethnic minority youth must also deal with multiple forms of marginalization; structural racism may constrain their life opportunities in general (Villarreuel & Walker, 2003) as well as provide circumscribed models of sexual expression. In the following sections, we consider patterns of gender, sexual identity, and race/ethnicity, and we close with recent examples of youth who are challenging dominant conceptualizations of their sexualities.

Developmental Changes and Gendered Sexual Trajectories

Due to physically observable and physiological changes during puberty, with subsequent increases in sexual arousal and desire, adolescents gain awareness of the social dimensions of sexuality. Additionally, during mid- to late adolescence, young people's cognitive capacities mature in ways that enable them to reflect on their sexual feelings and behavior; they also begin to understand, interpret, and enact the sexual scripts in their communities and cultures. Social norms for gender intensify during adolescence (Galambos, Almeida, & Petersen, 1990) such that boys and girls typically have different scripts for sexual expression and behavior available to them.

Most societies socialize their children regarding sexuality by encouraging them to abstain from sexual behavior until they are married or in committed romantic relationships. However, even in the West, where gender differences in opportunities are increasingly muted, girls and boys are generally given radically different messages about the sexual experiences that are appropriate for and available to them. These messages influence the degree to which they feel empowered to experience and explore their sexuality. Emerging sexuality in boys is accepted and boys are allowed freedom for sexual exploration; girls' displays of sexual feelings and behaviors are typically met with disapproval and regulation. Most boys are expected to develop a strong sex drive, and they often feel pressure to assert their sexual prowess to prove their manhood (Tolman, Spencer, Harmon, Rosen-Reynoso, & Striepe, 2004). Girls, on the other hand, are kept largely ignorant of their sexual anatomy and physiology, their capacity for sexual pleasure, and skills that would ensure their sexual safety (Impett et al., 2006). They are discouraged from becoming sexually active until they are married, or at least until they are in committed romantic relationships. These socialization practices assume that all children are heterosexual and, accordingly, must be prepared to participate in romantic relationships according to accepted gender norms (see Green, this volume).

Expectations about gender further dictate how individuals should behave in sexual situations. Girls are pressured to behave in feminine ways in their relationships with others, such as suppressing their anger, avoiding conflict, and being "nice" regardless of how they feel inside (Impett et al., 2006). They are also taught to manage their bodies to conform with ideal standards of female beauty, such that many internalize societal objectification and eventually learn to evaluate and assess their bodies rather than to feel and experience them. Boys, on the other hand, are socialized to adopt masculine norms such as acting tough in public, avoiding the disclosure of feelings, and hiding distress or vulnerability (Oransky & Maracek, 2009). As they progress through adolescence, many learn to regulate both their own and other boys' emotional expression to maintain a tough persona and avoid stigmatization or ridicule. These ideologies get internalized at young ages and are perpetuated through external rewards and punishments by family, teachers, coaches, peers, religious leaders, and the mass media (Laub, Somera, Gowen, & Diaz, 1999). The internalization process happens so early that most young people cannot recognize the social forces that influence the construction of gender ideologies; instead, youth come to think of these sexual scripts as normal and natural.

One way that pubertal changes intersect with gendered sexual socialization to shape sexual trajectories can be seen in the controversial issue of sexual desire. Despite evidence that girls may experience genital arousal to similar degrees as boys, girls often report lower rates of sexual desire (Laan & Janssen, 2007). One reason for this discrepancy is anatomical and physiological: penile erections provide boys with a distinct anatomical cue that allows them to detect and attribute meaning to physical arousal. Consequently, boys may have more opportunities to produce or re-create arousal (e.g., through masturbation). Some neurological evidence exists that men may be more sensitive to sexual stimuli than women; women may need greater amounts of stimulation in order to experience arousal. However, girls not only have fewer anatomical cues, but they also are socialized to restrict knowledge of their genitalia and to mistrust their bodily cues of physiological arousal (Horne & Zimmer-Gembeck, 2005). These socialization practices may offer another reason for sex differences in desire.

A recent and growing body of research suggests that female sexuality is more "fluid"—that is, more responsive to social and cultural factors—than men's (Diamond, 2008b). Therefore, females may be more likely to enjoy different kinds of sexuality and to change sexual identities over the life course. The concept of sexual fluidity partly explains the finding that males' and females' subjective appraisal of their sexual arousal (i.e., desire) seems to be determined by different factors. For both men and women, the sexual meaning of a sexual stimulus will generate a genital response; however, men will view that genital response as a more important source of information about their sexual desire than will women (Laan & Janssen, 2007). Women's subjective arousal appears to be more determined by the kinds of meanings (both positive and negative) they attribute to the sexual stimuli. In this sense, at least in contemporary times, women's sexual responses and behaviors seem to be more shaped by cultural, social, and situational factors than men's (Diamond, 2008b).

The tendency for men's and women's sexual trajectories to diverge throughout the life course reveals how cultural and gendered scripts may constrain young people's sexual choices to produce less than optimal sexual and relational experiences and consequences. A narrow framework regarding sexuality puts boys and girls at a disadvantage in their sexual experiences, but in different ways. Girls who have depressed or truncated awareness of sexual feelings may not be able to be guided by those feelings (Tolman, 2002). Their sexual agency thus compromised, young women are more at risk of putting themselves in potentially dangerous situations. In fact, many girls report unwanted or coercive intercourse, low sexual desire, and high rates of STIs (Fine & McClelland, 2006). Boys, on the other hand, are often forced to choose between securing their masculinity or having satisfying, emotionally intimate relationships (Tolman et al., 2004). Many succumb to pressures to create public images as sexual "players" in pursuit of heterosexual sex. In doing so, they often end up hurting others by engaging in heterosexist behavior such as objectifying female bodies or boasting of heterosexual escapades; they also participate in homophobic behavior such as name-calling of boys who show signs of weakness or vulnerability (Pascoe, 2007).

Gendered scripts can be problematic for male adolescents in other ways. For example, the social costs of behaving in gender-atypical ways are higher for males than for females. During childhood, engaging in gender-based sexual scripts such as those based on masculine self-efficacy or feminine relationality is linked to self-esteem for both sexes (Allgood-Merten & Stockard, 1991). During adolescence and young adulthood, however, it is easier for girls to act in masculine ways than for boys to act in feminine ways. In fact, boys who do not conform to traditionally masculine gender norms are less likely to gain peer acceptance than their conforming male counterparts. These gender-atypical boys are considered deviant and suffer from greater self-image problems than boys who believe males should act "masculine"; however, the latter group is more likely to be involved in high-risk sexual behavior including having more sexual partners and more negative views about condom use (Pleck, Sonenstein, & Ku, 2004).

Queer Sexualities

Only during the last two to three decades have the social and behavioral sciences paid attention to lesbian, gay, bisexual, transgender, or queer (LGBTQ) adolescents.[1] From the earliest studies, research on same-sex sexuality in adolescence has focused on problems stemming from development in a heteronormative and homophobic society with a dominant focus on risk behaviors and negative health outcomes (Martin & Hetrick, 1988). Research clearly shows that LGBTQ adults are at disproportionate risk for emotional, behavioral, and physical health problems across the adult life span (Meyer, 2001). These disparities are presumed to have their origins in adolescence given the similar statistics about the health and well-being of queer adolescents.

The risk focus of the earliest research was consistent with the social invisibility and marginalization of queer people in the 1980s and 1990s. Although discrimination and inequality persist, social change since then has been dramatic. There have been large shifts in societal attitudes regarding same-sex sexuality alongside increasing visibility of queer people in the media and growing public attention to multiple LGBTQ issues. A decade ago the possibility for same-sex marriage may have seemed unlikely, but several U.S. states now issue marriage licenses to same-sex couples, and other states provide legal state-level spousal rights to unmarried couples. Conversely, a number of states have enacted laws defining marriage in heteronormative terms, as a union solely for a biological man and woman, resulting in increased tension and debate over the issue of same-sex marriage. These geographic differences matter for the well-being of adult gay and lesbian couples (Rostosky, Riggle, Horne, & Miller, 2009), and it is likely that these social changes make a difference for young people and their self-acceptance and willingness to "come out" (i.e., disclose their same-sex identities to family members, peers, or other adults) to others.

These social changes have created growing awareness of same-sex sexuality, and for adolescents the possibilities for understanding their developing sexuality as being queer. Indeed, studies document younger ages of coming out for recent cohorts of queer youth (Ryan & Futterman, 1998). A decade ago, Ryan and Futterman (1998) noted that queer youth for the first time had access to role models; prior generations had few queer role models or visions of happy and successful adulthoods from which to imagine their futures. Today there are many queer role models, along with growing access to information and resources for queer youth via the Internet (Russell, 2002). In light of these developments, Savin-Williams (2005) has argued that being queer in adolescence will cease to be—if it has not already—a distinctive or meaning-ful category of difference. However, these changes are defined by tensions and contestations of the authenticity, acceptability, and viability of queer identi-ties. In short, the life options and pathways into adult statuses that are taken for granted by many heterosexual youth—such as options for marriage or military service—remain truncated, blocked, or contested for queer youth.

Thus, in spite of recent social changes, it remains the case that queer youth are socialized to live heterosexual lives (see Green, this volume). Adolescents learn that romantic or sexual attraction for the "opposite" sex is privileged and assumed; historically, this normalization kept same-sex attractions largely invisible. Heterosexuality is normalized in the major institutions that shape adolescents' lives: family, school, faith, and mass media (Russell, 2002). Even the notion of "coming out" is based on the presumption of het-erosexuality. Coming out as an adolescent has historically been met with some form of family disturbance, even if only temporarily; ultimately, most families adjust to having a queer child (Heatherington & Lavner, 2008). Par-ticularly during the coming-out period, parent-adolescent relationships may be strained, and this family stress has negative repercussions for queer youth. A recent study found strong associations between a family's rejection of a child based on sexual orientation and dramatic health risks among LGBTQ adolescents and young adults (Ryan, Huebner, Diaz, & Sanchez, 2009).

Other developmentally normative adolescent sexuality experiences, such as dating and romance, remain elusive for young people who are queer and questioning, as well as for those who may be asexual or celibate (Don-nelly et al., 2001; Savin-Williams, 1994). Dating and romance are typically thought to be developmentally normal, meaningful, and important for ado-lescents' interpersonal development. The initiation of intimacy and romance is understood to be a core developmental task during the adolescent years; it provides young people with experiences to learn about trust, communi-cation, commitment, mutuality, and emotional expression, capacities that will serve them the rest of their lives. Yet, queer youth have historically been unable to form and maintain romantic relationships openly and easily. Due to the primacy of heterosexual dating scripts for teens, many LGBTQ ado-lescents may participate in heterosexual dating despite or because of their same-sex desires (Savin-Williams, 1994). However, Russell and Consolacion (2003) found that same-sex dating was associated with positive well-being: same-sex attracted youth who dated same-sex partners reported lower levels of anxiety and depression compared to those same-sex attracted youth who were single or who dated heterosexually.

In short, romantic relationships and intimacy play important roles in adolescence, and they have some of the same developmental benefits for LGBTQ youth that they do for young heterosexuals. Yet when LGBTQ adolescents conform to scripts for heterosexual dating, they appear to experience more anxiety and depression (Russell & Consolacion, 2003). Little prospective research exists that follows queer youth into adulthood, but we have reasons to suspect that adolescent dating and romantic experiences have lasting influence on their adult relationships.

Race, Ethnicity, Culture, and Youthful Sexualities

At a basic descriptive level, early sexual activity is associated with behaviors that place young people at high risk for negative health outcomes. Compared to their White counterparts, African American adolescent females tend to initiate sexual activity earlier, Latina adolescents experience sexual activity with partners who are "substantially older" (four or more years), and both are less likely to use any method of contraception (Centers for Disease Control and Prevention [CDC], 2009a). Further, African American youth are at disproportionately higher risk for STIs, HIV/AIDS, and teenage pregnancy than all other groups, and Latino and American Indian/Alaska Native adolescents also have higher risks of STIs, HIV/AIDS, and pregnancy than White youth. On the other hand, Asian American youth are more likely to delay sexual intercourse (Tosh & Simmons, 2007) and thus less likely to have negative sexual health outcomes than other racial and ethnic groups (CDC, 2009a). A growing body of research has identified social oppression, including prejudice and discrimination, persistent poverty, and homophobia as mediators of these sexual health disparities (Rangel, Gavin, Reed, Fowler, & Lee, 2006). In other words, dominant sociocultural forces shape the sexual scripts and trajectories of marginalized youth in ways that are characterized by disadvantage and oppression. Within that context, culturally distinctive practices of sexual and gender socialization play a role in adolescent sexuality development.

Sexual health disparities evident among ethnic minority adolescents have their origins in, and are reinforced by, dominant cultural images and scripts for sexuality among marginalized youth. Crude stereotypes often dramatically contradict personal realities. For example, in music videos featuring African Americans, young women are often objectified, reduced to body parts, and viewed with contempt or as sexual objects at the service of men's desires; young men are typically depicted as out-of-control violent criminals or lust-filled rapists (Jhally, 2007). In addition, many television shows portray African Americans as gangsters, natural athletes, or figures of comic relief (Ward, 2004). In video games, Native Americans are invariably adorned with tribal gear such as feathers and bows and arrows (Huntemann, 2000). On television, Latino youth are often pictured as hot-tempered and sexually aggressive lovers with heavy accents, although males appear groomed and professionally dressed while women seem disheveled and unkempt (Mastro & Behm-Morowitz, 2005). These examples suggest that for youth from nondominant racial and ethnic groups, dominant cultural factors influence sexual scripts in ways that lead to vulnerability in sexual health outcomes.

Cultural variations in gender and sexual socialization practices also shape sexuality development in distinct ways for ethnic minority youth. For example, most of the research on family sexual socialization is based on studies of European American families, for whom direct verbal communication is a dominant cultural feature. However, scholars have pointed out that in collectivist or interdependent (as compared to individualist) cultures, the meanings received through communication are often based on the physical context, external cues, and social relationships of the communicators (Gudykunst, 2004). This "high-context" communication may be nonverbal and rely on indirect messages to communicate meaning. In one recent study of sexual socialization in Asian American families, most women emphatically reported that their parents did not speak to them about sexuality, yet the young women perceived clear, consistent messages about their parents' values and expectations for their sexual behavior through nonverbal and indirect cues (Kim, 2009). Across the diverse sample (including women with Indian, Asian, and Pacific Islander ethnicities), the young women perceived their parents' sexual socialization goals through gossip, restricted social activities, and closely monitored behavior (see also Espiritu, this volume). When direct communication from parents did occur, its purpose was not perceived to be for education, but for probing and monitoring their daughters' behavior.

Such high-context communication is rooted in several cultural factors, including the hierarchical nature of social relationships, particularly family relationships, in many Asian and Hispanic cultures. Adolescents are expected to defer to their parents and not to question them; communication in a direct manner may be understood as challenging parental authority. This may explain why, compared to White mothers, Latina mothers are more dominant in conversations with their children about sexuality and give them fewer opportunities to ask questions (Lefkowitz, Romo, Corona, Au, & Sigman, 2000). The role of gender and sexuality is also important; in many cultures, persistent control of girls' innocence or purity often stems from concerns about family reputation (Raffaelli & Ontai, 2004). Thus, cultural beliefs may lead some Latino families to engage in more direct messages about sexual expectations for daughters (Raffaelli & Green, 2003). Mexican American as well as Filipino families may also restrict daughters' behavior, particularly regarding socializing with boys (Raffaelli & Ontai, 2004; Espiritu, this volume). In many Asian cultures, a strongly held taboo against recreational sexual activity, particularly for unmarried women, is coupled with a concern for "saving face" or remaining in good social standing. As a result, parents have strong motives for communicating expectations for their daughters' sexual conduct, even in the context of pressure to avoid direct discussion (Kim, 2009). Despite Asian American women's perceptions of clear sexual socialization messages from their parents, a recent study showed that mothers' reports of sexual communication with their children significantly predicted noncoital sexual activity for European American but not Asian American adolescents (Lam, Russell, & Leong, 2008).

For African American youth, close, extended family relations are a salient feature in sexual development and relationship behavior. More than other young people, these youth are likely to live in low-income, single-parent, female-headed households; parents typically exert high levels of supervision and strictness over their behavior (Giordano, Manning, & Longmore, 2005). Most likely because of parental messages to retain a certain level of independence from peers, African American adolescents are more likely than other teen populations to have stronger attachments to family than friends. This reliance on families may explain why African American youth tend to have longer lasting but less intimate romantic relationship styles than other youth (Smetana & Gettman, 2006).

Cultural differences in gender socialization are important for understanding adolescent sexual scripts. The obligation to adhere to traditional gender norms may be stronger in some cultures than others. In Latino cultures, family closeness, unity, and loyalty are highly valued, and girls are encouraged to be submissive, chaste, and relationship-oriented, while males are more dominant and given greater freedom to explore their sexuality (Garcia, 2009). Latino boys who adhere to more traditional masculine identities report having less intimate relations, more adversarial relationships, and more risky sexual behavior (Pleck et al., 2004). Many youth who immigrate from less-developed to highly developed societies experience tensions with their families as they acculturate to the dominant society. The new society offers Latina girls unprecedented opportunities to experience greater sexual and relational autonomy, and girls whose parents restrict the development of autonomy are more likely to report serious mental health problems, including suicide ideation and attempts (Zayas, Lester, Cabassa, & Fortuna, 2005). Dimensions of sexual socialization are also associated with gender ideologies among African American adolescents. In one study, most young African American women idealized being economically independent and emotionally strong, while they also believed that they should be emotional caretakers of their male partners; such beliefs may be linked to a tolerance of male sexual risk behavior (Kerrigan et al., 2007). In the same study, young African American men identified financial productivity, toughness, and sexual prowess as the cornerstones of manhood, but they tended to adhere more strongly to the latter two qualities because of their perceived inability to fulfill their role as economic providers.

Social Class, Sexuality, and Marginalization

Finally, social class also contributes to the marginalization of young people's sexuality. Research aimed at studying sexual conduct among adolescents often focuses on poor, urban populations because of the assumption that these adolescents are more sexually active and at increased risk for negative outcomes (Tolman, 2002). In fact, few studies directly examine the impact of social class on adolescent sexual behavior. (More research has documented the link between social class and adult sexual behavior.) Most existing work has focused on young women. Lack of voice in sexuality is a theme that runs through the lives of many low-income female youth, leading to negative sexual outcomes. Tolman (2002) showed that girls from urban environments who struggled with poverty and racism felt less freedom to express their sexuality and less comfortable talking about sex in front of their peers and parents than girls from suburban areas. In addition, nearly all adolescents living with AIDS are impoverished youth, runaways, or prostitutes victimized by adults. Irregular or nonuse of contraception is correlated with lower social-class status, which may be explained by other correlates including low educational aspirations, high family conflict, and low parent-adolescent sexuality communication (Brooks-Gunn & Furstenberg, 1989). Higher social class also comes with consequences for female sexuality. Evidence shows, for example, that the higher the social class, the more emphasis placed on being thin, a situation that can lead not only to lower self-image and negative outcomes such as eating disorders and malnutrition (Dornbusch et al., 1984), but also to more heterosexual dating and sexual activity (Halpern, Udry, Campbell, & Suchindran, 1999).

Youth, Agency, and Resistance

Thus far we have pointed mostly to the constraints of gender, sexual identity, race, ethnicity, and social class. However, several examples of sexual agency illustrate possibilities for youth, particularly those at the margins, to actively resist dominant sexual scripts or ideologies and create new sexual scripts. Several studies of young women point to possibilities for transcending traditionally gendered sexual scripts. An analysis of the (mostly White) Riot Grrrl movement in the 1990s showed how young women aimed to upset existing meanings of sexuality by reclaiming the word "slut" on their own terms (Attwood, 2007). A study of the sexuality discourses among (mostly racial-ethnic minority) female gang members reveals that "home girls" perceived a need to assert their sexual agency and develop autonomy from others; in addition to the classic tension between "good" girls versus "sluts," these female gang members engaged in a discourse about sexual autonomy that focused on girls' sexual needs, choices, and independence (Schalet, Hunt, & Joe-Laidler, 2003). Interestingly, the good girl/slut discourses intersected with race and poverty; Latina girls from traditional families with close economic ties endorsed the classic respectability discourse, while African American girls, many of whom reported family estrangement, emphasized sexual autonomy.

What are the possibilities for sexual agency for queer youth? In the context of heteronormativity (at best) and homophobia (at worst), how do LGBTQ youth navigate adolescence to develop agency that can set the stage for optimal sexual expression and health throughout the adult life course? The empirical studies of queer youth described above were strongly informed by psychological theories of identity development and notions of health and risk. However, recent work, much of it drawing from social movements literatures, has focused on the possibilities of agency (including sexual agency) for LGBTQ adolescents. Like the literature on positive sexuality development, this research emphasizes resilience and agency. For example, recent studies of high school gay-straight alliance (GSA) clubs illustrate how the development of personal and political awareness of sexual identity—including heterosexual (or "straight") identities—may be turning points in the early life course (Russell, 2002). Importantly, GSAs engage and are meaningful for heterosexual youth as well as for queer youth. Some heterosexual members of GSAs join because they are friends with a queer member of the club, because they themselves do not strictly adhere to society's notions of what it means to be masculine and feminine, and/or because they disagree with and want to stop discrimination (Herdt et al., 2007). The community within a GSA can be liberating for members who feel that they are voiceless in the greater community of their school, city, or country. GSAs foster empowerment through processes of personal, relational, and strategic empowerment (i.e., having and using knowledge to achieve collective ends). GSAs offer members a politicized space to openly discuss what is important to them (Russell, Muraco, Subramaniam, & Laub, 2009) and, in doing so, to promote civic engagement.

Concluding Remarks

We have discussed the distinctiveness of adolescence as a crucial life stage for the development of sexual awareness and identities that set the stage for sexualities across the adult life course. We have considered culture, gender, and sexual socialization and their roles in shaping the sexual scripts of adolescence. Our goal has been not only to point out the importance of reframing sexuality development in adolescence as positive sexuality development, but also to argue that understanding sexuality in adolescence requires refocusing attention on agency. We advocate a shift from the historical focus on the problems of adolescent sexuality to normative or typical development and argue that youthful agency is the basis for positive sexuality development.

We are hopeful because we have seen promising examples of youthful agency and resistance to dominant sexual scripts, as well as changes in the way that scholarly literature documents adolescent sexuality. Researchers are beginning to challenge the construction of adolescents as lacking the ability to take responsibility for and ownership of their sexualities and to assert that this false assumption about adolescents constrains their positive sexuality development (Lehr, 2008; Russell, 2005). Based on years of HIV prevention experience, Laub and colleagues (1999) assert that effective adolescent interventions need to address sexual pressure from peers to conform to sexual scripts and expectations about how men and women should behave in sexual situations. New models of adolescent sexual health advocate that young people develop both a critical perspective on romantic conventions that regulate heterosexual relationships and a sense of entitlement to make active choices in romantic relationships (Tolman, Striepe, & Harmon, 2003). Empowering young people to think critically about constructions of adolescence and adolescent sexuality may be the best strategy for broadening the range of sexual trajectories that are available for young people. This empowerment will be possible when societies publicly approve discourse on adolescent sexuality that includes the possibility of positive sexuality development (Russell, 2005).

NOTE

1. We use the term "queer" to be inclusive of individuals who have same-sex sexual and romantic feelings and who self-identify as lesbian, gay, bisexual, or transgender; who identify as queer; or for whom these sexual or gender identity labels are meaningless (Russell, Clarke, & Clary, 2009).

4

The Life Course Consequences of Childhood Sexual Assault

Effects on Relationship Formation and
Intimate Violence across Relationships

KRISTIN CARBONE-LOPEZ

Research on the prevalence, risk factors, and consequences of childhood sexual abuse (CSA) has increased a great deal in the past four decades (for reviews, see Beitchman et al., 1992; Finkelhor, 1994). Such inquiries have produced three important conclusions for researchers, policy makers, and clinicians (Fergusson, Lynskey & Horwood, 1996). First, a large number of children are exposed to sexual violence of some sort.[1] In a meta-analysis of 22 studies published between 1980 and 1998, Bolen and Scannapieco (1999) suggest a "reasonable estimate" is that between 30 and 40% of females and upwards of 13% of males experience sexual abuse—which includes both contact (e.g., fondling) and noncontact (e.g., genital exposure) forms of abuse—in childhood. Rates of *sexual assault* or rape in childhood are somewhat lower, yet still substantial; between 5 and 15% of females and between 1 and 10% of males have been victims of actual or attempted sexual intercourse by the age of 18 (Ageton, 1983; Fergusson et al., 1996; Finkelhor, Hotaling, Lewis, & Smith, 1990).

Second, the risk of CSA is associated with important individual and family factors. Both gender and age appear to be related to the risk of CSA; the risk of abuse is higher among girls and among children 7 to 13 years of age. In contrast, race, ethnicity, and socioeconomic status are not generally associated with children's risk of sexual abuse, at least not in any systematic manner. Those risk factors that show up most consistently are environmental elements such as parental inadequacy or unavailability, family conflict, and poor parent-child relationships. In particular, children who are separated from parents or who have parents with problems attending to and supervising them (e.g., as a result of alcohol or drug addictions) are at greater risk of sexual victimization at young ages (Finkelhor, 1994).

Third, sexual abuse experiences in childhood are frequently associated with a range of adjustment and psychological problems, both in the short term and across the life course.[2] For example, CSA experiences generally have been related to behavioral and emotional problems within childhood such as nightmares and generalized fear, posttraumatic stress disorder (PTSD), withdrawn behavior, self-injurious behavior, precocious sexualized behavior, and other behavior problems such as running away and delinquency (Kendall-Tackett, Williams, & Finkelhor, 1993). Yet, the consequences of sexual abuse are not limited to childhood; anxiety, fear, depression, suicidality, and personality disorders in adulthood are all associated with childhood experiences of sexual abuse (Beitchman et al., 1992). Moreover, there is some suggestion that these effects differ by type of abuse. Sexual acts involving the use of force or penetration have a more detrimental impact on victims and are associated with more serious long-term outcomes (Browne & Finkelhor, 1986; Kendall-Tackett et al., 1993).

Child Sexual Abuse, Revictimization, and Effects on Relationships

Increasing attention has also been paid to the link between CSA and subsequent victimization experiences in adolescence and adulthood. Victims of early sexual abuse are at heightened risk of experiencing subsequent sexual violence both as adolescents and in adulthood, a phenomenon known as "revictimization" (Browne & Finkelhor, 1986). Early sexual victimization also influences a variety of "risky" behaviors, including running away, involvement in prostitution, and other forms of delinquency that, in turn, may increase one's risk of future sexual assault (Whitbeck & Simons, 1990). However, the increased risk of later victimization is not confined to sexual violence. Women with histories of sexual abuse in childhood are at an increased risk of experiencing intimate violence by a partner in adulthood as well (DiLillo, Giuffre, Tremblay, & Peterson, 2001).

Less is known about other, broader consequences of early CSA experiences, particularly in terms of relationship formation and functioning over the life course. Yet, there is some suggestion that sexual victimization in childhood is associated with later sexual and relational adjustment. For example, individuals who have been sexually abused as children may initiate sexual activity earlier and have more frequent and riskier sexual encounters, leading to higher rates of sexual and interpersonal dysfunction in adulthood as well as increased risk of revictimization within intimate relationships (Browning & Laumann, 1997; Cherlin, Burton, Hurt, & Purvin, 2004). In addition, childhood sexual abuse has been linked to distrust of others, concerns about abandonment, and intimacy problems including ambivalence and fear of intimacy. Survivors of CSA report less satisfaction with their relationships overall and more maladaptive interpersonal patterns (Briere & Elliott, 1994). Adults with CSA histories are more likely to remain single and, if married, report less satisfaction with their marriages. They are also more likely to divorce or separate, suggesting less commitment to relationships or greater difficulty in negotiating them (Finkelhor, Hotaling, Lewis, & Smith, 1989; Russell, 1986).

Explaining Violence across the Life Course

Various theoretical models have been proposed to explain the relationship between CSA and later victimization, including learning theory, learned helplessness, relationship choices, and traumatic sexualization (Messman-Moore & Long, 2003). However, as Browning and Laumann (1997) suggest, broader theories of the life course can also provide a framework for understanding the far-reaching consequences of early traumatic sexual experiences.

Life course theory generally examines how individual lives unfold over time. Understanding the social forces that influence the life course as well as its developmental consequences is key (Elder, 1995). Individual trajectories or pathways through the life course develop over time and are marked by positive or negative transitions or life events. Some transitions may generate a turning point, consequently altering the life trajectory (Clausen, 1995). Browning and Laumann (1997) conceptualize adult-child sexual contact as a transition into sexual activity that may then influence subsequent sexual experiences. Children who experience early sexual interaction may develop negative "sexual scripts" (Gagnon & Simon, 1973), which, in turn, influence subsequent sexual behavior, relationships, choice of partners, and even future risk for violence. In some cases, the transition to sexual activity and its associated sexual scripts may manifest in terms of multiple sex partners or a series of fleeting intimate relationships in adolescence and adulthood (Browning & Laumann, 1997; Elliott, Avery, Fishman, & Hoshiko, 2002). These brief sexual relationships may end when intimacy develops, precluding one's involvement in long-term committed relationships. More partners may increase the probability of violence—due, in part, to exposure to many potential offenders.

Life course theory also addresses patterns of change and continuity between early and later life stages. The concept of *state dependence* can be used to explain the continuity of victimization experiences over time. State dependence suggests that individuals are altered by past events, which have implications for their future behavior and experiences. Adverse experiences, such as victimization, can have lasting effects on an individual because they produce an "accentuation effect" that perpetuates further adverse experiences (Caspi & Moffitt, 1993). Thus, victimization may increase the likelihood of further victimization by way of negative self-cognitions as well as negative interactions with others. Lauritsen and Davis Quinet (1995) suggest that victims of crime may experience a labeling process; following victimization, others may perceive them as vulnerable or even attractive as a victim and this attractiveness makes them more likely to be revictimized. Conversely, individuals may self-label as victims and behave in ways that elicit more aggressive responses from others (Schwartz, Dodge, & Coie, 1993). Individuals who expect others to be hostile may actually behave in ways that elicit that hostility. This *interactional continuity* (or self-fulfilling prophecy) suggests that an individual's behavior evokes reciprocal, sustaining, and perhaps violent responses from others (Caspi, Bem, & Elder, 1989).

Continuity can also be seen in relationship processes. Experiences in our previous interpersonal relationships provide a template for action in the construction of new relationships (Hartup, 1985) as well as for behavior in those relationships (Reis, Collins, & Berscheid, 2000). Thus, the negative self-images and corresponding negative perceptions of others resulting from victimization in earlier relationships or at earlier stages in one's life course may impact one's subsequent relationships (or the lack thereof). Early experiences of violence may influence with whom one becomes involved in a relationship as well as the quality of interactions within that relationship. Similarly, subsequent exposure to intimate partner abuse in adulthood may lead to emotional distance and hesitancy to make long-term commitments, which may also increase risk of violence within those and future relationships. Victimization experiences then may transcend relationships, with individuals experiencing "serial victimization," whereby they are unable to develop and maintain nonviolent intimate relationships.

In sum, the consequences of CSA appear to be diverse and far-reaching and more severe forms of abuse, particularly those involving force or penetration, appear to be related to more harmful outcomes. Although much work has focused on intrapersonal aspects, such as clinical symptomatology, researchers are now beginning to explore systematically the impact of CSA on *interpersonal* functioning. Such inquiries have demonstrated that CSA is not only a risk factor for subsequent victimization experiences but also has deleterious effects on an individual's ability to form and maintain nonviolent intimate relationships. A full understanding of the broad and cumulative impact of CSA experiences, however, requires further examination of the ways in which early sexual victimization experiences affect relationship patterns and trajectories across the life course.

Expected Associations between Childhood Sexual Assault, Relationship Trajectories, and Intimate Partner Violence

Although much of the existing literature focuses broadly on sexual abuse experiences in childhood, I am interested more specifically in childhood sexual *assault* experiences. Using data from a national survey of male and female adults living in the United States, I examine the broader life course sequelae of child sexual assault, beyond sexual revictimization. In particular, I focus on the extent to which such experiences in childhood are related to relationship formation and dissolution patterns across the life course. Second, I examine the risk of violence within these subsequent intimate relationships and assess the extent to which such victimization occurs within multiple relationships.

Based on existing research, I anticipated a number of associations. First, because of the impact of traumatic sexual experiences on interpersonal functioning, I expected child sexual assault to be related to a decreased likelihood of sustained, stable relationships; thus, sexual assault should be associated with an increased likelihood of divorce or separation during adulthood, as well as an increased likelihood of multiple intimate relationships. Second, in line with research demonstrating the continuity of victimization, or revictimization, I expected experiences of child sexual assault to be related to increased risks of experiencing intimate partner violence (IPV) in adulthood and—importantly— to IPV within multiple relationships. The relationship between childhood experiences and relationship trajectories and violence, however, should vary depending on the age at first experience and gender of the victim. Specifically, I expected the associations to be stronger among females and those who were first victimized in adolescence compared to those victimized at younger ages.

Data

The National Violence Against Women Survey (NVAWS) was completed between the years 1995–1996 and was co-sponsored by the National Institute of Justice (NIJ), the National Center for Injury Prevention and Control (NCIPC), and the Centers for Disease Control and Prevention (CDC). Participants included 8,000 women and 8,005 men 18 years and older residing in households located within the United States. The participation rate was

72%, consistent with other surveys of crime and violence. Respondents were interviewed over the telephone. Due to the sensitive nature of the questions, females interviewed female respondents. Approximately half of the men were interviewed by males and the other half by female interviewers to test for a possible bias due to interviewer gender (Tjaden & Thoennes, 2000).

One of the unique features of this survey was its breadth of measurement. Individuals were asked about lifetime experiences of physical and sexual assault (including in childhood), emotional abuse and controlling behavior by intimate partners, and physical, sexual, and stalking violence in adulthood. To elicit this information, respondents were first asked a series of behavior-specific screening questions (e.g., "after you became an adult did any other adult, male or female, ever throw something at you that could hurt you?"). They were then asked a series of more detailed questions pertaining to the incident, including their relationship to their attacker. If the perpetrator was a spouse or intimate partner, respondents were asked to identify whether it was a current or ex-partner (and if an ex-partner, whether it was the first, second, third, etc., partner). This information is presented in an "offender grid" linking specific acts with specific perpetrators. These data offer a unique opportunity for analyzing experiences across relationships because they differentiate between acts involving former intimate partners and those involving current partners and allow for the identification of specifically which former partner (i.e., first ex, etc.) was the perpetrator.

Because this investigation was interested in patterns of union formation and violence within heterosexual intimate relationships as an outcome, I restricted the analyses to those men and women reporting at least one current or prior intimate relationship with a partner of the opposite sex (N = 14,092, including 6,885 males and 7,207 females).

Measures

Childhood Sexual Assault

The NVAWS measure taps more aggravated forms of sexual victimization in childhood and adolescence and excludes contact experiences such as fondling and noncontact experiences such as flashing or exposure. NVAWS respondents were asked whether they had experienced sexual assault at any time during their lifetime. This includes attempted and completed acts of forced sexual intercourse as well as other forms of sexual assault such as someone inserting objects into their anus or vagina. If respondents indicated any experience of sexual assault, they were asked the age at which it occurred. If there were multiple assaults by a single perpetrator, they were also asked their age at the first and most recent sexual assault. Using this information, I created two dichotomous indicators identifying individuals who had experienced sexual assault in early childhood (up to age 12) and those who had experienced sexual assault in adolescence (from age 13 to 17).

Patterns of Union Formation and Relationship Trajectories

To create indicators of relationship status and history, I aggregated information from a number of questions about respondents' current and previous marital status. I coded individuals with *current relationships* as those who were married, in a common-law marital union, or cohabiting with a member of the other sex at the time of the survey.[3] *Previous relationships* included individuals who were, at the time of the survey, divorced, separated, or widowed as well as those who reported that they had been previously married or involved in a heterosexual cohabiting relationship. Based on these initial indicators, I distinguished respondents who reported only a current intimate partner with no previous relationships (*current partner only*) from those who reported only previous relationships and were not currently intimately involved (*no current partner*). These suggest two very different patterns of union formation across the life course. The first represents those who moved from being single into a sustained intimate relationship. The second group represents those who, for one reason or another, are not currently involved with an intimate partner although they had been previously. To examine previous relationships in greater depth, I also created indicators for respondents who had been married previously (*previous marriage*), those who had multiple previous marriages (*multiple previous marriages*), those who had cohabited with an intimate partner before (*previous cohabitation*), and those who had previously cohabited multiple times with intimate partners (*multiple previous cohabitation experiences*). These relationship trajectories all involve relationships that were not sustained and, in some cases, movement into (multiple) new intimate relationships.

IPV Measures

Using items derived from the modified Conflict Tactics Scale (CTS) (Straus, 1979, 1990), respondents indicated whether they had experienced a number of violent acts as an adult. These questions measure specific behaviors, allowing researchers to determine whether respondents have been the victim of violent acts regardless of whether the respondents themselves describe their experience as "abuse." IPV includes any reported experiences of victimization by partners. Using information from the offender grid completed during the survey, I created indicators of victimization by a current spouse or intimate partner, by a "first ex" partner, and also by more distal (i.e., second or third ex) partners. I further separated IPV into "minor" and more "severe" forms. *Minor physical violence* includes pushing, grabbing, or shoving; pulling hair; having something thrown at them that could hurt; or slapping or hitting. *Severe violence* includes kicking or biting; choking or attempted drowning; having been hit with an object; being beaten up; threats made with a gun, knife, or other weapon; or the use of any weapon on them. *Sexual assault* measures attempted and completed acts of forced sexual intercourse or activity by a current or previous intimate partner. Additionally, I created a separate indicator of *any intimate violence*, physical or sexual, by any current or former partner. Finally, to address the question of whether early experiences of violence are associated with repeated victimization across the life course and across multiple relationships, I included a measure of *repeat intimate violence*, which taps violence within two or more adult intimate relationships.

Covariates

Various factors that are related to IPV are controlled in these statistical models. First, I examined separate models for males and females, which allowed me to directly compare the consequences of CSA for males and females. Because CSA is associated with other forms of childhood victimization (Taylor et al., 2008), a measure indicating physical violence by parents or guardians before the age of 18 was also included.[4] *Childhood victimization* experiences are included as a dichotomous variable where "1" indicates any form of physical violence and "0" represents no physical violence in childhood by a parent or guardian. Other factors included *age* (ranging from 18 to 95) and *race/ethnicity* (where white, non-Hispanic is the reference). In addition, I included *educational attainment* (ranging from no schooling to postgraduate degree), *household income*[5] (ranging from $0 to over $100,000), and a proxy indicator of *poverty* (whether a respondent has lost phone service in the past 12 months).

Sample Description

Descriptions and univariate statistics for all measures can be found in table 4.1. There are few demographic differences between females and males in the national sample. Respondents are on average 45 years of age, white, non-Hispanic, and have educational levels beyond high school. The majority of respondents reported being married; however, more of the men in the sample

TABLE 4.1

Descriptive and Univariate Statistics, by Sex—NVAWS (1995–1996)

Variable	Description	Males N	Males Mean/%	Females N	Females Mean/%
Respondent age	Age in years	6822	44.66 [14.64]	7084	45.57 [15.69]
Race/ethnicity	Respondent self-reported race				
White, non-Hispanic	[1=white, non-Hispanic; 0=other]	6680	82.19%	7079	80.66%
Black, non-Hispanic	[1=Black, non-Hispanic; 0=other]	6680	7.32%	7079	8.21%
Other, non-Hispanic	[1=Asian or American Indian or mixed, non-Hispanic; 0=other]	6680	4.87%	7079	4.12%
Hispanic	[1=Hispanic/Latino; 0=other]	6680	5.22%	7079	6.50%
Education level	Highest education received [1=no schooling; 7=Postgraduate]	6872	4.92 [1.25]	7177	4.72 [1.18]
Current marital status	Respondent current marital status				
Married	[1=Currently married; 0=other]	6885	76.85%	7207	68.91%
Divorced or separated	[1=Currently divorced or separated; 0=other]	6885	11.58%	7207	14.35%
Cohabiting	[1=Currently living as couple with man/woman; 0=other]	6880	8.63%	7201	7.40%
Household income	Total household income [1=less than $5,000; 10=more than $100,000]	4729	6.87 [2.03]	4248	6.36 [2.21]
Poverty proxy	Lost telephone service in last 12 months [1=yes; 0=no]	6866	3.68%	7203	3.64%
Childhood physical abuse	Experienced physical assault by parent/guardian prior to age 18 [1=yes; 0=no]	6885	33.58%	7207	23.07%
Childhood sexual abuse	Experienced sexual assault prior to age 13 [1=yes; 0=no]	6877	1.37%	7148	4.42%

		N	%	N	%
Adolescent sexual abuse	Experienced sexual assault between ages of 13 to 17 [1=yes; 0=no]	6877	0.49%	7148	4.92%
Patterns of union formation	Relationship patterns in adulthood				
Current partner, no previous	Currently married or cohabiting, no previous relationships [1=yes; 0=no]	6849	59.79%	7171	54.30%
No current partner	Previously married or cohabiting, no current relationship [1==yes; 0=no]	6849	14.54%	7171	23.78%
Previous marriage	One or more previous spouses [1=yes; 0=no]	6868	30.84%	7184	34.17%
Multiple previous marriages	Two or more previous spouses [1=yes; 0=no]	6868	6.68%	7184	7.31%
Previous cohabiting relationship	One or more previous cohabitations [1=yes; 0=no]	6849	19.70%	7199	12.79%
Multiple cohabiting relationships	Two or more previous cohabitations [1=yes; 0=no]	6849	7.87%	7199	3.60%
Adult experiences of IPV	Experiences of physical violence in adulthood by intimate partner based on CTS				
IPV (mild) by current partner	[1=yes; 0=no]	6798	2.18%	7102	4.51%
IPV (severe) by current partner	[1=yes; 0=no]	6820	1.04%	7127	1.89%
Sexual assault by current partner	[1=yes; 0=no]	6805	0.03%	7111	0.21%
Any IPV by current partner	Mild or severe IPV or sexual assault [1=yes; 0=no]	6770	2.27%	7087	4.76%
IPV (mild) by 1st ex partner	[1=yes; 0=no]	6827	35.08%	7139	26.61%
IPV (severe) by 1st ex partner	[1=yes; 0=no]	6824	19.68%	7130	15.82%
Sexual assault by 1st ex partner	[1=yes; 0=no]	6805	0.04%	7111	2.32%
Any IPV by 1st ex partner	Mild or severe IPV or sexual assault [1=yes; 0=no]	6777	36.05%	7095	27.54%
IPV by any partner, current or ex	Mild or severe IPV or sexual assault [1=yes; 0=no]	6769	40.96%	7087	28.74%
IPV across multiple relationships	IPV in at least two relationships [1=yes; 0=no]	6769	3.52%	7087	7.49%
TOTAL		6885		7207	

Note: Standard deviations given in brackets.

were currently married. Patterns of union formation also differed by gender. A larger proportion of women than men had exited intimate relationships (i.e., were not currently involved with an intimate partner) and a slightly larger proportion of women reported previous marriages compared to men. In contrast, more men than women reported previous cohabiting relationships, including multiple cohabiting relationships. In addition, more men reported some form of physical assault by a parent or guardian before the age of 18.

Consistent with existing literature, a larger proportion of females reported childhood experiences of sexual assault, both in early childhood (4% compared to 1% of males) and in adolescence (5% versus less than 1% of males). Females were equally likely to report victimization prior to age 13 and between the ages of 13 to 17. However, males were somewhat more likely to experience violence in early childhood than in adolescence. This may be because once males go through puberty, they are better able to defend themselves physically against attack.

Table 4.1 also shows that IPV, particularly violence in dissolved relationships, was relatively prevalent among respondents. Physical victimization by current partners was experienced by between 1 and 5% of respondents; a larger proportion of women, as compared to men, were *currently* involved in a relationship that entailed intimate violence. Larger proportions of both males and females reported experiencing mild as opposed to more severe forms of IPV within their current intimate relationship and less than 1% of both males and females reported sexual assault by their current partner. In contrast, between 16 and 35% of respondents reported some form of physical violence by their most recent ex-partner. Interestingly, a greater proportion of males reported experiencing IPV in previous relationships, particularly mild forms.[6] A small proportion of respondents experienced sexual assault by a previous partner, with women more likely to report sexual victimization than men. Overall, 41% of males and 29% of females reported experiencing IPV within *any* adult relationship and 4% of males and 7% of females reported IPV in *multiple* relationships.

Analytic Strategy

To describe the association between childhood experiences of sexual abuse and later adult experiences, I modeled the relative odds of particular consequences using multivariate logistic regression (Long, 1997).[7] In each of the models presented in table 4.2, I focus on the increase or decrease in the odds of a particular outcome associated with experiences of CSA, while controlling or adjusting for various covariates. Table 4.2 provides adjusted odds ratios (AORs) and 95% confidence intervals (CIs) for the estimates.[8] These odds ratios are interpreted as the increase or decrease in the odds of a respondent who experienced child sexual assault reporting a particular relationship trajectory or IPV experience relative to those who did not experience sexual assault in childhood. Using a statistical Z-score test (see Paternoster, Brame, Mazerolle, & Piquero, 1998), I assessed whether the coefficients (or effects) for child sexual assault differed significantly across men and women or by age at victimization.

Results

Table 4.2 provides evidence of a significant association between experiencing sexual assault in childhood or adolescence and relational experiences in adulthood. Controlling for demographic characteristics,[9] female victims were more likely to report disrupted unions. Women assaulted in childhood were 1.6 times more likely and women who experienced sexual assault in adolescence were 1.3 times more likely to be currently divorced or separated and had correspondingly lower odds of being married at the time of the survey (AOR = .603). Males and females sexually assaulted in childhood (males AOR = .641; females AOR = .630) and females who experienced sexual assault in adolescence (AOR = .498) had lower odds of reporting a current, sustained relationship with no previous relationships. Women who experienced child sexual assault were between 1.3 and 1.6 times more likely to be in no relationship at the time of the data collection. Conversely, males and females who experienced child sexual assault and females assaulted in adolescence had greater odds of involvement in multiple previous cohabiting relationships. Child sexual assault increased the odds of previous cohabiting relationships and multiple prior marriages by 1.3 to 2.5 times. In sum, these results suggest that child and adolescent sexual abuse is associated with a greater number of relationships and relationships that are not sustained across the life course for both males and females.

Moreover, child sexual assault is significantly related to IPV among both males and females. Female victims of sexual assault in adolescence are between 1.5 and nearly 5 times more likely to experience violence—physical or sexual—by any intimate partner in adulthood. Women who experienced sexual assault at earlier ages (i.e., prior to age 13) were no more likely than women who did not experience sexual assault to report violence within their current relationship, but did have higher odds of violence within previous relationships. For men, however, the effects were less consistent. Males who experienced sexual assault in early childhood had elevated odds (between 1.7 and 2.1) of reporting physical violence by a previous partner, but such experiences had no effect

TABLE 4.2

Adjusted Odds Ratios and Confidence Intervals for Relationship Patterns and IPV Victimization—NVAWS (1995–1996)

| | MALES | | | | FEMALES | | | |
| | Early childhood sexual assault | | Adolescent sexual assault | | Early childhood sexual assault | | Adolescent sexual assault | |
	AOR	CI	AOR	CI	AOR	CI	AOR	CI
Current relationship status								
Married	.645	.409 – 1.018	1.278	.539 – 3.028	.796	.620 – 1.023	.603	.478 – .762*
Divorced or separated	1.286	.720 – 2.297	.935	.326 – 2.683	1.623	1.221 – 2.157*	1.326	1.003 – 1.753*
Cohabiting	1.410	.751 – 2.646	.924	.269 – 3.173	1.030	.686 – 1.547	1.218	.871 – 1.705
Relationship trajectories								
Current partner, no previous	.641	.419 – .981*	1.207	.593 – 2.455	.630	.496 – .799*	.498	.396 – .627*
No current partner	1.403	.828 – 2.377	.742	.258 – 2.133	1.331	1.006 – 1.761*	1.558	1.197 – 2.028*
Previous marriage	1.546	1.001 – 2.387*	.907	.425 – 1.935	1.503	1.179 – 1.914*	1.456	1.153 – 1.840*
Multiple previous marriages	2.014	1.051 – 3.861*	—		1.780	1.227 – 2.581*	1.581	1.077 – 2.319*
Previous cohabiting relationship	1.972	1.246 – 3.121*	1.191	.534 – 2.658	1.813	1.369 – 2.400*	1.841	1.422 – 2.384*
Multiple cohabiting relationships	2.476	1.454 – 4.218*	1.950	.783 – 4.858	1.601	1.017 – 2.519*	1.874	1.257 – 2.793*
Intimate partner violence								
IPV (mild) by current partner	.689	.166 – 2.863	3.738	1.109 – 12.600*	1.206	.771 – 1.887	1.526	1.033 – 2.253*
IPV (severe) by current partner	.686	.092 – 5.092	2.424	.319 – 18.431	.878	.419 – 1.842	2.095	1.259 – 3.484*
Sexual assault by current partner	—		—		—		4.562	1.271 – 16.374*
Any IPV by current partner	.669	.161 – 2.783	3.741	1.107 – 12.646*	1.139	.729 – 1.780	1.725	1.192 – 2.498*
IPV (mild) by 1st ex partner	1.694	1.066 – 2.694*	1.955	.930 – 4.111	1.868	1.461 – 2.389*	2.459	1.945 – 3.107*
IPV (severe) by 1st ex partner	2.120	1.337 – 3.360*	2.408	1.138 – 5.095*	1.647	1.261 – 2.149*	2.933	2.311 – 3.723*
Sexual assault by 1st ex partner	—		—		1.841	1.077 – 3.147*	4.853	3.203 – 7.354*
Any IPV by 1st ex partner	1.754	1.095 – 2.810*	1.876	.869 – 4.050	1.857	1.452 – 2.376*	2.597	2.052 – 3.286*
IPV by any partner, current or ex	1.768	1.090 – 2.867*	2.085	.936 – 4.645	1.892	1.479 – 2.421*	2.545	2.011 – 3.221*
IPV across multiple relationships	2.258	1.099 – 4.639*	2.137	.635 – 7.191	1.265	.885 – 1.807	2.344	1.743 – 3.151*

AOR = adjusted odds ratio; CI = 95% confidence interval; * p < .05.

Note: Because of small cell counts, particularly for sexual assault within current relationships, some of the full models were not estimable.

on violence within a current, sustained relationship. In contrast, males who were adolescents at the time of the sexual abuse had elevated odds of IPV within a current relationship and increased odds of severe violence by a previous partner (OR = 2.408). Finally, both men and women who had experienced sexual assault had increased odds of violence within *multiple* intimate relationships; however, this depended on the age at which sexual victimization occurred. Males who were victimized in childhood and females victimized in adolescence were significantly more likely to report violence by more than one intimate partner in adulthood. In general, then, child sexual assault appears to contribute similarly to females' and males' revictimization experiences, including within multiple relationships, in adulthood.

There were few significant differences in the magnitude of the effect of sexual assault by gender and by age at victimization. Females victimized in adolescence were significantly less likely to be married or to report no previous relationships compared to males who were victims of sexual assault in adolescence. Thus, the prediction that females would experience more detrimental consequences related to sexual assault in childhood did not appear to be borne out. The Z-tests also indicate that the timing of victimization mattered, but only in terms of revictimization experiences. As predicted, sexual assault in adolescence had significantly greater impact than sexual assault in childhood on later IPV experiences for both males (with current partners) and females (for current and previous partners, as well as multiple relationships).

Conclusion

I used data from a nationally representative sample of individuals in the United States to examine the relationship between childhood sexual assault, relationship trajectories, and victimization across the life course. In general, the results suggest that, although males are somewhat less likely than females to report sexual assault experiences during childhood and adolescence, they too suffer from the long-term consequences of those victimization experiences. Among both men and women, early traumatic sexual experiences are related to specific trajectories of relationships in adulthood as well as violence by intimate partners.

Two general conclusions can be drawn from these findings, as well as important implications for policy makers and practitioners. First, existing research on child sexual abuse and its consequences has largely focused on females. Although my analyses provide evidence that females are more likely than males to experience (or to report) serious acts of sexual violence in childhood and adolescence, the finding that male victims of sexual assault experience similar consequences as female victims in their later adult experiences of intimate violence suggests that greater future attention to men is necessary. In contrast to the conclusions drawn by Rind and Tromovitch (1997), the size and magnitude of the effect of childhood sexual assault differed little by gender. This may be, at least in part, because I have focused here on the more severe cases of child sexual abuse—those involving attempted or completed sexual intercourse. Such experiences, when they occur, may have devastating effects on victims regardless of gender.

Second, these results highlight the negative consequences that early experiences of violence can have, not only in the short term, but across the life course. Child sexual assault has distinct implications for the development of intimate relationships in adulthood. Specifically, such experiences in childhood were related to a lower likelihood of involvement in sustained relationships at the time of the data collection for both men and women. Further, victims of child sexual assault were more likely to report involvement in multiple previous relationships, particularly cohabiting relationships. Thus, it appears that early experiences of sexual assault may diminish an individual's capacity to maintain committed intimate relationships as adults.

Of course, sustained relationships are not always desirable. To some degree, these analyses presumed that a sustained relationship is healthy and does not involve violence; this is not always true and, in such cases, divorce or separation would clearly be a healthier alternative. Indeed, a significant proportion of divorces are related to previous domestic violence (DeMaris, 2000; Kurz, 1996). However, given that the majority of IPV experienced by respondents occurred in previous (i.e., not current) relationships, it does not appear within the national sample that individuals necessarily remain in violent relationships. Research with women who do leave abusive partners and studies documenting low marital satisfaction within violent relationships has suggested that some respondents may have left a partner or remained single following a previous relationship *because of the violence*. Unfortunately, the NVAWS data do not include information on why relationships ended, so I am unable to test this directly.

Going beyond the existing literature's focus on the impact of CSA on *sexual* revictimization in adolescence and adulthood, these analyses also provide evidence that one's risk of victimization in other realms, such as within intimate relationships, is also heightened following traumatic sexual experiences. Individuals with a history of sexual assault in childhood or adolescence were at increased risk of experiencing violence, including severe physical violence, by an intimate partner as adults. Importantly, child sexual assault was also related to increased risk of involvement in multiple violent intimate relationships—or "serial victimization"—among both males and females. However, this effect was conditioned by gender and age at victimization. Among men, only those who experienced early sexual assault had increased risks of serial victimization within intimate relationships. That adolescent victimization of males was not significantly related to multiple IPV experiences is likely due to the small number of males who reported adolescent experiences of sexual assault. On the other hand, women who experienced sexual assault as adolescents, but not in early childhood, were significantly more likely to report violence by more than one intimate partner in adulthood. One possible explanation for this may lie in a differential impact on risky (and sexual) activities based on the timing of victimization. Violence occurring in early childhood may be less likely to be associated with early sexual involvement and risky sexual encounters whereas victimization in adolescence may be more likely to result in early and heightened sexual activity. Future research should continue to examine these mediating factors.

As with all research, these analyses have limitations. Although I have suggested one process by which child sexual assault impacts later experiences of intimate partner violence and involvement in relationships across the life course, it is impossible to test this framework directly. The NVAWS does not include information on many of the mediating factors that may help to explain the association between child sexual assault and subsequent relational experiences. For example, perhaps individuals have disrupted unions (e.g., divorce or separation) or a series of cohabiting or nonmarital relationships because of negative sexual scripts developed after the initial victimization experience, wherein they link pleasure with loss of control within the relationship or simply have expectations of violent behavior. Browning and Laumann's (1997) work suggests that childhood sexual contact with adults increases the likelihood that individuals will initiate sexual relationships in adolescence and have multiple sexual partners, both of which then have long-term consequences for sexual dysfunction and relationship satisfaction. Sexual assault in childhood may also increase one's likelihood of developing PTSD symptomatology, which may be related to the decreased ability to recognize potentially risky situations, including potential danger within interpersonal relationships (Chu, 1992). Similarly, childhood experiences of sexual assault may also increase the use of alcohol and drugs in adolescence or adulthood. Not only does substance abuse impair the ability to protect oneself, but frequenting places where alcohol is served (or where individuals are using drugs) also results in a greater likelihood that the people one meets and associates with also drink or use drugs; these encounters can then increase one's risk of subsequent victimization. Finally, experiences of sexual victimization in childhood or adolescence may decrease one's relationship efficacy. Victims may be unable to assert themselves or have difficulty trusting potential partners. Such emotional distancing, resulting from earlier traumatic experiences, may then increase the potential for further violence. Unfortunately, the NVAWS data do not include indicators (such as the quality of respondents' interactions with their intimate partners or cognitive beliefs about themselves) to test these pathways. Future research efforts should focus on collecting longitudinal data that follow individuals through key relationships and through key life stages. In particular, it is clear that there is great need for *qualitative* research on the long-term effects of childhood sexual assault on life choices to address some of these outstanding questions.

Generalizability of my findings may also be limited with respect to race because the majority of the sample is white. My results indicated that women (but not men) of color are at somewhat greater risk of intimate violence, particularly by previous partners, when controlling for experiences of child sexual assault. Further, relationship patterns are very much tied to race in these data; consistent with national patterns, Black men and women were more likely to report multiple relationships and to be divorced or separated at the time of the survey. Such differential family patterning by race in the United States may make it difficult to tease out the effects of child sexual assault. These analyses also only examine heterosexual relationships. Indeed, analyses using the same data offer some evidence that women who had lived with same-sex partners were more likely than those who had been in only heterosexual relationships to have experienced sexual assault as children and adults (Tjaden, Thoennes, & Allison, 1999). Finally, the relatively small number of child sexual assault victims precluded more detailed analyses as to whether consequences differ depending on the characteristics of the assault. For example, the NVAWS obtained information on the number of times the victimization took place, the perpetrator's relationship to the victim, where the incident took place, whether the victim or offender was using drugs or alcohol prior to the incident and, for females, whether the assault resulted in a pregnancy. Although there is some evidence that the impact of childhood sexual violence differs depending on the perpetrator and aggravating characteristics, it is unclear how or why such characteristics may be related to relationship trajectories and later experiences of violence in adulthood.

The data used for these analyses were collected more than a decade ago. The majority of the respondents at that time were over the age of 35, meaning that they were adolescents during the 1960s and 1970s. This may have implications for their ability to recall experiences that had happened, for them, many years prior. Related, the sociohistorical context in which the data were collected may have limited my ability to study extended patterns of relationships over time. Very few respondents reported more than one previous intimate relationship, thus limiting the extent to which I could track victimization experiences with multiple partners. Marital patterns continue to change in this country, particularly among younger generations, and individuals today are more likely to cohabit before marriage and to marry later. Thus, increasingly individuals are involved in multiple relationships across their life course. Including additional and more systematic information on earlier relationships may indicate more persistent revictimization effects. In other words, as individuals are more likely to be involved in multiple, short-term relationships today, and because cohabiting couples are at increased risk of intimate violence in comparison to married couples (Stets & Straus, 1989), there may be a greater prevalence of serial intimate victimization occurring, particularly among the most vulnerable individuals. Further, only *adult* intimate relationships were considered here. Dating and courtship relationships in adolescence are also related to both childhood violence and subsequent IPV within adult relationships (Smith, White, & Holland, 2003). Additionally, there is some evidence that other early violent experiences (i.e., physical abuse by parents) are associated with victimization by a whole host of perpetrators in adulthood, including strangers, dates, and acquaintances (Kruttschnitt & Macmillan, 2006). To what extent child sexual assault is related to violence outside of intimate relationships is unclear; whether victims of assault in childhood are more likely to experience victimization by multiple and varying perpetrators, perhaps as a function of their involvement in risky activities, is an important question for further examination. Taken together, these considerations for future research on intimate and family violence suggest that data collection techniques must be designed to account for these dynamic relational patterns in order to untangle the complexities of relationship involvement and violence across the life course.

In sum, experiencing sexual assault in childhood has profound implications for the development and maintenance of intimate relationships in adulthood, as well as experiences within those relationships. Policy makers and practitioners should be urged to continue their efforts to try and diminish these negative consequences to the best of their abilities. It appears clear that early intervention and the provision of extensive services—both at the time of discovery of the abuse as well as throughout the life course—are necessary. Such treatment efforts should focus in particular on repairing the damage to victims and to their interpersonal relationships. With such intense treatment, it is hopeful that the damaging sexual scripts of fear and dysfunction can be revised to allow victims to learn to develop and maintain healthy intimate relationships.

1. Obtaining an accurate estimate of the number of individuals who experience sexual violence in childhood is difficult. Existing estimates vary considerably because of methodological and sampling differences, as well as differences in what age represents the end of childhood (16 or 18), whether victimization by same-age peers is included, and what types of experiences are defined as "abuse." Although some studies include only rape or attempted rape, others include other types of contact abuse (e.g., fondling) as well as noncontact experiences such as genital exposure. In discussing the conclusions drawn in this field, I find it necessary to differentiate estimates of *child sexual abuse (CSA)*, broadly defined, from those of *child sexual assault*, which is limited to acts of attempted or completed sexual intercourse. In this chapter, I am interested in the latter and focus on the life course consequences of sexual assault—involving attempted or completed sexual intercourse—experienced before the age of 18. Yet, because less research has focused specifically on child sexual assault, I draw on findings from the broader literature on CSA to develop hypotheses and interpret my findings.

2. In general, scholars agree that CSA is associated with a range of negative consequences. One exception is the widely publicized review by Rind and Tromovitch (1997). They believe that four conclusions about CSA are misguided: (1) CSA is *causally* related to subsequent psychological adjustment; (2) the consequences of CSA are pervasive within the population; (3) the harm from CSA is "intense"; and (4) effects are equivalent across gender. Noting that previous research largely focused on clinical or community samples, they argue that these conclusions do not hold up in their review of results from large, national probability samples.

3. Respondents were also asked whether they were currently cohabiting with a same-sex partner or had in the past. These relationships are excluded from the present analysis because less than 1% of the sample reported lifetime same-sex cohabitation.

4. Respondents in the NVAWS were asked about physical violence they may have experienced as a child, using the same modified Conflict Tactics Scale, with parents/guardians rather than intimate partners as the reference.

5. Mean substitution was used to replace missing values for household income.

6. Further investigation into these gender differences reveals that men were more likely to report experiencing acts such as thrown objects, pushing, slapping, kicking, hitting, and the use of weapons in their previous relationships. In contrast, women had greater likelihoods of hair pulling, choking or strangling, and being beaten up by a previous intimate partner.

7. "Odds" is the frequency of being in one category relative to the frequency of *not* being in that category (Bohrnstedt & Knoke, 1994).

8. Confidence intervals are a range of values constructed around a particular point estimate. They make it possible to state that the interval contains the actual value between the upper and lower limits (Bohrnstedt & Knoke, 1994). Importantly, they also provide information on whether the odds ratio is statistically significant; if the interval contains 1, the odds ratio is not significant.

9. The models estimating relationship trajectories control for age, race/ethnicity, education attained, household income, a proxy indictor for poverty, and childhood physical victimization by a parent or guardian.

— PART III —

Sexualities from Young Adulthood through Midlife

5

A Meta-Analysis on the Relationship between Parental Divorce Family Structures and Adolescents' Attitudes and Behaviors Regarding Premarital Intercourse

WILLIAM JEYNES

Over the last 35 years social scientists have made considerable advances in understanding the effects of parental family structure on children's behavioral, academic, and attitudinal outcomes. Of these outcome measures, the relationship between parental family structure and academic achievement was most aggressively established by researchers during the 1970–2005 period (Jeynes, 2002a; McLanahan & Sandefur, 1994; Wallerstein & Lewis, 1998). More recently, social scientists have expanded their sphere of exploration to include the association between parental family structure and youth attitudes and behavior toward nonmarital sexual intercourse. Life course scholars are interested in examining how parental marital transitions both result from and initiate new kinds of trajectories (Rossi, 1994; Wertlieb, 1996). They are also cognizant of the fact that the life course decisions that parents make ultimately will affect their children. Wertlieb (1996) and others point out that youth who experience their parents' marital dissolution are at risk and may remain so for many years after the divorce has taken place. This is not to say that these youth are destined to experience difficulties, but it does mean that they on average possess certain propensities and that it is important for those around these young people to be sensitive to the challenges they face in order to help them realize their potential (Jeynes, 2003a, 2003b, 2007b).

One of the great strengths of a life course approach is that it regards life as an ongoing course rather than as an isolated series of events (Rossi, 1994). Life is best understood as a long interconnected series of causes and the effects and responses that emerge from them. On this basis, then, one can argue that individuals' actions and attitudes are best understood through becoming familiar with their experiences over the life course. Using a life course perspective therefore not only has the intellectual advantage of developing a more accurate understanding of why people behave the way that they do, but also hopefully yields a certain degree of compassion toward every individual (Jeynes, 2003b; Rossi, 1994).

The life course perspective provides two vitally important advantages for understanding children from a variety of family structures. First, life course theory is in many respects less "judgmental" than Freud-based psychoanalytic theories. As time has passed, many psychologists and sociologists have increasingly regarded psychoanalytic views as unnecessarily dogmatic and judgmental. This is true for a number of reasons. First, Freud and even Erikson are quite dogmatic when it comes to connecting adult problems with unsuccessful youth transitions (Allers, 1998; Storr, 1996). Psychoanalytic theories contend that nearly all the key turning points that a person encounters occur early in his or her development (Wertlieb, 1996). Consequently, they do not give enough attention to challenges that people face later in the life course and, therefore, they may make invalid causal attributions to early life events (Allers, 1998; Storr, 1996). A second major advantage of the life course approach is that it promotes a perspective that life, as a whole, is in many respects a series of transitions. Moreover, it facilitates a general understanding that the intensity and duration of these transitions can influence later transitions, opportunities, and constraints. Ultimately, what results from this perspective is a more realistic and compassionate assessment of people and a conviction that people are not helplessly bound by experiences in their youth but that they can learn and be guided into making better decisions than in their past for the remainder of their life course.

Youth can especially benefit from the use of life course theory, because this theory not only appreciates the extent to which parents influence children, but also respects the fact that children affect their parents (Jeynes, 2005, 2007b; Wertlieb, 1996). Ultimately, life course studies may help produce an environment in which youth whose behavior and attitudes might at first concern and even frighten adults are viewed more sensitively as individuals who have been affected by their own and their parents' life course experiences. It is within this context of compassion and comprehension that youth from a variety of living situations can be better understood and helped to make choices in life that will fulfill rather than constrain them.

Although a variety of parental family configurations exist, social scientists have concentrated their efforts on examining the influence of parental divorce and remarriage because these are the most common nontraditional family structures. Various family and psychological theories predict that parental divorce would increase the likelihood that the progeny, given their own nontraditional family background, would engage in behavior that would yield a nontraditional family structure. There is considerable evidence that people who have grown up in a nontraditional family structure are more likely than their counterparts from intact families to live in a nontraditional family structure themselves (Cherlin, Kiernan, & Chase-Lansdale, 1995; McLanahan & Sandefur, 1994). Moreover, these same progeny living in nontraditional households are also more likely to maintain less traditional views about family structures and about engaging in sex outside of marriage than their counterparts from nondivorced families (Cherlin et al., 1995; Wallerstein & Lewis, 1998). It is well established that one's attitudes influence one's sexuality- and family-related behaviors (Wallerstein & Blakeslee, 2003).

Despite the strong consensus that being raised in a postdivorce family structure opens one's mind to the possibility of living in such a family structure as an adult, there is less agreement about the precise mechanism(s) that often can make this the case (McLanahan & Sandefur, 1994; Wallerstein & Lewis, 1998; Wallerstein & Blakeslee, 2003). Some of the mechanisms proposed by researchers include: (1) the void that many youth feel as a result of a rupture in their relationship with their parents will cause adolescents to seek filling that void through a relationship (Cherlin et al., 1995; Hetherington, Henderson, Reiss, & Anderson, 1999); (2) the lesser parental monitoring and discipline will cause the children, impressed by the parental example set before them, to develop permissive opinions about intercourse outside of marriage (although this can occur in other family structures as well) (McLanahan & Sandefur, 1994); and (3) to the degree that the children in a family might perceive an act of parental divorce as an act of self-orientation rather than an act of sensitivity toward children, this could cause them to act insensitively toward any children they might have on their own (Jeynes, 1999, 2003b, 2010).

Other social scientists assert that parental divorce will not cause children to engage in sex outside marriage or to possess attitudes that are conducive to doing so (Amato & Sobolewski, 2001; Hanson, 1999; Morrison & Coiro, 1999). They either believe that parental divorce on average will not yield such beliefs and behaviors or that these parental actions will not necessarily yield these specific results in their children (Amato & Sobolewski, 2001; Hanson, 1999; Morrison & Coiro, 1999).

Research has generally confirmed the prediction that children in never-married single-parent family structures are, on average, more prone to engage in sex outside of marriage and to have children outside of marriage than children in intact households (McLanahan & Sandefur, 1994; Wallerstein & Lewis, 1998). It is, however, not as intuitive that a child from a divorced single-parent family structure would necessarily be inclined to be more likely to approve of, or engage in, sex outside marriage. This particular important research question has not been resolved.

One reason why this issue has not been resolved is because so much of the research on the influence of parental family structure has focused on children's educational outcomes. The influence of family structure on the scholastic progress of youth historically received more attention than its potential impact upon psychological and behavioral dimensions for several reasons. First, academic outcomes are probably the easiest to measure. Educational measures are frequently taken, can be administered within a matter of days, and are easily quantified (Lerdau & Avery, 2007; Wittberg, Northrup, & Cottrel, 2009). Second, scores on the Scholastic Aptitude Test (SAT) declined an unprecedented 17 consecutive years between 1963 and 1980, which raised concerns among parents, politicians, and educators (U.S. Department of Education, 2005). Over time, researchers and the College Board (the designers of the SAT) itself concluded that the nation's divorce rate played a major role in the plummeting SAT scores (Jeynes, 1999, 2007a; Wirtz, 1977). Such conclusions were logical and compelling particularly because, after declining from 1948 to 1962, divorce rates started to increase steadily from 1963 through the same consecutive 17 years in which SAT scores fell (Jeynes, 2006a, 2010). Third, many psychological and behavioral results take time to emerge and are more likely to manifest years after a family transition has taken place (Shek, 2007).

Over time, results consistently emerged indicating that youth from non-traditional family structures underperformed academically when compared with their counterparts from intact families (Jeynes, 2000, 2006b; Pong, Dronkers, & Hampden-Thompson, 2003; Rodgers & Rose, 2002). Initially, most of the research on this topic focused on the effects of parental divorce (McLanahan & Sandefur, 1994; Wallerstein & Lewis, 1998), since this was the first nontraditional family structure to become common in the United States (Bennett, 2001; Coontz, 1997). As Ganong and Coleman (2004) pointed out, the examination of remarriage emerged later than did the study of divorce, in part because it took academics some years to realize what seemed like common knowledge among the American public—that parental remarriage represented another family transition to which children needed to adjust (Hetherington, 2003; Jeynes, 2006b). Such adjustments are likely to cause negative effects, at least in the short term. Over time, the study of parental family structures also expanded to include an even wider variety of relational arrangements, including cohabiting parents, nonmarried single parents, and widowed parents (Jeynes, 2000, 2010; Nonoyama, 2000).

As the gamut of family structures examined expanded, so did the range of topics addressed; new research increasingly included divorce's effects on psychological and behavioral outcomes. At first, the focus remained on the couples themselves, but it eventually expanded to include the influence of marital dissolution on children's psychological welfare and behavioral patterns (Corsaro, 2005; Ganong & Coleman, 2004).

In sum, social scientists have yet to reach a consensus regarding the relationship between youth coming from a divorced home and their proclivity for engaging in sex outside of marriage, whereas the effects of being raised in nonmarital family formations are fairly well established (Amato & Sobolewski, 2001; Jeynes, 2002a; Morrison & Coiro, 1999). Over the last couple of decades, in particular, interest in how parental divorce could affect adolescent sexual behavior has increased. Thus, a meta-analysis to resolve this debate seems both timely and logical. Moreover, discerning whether there is a relationship between parental divorce and adolescent sexual behavior, and establishing the extent of that relationship, is crucial if one is to know how to best help youth from this type of family structure and in order to educate parents, teachers, and the general populace.

The meta-analysis presented in this chapter examined the following questions: (1) Is there a general relationship between coming from any type of divorced family structure (divorced or divorced and remarried) and behavior and attitudes regarding adolescent intercourse outside of marriage? (2) Does coming from a divorced single-parent family structure have a different potential relationship to behavior and attitudes regarding adolescent intercourse outside of marriage than coming from a remarried-following-divorce family structure? (3) Do the results differ when only high-quality studies are included in the analysis?

Methods

Analytical Approach

This meta-analysis examined the relationship between parental family structure, on the one hand, and their children's attitudes and behaviors regarding premarital sex on the other. The first analysis entailed determining effect sizes for the overall parental divorce and remarriage variables for all those studies examining *either* children's behavioral *or* attitudinal outcomes (research question #1). The second analysis examined the association between parental divorce and remarriage and behavioral and attitudinal outcomes individually (research question #2). The third analysis examined the association between these variables using only the results of the highest quality studies, that is, those rated 3 on a 0–3 scale (research question #3). The procedures employed to conduct the meta-analysis are outlined below.

Each study included in this meta-analysis met the following criteria:

1. It needed to examine parental divorce and remarriage in a way that could be conceptually and statistically distinguished from other primary variables under consideration. For example, if a researcher examined only nontraditional family structures generally and did not distinguish among the types examined in this analysis, the study was not included in the analysis.
2. It needed to include a sufficient amount of statistical information to determine effect sizes. That is, a study needed to contain enough information so that test statistics, such as those resulting from a t-test, analysis of variance, and so forth (each of which are statistical methods of comparing means from different groups), were either provided in the study or could be determined from the means and measures of variance listed in the study.
3. If the study used a control group, it had to qualify as a true control group and therefore be a fair and accurate means of comparison. For example, if youth from the "control" and the "experiment" groups differed both socioeconomically and in past achievement history this was not considered a fair and accurate comparison. If the research used a control group at some times but not others, only the former comparisons were included in the meta-analysis.
4. The study could be a published or unpublished study.

Given the nature of the criteria listed above, qualitative studies were not included in the analysis. Although qualitative studies are definitely valuable, they are difficult to code for quantitative purposes (and they generally do not include findings equivalent to effect size), so doing so might bias the results of the meta-analysis.

Data Collection Method (Coding and Rater Reliability)

In order to obtain the studies used in the meta-analysis, I undertook a search to locate the research on the relationship between children coming from a divorced family structure (divorced or divorced and remarried) and the children's attitudes and behaviors regarding intercourse before marriage. The first procedures used to locate these studies involved a computer search using 25 research databases (e.g., PsychInfo, ERIC, Dissertation Abstracts International, Wilson Periodicals, Sociological Abstracts, and so forth). The search terms included divorce, remarriage, family structure, marital dissolution, premarital intercourse, premarital sex, attitudes toward sex, and many other similar terms. Reference sections from journal articles on divorce and premarital intercourse were also examined to find additional research articles. In addition, my research team and I contacted 50 deans of colleges or departments of psychology or sociology at Research 1 institutions and requested that they ask their faculty to share with us any research they had completed relevant to parental divorce, parental remarriage, and the sexual behavior and attitudes of their children.

Although this search yielded more than 100 articles and papers on the topics of interest, few of these articles were quantitative in nature. Ultimately, our winnowing yielded a total of 20 nonduplicate studies that quantitatively examined the relationship between parental divorce and remarriage and children's sexual behavior and attitudes. Of these 20, 13 possessed a sufficient degree of quantitative data to include in this meta-analysis.

A number of different characteristics of each study were recorded for use in this analysis. These characteristics included: (a) report characteristics, (b) sample characteristics, (c) the intervention type, (d) the research design, (e) the grade level or age of the students, (f) the outcome and predictor variables, (g) the attrition rate, and (h) the estimate of the relationship between parental marital status and their children's sexual attitudes and behavior.

Report Characteristics

Each study entry began with the name of the author of the study. Then the year of the study was recorded, followed by the type of research report. Research reports were defined either as a journal article, book, book chapter, dissertation, master's thesis, government report, school paper, private report, conference paper, or other type of report.

Sample Characteristics

These included the number of youth sampled, their locations, and how they were selected (e.g., via random selection, stratified random selection, or advertisement).

Intervention Type

We recorded the experimental or procedural manipulation used, if any, to determine the relationship between parental divorce and remarriage and the sexual behavior and attitudes of their children. We noted whether a study obtained family structure information from self-reports or written records, as well as how sexual attitudes were measured.

Research Design

The studies in this meta-analysis were categorized into three basic types of designs. First, we noted the studies that employed some type of experimental manipulation to assess the effects of parental family structure. For example, some clinical studies may examine the effects of family structure only upon certain types of youth. The second type included studies that took cross-sectional measures of the variables under study. The third type involved the calculation of a correlation coefficient between the parental family structure under study and the sexual behaviors and attitudes of their youth. For the cross-sectional and correlational studies, if it was available, we also recorded (a) the socioeconomic status of participants in the sample and (b) the types of behavioral and attitudinal measures that were employed.

Grade Level or Age

The grade level or age of the students was coded, including means and standard deviations when they were available.

Outcome and Predictor Variables

The outcome and predictor variables from each study were coded. These included such outcomes as attitudes toward engaging in intercourse outside of marriage.

Attrition Rate

When available, the attrition rate of each study was coded.

Relationship Estimate

This is the estimate of the relationship between divorce and remarriage on the one hand and sexual behavior and attitudinal outcomes on the other. The process of the effect size estimation is described in the next section.

Statistical Methods and the Effect Size Statistic

Among the 13 studies that possessed a sufficient degree of quantitative data to include in this meta-analysis, the total number of participants exceeded 50,000. Effect sizes from data in such forms as t-tests, F-tests, p-levels, frequencies, and r-values were computed via conversion formulas provided by Glass, McGaw, and Smith (1981). (Effect sizes are numbers, based on the analysis, that summarize the strength of the relationship between two variables.) If any results were not significant and the direction of these not-significant results was not available, the effect size was calculated to be zero.

For studies with manipulations, we used the standardized mean difference to estimate the effect of parental divorce and remarriage.[1] The d-index (Cohen, 1988) is a scale-free measure of the separation between two group means. Calculating the d-index for any comparison involves dividing the difference between the two group means by either their average standard deviation or by the standard deviation of the control group.[2] In the meta-analysis, we subtracted the control group mean from the experimental group mean and divided the difference by their average standard deviation. Hence, positive effect sizes indicate that students who were from divorced or remarried parental family structures were more likely than their counterparts in intact families to have attitudes and behaviors that were more conducive to engaging in premarital intercourse and becoming pregnant outside marriage.

For studies that involved cross-sectional measures of the effects of parental divorce and remarriage as related to behavioral and attitudinal outcomes, we undertook the following procedures. For those studies that attempted statistically to equate students on other variables, our preferred measure of relationship strength was the standardized beta-weight, ß. This is simply a means of assessing the strength of a relationship using certain statistical techniques (e.g., regression analysis). The researchers determined these parameters from the output of multi-variate regression analyses. In a few instances, beta-weights could not be obtained from study reports, so the most similar measures of effect (e.g., unstandardized regression weights) were retrieved.

For studies that involved cross-sectional measures but included no attempt to equate students statistically on third variables, we used the results from the t-tests, F-tests, and correlations provided by the researchers. Probability values were used as a basis for computation only if the researchers did not supply any information on the test statistics just mentioned.[3]

Calculating Average Effect Sizes

We used a weighting procedure to calculate average effect sizes across all the comparisons. First, each independent effect size was multiplied by the inverse of its variance. The sum of these products was then divided by the sum of the inverses. Then, 95% confidence intervals were calculated.[4]

Fixed and Random Error

As Hedges and Vevea (1998) recommend, we conducted all our analyses using fixed-error assumptions in one analysis and applied random-error assumptions in the other.[5] The advantage of undertaking both fixed and random effects analyses is that we can examine the effects of different assumptions on the outcomes of the synthesis, such as whether the effects of parental family structure are fixed over time or whether they change and whether the response of children to a given family transition is static or changes over time.

Study Quality Rating

Two researchers coded the studies independently for quality, the presence of randomization, and whether the definitional criteria were met for parental divorce, remarriage, and attitudes and behaviors regarding premarital intercourse. Study quality and the use of random samples were graded on a 0 (lowest) to 3 (highest) scale. Quality was determined using the following criteria: (1) Did it randomly assign subjects to control and treatment groups (if applicable)? (2) Did it avoid mono-method bias? (3) Did it avoid mono-operation bias? In both the case of methods and operations undertaken in the study, it is ideal to use more than one means of doing each to know that the findings are the same or very similar using at least two different methods or operations, that is, they are robust and broader than those that emerge using one particular method or operation. Other criteria were (4) Did it avoid selection bias, so that certain types of people were not disproportionately more likely to be chosen than others? (5) Did it use a specific definition of family structure through which parental family structure could easily be identified? We calculated inter-rater reliability by computing the percentage of agreement on each of these measures of quality.[6] Inter-rater reliability was 100% on whether a study examined the relationship between parental family structure and the sexual behaviors and attitudes of their children and 92% for the quality of the study. For the specific components of quality, inter-rater agreement percentages were 100% for randomization, 92% for avoiding mono-method bias, 92% for avoiding mono-operation bias, and 83% for avoiding selection bias. A supplementary analysis was performed using only those studies with quality ratings of 3.

Defining Variables

Independent Variable
For the purposes of this study, parental divorce was defined as any family in which divorce had taken place as determined by each study, either as officially proclaimed by law or via lengthy separation. Parental remarriage was defined as the formal matrimonial union between a man and a woman following divorce. Although some individuals choose to participate in a relationship of cohabitation rather than to remarry after divorce, research indicates that a considerable majority eventually remarry (DeWilde & Uunk, 2008). Largely because of this, the vast majority of studies analyzed in this meta-analysis did not include a variable for cohabitation following divorce. Consequently, too few studies included this variable to allow for a meta-analysis.

Dependent Variables
Behavior associated with premarital sex was defined either as engaging in sex or becoming pregnant as an unmarried adolescent. Each of the studies included in this analysis equated sex with vaginal-penile intercourse between a male and a female. An attitude associated with premarital sex was defined as maintaining a belief system that held such behaviors to be morally acceptable.

Results
Effects from Individual Studies and Homogeneity Tests

Table 5.1 lists the average effects for the studies included in the meta-analysis, beginning with the study with the largest effect and continuing to the smallest, measured in standard deviation units. (Standard deviation is a statistical measure that provides the researcher with a common method of depicting

TABLE 5.1

Average Effect Sizes for the Studies Included in the Meta-Analysis

Study	Sample	Effects*
Jonsson et al. (2000)	N=179	.57
Kinard & Gerrard (1986)	N=90	.49
Moore & Chase-Lansdale (2001)	N=289	.39
Axinn & Thornton (1996)	N=679	.34
Whitbeck et al. (1996)	N=499	.33
Jeynes (2002b)	N=18,726	.30
Ferguson et al. (1994)	N=935	.23
Aseltine & Doucet (2002)	N=11,208	.18
Rodgers (1994)	N=5,362	.18
Anda et al. (2002)	N=7,399	.16
Jeynes (2001)	N=24,599	.14
Dorius et al. (1993)	N=1,147	.14
D'Onofrio et al. (2006)	N=2,554	.12

* The effects listed are overall effects without the use of sophisticated controls.

results among a set of studies; this makes it possible to adequately compare different measures with one another.) These effects depict the average influences for the family structures included in each study, that is, either single-parent divorced families or remarried parents following a divorce or both. One of the most pronounced trends in the data is that in every single study examined, parental divorce was associated with a greater likelihood of children engaging in premarital sex or maintaining attitudes that are conducive to doing so. The effects ranged from a high of .57 to a low of .12 of a standard deviation unit.

Research Question #1: Is there a general relationship between coming from a divorced family structure (divorced or divorced and remarried) and behavior and attitudes regarding premarital intercourse?

The results of the first meta-analysis appear in table 5.2. The findings were very similar for both random and fixed effects analyses. Therefore, only the results from the latter, the more conservative of the two, are included in the tables. Table 5.2 lists the effect sizes for the studies on sin-

TABLE 5.2
Effect Sizes for the Studies Included in the Meta-Analyses

	Family Structures Combined	Divorce	Remarriage Following Divorce
Behavioral & Attitudinal Measures Combined without Sophisticated Controls	.21*	.20*	.31*
Behavioral & Attitudinal Measures Combined with Sophisticated Controls	.13	.12	.28
Behavioral Measures Combined without Sophisticated Controls	.20*	.19*	.19*
Behavioral Measures Combined with Sophisticated Controls	.12	.11	—
Attitudinal Measures Combined without Sophisticated Controls	.24*	.23*	.32*
Attitudinal Measures Combined with Sophisticated Controls	.22*	.21*	.28*

*p <.05

gle-parent and remarried divorced families overall, and then for these family structures separately. The effect sizes are also listed separately for those studies that included sophisticated controls in the analyses, for example controlling statistically for differences in socioeconomic status (SES). For both divorced and remarried after divorce families/children, the combined effect size was .21 for all behaviors and attitudes related to premarital intercourse when there were no sophisticated controls included. This was statistically significant at the p < .05 level of probability. For those studies that did include sophisticated controls, the effect size was .13, which was somewhat short of statistical significance, p > .05. For those studies that did not include sophisticated controls, the effect size was .20, p < .05, for the relationship between these family structures and premarital sex and .24, p < .05, for attitudes related to premarital intercourse. For those studies that did include sophisticated controls, the effect sizes were .12, p = ns and .22, p < .05, respectively.

Research Question #2: Is there any potential relationship between coming from either a divorced or a remarried following divorce family structure and behavior and attitudes regarding premarital intercourse?

For parental divorce specifically, when sophisticated controls were not included in the studies, the effects sizes for both behaviors and attitudes about premarital intercourse were .20, p < .05. For the relationship between parental divorce and premarital sex the effect size was .19, p < .05, and for attitudes related to premarital intercourse the effect size was .23, p < .05. For those studies that did include sophisticated controls, the pattern of results was similar as when both family structures were included in the analysis.

Table 5.2 also indicates the effect sizes measuring the relationship between parental remarriage following divorce and behaviors and attitudes regarding premarital intercourse. These results consider the influence of a combination of two family transitions: parental divorce and remarriage. The effect size of parental remarriage following divorce on combined measures without controls was .31, p > .05. The effect size on measures of premarital intercourse without controls was .19, p > .05, and on measures of attitudes was .28, p > .05. With sophisticated controls, the effects size on combined measures was .28, ns; on attitude measures, it was .32, p > .05. The effect sizes were just slightly higher for attitudes related to premarital sex than they were for the actual behaviors themselves. These differences were very small and were not different from each other to a statistically significant degree.

Research Question #3: Do the results differ when only high-quality studies are included in the analysis?

Additional analyses (see table 5.3) were undertaken to discern if any different patterns emerged when the quality of the study was considered. The results indicate that the effect sizes that emerged when only the studies with a 3 rating were included were generally just slightly higher numerically than when all the studies were included in the meta-analyses. None of these differences were statistically significant.

Discussion

The results from this study indicate that there is a consistent relationship between parental family structure and the likelihood that adolescents from particular types of families will approve of and/or engage in premarital intercourse. Specifically, this study indicates that parental divorce and remarriage following divorce are related to these beliefs and behaviors. Every study in the meta-analysis yielded a positive effect size. This is highly unusual and

TABLE 5.3

Effect Sizes for the High Quality Studies (rated 3 on 0-3 scale) Included in the Meta-Analyses

High Quality Studies: Family Structures Combined	Effect Sizes
Behavioral & Attitudinal Measures Combined without Sophisticated Controls	.22*
Behavioral & Attitudinal Measures Combined with Sophisticated Controls	.13
Behavioral Measures Combined without Sophisticated Controls	.21*
Behavioral Measures Combined with Sophisticated Controls	.12
Attitudinal Measures Combined without Sophisticated Controls	.25*
Attitudinal Measures Combined with Sophisticated Controls	.23*
Specific Measures	*Effect Sizes*
Age at First Experience of Premarital Intercourse	.23*
Tendency to Have Sexual Intercourse as an Unmarried Youth	.23*
Became Pregnant While Unmarried and Before Age 20	.16*

demonstrates the extent to which a relationship exists between parental divorce and the attitudes and the behaviors of their children.

The effect sizes that emerged from the meta-analyses tended to be greater for attitudes toward engaging in premarital intercourse than they were for the actual act of premarital intercourse. This finding is both notable and logical. In the case of what is viewed as a highly pleasurable physical experience, such as sexual intercourse, one would anticipate that if young people believe that there is nothing wrong with sex outside of marriage, then they will be fairly likely to engage in this behavior. However, the pleasure associated with sex will likely prompt some adolescents who believe it is morally wrong to act contrary to their beliefs. Hence, it is probably inevitable that the effect sizes for adolescent and single-young adult attitudes toward sex before marriage will be larger than for their actual behavior.

The fact that engaging in sex before marriage can affect several lives coupled with the results of this study suggest that it would be advisable for parents, educators, and society as a whole to discourage adolescents and young adults from engaging in unprotected sexual intercourse (outside contexts when having children might be acceptable or desirable). Nevertheless, it is also important to acknowledge that even if one instructs youth and young adults to have responsible attitudes regarding premarital intercourse these attitudes may not be internalized and it will not yield a 100% change in behavior. One should also note that the relationship between attitudes and behaviors is not quite as strong as one would think (Jeynes, 2007b).

The results of this study also indicate that the relationship between divorced parental family structures and the behaviors and attitudes of the family's progeny, as measured by effect sizes, is less strong in those studies that use sophisticated controls. The most frequent difference between those studies that incorporated sophisticated controls and those that did not was the inclusion of SES. Therefore, there is some degree of evidence that part of the relationship between parental family structure and the attitudes and behaviors of the family's children regarding premarital sex can be accounted for by SES. As research indicates, however, in the case of family structure, attributing causation to SES is unwise, because changes in family formation nearly always affect the income component of SES (Jeynes, 2002a, 2005, 2007b). Therefore, it is difficult to know how much significance to attribute to those studies that control for SES. If this line of research is correct—and it does appear both logical and intuitive—it may be that such studies essentially over-control for SES.

It is also interesting to note that sophisticated controls had a greater influence on findings about sexual behavior than about sexual attitudes. This difference was small but worthy of mention. To the extent that the additional sophisticated controls were largely in the form of controls for SES, one possible explanation is that in socioeconomically depressed neighborhoods, and other locations as well, there may not be sufficient family, neighborhood, and community supports necessary to keep youth from engaging in sex before marriage. One must be careful to understand that the data do not necessarily indicate this explanation, but the pattern of results is such that this is one hypothesis worthy of investigation.

The effect sizes that emerged for the studies rated the highest in quality (3 out of a possible 3 points) were slightly higher than for those that emerged for all of the studies combined. This indicates that one may have a high degree of confidence that the findings that emerged appear to reflect the overall body of research pretty accurately and that even if certain studies could have been done in a way that reflected higher levels of quality, the results would unlikely be any different.

Limitations of the Study

The primary limitation of this meta-analysis, or any meta-analysis, is that it is restricted to analyzing the existing body of literature. Therefore, even if the researcher conducting the quantitative integrations sees ways that the studies included could have been improved, there is no way to implement those changes. For example, most studies did not address the issue that divorce really takes place in stages and there is de facto parental divorce well before the final papers have been signed. A second limitation of a meta-analysis is that the social scientist is limited to addressing the same research questions addressed in the aggregated studies, even if one recognizes that others are worthwhile. Third, within the past few years the phrases "premarital sex/intercourse" and "sex outside marriage" have become more problematic as various states have asked their voters to consider the issue of marriage between same-sex partners. The fact that Americans commonly use the term "premarital sex" to refer to relations between young heterosexuals is a reminder that in a number of respects the term is heteronormative. It is also true that even in those states that allow marriage among same-sex couples, some concerns regarding premarital intercourse are likely to be greater for heterosexual youth than gay and lesbian youth because children can be conceived as a result of heterosexual intercourse (Stein, 1999). There is little question, for example, that parents are more concerned when their unmarried adolescent son informs them that he has just impregnated a girl versus that he has engaged in coitus. Therefore, for a variety of reasons, physical activities that can conceive children outside marriage are often of great concern to society.

Conclusion

The results of this study indicate that coming from a divorced or divorced and remarried family structure is associated with a greater likelihood of engaging in premarital intercourse and becoming a single adolescent parent. The body of research also indicates that if one comes from either of these family structures he or she is more likely to accept or approve of this type of behavior. Further research should be undertaken to test some of the possible reasons why these relationships exist. Additional studies should also examine the extent to which decisions regarding intercourse during adolescence affect the lives not only of the couple engaging in sex, but also of any children that might result from intercourse and of others among family, friends, and the community at large.

APPENDIX: STUDIES INCLUDED IN THE META-ANALYSIS

Anda, R. E., Chapman, D. P., Felitt, V. J., Edwards, V., Williamson, D. F., Croft, J. B., & Croft, W. H. (2002). Adverse childhood experience and risk of paternity in teenage pregnancy. *Obstetrics & Gynecology, 100*(1), 37–45.

Aseltine, R. H., & Doucet, J. (2002). The impact of parental divorce. *Adolescent & Family Health, 3*(3), 122–129.

Axinn, W. G., & Thornton, A. (1996). The influence of parents' marital dissolution on children's attitudes towards family foundations. *Demography, 33*(1), 66–81.

D'Onofrio, B. M., Tunkheimer, E., Emery, B. E., Slutuke, W. S., Heath, A. C., Madden, P. A., & Martin, M. G. (2006). A genetically informed study of the processes underlying the association between parental instability and offspring adjustment. *Developmental Psychology, 42*(3), 486–499.

Dorius, G. L., Heaton, T. B., & Steffen, P. (1993). Adolescent life events and their association with the onset of sexual intercourse. *Youth & Society, 25*(1), 3–23.

Fergusson, D. M., Horwood, J., & Lynskey, M. T. (1994). Parental separation, adolescent psychopathology, and problem behaviors. *Journal of the American Academy of Child & Adolescent Psychiatry, 33*(8), 1122–1131.

Jeynes, W. (2001). The effects of recent parental divorce on their children's sexual attitudes and behavior. *Journal of Divorce & Remarriage, 35*(1/2), 115–134.

Jeynes, W. (2002b). The predictive value of parental family structure on attitudes regarding premarital pregnancy and the consumption of marijuana. *Journal of Human Behavior in the Social Environment, 6*(1), 1–16.

Jonsson, F. H., Njardvik, U., Olafsdottir, G., & Gretarsson, S. J. (2000). Parental divorce: Long-term effects on mental health, family relationships, and adult sexual behavior. *Scandinavian Journal of Psychology, 41*(2), 101–105.

Kinnard, K. L., & Gerrard, M. (1986). Premarital sexual behavior and attitudes toward marriage and divorce among young women as a function of their mother's marital status. *Journal of Marriage and Family, 48*(4), 757–775.

Moore, M. R., & Chase-Lansdale, P. (2001). Sexual intercourse and pregnancy among African American girls in high poverty neighborhoods: The role of family and perceived community environment. *Journal of Marriage and Family, 63*(4), 1146–1157.

Rodgers, K. B. (1994). Pathways between parent divorce and adult depression. *Journal of Child Psychology, 35*(7), 1289–1308.

Whitbeck, L. B., Simons, R. L., & Goldberg, E. (1996). Adolescent sexual intercourse. In R. L. Simons (Ed.), *Understanding differences between divorcing and intact families* (pp. 144–156). Thousand Oaks, CA: Sage.

1. The standardized mean difference is a measure of statistical dispersion equal to the average absolute difference of two independent values.

2. The average standard deviation is the average of the average amounts by which individual items in a data set differ from the arithmetic mean of all the data in the set.

3. Probability values statistically determine the likelihood that a certain event will happen.

4. This type of analysis indicates that there is a 95% degree of confidence that the actual relationship between two variables exists within a certain numerical range.

5. Fixed error models assume that the effects of certain variables do not change, while the random effects model assumes greater change in these variables' effects.

6. A measure of the degree to which raters agree with one another in their ratings.

Hooking Up and Opting Out

Negotiating Sex in the First Year of College

LISA WADE AND CAROLINE HELDMAN

I wanted to explore, experiment, have fun, be a 19-year-old freshman in college.

—Ramona

Ramona's optimistic remark, already in the past tense, captures the hopes and disappointments of many first-year college students. Ramona had a worse year than most. After surviving two attempted sexual assaults and one successful one, she decided to transfer to another college. "I don't know where I will feel safe," she explained, "but it's not at this school."

Traditional students in their first year at many residential colleges find themselves in a highly sexualized environment with great freedoms and few protections. This is a critical age-related transitional period during which many students reconsider their sexual values and initiate or change their sexual behaviors. They do so in negotiation with other students undergoing the same transition, as well as with older students who already have some college experience behind them. In this chapter, we summarize the observations of 44 first-year students who were enrolled in a sexuality-related course and who were undergoing this life course change.

With the transition to campus, students encountered an institution that enabled casual sex and peers who offered social support for "hooking up," the term commonly used to describe casual sexual activity among college students. Almost two-thirds of students reported at least one hookup, acquiring up to 13 new sexual partners in their first year. These hookups involved nonrelational sex with strangers, acquaintances, or friends, usually under the influence of alcohol. More than simply casual, students reported a compulsory carelessness: norms of sexual engagement required students to have sex without caring for their sexual partner. Our analysis also confirms previous findings about the presence and normalization of men's sexual coercion of women on contemporary U.S. campuses.

In addition to corroborating previous findings, we offer two new insights. First, we add to the understanding of the nature of cross-sex friendships within hookup culture. Students found that friendships were difficult to establish and maintain because many cross-sex friends were also past or potential sexual partners. Second, we clarify the role of alcohol in preserving the meaninglessness of sexual activity. More than simply disinhibiting students, alcohol functioned to establish the illusion of carelessness required by the hookup script.

Most respondents, both those who did and did not participate in hookup culture, were highly dissatisfied with sex on campus. Students expressed the desire for sex to offer them one of three things: meaningfulness, empowerment, or pleasure. However, most students, especially women, had difficulty achieving any of these things. In response, some clarified their sexual values and changed their behaviors. The first year of college, then, can help students to become more autonomous sexual adults.

Hooking Up on College Campuses

A life course perspective on sexuality brings the changes that occur as one ages into dialogue with one's biography, demographic characteristics, and the cultural and historical context in which one lives (Carpenter & DeLamater, this volume). The first year of college is a life stage transition and, for many college students in the United States today, this transition requires the negotiation of a new script for sexual expression dictated by hookup culture.

Research indicates that two-thirds to three-quarters of students hook up at least once during college (Armstrong, England, & Fogarty, 2009; England, Shafer, & Fogarty, 2008; Paul, McManus, & Hayes, 2000). A "hookup" is a non-romantic encounter with a friend or acquaintance that involves an unspecified degree of sexual interaction. While hooking up at college is not new, a *culture* of hooking up likely began to emerge in the 1980s or 1990s (Heldman & Wade, 2010). What differentiates contemporary hookup culture from the occurrence of casual sex is the virtual disappearance of the "going steady" dating culture (or script) that was dominant from the postwar period forward (Armstrong et al., 2009; Bogle, 2008). With dating no longer a socially sanctioned option, casual sex has become the dominant type of sexual activity and the primary "pathway into relationship" (England et al., 2008, p. 540).

Compared to previous generations, then, students today are participating in more sexual activities with more partners and having less emotional intimacy. Rates of penile-vaginal intercourse have declined slightly (Kaiser Family Foundation, 2006), with about one-third of hookups involving intercourse (Armstrong et al., 2009; England et al., 2008). This, however, has been accompanied by a shift in the perceived hierarchy of intimacy (Gagnon & Simon, 1973; Rubin, 1984), such that oral sex is seen as being less intimate than intercourse (Pitts & Rahman, 2001; Sanders & Reinisch, 1999). Consequently, oral sex has become an increasingly common sexual behavior on college campuses (Gates & Sonenstein, 2000; Lindberg, Jones, & Santelli, 2008).

Students bring different personal characteristics to hookup culture and not all types of students participate in hookup culture to an equal extent. Evangelical Christian students often save sex for serious relationships or marriage (Freitas, 2008; Wilkins, 2008). Data on participation in hooking up by gay and lesbian students are mixed. Freitas (2008) found that gay and lesbian students at Catholic and secular colleges participated in hookup culture at about the same rate as heterosexuals at those institutions, but Bogle (2008) found otherwise, suggesting that gay and lesbian students hook up less often because the activities that facilitate hooking up (e.g., fraternity parties) are not always "gay safe."

Quantitative research has found that White students are more likely than students of color to engage in casual sex (Owen, Rhoades, Stanley, & Fincham, 2010). White youth, even those who flout mainstream values, like Goths (Wilkins, 2008), can experiment with sexuality without the concern that it will be used to affirm a stereotype that Whites are sexually promiscuous (White, 2001). Confirming this, Black and Latino students interviewed by Kimmel (2008) expressed a reluctance to hook up for fear that their behavior would entrench racism.

Upper- and middle-class female students hook up at higher rates than working-class students. Hamilton and Armstrong (2009) found that class-privileged women prefer hooking up because it allows them to experiment with sex without forming relationships that might interfere with their career plans. In contrast, these researchers argue, working-class women may not envision the same degree of occupational success for themselves and, therefore, may cultivate the "feminine capital" of sexual inexperience instead. Working-class women may choose to opt out of hooking up in favor of monogamy and marriage, especially if such choices are reinforced by families and friends at home.

Gender is the most-studied variable in research on hooking up. Men and women hook up at similar rates (England, 2009; Owen et al., 2010; Paul et al., 2000) and some students of both genders enjoy hookup culture (Armstrong & Hamilton, 2009). Nevertheless, the rewards and punishments for hooking up are gendered. Men's sexual pleasure is prioritized over women's and only women risk being labeled a "slut" (Armstrong et al., 2009; Bogle, 2008; Paul, 2006). Women also report unpleasant, psychologically manipulative, and coercive sexual experiences, which appear to be facilitated by hookup culture (Flack et al., 2007; Littleton, Tabernik, Canales, & Backstrom, 2009). College students are more likely to be sexually assaulted than their same-age peers who are not in college (Karjane, Fisher, & Cullen, 2002). Although the distribution of risks and rewards favors men, there is some evidence that men, too, find hookup culture dissatisfying and oppressive (Kimmel, 2008).

Women's negative experiences with hooking up may be less related to its casual nature than to the fact that it occurs within a system of gender inequality that makes women vulnerable to men generally. Armstrong and Hamilton (2009) followed 58 college women for a year, finding that relationships also posed many problems. Stalking and emotional abuse by boyfriends led to anxiety or depression. Women could spend months attempting to repair or end a relationship. Accordingly, many women said they preferred hooking up because it did not carry the same investment and risk (see also Kimmel, 2008). Edin and Kefalas (2005) find that many low-income women not enrolled in college avoid marriage, even if they become pregnant, because the men in their lives are frequently drug- or alcohol-dependent, violent, unfaithful, or involved in criminal activity. Those same poor and working-class women who prioritize relationships, then, may find it difficult to establish healthy partnerships. From this perspective, hooking up may actually make women less vulnerable to men than establishing monogamous relationships or getting married. Wilkins (2008), likewise, argued that evangelical Christian women's delay of both sex and dating protected them from gender inequality, at least for a time.

While the harmful outcomes of hookup culture are well documented, a life course perspective asks us to consider how life experiences shape life trajectories. There is evidence that women adjust their sexual attitudes and behaviors in response to disempowering sexual experiences. The poor women studied by Edin and Kefalas (2005) shied away from marriage because of negative experiences with men. Meadows (1997), however, was optimistic about women's life trajectories based on her study of thirty-something women from a variety of economic backgrounds. She found that many of these women had developed strategies for self-empowerment and a positive relationship to their sexuality. In fact, women in their first year of college appear to embrace hookup culture more wholeheartedly than even sophomores, who put more emphasis on intimacy (Bogle, 2008; Freitas, 2008; Gilmartin, 2006). Meanwhile, men may become aware of this changing terrain and develop strategies for avoiding women's increased interest in relationships, including dating first-year students (Bogle, 2008; Kimmel, 2008).

In sum, hooking up has largely replaced dating and relationships on today's college campuses. Necessarily, then, first-year college students must learn to negotiate their sexualities within or alongside hookup culture. Individual characteristics and prior and ongoing experiences will shape students' feelings about that culture. Some may be attracted to the sexual opportunities that college may provide; others may be repulsed or have mixed feelings. Once arriving at college, students' new experiences prompt them to further refine their feelings about the hookup script. In this chapter, students discuss anticipating college, describe their experiences with hookup culture, and reflect on their first year.

Methods

Data for this project were collected from 48 first-year students who were enrolled in a second-semester, sexuality-related writing course cotaught by the authors of this chapter. Participants wrote two narratives (one at the beginning of the semester and one at the end) in which they reflected on how and why their sexual attitudes and behaviors did or did not change over the course of their first year. One woman and one man chose not to participate, one woman dropped the course, and one man took an incomplete. Our final sample, then, consisted of 44 students: 33 women and 11 men.

Three women identified as bisexual; no respondents identified as gay or lesbian. The respondents were moderately diverse and included 22 Whites, eight Latinos, seven Asians, two Blacks, and one mixed-race individual. All our respondents know each other, so preserving confidentiality requires extra caution. Accordingly, in addition to using pseudonyms, throughout the discussion we refrain from offering biographical or demographic information about the respondents (with the exception of gender).

Our sample is nongeneralizable for at least three reasons. First, our respondents are not representative of college students: they are more likely than typical college students to be female, from California, and

TABLE 6.1

Participation in Hookup Culture

	Women	Men	Total
Degree of Participation	*n (%)*	*n (%)*	*n (%)*
Participated	21 (64)	6 (55)	27 (61)
Enthusiastically	3 (9)	2 (18)	5 (11)
Reluctantly	18 (55)	4 (36)	22 (50)
Opted Out	10 (30)	4 (36)	14 (32)
In a Relationship for Duration	2 (6)	1 (9)	3 (8)
	33	11	44

from the upper and upper-middle classes. They also score better on academic measures than the average college student. Second, our respondents self-selected into a course that required them to think intently about sexuality. Third, their responses are shaped by the class readings, lectures, discussions, and assignments. This is not to be underestimated; in their narratives, 24 students (55%) discussed the influence of the course. The experiences of our respondents, then, are the stories of students who were especially motivated, equipped with some sexuality-related knowledge and theory, and willing to dedicate several months to thinking about sexuality.

Table 6.1 shows how many of our students participated in hookup culture, opted out, or were in a monogamous relationship for the duration of their first year. Reluctant participators expressed shame, remorse, or a desire to have sex only within a relationship, while enthusiastic participators expressed mostly positive experiences with hookup culture.

Only three (8%) students were interested in and/or able to sustain monogamous relationships during their first year of college (see table 6.1). A substantial minority of students rejected participation in hookup culture (32%); the majority (61%) participated, if reluctantly. .

In our nonrepresentative sample, women were more likely to participate in hookup culture than men (64% and 55%, respectively). Because most studies find no gender difference in participation, this likely reflects the way we gathered our respondents. Overall, about two-thirds of students were hooking up, consistent with the existing literature.

To highlight the fact that the first year of college is a transition, our findings are divided into four parts: anticipation, transition, experience, and reflection. As recommended by feminist methodologists (DeVault, 1999), we reproduce the respondents' own words and narratives as written in order to allow them to speak for themselves (quotations are unedited for typos, spelling, and grammar mistakes, except when required for clarity).

Findings

Anticipating College Sexual Culture

Our students' anticipation of their first year was shaped by media portrayals of college life. Sixteen students (36%) volunteered their impressions of college. Joel said, "I couldn't even begin to list all of the movies that I have seen that depict a 'live free,' party hard, and sexually overloaded college scene." Students mentioned *Girls Gone Wild*, *Superbad*, *American Pie*, and cable television channels like MTV, Comedy Central, and Spike. They anticipated that college would be, as Kariann articulated it, "a wild, sexual party scene [filled with] alcohol, weed, and sex." Tyler thought college would involve "countless nights in which I would be totally hammered and have sex with extremely attractive girls . . . not a week would go by in which I would not have sex at least a dozen times."

For some, expectations were so high that it caused them to change their behavior in advance. Reflecting the attitudes of those who saw virginity as a stigma in Carpenter's (2005) study of virginity loss, Kariann and Sarah discussed embarking on a mission to lose their virginity because they anticipated a need to be sexually active people to fit into college life. Kariann, for example, wrote, "The thing I feared the most about going off to college? Being a virgin. . . . I thought that only nerds, religious nuts, and momma's boys were untouched when they started college." Not all respondents, however, eagerly anticipated hookup culture. Thirteen were in relationships when they completed high school, six were committed to having sex only in relationships, and three believed that sex was best saved for marriage.

The Transition

The transition to life on campus changed the terrain on which students enacted their sexuality. Rebecca pointed out that "it's extremely easy to have someone of the opposite sex in your room." Both Rebecca and Julia noted that, since students were not in classes all day, there was plenty of time in which to hook up. Sex is just "logistically easier [than in high school]," explained Charlotte, who also discussed the lack of a curfew. Fifteen students (34%) discussed the absence of parents and the resulting lack of both protection and accountability.

Charlotte, Paige, Joel, and Sondra all explained that their secondary schools included too few students to facilitate hooking up. Either they were uninterested in the partners who were available or rumors spread too quickly. In college, the sheer number of young people translated into greater opportunity for sexual activity. Ramona said, "There are 100 horny 19-year-olds stuffed into small dorms together, and hormones are just raging."

At our institution, students are required to live on campus for their first two years, so escaping the presence of hookup culture was nearly impossible. This troubled Lauren: "During high school you could go home or stay away from the crowd for a while and you would not have any pressure on you. . . . [Here,] if you do not socialize you are automatically excluded from anything and everything." Because hookup culture pervaded dorm life, living in the dorms meant that hookup culture was one's life. Opting out of hookup culture felt, to many, like opting out of socializing entirely. No students mentioned subcultural sexual alternatives like those embraced by evangelicals and Goths (Wilkins, 2008) or those found back home among working-class students (Hamilton & Armstrong, 2009).

In addition to the institutional features that facilitated hooking up, there is substantial social support for casual sex. Greg pronounced hookup culture as "definitive of sexual relations between college students." Lauren explained that "expectations to hook up at a party are over the charts. Many times that is the only reason students socialize." Notably, this social support for hooking up was relentlessly heterosexual.

The transition to college, then, involved a move to a new institutional environment that enabled hooking up. Three students, Ramona, Greg, and Lucy, made sociological arguments, explaining changes in their sexual values and behaviors with their new social context. Ramona wrote, "For whatever reason, it's the atmosphere of college that actually changes how you feel about sex." Greg explained (his emphasis): "It is not merely just deciding to become more liberal or conservative toward ideas of sexuality, it is the fact that college students are so bluntly given the *opportunity* to change that makes it so tempting to do so."

Greg believed that even those with nonpermissive values would be influenced by hookup culture. Indeed, two of the three students who entered college believing that sex should be saved for marriage ended up changing their minds in their first year (albeit with mixed feelings). Other students seemed to feel powerless to resist their context. Ramona wrote, "I had values. College seemed to strip them away from me." Frank confessed that he "went from not being open to anything to basically open to a full blown orgy." And Hannah reflected: "I arrived on campus with my innocence in my left hand, my morals in my right. I dropped them within two weeks of my arrival and they fell to the ground and crumbled."

Experiences with Hooking Up: The Script

Our respondents confirmed that hooking up typically begins with a social event from which partners retreat to a private or semiprivate location and engage in some form of sexual activity. After the hookup, students return to being friends or acquaintances, though sometimes they find themselves estranged from one another. In this section, we discuss three key features of the hookup script.

Troubled Cross-Sex Friendships

Because hookup culture positioned everyone as a potential sexual partner, friendships were sexualized. Female students reported that it was nearly impossible to have male friends. Ultimately, they believed that all men wanted sex from all women and, despite the "friends with benefits" language often used to describe friendship that included sexual activity, sex and the potential for sex seriously undermined friendship. Sondra explained:

> They all have sex on their minds. Every guy I connect with here on a purely friendly level has sent me numerous texts around 2 am asking, "Hey you. What are you up to?" . . . straight guys rarely want to be just friends with women. Even if the girl is ugly, he could drink enough to make her pretty.

Some women experienced friendship from men as simply a ploy to facilitate a future hookup. Sondra and Lauren both described unintended hookups with platonic male friends that resulted from persistence and an alcohol-induced opportunity. Lauren wrote:

> We have been friends since the summer and he always attempted to have a relationship with me but we are too different from each other so nothing ever happened between us. . . . [One day w]e were drinking and relaxing and every time he would get closer to me. After talking about random

topics and just having a good time, things led to other things and we ended up kissing. He tried to have sex that same day, but I refused. He insisted, so I decided to leave. The next day [a] couple of our friends had a party. So, I went and drank a good amount. The party began to get pretty boring so we decided to leave together. We went to my room and some things led to other things and we ended up having sex.

Lauren's story illustrates how friendships carried a sexual potential even when one party was uninterested in sex.

Danielle, who embraced hookup culture, was nonetheless disturbed by this aspect:

None of the guys here want to be my friend . . . only my fuck buddy. But not even that, just a girl that they can have a one-night stand with. . . . After they do that, they don't care. . . . With all the guys from last semester, the ones that were just random hookups 2 of those were still nice to me . . . aka they want to fuck me again. All the others could care less about what I do with my life or if I ever see them again.

Many women reported that, no matter how close they and a male friend appeared to be, their friendship was compromised when they hooked up. Danielle continues: "Many times afterward the guy will not say hello or even acknowledge my presence." Traci, who has only had one hookup, said that now it is "just this awkward 'I'm not gonna acknowledge you' thing." Hannah, describing one of her regular hookup partners, summed it up: "You could have labeled it friends with benefits, without the friendship maybe?"

The Normalization of Male Sexual Coercion

The hookup script involved, and even normalized, sexual pressure from men. Women reported emotional and psychological coercion and sexual assault. Rose told of two instances in which men had repeatedly ignored her when she said "no" because, she wrote, "according to them, they liked to hear me say no." Lauren observed: "Many first-year girls lose their virginity the first semester of college because they were too drunk to say no." Hilary said, "A lot of boys . . . feel that it is necessary to drink hardcore and when they are drunk they try to push you into engaging in sex." Charlotte echoed her when she said that even nice guys "feel pressured into having sex and thus pressure women into having sex with them."

In addition to the constant need to rebuff the advances of men in whom they were not interested, women reported having a difficult time shaping sexual activity once it had begun. Brooke had such an experience:

[He] was much more experienced and aggressive than the other guys I dated . . . we did stuff almost every day we hung out and it became very hard for me to say no to having sex because we had already done everything else I was comfortable with. He tried to pressure me into it [penile-vaginal intercourse] just like he pressured me into doing other stuff that I normally wouldn't do so soon or as often.

Several women reported being manipulated into performing fellatio. Kariann told this story: "[H]e didn't have a condom, and he said he 'didn't want to get off inside me.' . . . I ended up giving him a blow job because he wouldn't leave me alone." Many female students recalled consenting to sexual activity they did not desire, seeming to feel it was their only option, despite the absence of physical coercion, threats, or incapacitation.

Indeed, our students often felt uncertain about whether sexual coercion from men was acceptable. Some students identified coercion as highly problematic. Sarah, for example, who opted out of hookup culture, wrote, "This school seems to have a culture where guys get girls drunk and 'have their way with them.' . . . I feel so disgusted when I see my male peers shamelessly taking advantage of drunk and vulnerable females at dances." Other students, however, normalized sexual coercion. Rachelle, for example, told a story in which she hooked up with two guys to try to prevent her unconscious friend from being raped. Ultimately, she had intercourse with one because she was "too wasted to say no when he pulled off [my] pants" and the other assaulted her friend while Rachelle was unable to protect her. Reflecting on the night, Rachelle said that it had "bad moments," but it "overall wasn't bad," even as she questioned whether she was raped.

Eight women and one man volunteered stories in which they were sexually assaulted. Four of the women were unsure or did not believe that their experience qualified as sexual coercion. The man was assaulted as a freshman by a female upperclassman who took advantage of his inebriation. He did not define his experience as rape but instead as being "sniped." He wrote, "I told this story to my football brethren, who told me that I had gotten 'sniped,' when a girl solicits a drunk guy to have sex with her. From then on I learned to watch how much you drink." Sexual coercion, then, was a routine feature of hookup culture that, for many students, seemed normal or inevitable.

Alcohol as an Indicator of Carelessness

Twenty-three students (52%) remarked upon the intersection of heavy drinking and sexual activity. More than simply disinhibiting students or excusing their behavior, alcohol replaced mutual attraction as the supposed fuel for sexual interaction. For example, Sondra, when discussing how her male friends in high school were not interested in her sexually, explained that "there was never any sexual tension because sex was never on the table." Explaining further, she said that she and they *only* made out when they were drunk, "but nothing more." Trying to reaffirm the nonsexual nature of these male friendships, she explained that neither of her best male friends "have ever made sexual advances sober." Based on this, she concluded that her friends have never made sexual advances. Only sober advances are considered "real." Another student, Rachelle, dismissed sexual contact with other women as simply being "drunk and horny." In these cases, she said, "Why bother discriminating by gender? . . . The way I figure it, that doesn't mean that I'm not straight." Her same-sex contact, then, was made meaningless because alcohol was involved.

Because they could attribute sexual activity to the influence of alcohol, its presence allowed students to preserve the illusion, required by the hookup script, that they were engaging in sex carelessly. That is, one was not to choose their partner carefully, think carefully about whether to have sex, or care for their partner. This finding resonates with Kimmel's (2008) observation that alcohol is used to preserve an appearance of spontaneity that denies a sustained interest in any given person. Insightfully, Charlotte wrote, "A sober hook up indicates one that is more serious, which either no one is interested in or no one is brave enough to admit they want." Charlotte's comment reveals that the script required not only that you enjoy casual sex but also that you have an active *dis*interest in your sexual partner. May echoed her comment: "Even if both partners feel attracted to each other, not physically but emotionally, they do not tell each other that." Emotional connections are avoided; they are off-script. Alcohol, then, functioned to allow all parties to deny that their sexual contact indicated any interest in an emotional bond.

In sum, prior research has shown that the hookup script involves casual sex, the use of alcohol, and pressure and coercion from men. Our respondents have confirmed these findings, but they have also clarified the role of alcohol in protecting the meaninglessness of hooking up and have revealed how friendship dynamics are changed when all members of the other sex are potential sexual partners. In the next section, we discuss students' evaluations of hookup culture as their first year of college comes to a close.

Reflecting on Their First Year

Three women and two men expressed unequivocal enjoyment of hookup culture. Bianca said, "I feel that if both parties are using each other in the same ways and have established a set of rules, then a sexual relationship can work" and "I love open relationships." Jon wrote that, in contrast to monogamous relationships, "[A] much more logical approach . . . would to simply be friends with benefits as it is called today, where people are friends with no real emotional attachment . . . when someone needs a sexual release they simply call the other person and setup a time to have a little fun." Enthusiastic participators, however, were in the minority. Most students, both men and women, were dissatisfied with hookup culture because it largely failed to deliver even one of the three things that students wanted from sex: meaningfulness, empowerment, and pleasure.

Meaningfulness

Articulations of a desire for meaningful sex filled many of the narratives of both men and women. Thirty-three respondents (75%) discussed wanting sex to be meaningful, including the 14 who had opted out of hookup culture, the 6 in monogamous relationships, and 13 of the 22 students who were still participating in hookup culture at the end of the year. By meaningful, however, students did not necessarily mean love. Students used terms like "emotion," "intimacy," "trust," and "care." May and Lauren, for example, wanted to share a "bond"; Kelly wanted it to be "special"; Rebecca and Charlotte simply wanted to have "feel[ings]" for the person; and Evelyn and Danielle discussed a desire for a "connection" even if, as Danielle put it, it was not "a romantic one." Jessica agreed that love was unnecessary but thought that some sort of "sentiment" would be nice: "Like, you make me feel optimistic or you make me feel alive or you make me feel safe. Or you inspire me." Many students, then, did not require love, but they wanted some sort of positive emotion or meaningful connection. For example, Alexis explained, "It's not that I think sex has to be really intimate and full of emotion, it's just I wanna at least know the person. If only just a little bit." Danielle just wanted sex to mean "something."

Our overall impression is that 29 of the 44 respondents (66%), including many who had opted out of hookup culture, would have been content simply having sexual contact with someone with whom they were "in like" so that they could explore their sexuality in the context of benevolence. Still, our single students reported difficulty achieving even this level of intimacy.

Empowerment

Many of the women in our sample felt that they had inherited a right to express their sexuality from the women's movement. Freedom to have sex was a measure of their liberation and they saw college as an opportunity to enact it. However, the stories of unwanted sex and sexual assault suggest that many of our female respondents felt disempowered instead of empowered by sexual encounters.

Women disliked feeling pressured by men, but they appeared rather helpless to resist it. Options such as providing manual stimulation, saying "no," asking him to masturbate, leaving the situation, or abandoning the friendship or relationship did not seem to occur to them. If male pressure were not so normalized, it might have been experienced as outrageous or unacceptable, and noncompliant responses like these might have seemed appropriate. But some women, at least some of the time, simply could not assert their own preferences. Ironically, then, women were engaging in sex because they felt that the playing field was even, although it was not. This left them feeling "horribly discourage[ed]" like Jessica or even vulnerable like Ramona who, despite the optimistic quotation that begins this chapter, had decided to transfer to a school where she hoped she would feel more "safe."

Pleasure

Sexual pleasure, often conflated with "fun," was highly valued by many respondents and considered a good reason to engage in sexual activity. For example, Brooke wrote, "Sex is supposed to be about pleasure" and Meg liked the "opportunity to explore sex now and have a little fun." Many other students concurred.

Yet, even when sex was both consensual and wanted, students often reported highly unsatisfying sexual encounters. This was especially true for women, who discussed their sexuality as something they served up to men. Virginia wrote, "Having sex was entirely for his enjoyment, when he wanted it, where, and how," and Lauren simply said, "Anything we did was not pleasurable to me. I could not be satisfied by him in any way." Several women reported feeling like an object. Rebecca opined, "I was just a warm body being used to make a guy have an orgasm"; Lorelai explained that she felt like a "sex toy" with "three holes and two hands"; and Danielle railed, "I am just seen for my body, nothing else . . . a masturbation toy."

Women were dissatisfied with the sexual skills of their partners, but they also often deprioritized their own pleasure. Brooke said, "My sexuality was filled with anxiety and my need to please the guy instead of worrying about my own pleasure"; Rebecca explained, "I used to base my actions in sexual encounters on what I thought my male partner wanted"; and Bianca stated, "I want to please not myself but my boyfriends . . . even if I was in charge I did not make sure I was being pleased." Danielle, who had hooked up with 13 men in her first year, confessed that she had not been given a single orgasm: "The guy kind of expects to get off, while the girl doesn't expect anything." The depth of Danielle's dissatisfaction is revealed by her choice of words. She did not write that women do not expect an orgasm, or pleasure, or connection, or a relationship; she wrote that women do not expect "anything" at all.

These data suggest that, even from a purely physical perspective, women's experiences of hookups were often unsatisfying. This led some to start questioning the hookup script. Alexis, for example, reflected on whether she liked performing fellatio:

> I['ve] talked about how I enjoy giving head. . . . But now I'm not so sure. I gave them a lot to my ex-boyfriend but I don't really remember wanting to . . . in retrospect I'm not exactly sure if it was ever a willing activity. I don't mean to say that I was coerced into giving them, because that is not the case at all. I more mean to say that I can't recall ever going up to him and going down on him on my own accord. It was more like he would casually suggest it, or motion to his penis. And I would do it and "enjoy" it. But . . . I'm not so sure if my enjoyment was actually real. I feel like I learned somewhere that girls are supposed to enjoy giving head. . . . And so I did. I mean I really did . . . [but] I've come to the conclusion that I got really good at acting like I liked it. . . . But I don't think that I did. In fact, I think I kinda have an aversion to them . . . in retrospect, I really don't like how good I was pretending that I enjoyed blowjobs so much. It's kinda scary.

Many students, like Alexis, were rethinking the hookup script after experiencing unpleasant or unpleasurable sex.

In sum, most respondents wanted their sexual activity to be fun and pleasurable, empowering, or meaningful, but it was not. Facing a disconnect between their desires and their experiences, many students reported mixed or negative feelings about hooking up. Rebecca, for example, felt "good about [her]self but it was an empty sort of good." Elsewhere, she wrote that sometimes "[i]t just felt animalistic and worthless." Zoey described a bout of "extreme shame." Danielle called herself "pathetic." Traci both did and did not "regret" her sole hookup: "I don't necessarily wish that I hadn't spent that night with him, but at the same time, I do wish that I hadn't done anything. . . . I guess I feel like I might have enjoyed it more with someone I knew and liked. I think that's the real reason that I regret doing it with him."

Similarly confused, Hannah went back and forth, committing to contradictory sentences. She wrote, "I am no perfect angel, and quite honestly I like it this way." One sentence later, she said,

> I have lost self respect, self worth and confidence. Sometimes I feel I don't matter, and my actions have few repercussions on anyone but myself. . . . I have ended up in many intimate situations which were unplanned and rather "random." To state it bluntly, I have "slept around."

Then she returned to her previous position:

> That sounds so demeaning and harsh, right? Yet, I don't understand why. I have had fun, and been safe during the process, so quite honestly I don't see the problem? I understand the prizing and worth of one's virginity, but once the cherry is popped, what's the big deal about one more guy, one more night, one more experience?

These final question marks plead with the reader to help her make sense of her experiences. She wanted to feel good about her choices, and she could marshal up logic to justify feeling good, but she still felt at least a little bit bad. Carpenter (2005) documents a similar loss of boundaries and ambivalence about sex after virginity loss, especially for people who view virginity as a gift or as a stigma.

Several men also reported remorse. Tyler, who said that he engaged in a "collection of one night stands" during his first semester of college, labeled them "mistakes," and he said that he "was not proud the following morning[s]." Similarly, Joel wrote,

> At [first] I felt free and life seemed to be so great. When my experiences became more intimate, however, I found that I actually had a lower sex drive than I did in high school. Even oral sex seemed to just not be right deep down inside, even though on the surface it was extremely pleasurable.

After these experiences, Joel decided to opt out of hookup culture and reported no sexual activity during his second semester.

Many students, like Joel, felt that the first year had been an important learning experience. Ramona explained, "I don't think that you really develop a sense of how you feel about sex until after your first year. Then you've been through all of your experiences, whether they are good or bad, and can finally decide how you think differently about sex." And Lorelai reflected: "I would not give up . . . any of my experiences this year because they all taught me something about myself, through sex. Some were good, some were hard and some were painful, but I truly think that I am better for it."

Five students who had initially participated in hookups had decided over the course of the year that they would no longer do so. Charlotte opted out after reading feminist theory about sexual consent; Joel and Alexis had negative experiences at the beginning of their first semester; Traci was embarrassed by her hookup partner; and Virginia was scared by her friend's unplanned pregnancy. Another three were actively questioning whether to continue participating. Danielle, for example, had a deeply positive sexual experience that made her reevaluate the value of all her previous hookups. Tyler's year was complicated after hooking up with someone who may have been mentally unstable, leading him to wonder whether casual sex was worth the risk. Many were questioning the sexual script that they were offered.

But the alternative to hooking up on our campus was to opt out of sexual relationships altogether. Traditional dating was considered passé and relationships were stigmatized such that students seemed unable to imagine alternative ways to engage sexually. Opting out of hookup culture, then, meant opting out of sex. This also explains why so many who would have preferred not to have casual sex did so anyway. For them, hooking up was a price they were willing to pay for the opportunity to have sex and the small possibility that hookups would lead to pleasure, empowerment, or a relationship.

Conclusions

Our findings confirm previous research indicating that the hookup script includes alcohol use, an open-ended sexual encounter, and a casual attitude toward sex. The narratives also add new texture to what we know about hookup culture. Alcohol functioned not simply to disinhibit students but also to affirm (the illusion) that sexual partners do not care about each other. In such a context, men and women may orient toward one another antagonistically, making it difficult to establish and maintain cross-sex friendships. Few students expressed enthusiastic appreciation for hooking up. Most reported that it failed to offer them any of the things that they wanted from sex. Instead, students described disconnection from their sexual partners, feelings of objectification and disempowerment, and unpleasant and unpleasurable sex.

Many analyses of hookup culture draw similarly dire conclusions based on the script and its enactment (Flack et al., 2007; Littleton et al., 2009; Paul, 2006)—and rightly so. Some of our students have been or will be sexually assaulted, some will contract serious sexually transmitted infections, and the gendered antagonism will, no doubt, cause emotional trauma for many. Our findings, however, in addition to confirming that hookup culture is not a safe space, especially for women, suggest that for some students it provides an opportunity to clarify their values and practice asserting their boundaries. Students report reevaluating hookup culture and the hookup script, shifting their priorities and changing their behaviors accordingly. Because hookup culture is hegemonic and pervasive, however, they have little vision of an alternative and, so, dissatisfied students simply choose to opt out of sexual relationships altogether—at least for the duration of their college careers.

NOTE

We are grateful, first and foremost, to our respondents. Their honest, heartfelt, beautifully written, and often funny narratives touched us both as humans and as scholars. We are also thankful for the time and effort of our anonymous reviewers.

7

The Symbolic Power of Civil Marriage on the Sexual Life Histories of Gay Men

ADAM ISAIAH GREEN

The institution of marriage has had a profound and enduring impact on intimate life. Marriage, for instance, confers a wide range of benefits, rights, and obligations that support the marital couple, including resources for the protection of the couple's health, property, and dependents, and the imposition of a legal protocol that discourages capricious dissolution of the marital relationship. Somewhat less obvious, however, is the symbolic power of the institution, including the legitimacy it confers upon spouses and those with whom the spouses interface, such as friends, family, and employers. Moreover, because marriage in North America represents one of the most profound rites of passage in adulthood, its effects are not localized to the point at which one becomes married but, rather, bear on individuals' sensibilities and expectations as early as childhood. For example, little girls may learn about the wonderment of becoming a bride in films and fairy tales, and little boys begin to anticipate being a married dad with their own children. Irrespective of the actuality of these ideations, the institution of marriage situates most individuals along a marital trajectory well before reaching the altar, producing expectations and value commitments that establish the template of a "successful" intimate life (see Ingraham, 1996).

Precisely because of the significance of civil marriage in the life course, those who do not marry are typically regarded as "failed" men and women. For instance, despite the tremendous gains women have made in the paid workplace over the past century, women who do not marry by midlife are often stigmatized or regarded with pity. Never-married men in midlife fare little better in the court of public opinion; they are regarded as playboys or, worse, as homosexuals. The social scientific literature, too, reproduces the marital norm by creating categories of men—"marriageable" and "unmarriageable"—the latter of whom are men who poverty and underemployment have rendered incapable or unwilling to enter into marriage. The implication is, of course, that men with economic wherewithal will choose marriage over bachelorhood. That is, put differently, a never-married, middle-class man in midlife is deviant.

In this chapter, I consider yet another contingent of historically "unmarriageable" men—*gay* men. Unlike heterosexual men, gay men have occupied a unique structural position (along with lesbians) in that, until very recently, the law blocked them wholesale from entering into civil marriage (and it still does in the majority of states in the United States). As I argue elsewhere (Green, 2006, 2010), *both* access to and exclusion from civil marriage have powerful effects that resonate throughout the life course of heterosexual and homosexual men, respectively. In fact, differential access to marriage may be the single most important historical factor that produces patterned distinctions in the sexual careers of working-and middle-class heterosexual and homosexual men in North America, including both norms and practices related to monogamy and the rate of partner change.

But the effects of marital exclusion for homosexual men are not confined to the past, not even among those who can now marry legally in the United States and Canada. Rather, I argue in this chapter that the historical exclusion from marriage has established the structural conditions of a "meaning-constitutive" dialectic (Gross, 2005) whereby a queer cultural tradition has emerged in opposition to the traditional, romantic meaning-constitutive tradition. That is, heterosexual access to and homosexual exclusion from civil marriage have produced the institutional backdrop against which a gay sexual subculture has emerged with a value system concerning intimate life forged in direct opposition to its heterosexual counterpart. Whereas the predominant, heterosexual, romantic meaning-constitutive tradition is anchored to the institution of heterosexual marriage (Gross, 2005), the queer meaning-constitutive tradition is anchored to the institutions of sexual sociality, including bars, nightclubs, and bathhouses. And whereas the institution of marriage promotes and valorizes monogamy and reproduction, the institutions of sexual sociality promote and valorize sexual exploration, nonmonogamous norms, and extended bachelorhood. Consequently, same-sex couples today arrive at the doorstep of marriage having traveled along a very different pathway from their heterosexual counterparts, and this difference is likely to materialize in the dyadic norms and practices of their marital relationships.

In the following section, I ground these insights in the findings of two studies I conducted on intimate life. A data section provides a discussion of the respective samples of this research. Then, drawing on the first study of the sexual life histories of gay and straight men in New York City, I examine how exclusion from civil marriage is likely to bear on working-and middle-class homosexual men from youth to midlife, paying special attention to sexual norms and practices. A subsequent section of the chapter sketches the historical process by which a queer meaning-constitutive tradition has taken form, less as a consequence of an intentional, politicized lifestyle than as a consequence of structural exclusion from civil marriage. In the last section of this chapter, I draw on suggestive data from the second study—an exploratory study of same-sex marriage in Toronto, Canada—to demonstrate how this queer meaning-constitutive tradition may continue to bear on same-sex civil marriages today.

Data

The analysis in this chapter is drawn from two studies that I conducted over the previous ten years. In the first, I performed a comparative study of the intimate lives of New York City gay and straight men. In this research, I interviewed 60 gay and 50 straight men who lived or worked in New York City for at least a year before the interview. They ranged in age between 21 and 52 years old. The majority of respondents identified as middle-class and had obtained college degrees, while about one quarter had obtained graduate degrees. To maximize the possibility of identifying racial patterns in the sexual career, I restricted study participants to those identifying as either "black" or "white." In total, one half of the homosexual respondents identified as black; the other half as white. Despite my best efforts to recruit heterosexual black men, the heterosexual respondents were almost entirely white. At the time of the interview, about half of the heterosexual and homosexual men were in relationships. Notably, my data do not allow a consideration of how poor or upper-class gay men experience marital exclusion, nor do they permit a comparison of black homosexual and heterosexual men. In the case of poor, black heterosexual men, research suggests that such men are less "marriageable" than their wealthier counterparts (West, 2001; Wilson, 1987) because they are less able to provide for a wife and children. In this regard, it remains an empirical question whether poor homosexual men would also marry less often, because these men do not generally carry the expectation of supporting a family. As well, it is not clear how much of the unmarriageable effect is due to racial factors or income (Battle, Bennett, & Lemelle, 2006). Thus, how race and income bear on the experiences of exclusion from and, more recently, inclusion in, civil marriage among gay men remains unknown.

The second study upon which I draw represents an exploratory piece of research examining same-sex marriage among 30 lesbian and gay Canadians. The participants, 15 lesbians and 15 gay men, had been married for at least one year prior to the interviews I conducted with them, and they ranged in age between 26 to 61 years old. With the exception of two spouses in two marriages, the same-sex spouses of this study identified as white. The vast majority of study participants were university-educated and characterized themselves as earning a yearly combined income of $80,000 or more.

Next, I turn to the first study to discuss the impact of inclusion in and exclusion from civil marriage.

The Uninvited Guest: Same-Sex Desires in Adolescence

In my study of heterosexual and homosexual working- and middle-class men of New York City, I was struck by the extent to which both straight and gay respondents recalled anticipating marriage and fatherhood in childhood and adolescence (Green, 2006). These expectations were part of a larger heteronormative *script* (Gagnon & Simon, 1973) that prescribes a set of lifestyle choices—including monogamous marriage and parenting—as the definition of a normal, satisfying romantic life. This was particularly surprising from a sample of men who reside in the nation's most cosmopolitan metropolitan center—men for whom one might expect the *least* traditional lifestyle commitments. But, in fact, with only a few exceptions, both groups of men had adopted the "marital template"—that is, a sexual road map that, by design, was to culminate before midlife in monogamous marriage and fatherhood.

Perhaps this should not have been a surprise. Despite significant changes over the past 50 years in the ages at which people marry and divorce, the vast majority of North Americans still marry by midlife and the majority of people who divorce get remarried within 4 years (Coleman, Ganong, & Fine, 2000). As well, both ideologically and behaviorally, marital monogamy continues to be the norm (Laumann et al., 1994). In fact, despite what some may perceive to be increasing sexual permissiveness following the sexual revolution of the 1960s, attitudinal support for marital monogamy *increased* in the United States between 1972 and 1998 (Cherlin, 2002). Put differently, a meaning-constitutive tradition that is anchored to marriage, monogamy, and parenthood is still by far the dominant tradition of working- and middle-class America (Gross, 2005), both in practice and ideation.

But although the men in my study reported childhood commitments to the martial template, this changed quite dramatically with the arrival of, as one respondent put it, the "uninvited guest"—that is, same-sex attraction. Indeed, like many queer youth (Fergusson, Horwood, & Beautrais, 1999; Savin-Williams, 1995), the gay men in my study struggled with their homosexual desires during adolescence; they ignored them, repressed them, or tried to dissolve them through drug and alcohol use. Nevertheless, eventually, the uninvited guest prevailed, and these men sought out an openly gay lifestyle.

The acceptance of homosexual orientation is typically a powerful turning point in one's life history, but its implications are not reducible to an individual choice revolving around the sex of one's romantic partner. In fact, accepting one's homosexuality represents a much broader, structural transition in queer lives (Herdt, 1992). For instance, among the men of my study, "becoming" gay meant seeking out an entirely new set of peers with whom one could bond and forge friendships and sexual partnerships. As well, one's relationships to old friends and family were subject to change. Perhaps most importantly, before the emergence of same-sex civil marriage, gay men understood that their sexual desires rendered them unmarriageable. No longer candidates for the marital template, these gay men had to "unlearn" (Herdt, 1992) the heteronormative[1] meaning-constitutive tradition that they had acquired at home, school, and church, and they had to realign their identities—present and prospective—with the structural conditions attendant to homosexual status. Put differently, like Weber's switchmen (1915/1958), being a homosexual directed newly identified gay men onto a new set of train tracks, away from marriage and parenthood, and toward gay culture and community (Herdt & Boxer, 1992). This transition is still likely to operate today among gay men for whom same-sex marriage is not a possibility.

In the next section I draw again from my study of heterosexual and homosexual life histories to highlight the formation of an alternative queer tradition that formed at a time when same-sex marriage was not legally possible anywhere in the United States or Canada. Here, I show how access to and exclusion from marriage shaped the sexual lives of these respondents as they sought out the gay metropolis of New York City.

The Queer Meaning-Constitutive Tradition: Adult Gay Male Adaptations

Because "becoming" gay is at once an individual transformation and a change in structural location, "new" gay men in my study found that the rites and passages that defined the heterosexual life course were now irrelevant to them. Blocked from accessing the institution of marriage and, in turn, the normative sexual trajectory out of bachelorhood, generations of gay men built an adult intimate life in the absence of the traditional, heterosexual meaning-constitutive tradition. As one respondent put it:

> I knew that, o.k., if I am going to be gay, I am not going to be married. The whole children thing—well, there goes the kids! . . . There's no kids in the picture! . . . And I fully believed that a monogamous relationship was far less possible.—*Gary,*[2] *white, 30s*

In the short term, for each individual gay man, meeting sexual partners is often of paramount importance upon "coming out." This is not unlike heterosexual men entering late adolescence and early adulthood, whereby sexual relations with multiple partners are often highly desired (Kimmel, 2008). In my own study, heterosexual men in this latter age group articulated a strong interest in "hooking up" with female peers. Although some of these men were involved with dating and longer-term relationships, most of these relationships were, in fact, relatively short in duration—a few months to a year or two at most. For these heterosexual men, the early and mid-twenties, by and large, were occupied with sexual relationships and sporadic dating.

But by their late twenties and early thirties, the marital template bore down upon them as a consequence of their internalization of the traditional romantic meaning-constitutive tradition and its associated scripts, the example of peers, and the pressure of family members and girlfriends. Even self-identified "playboys" began to construct their bachelorhood as a waning "phase" that would end upon meeting the "right" girlfriend. Here, libidos were tempered on the pathway toward an "age-appropriate" intimate relationship that paired desire, long-term commitment, and ultimately marriage (Settersten, 2003). Indeed, in a very real sense, these men had been training for this transition all their lives.

By contrast, among homosexual men entering their late twenties and thirties, this life course transition had no relevance. In fact, while straight men were increasingly subject to the gravitational pull of the institution of marriage upon entering their late twenties and thirties, gay men in my study were subject to a different and opposing gravitational pull—that exerted by institutions of sexual sociality and a queer meaning-constitutive tradition.

The formation of a queer meaning-constitutive tradition is itself a historical process that was institutionalized in most large North American gay communities by the early 1970s (Adam, 1987; Fitzgerald, 1987; Levine, 1998; Murray, 1996). Here, generations of "unmarriageable" gay men traveled to or set up residence in urban centers such as San Francisco, New York, Chicago, Los Angeles, Montreal, and Miami. The unmarriageable status of each newcomer would, over time, materialize into networks of unmarriageable men with attendant subcultural forms predicated on sexual freedom, sexual exploration, and long-term bachelorhood. Commercialized gay spaces such as gay bars, bathhouses, and nightclubs facilitated and accelerated the formation of these gay networks in the spatial context of gay-identified enclaves (Adam, 1987). The sexual institutions of the gay enclave magnified the unmarriageable status of each individual participant in a process of cultural intensification (Fischer, 1980). What resulted was a distinct queer sexual culture and a queer meaning-constitutive tradition defined by sexual exploration and a robust sex-positive ethos (Adam, 1987; Bech, 1997; Fitzgerald, 1987; Levine, 1998). Institutionalized in a range of subcultures revolving around particular sexual scenes—for example, leather, jock, clone, and bear—the queer meaning-constitutive tradition was imparted in bars, bathhouses, dance clubs, circuit parties, the major thoroughfares of gay enclaves, coffee shops, private parties, sex shops, bookstores, and queer media.

For many men in my study, the arrival in New York City entailed participation in this queer meaning-constitutive tradition, and it was the occasion for great joy. Now a gay life, with gay friends and sexual partners and open discussions about one's desires and interests, was finally possible:

> So I started coming every weekend after that, staying at the Chelsea Hotel—right there in the citadel of young gaydom—and just embracing it! And it was like wild! I was just like free! I mean the first weekend I was here [in Manhattan] I went to the Eagle, and I went to the Spike, and I went to the Lure! And I was like "wow!"—I am walking up Eighth Avenue being exhilarated. I am in the deep West Village, seeing these huge, massive guys hugging and kissing while roller-blading and I just couldn't stop smiling! Everywhere—at the bus, at the train station, at the ATM machines, in restaurants on the streets, in the park—I mean everywhere, there was this complete acceptance and normalization of everything I had thought was deviant and wrong. It was wonderful! [laughs with joy]—Paul, white, 30s

But although the gay metropolis permits many gay men to build a life of their choosing, it at the same time generates a social system with its own set of norms, traditions, institutions, and, in turn, pressures. That is, the queer meaning-constitutive tradition and its associated sexual institutions pull gay men into lifestyle forms predicated on sexual exchange, long-term bachelorhood, an emphasis on sexual freedom over norms of monogamy, and the development of sexual identities and practices organized by the sexual fields of gay enclaves (Green, 2008). In fact, the very queer meaning-constitutive tradition that developed as a consequence of exclusion from the institution of marriage itself establishes a new social imperative—sexual sociality. Indeed, if late twentysomething heterosexual men adjust their sexual and dyadic practices to the gravitational pull of the traditional, heteronormative meaning-constitutive tradition, so their gay counterparts adjust their own sexual and dyadic practices to the gravitational pull of the queer meaning-constitutive tradition.

For some gay men, the queer meaning-constitutive tradition is both a source of pleasure and a source of frustration. Those who prefer a monogamous, long-term relationship, for instance, can find the normative emphasis on sexual opportunity over relationship building problematic (Green, 2006):

> I think it would be nice to have someone eventually I could connect with. . . . But it's . . . I don't know . . . maybe I am losing hope. . . . No, I don't think I am losing hope of that . . . I think I'll find that someday. I think I would like to find that someday. It just feels that everyone is always looking for the next best thing . . . y'know . . . I think because there isn't a model in the gay community of steady relationships. No one knows how to do it. . . . In the gay community, there's always a way out. There aren't many people who are like, "No, we need to stay together." Usually, it's like, "Oh, I'm attracted to somebody else."—*Jim, white, 20s*

Assimilation to the queer-meaning constitutive tradition entails reorganizing one's sexual and dyadic expectations, including nonheteronormative possibilities, such as nonmonogamy:

> I would have to see [about an open relationship]. I would be open to discussing it. I don't know how I would work in an open relationship. . . . I still have problems with it. I only take this attitude because I look at what is going on in the community and I see very few monogamous relationships. That's the only reason I'd say I'm even open to considering it.—*Derek, black, 30s*

Over time, although some gay men may feel initially uneasy about open relationships, the queer meaning-constitutive tradition can transform how they conceive of a meaningful relationship and the role of sexuality within it:

In the beginning, when we started this [open relationship], I was jealous. And then it wore off quickly when I started seeing the benefits for myself. . . . Stan introduced me to the bathhouse. I think because of him I became more involved in the whole gay sexual experience. He told me that in every relationship he's ever been in, he, after a while, just wants to have sex with other people. . . . So I would come to New York City to visit him, and if I was here for an extended period of time, he would have no problem letting me borrow his bathhouse club card . . . so there were perks.—*Kevin, black, 20s*

A powerful agent of socialization, the queer meaning-constitutive tradition may also shape how gay men imagine gay marriage, were it ever to become a reality.

I would be interested in marriage [to a man]. . . . It would not be a traditional monogamous one, though. It would possibly be more like the relationship I have. More and more, I don't understand how anyone could expect [that] the person they're marrying is never going to sleep with another person, or why that should have to be the case.—*Andy, black, 20s*

In sum, both working- and middle-class gay and straight men start out in roughly similar places with regard to how they imagine their adult sexual careers. Over time, however, sexual orientation distinguishes these two groups of men. The effects become observable in their late twenties and thirties as heterosexual men are winding down bachelorhood and gay men are transitioning to a fully realized queer sexual lifestyle. Each of these turning points involves a reconceptualization of the sexual life path and a reconfiguration of sexual scripts, norms, and practices. Thence, heterosexual playboys begin to see a life of bachelorhood as deviant, and homosexual monogamists begin to see a life with only one sexual partner as unrealistic and antiquated. Importantly, it would be wrong to suggest that either sexual career is "ideal"; in fact, both are fraught with contrasting frustrations. Heterosexual men may, for instance, feel sexually unfulfilled in their marriages and wish for more sexual diversity and exploration. They may also feel burdened by the responsibilities of marriage and parenthood. Their gay counterparts, by contrast, may grow frustrated by what they perceive to be a lack of dyadic commitment in the gay community and a lifestyle that emphasizes sexual opportunism over long-term, intimate connections.

Theoretically, these sexual careers must be understood as the result of individual decision-making processes within the bounded possibilities of social structure. That is, working- and middle-class heterosexual men have been trained since childhood to follow the marital template, and to align their wants and desires with it when bachelorhood is no longer considered age-appropriate. As Gagnon and Simon (1973) have noted, even young men who falsely profess affection in exchange for sex learn to invest in the rhetoric of dyadic commitment. In fact, most heterosexual men in my study not only learned to accept monogamy and marriage, but they also came to *desire* it.

Conversely, as a consequence of their structural exclusion from civil marriage, working- and middle-class gay men *unlearn* the heteronormative meaning-constitutive tradition and its associated dyadic scripts, eventually refashioning this tradition or rejecting it altogether to develop new sexual careers in the context of the sexual institutions of the gay metropolis. Like their heterosexual counterparts, gay sexual careers are a product of individual decisions, but these decisions are embedded in the context of the queer meaning-constitutive tradition and associated sexual institutions. To wit, gay sexual careers are guided as much, if not more, by the strong arm of institutional impingement as by individual preferences for monogamy, sexual opportunity, or ideologies of sexual liberation (Green, 2006).

Having established the historical basis of the queer meaning-constitutive tradition and its relationship to "becoming gay," I turn below to a consideration of new possibilities for intimate life afforded by same-sex marriage. I argue that even as civil marriage permits gay men in some areas of the world to enter marital relations, the history of exclusion from the institution and the queer meaning-constitutive tradition that resulted are likely to continue to bear on queer relationships, married and otherwise.

Same-Sex Marriage: A Queer Union

Because same-sex civil marriage is only a very recent phenomenon in North America, today's contingent of lesbian and gay married spouses came of age in an era when state-sanctioned marriage was not yet possible. As I have argued above, historical exclusion from civil marriage and the marital template has had a profound effect on queer sexual careers—perhaps most on gay men for whom, by dint of masculine socialization or male physiology or a combination thereof, the institutions that regulate sexuality have the most tangible impact.[3] Consequently, when contemporary gay male couples enter into civil marriage, they do so from a historical and structural pathway distinct from that followed by their heterosexual male counterparts. From a sociological perspective, same-sex marriages are likely to be broadly distinguishable from their heterosexual counterparts on characteristics such as the domestic division of labor (Blumstein & Schwartz, 1983; Dunne, 1997) and sexual norms and practices. Part of this difference is likely to emerge out of the fact that same-sex marriages are composed of partners of the same gender, in which case the traditional gendered marital script may no longer apply (though see Carrington, 1999). Nevertheless, the symbolic significance of state-sanctioned marriage on these relationships should not be underestimated as lesbians and gay men enter into conjugal relations and reimagine their relationships and themselves in this new light.

For the present purpose, I will restrict my discussion to male same-sex marriages, though the themes I discuss below—including the symbolic power of civil marriage and a practical queer orientation to marital fidelity—are not uniquely gay male phenomena.

Overwhelmingly, gay married men report feeling an added sense of commitment to their relationship following civil marriage. Often enough, gay spouses are surprised by the emotional impact of the act of getting married, which provides them with a new sense of "emotional security." Thus, on the meaning of getting married, Greg states,

> I think it's only partially intellectual but there's something emotional as well. I think it's a partnership. A partnership of trust. And security, not financial security, (but a) kind of emotional security. . . . Yeah, about cementing the relationship and declaring it to one another. . . . I think it's more of a psychological advantage than a real financial or actual tangible advantage.—*Greg, white, 30s*

As well, marriage has a legitimating function in the eyes of others. Thence the married couple peers into the looking glass (Cooley, 1908) and finds a new sense of significance as a couple.

> They started recognizing, wow, this isn't just a gay relationship—this is a relationship. And the parallels between a heterosexual and a homosexual relationship haven't been thought of in that sort of light and the way it is perceived by some family members and even friends. . . . So the language we're using, doing the (wedding) planning, setting up the stuff we're talking about—it magnified it. It really changed the whole concept of gay rela-

tionships for a lot of these different people. . . . We would have had a strong relationship regardless of being married or not, but what we've learned from the process of being in marriage to each other and how it has affected the people around us, is that the support group has become magnified in terms of their acceptance of us.—*Larry, white, 40s*

Nevertheless, although civil marriage provides gay married couples a powerful sense of societal integration and social significance, it is quite possible that same-sex male marriages and heterosexual marriages will reveal important differences. For instance, one of the clearest distinctions between male same-sex and heterosexual marriages may be marital norms and practices regarding fidelity. While nearly 100% of U.S. heterosexual married partners were found to expect sexual exclusivity from their partners (Laumann et al., 1994), and support for marital monogamy among the American public has actually *increased* to 92% over the last three decades (Cherlin, 2002)[4]—three fifths of the male couples in my study do not believe that marriage need always be monogamous. In fact, marital fidelity is not taken for granted but instead emerges in a reflexive process organized more by the personal needs and wants of the partners than by the heavy hand of heteronormative tradition.

I don't [think] marriage should always be necessarily [monogamous]. . . . I can't see any argument in the abstract against polygamy. . . . I can't see any argument in the abstract against an asexual couple being married. . . . They should be faithful by whatever definition the people involved chose to define fidelity. And for us, monogamy is the route we have taken.—*Ian, white, 50s*

As well, even currently monogamous marriages are not regarded as set in stone. Once again, the sexual needs of the couple are to be negotiated over time:

INTERVIEWER: Do you think your marriage will always be this way [monogamous]?
ALEX: We don't know that, and we understand that at the moment we are very happy with that. I don't think either of us thinks about going the other way. We have everything we want at the moment. In other words, it's not like "forever and ever," just let's do it and it works, so let's keep doing it.—*Alex, white, 50s*

And, in a fascinating twist, for some of these couples, state-sanctioned marriage created the very conditions under which nonmonogamy was *first* imaginable. That is, the increased sense of commitment and emotional security rendered by civil marriage allows some gay partners to open up their relationships to sexual exploration, thus drawing from and reintegrating the queer meaning-constitutive tradition into this most conservative institution:

> The fact that we are legally married to each other is a completely different ballgame for opening up the relationship. I would not have felt comfortable to do it, not being legally married. So, it sounds kind of backwards to the traditional model, but the fact that we're legally married to each other and permanently committed makes us both feel very secure about doing this.—*Karl, white, 40s*

Although my exploratory study was not designed to extrapolate more broadly to other male same-sex married couples, the findings above are not surprising. Coming of age in an era prior to legal access to same-sex marriage, the current generation of male same-sex spouses "unlearned" (Herdt, 1992, p. 30) and reworked (Adam, 2006) the dominant meaning-constitutive romantic tradition (Green, 2010). Socialized in the alternative, queer meaning-constitutive tradition, these men exercise what Woolwine and McCarthy (2005, p. 400) might call a queer "moral pragmatism," whereby no single moral code around sexual fidelity prevails (Green, 2010). Rather, these men adopt a kind of "morally pragmatic stand" (Woolwine & McCarthy, 2005, p. 400) that decouples sex and love and allows for the possibility of an "ethics of relating" centered on the negotiation of sexual needs and wants (Weeks, Heaphy, & Donovan, 2001, p. 148). This is not to suggest that all or even most male same-sex marriages will be nonmonogamous but, rather, that the structural and historical context from which gay men arrive at civil marriage will predispose them to dyadic alternatives from the traditional, heteronormative meaning-constitutive tradition and its emphasis on monogamy. Indeed, if gay men had to "unlearn" (Herdt, 1992, p. 30) heteronormativity to become gay, they may need to "unlearn" the queer meaning-constitutive tradition if they are to be faithful to the traditional marital norm of fidelity. But preliminary research suggests this is unlikely to be the case for all gay men, some of whom will bring together norms and practices from both meaning-constitutive traditions as they and their partners see fit. Indeed, in more than one sense, same-sex marriage may represent a *queer* union.

Conclusion: The Symbolic Impact of Civil Marriage on Gay Men

In this chapter, I have developed an analysis of the impact of marriage on working- and middle-class gay men in North America. Systematically excluded from the institution, gay men developed alternative lifestyles in a process of cultural intensification that diverged from the dominant, hetero-normative meaning-constitutive tradition from which they were legally and culturally disenfranchised. In its place, over time, a queer meaning-consti-tutive tradition materialized and was institutionalized in large urban centers across the country. Here, a robust, sex-positive norm anchored to sexual exploration, sexual freedom, and long-term bachelorhood replaced the for-merly hegemonic marital template to constitute new lifestyle forms. To the extent that the institution of marriage pulls most heterosexual men out of bachelorhood and into marriage by the early thirties, the sexual norms and institutions of large urban gay centers have the opposite gravitational effect, pulling gay men into sexual sociality and into a reevaluation of monog-amy and marriage. Hence, as much or more a consequence of institutional processes related to cultural intensification than of individual desires, this meaning-constitutive tradition has shaped the sexual life histories of genera-tions of urban gay men.

Recent developments in law now permit same-sex couples to marry in a few states in the United States, in the District of Columbia, and through-out Canada. This legal transformation represents at once a symbolic and a structural transformation as gay men move from being "unmarriageable" to "marriageable" citizens. Nevertheless, the effects of the queer meaning-constitutive tradition are unlikely to disappear, at least for the current gen-eration of married men. That is, in at least some cases, gay men are likely to create civil marriages by drawing from both the dominant heteronorma-tive and the queer-meaning constitutive traditions. This is evident in my own study of same-sex marriages wherein sexual fidelity was not taken for granted but, rather, appropriated or rejected in a process of pragmatic nego-tiation whereby the needs and wants of each marital partner are considered. Interestingly enough, for a few male couples, civil marriage supplied the very conditions upon which monogamy was abandoned.

Unlike heterosexual men, gay men arrive at the institution of marriage in the context of discordant meaning-constitutive traditions. But this is a structural, historical pathway that may change over time. That is, some gay men will come of age in an era that permits same-sex civil marriage, and it is unclear if the queer meaning-constitutive tradition will continue to have salience for them. In fact, one might well imagine an era in the not-so-distant future when young gay men no longer construe their sexual desires as being incongruous with the marital template. In this regard, one can expect the relationships of future generations of same-sex married men to overlap ever more closely with the relationships of their married heterosexual counterparts.

Future work on same-sex marriage among gay men would benefit from a closer examination of how race and class intersect with marital patterns. In my research, for instance, I found little difference between white and black middle-class and working-class men with regard to their experiences of exclusion from civil marriage and its attendant effects. Preliminary data from an ongoing study of same-sex marriage in Ontario, Canada, however, suggest that the vast majority of same-sex marriages are occurring among white men and women with working- and middle-class backgrounds. It may very well be that the marital traditions of gays' and lesbians' heterosexual communities are upheld and reproduced in their own lives. If this is so, how and why queer generations reproduce traditional marital patterns will require future investigation.

NOTES

1. "Heteronormativity" refers to the dominant set of mutually reinforcing norms, practices, and institutions that include heterosexuality, marriage, monogamy, and the nuclear family. For the original use of the term, see Warner (1991).

2. All participant names are pseudonyms.

3. Males and females cannot be considered identical units of analysis on the issues of concern in this chapter. That is, whether one takes a biological, psychological, or sociological perspective on sex and gender, the implication of difference is the same. Although it is impossible here to weigh in on the significance of these various potential factors for male and female sexuality, the point is that we should not expect institutions of marriage (or their absence) to have a comparable effect on gay men and lesbians. Rather, when it comes to questions regarding sexual orientation, the appropriate comparison groups are between heterosexuals and homosexuals of the same gender.

4. Unfortunately, no comparable Canadian data exist, with the exception of a World Values Survey conducted in 1990. In this survey, nearly three fourths of Canadian respondents reported that a marital affair was either never justifiable or rarely justifiable.

PART IV

Turning Points
throughout the Life Course

8

U.S. Colonialism, Migration, and Sexualities

The Filipino American Case

YEN LE ESPIRITU

Life course research on migration and sexuality treats migration as a key turning point in migrants' sexual lives. In her 1999 groundbreaking study, Espin observes that migrant women, free from the prescribed choices of their premigration life, reinvent their gendered and sexual selves in the new country. Subsequent research on sexuality and love in Mexican and Asian transnational families likewise indicates that migration, as an event that disrupts and determines one's life course, provides opportunities for negotiating and reconstructing ideals of marriage and sexual ideologies and practices (Espiritu, 2008; González-López, 2005; Hirsch, 2003; Manalansan, 2003). Together, these studies confirm that, far from being culturally determined, sexuality is fluid and complex and that sexuality transitions are intimately attuned to changes in the social organization of life related to migration.

Informed by the acculturation and assimilation paradigms, which prescribe cultural and economic adaptation and incorporation, immigration studies scholars often misidentify immigrant sexuality as a unidimensional entity that is transformed along a continuum—from the putatively traditional and conservative sexuality of the original country to the purportedly more modern and liberal sexual culture of the United States (Marin, Gomez, & Hearst, 1993). Challenging this unilinear sexual acculturation model, and the tradition/modern binary that extols the United States as the center of sexual freedom (at least in the Western hemisphere), scholars have concluded that immigrants' sexuality transformations involve social processes that have little to do with "sexual assimilation" and "becoming American." As Hondagneu-Sotelo (1994) and González-López (2005) contend, due to socioeconomic and racial segregation, Mexican immigrants reproduce, negotiate, and reinvent their sexual behavior within and by their own immigrant communities, not by the dominant culture. Similarly, Manalansan (2003) and Cantu (2009) argue that gay immigrant men do not move progressively and passively from tradition to sexual modernity, but rather they chart and rearticulate hybrid and complex paths toward sexual transformations that trouble seemingly stable borders.

When scholars pinpoint migration as the generator of sexual changes, they are presuming that the migrants' origin and destination countries are unconnected and that migrants encounter the latter's sexual beliefs only after migration. Focusing on Filipino immigrants, this chapter argues that, owing to the Philippines' (neo)colonial relationship with the United States, Filipinos occupy a comparatively unique position among immigrants because they encounter U.S. mores while *still in* the Philippines. As a result of a century of exposure to U.S. cultural practices and consumption patterns, Filipinos "[have] been prepared by the thoroughly Americanized culture of the homeland" (San Juan, 1991, p. 118). Thus, Filipino immigrants arrive in the United States "not to begin a process of Americanization but rather to continue and transform the ongoing engagement with America" (Manalansan, 2003, p. 13). A critical approach to Filipino migrants' sexuality decouples it from the process of migration and situates it within the larger history of U.S. (neo)colonialism.

Drawing on life stories of Filipinos in San Diego, I examine the ways in which Filipino sexualities are constituted by and constitutive of gendered, sexualized, and racialized discourses and practices that circulate between the Philippines and the United States. The first section focuses on first-generation immigrants, many of whom came to the United States when they were in their twenties, to examine the contradictory effects of U.S. (neo)colonialism on Filipino sexualities. The second section focuses on sexuality-related negotiations between immigrant parents and their children, contending that these domestic tensions must be understood within a historical and transnational framework.

It is not coincidental that Filipinos make up the largest Asian American group in San Diego. Until 1998, San Diego was the site of the largest U.S. naval base and the Navy's primary West Coast training facility, the Naval Training Center (NTC). The majority of Filipino Navy men received their basic training at the NTC. Filipino Navy families thus formed the cornerstone of San Diego's Filipino American community and provided the impetus for and sponsorship of subsequent chain migration (Espiritu, 2003). In the decades following the 1965 Immigration Act, new immigration helped to triple the county's Filipino American population from 1970 to 1980 and to double it from 1980 to 1990.[1] By 2004, more than 135,000 people, or about one in 20, in San Diego County were Filipino (Gaona, 2005). Filipino Americans in the county enjoy a median family income of $80,772, close to 70% own their own home, and only about 4% live in poverty.[2]

The data for this chapter come from two sets of in-depth interviews conducted between 1992 and 2002 with Filipinos living in San Diego County. The first was a set of interviews that I conducted with more than 100 Filipinos in San Diego from 1992 to 2000. The second was from a later study conducted with Diane Wolf between 2000 and 2002. With the assistance of a Filipina research assistant, we interviewed 20 Filipina women, 20 Filipino men, and 20 immigrant parents. Participants in both projects were chosen not randomly but through a network of Filipino American contacts whom the first group of respondents trusted (i.e., "snowball" referrals). Interview questions were open-ended and covered family and immigration history, ethnic identity and practices, family relations, and community development. Reflecting the average socioeconomic status of the county's Filipino American population, the majority of the respondents came from middle-class, college-educated, home-owning families. All of the immigrant parents self-identified as heterosexual; only a handful of the second generation identified as gay or lesbian.

U.S. Colonialism, Transnationalism, and Sexuality: The First Generation

The relationship between the Philippines and the United States originates in conquest, occupation, and exploitation. The U.S. imperialist drive into the Philippines at the turn of the twentieth century unleashed a consistent, disruptive, and well-articulated ideology depicting foreign rule over the Philippines as a blessing—a means to a higher form of civilization for a country and people deemed "incapable of self-rule." Sexuality, as a salient marker of otherness, has figured prominently in racist and colonialist ideologies (Stoler, 1995). The racialization of Filipinos as being biologically unfit for independence drew on stereotypes of Filipino men as sexually deviant (Hoganson, 1998). Images of sexual deviancy traveled with Filipinos to the United States and prescribed their racialization there. During the pre–World War II period, Filipino and other Asian immigrants met with widespread hostility upon their arrival in the United States. Conspicuous in that era's anti-Filipino tirades is a fear of Filipino male sexuality as excessive and animalistic in contrast to the supposedly restrained or "civilized" sexuality of white colonial men. In the classic *America Is in the Heart*, Carlos Bulosan (1946, p. 121) bitterly recounts the brutalities that Filipino migrant men experienced during the 1930s: "I came to know . . . that in many ways it was a crime to be a Filipino in America. I came to know that the public streets were not free to my people: we were stopped each time these vigilant patrolmen saw us driving a car. We were suspect each time we were seen with a white woman."

Attempts to manage sexuality through morality are bound to colonial rule: "The very identity and authority of the colonial project rested upon the racialization and sexualization of morality" (Alexander, 1991, p. 133). At stake in these stereotypes is the construction of colonized women as lacking sexual restraint and traditional morality. Filipinas—both in the Philippines and the United States—have been marked as desirable but dangerous "prostitutes" and/or submissive "mail-order brides" (Halualani,1995; Egan, 1996). These stereotypes emerged out of the colonial process, especially the extensive U.S. military presence in the Philippines. Until the 1990s, the Philippines housed some of the largest U.S. overseas airforce and naval bases. Many Filipino nationalists have charged that the "prostitution problem" in the Philippines stemmed from U.S. and Philippine government policies that promoted a sex industry—brothels, bars, and massage parlors—for U.S. servicemen stationed or on leave in the Philippines. During the Vietnam War, the Philippines was the "rest and recreation" center of Asia, housing approximately 10,000 U.S. servicemen daily. In this context, *all* Filipinas were racialized as sexual commodities, usable and expendable. Married to a Philippine-born Navy man, U.S.-born Connie Tirona[3] recounted the sexual harassment she faced in the late 1960s while visiting Subic Bay Naval Station in Olongapo City:

> One day, I went to the base dispensary. . . . I was dressed nicely, and as I walked by the fire station, I heard catcalls and snide remarks being made by some of the firemen. . . . I was fuming inside. The next thing I heard was, "How much do you charge?" I kept on walking. "Hey, are you deaf or something? How much do you charge? You have a good body." That was an incident that I will never forget.

As this incident indicates, the sexualized racialization of Filipinas always forms a backdrop to relations between Filipinas and Americans.

The century-old (neo)colonial association between the Philippines and the United States activated a transnational flow not only of information, capital, goods, and technology but also of people. Filipinos encountered the

United States not only through Americans who lived in the Philippines but also through Filipinos who visited, resided, or worked in the United States— people ranging from students to teachers, independent travelers to sponsored workers, and vacationers to permanent immigrants. My interviews indicate that the *transnational* terrain of the Philippines (re)shapes the knowledge, consciousness, and identities of local Filipinos, transforming sexual beliefs, practices, and standards of appeal.

Military Towns and Changing Sexual Rules and Practices

Military towns constitute one transnational space in which sexual rules and practices were often in flux. In these towns, where exposure to Americans was extensive, large numbers of Filipinas married U.S. servicemen every year. Many "respectable" Filipinas, who lived sheltered lives otherwise, met their American husbands through school-organized functions to welcome American servicemen to the Philippines. Luz Latus met her white American husband in the late 1950s when her nursing school was asked "to show them [recently docked sailors] around and tell them about the country." The honor of hosting American sailors outweighed the school's conservative policies of confining young female students to their dormitory and forbidding visitors. Luz vividly recalled the night they met:

> All the nursing schools were invited to participate, and the nursing students were asked to be the sailors' hostesses. All of us were very excited, because we seldom were allowed to leave our dormitory. We were picked up by these big buses and driven to Manila Hotel. . . . All these well-dressed and clean-shaven Navy sailors were there. There was entertainment—folk dances and all kinds of floor shows put on by the USO. That was where I first met [my husband].

Many other women met their American husbands while working on a base or at the local restaurants and entertainment establishments. For Cynthia Tosoc, who had a son "out of wedlock," working as a waitress near a base gave her an opportunity to start over—to marry a younger American serviceman and relocate to the United States in the early 1970s. Cognizant of the pervasive hypersexualization of the Filipinas who lived and worked in military towns, many women I interviewed were quick to claim that they were not "that kind of girl" and that they met their American husbands through "legitimate" means. In particular, women who grew up near the military bases often declared (unasked) that they did not frequent "that part of town." As Mona Ampon, who migrated to the United States in the mid-1960s, said, "Growing up [in the Philippines], . . . my dad wouldn't let us date an American [because] people will think that the only way you met was because of the base. I have never seen the inside of any of the bases because we were just forbidden to be there."

Filipino enlistees in the U.S. Navy constitute another group of desirable potential husbands. In the United States, many of these men were relegated to servile positions as Navy stewards, passed over for promotions, and racially harassed as brown men in a country that favors whites (Espiritu, 2003). However, in the Philippine context, U.S. Navy enlistees enjoy a high and enviable status, connoting U.S. citizenship and residence, a higher income, and access to desirable consumer goods. Thus many of these men can, in returning "home," reconstruct themselves as able economic providers and desirable sexual partners. Growing up in the Philippines, Vicente Rodriquez's poor circumstances hampered his ability to date women:

> I never had a chance to date in the Philippines. . . . Up to the age where I was in high school, I was . . . collecting leftover [sic], feed the pigs, I'd go to school. So kids are mean, you know, they called me names. They teased me. . . . Plus, I didn't have the chance to date because, you know, I'm helping run the stores and I'm going to school. In fact, I had to go to school at night to help in the morning. I didn't date, just a lot of looks and crushes. But I couldn't afford it, to make the money.

In 1968, 20-year-old Vicente joined the U.S. Navy because he was deeply impressed by the apparent success of those who had enlisted: "A Filipino sailor got it all! He got all the girls. . . . He got all the money. He got everything!" Although Vicente bitterly resented doing "housekeeping type of jobs" and experienced "lots of racism," he felt satisfied because he was earning good money—money to provide for his widowed mother and younger sister, to gain the respect and envy of his town mates, and to attract the "prettiest girls in town." Vicente was thrilled by the attention he received from young women in his town during his stays in the Philippines: "When I relocated to Subic, I had me a 1973 Pontiac Firebird. And I'm the only one who has a Pontiac Firebird in the whole Philippines! And I drive it in Angeles City, and everybody looks at it. And then, those pretty girls are all over me, see?" In 1976, Vicente married one of these "pretty girls" and brought her back to the United States. The discrepancy in Vicente's life—between his servile position in the United States and his exalted status in the Philippines—and its bearing on his sexuality shows how migrant lives are influenced by their ever-changing historical context.

The sailors' relatively higher social status, resulting from income and resource differentials between the Philippines and the United States, emboldened many returning Navy men to challenge local sexual norms by expecting "quick romances" and "Western-style dating" with local Filipinas. When Jose Abat, who joined the Navy in the 1950s, returned to the Philippines for a visit in the early 1960s, he asked his best friend to "hook [him] up" with the local women. His friend took him to an insurance office where there were "plenty of girls." According to Jose's wife:

> When we first met, he was aggressive. He was fresh. He just went to my desk and says "hi". . . . Who's this guy? As I told him, you need to be introduced formally. That's the way in the Philippines. That's how we met. He keeps coming back every year for vacation. Eventually it was a quick romance. Then we got married.

Another U.S. Navy enlistee, Nestor Balayan, who was stationed in the Philippines in the late 1960s, broke up with a Filipina girlfriend because she was too bound to traditional sexual mores, which he felt clashed with the "westernized" ways he acquired through his five-year stay in the United States:

> In the Philippines . . . back in the old days, when I had a girlfriend, I . . . I just couldn't kiss her you know, . . . or I am sure she wouldn't kiss me. I have to steal a kiss to kiss her, you know. And one time I was asking her for a date, like we can't go out. She wants to have someone to go with her, but I am already westernized. I've already been here for years and I go back. And that's what she wanted to happen and I didn't like it so I didn't get married with her.

Especially before the influx of post-1965 immigration, the shortage of Filipinas in the United States prompted many Filipino Navy men to return to their hometowns to marry. Because many Filipino enlistees returned to the Philippines with the express purpose of finding a wife, the courtship period was often truncated to accommodate the groom's short stay in the Philippines. When Lucy Gonzalez was dating her Navy husband who was stationed in the Philippines in the early 1950s, "he kept making hints that, you know, before I leave I'm going to have to be married. You know I'm back here to find a wife, and all this stuff." His relentless pressure succeeded: the couple shortened both their dating and engagement periods and married five months after their first date. Lucy recalled with glee her mother's relaxation of the family chaperon rule: "She let me go on dates with a chaperon at first, then without. Oh it was a big thing, because I went without a chaperon." In some instances, couples even eloped, breaking with tradition and defying their families' expectations. Connie Rodriquez reminisced about her rushed wedding, which was linked in part to her Navy husband's brief stay in the Philippines in the late 1950s:

> And then one day, my husband . . . he went to my house. I remember he went to my house and he asked me, "Either come with me to elope or you won't see me anymore.". . . . And I just went. . . . We eloped and he brought me back to his parents in Pampanga. And we got married.

Due to restrictive immigration policies and convoluted petition procedures, many of these marriages turned into transnational families, as wives (and children) waited, sometimes for as long as a decade, to reunite with their husbands (and fathers) in the United States. These long-distance relationships clearly affected the couples' sex lives. Ruth Balandra related that during the 12 years that her parents were separated during the late 1950s and early 1960s, "every time [my father] went home [to the Philippines], he got my mom pregnant. The first year was my sister. And then [in] '62 I was born and then my brother a year later."

Women Migrants and Newfound Sexual Independence

My analysis of Filipino Navy men's narratives suggests that their motivations for joining the U.S. Navy were gendered: to better represent themselves as able economic providers and desirable sexual partners. Women who migrate seem to have other desires and ambitions, which are equally gendered: to see the world and to experience untried ways of living. In my interviews, many of the women who migrated on their own did so to unshackle themselves from gender norms and family discipline. These single women were primarily health care professionals who entered the United States through the U.S. Exchange Visitor Program (EVP)[4] and the new occupational preference categories of the 1965 Immigration Act. In 1979, armed with a B.S. in nursing, Cecilia Bonus left for the United States through the EVP because "my family was just so protective. I just kind of wanted to get away and be independent." Being away from home enabled many young women to free themselves temporarily from strict parental control on their activities and movements. In the United States, they traveled freely, socialized widely, and lived on their own.

Perhaps most important, they reveled in their newfound freedom to date and to explore their sexuality. Given their relatively small numbers in the United States, single Filipinas were highly prized as sexual and marital partners by Filipino immigrant men—another example of the connection between individuals' sexual choices and the historical context in which they lived and loved. Maria Rafael, who came to San Diego in 1965 as a high school exchange student, related how she and her friend had to fend off unwanted sexual attention from the young Filipino sailors:

> Every time there was a Filipino function, Strela and I would go and the Navy people would be there. They always managed to get our names and phone numbers. It was just a big thing for them to see Filipinas. Everyone wanted to meet us. We tried to be nice; gave them our names and the phone never stopped ringing. . . .

Carmen Reynila described how she and her fellow nurses enjoyed the company of the Filipino sailors in the early 1970s: "There used to be lots of Filipino gatherings around. So you got to meet each other, and then the sailors, you know, they would come to our apartments, and then, you know, we would go out with them."

Many women also seized their newfound freedom to make more independent choices about marriage, with some choosing to marry on their own in the United States, partly to mute possible objections from their parents. Rosie Roxas, who met her Filipino Navy husband while studying in San Diego in the early 1970s, explained why she did not return to the Philippines to marry: "My parents would not have approved of him. . . . They wanted me to marry a professional. . . . He would not have passed." Paz Jensen, who met her white American husband in Hawaii in 1967 while working as a Peace Corps volunteer trainer, also married without her family's knowledge because she did not want her husband to be subject to her mother's harsh scrutiny:

> If he had to go through the kind of scrutiny that my mother would put every suitor of my sister and myself . . . he would not have passed. . . . They would not have approved of him. So we just got married here in San Diego. And then just send the announcements, and say, "Hey guys, I'm married."

The United States also provided a fresh start for women who had "messed up." When Carmen Santos was 20, she had a child with her boyfriend but she had not married him. Her family insisted that she migrate to the United States in order to "start over" and offered to care for her daughter while she was away. After 2 years of working as an exchange nurse in California, Carmen met and married an American man in 1975, which enabled her legally to send for her young daughter. Some Filipino critics have disparaged the more sexually permissive lifestyles of Filipina women abroad, charging that some Filipina migrants have become morally corrupt and licentious (Choy, 2003). These charges must be viewed as retaliatory moves to reassert patriarchal control over these women's bodies and newfound sexual independence.

In all, these narratives highlight the ways that Filipino sexual choices are shaped by the pervasive presence of the United States in the Philippines and the resultant transnational character of Philippine culture and life. Through the influence of American media and through actual transnational social ties among Filipino nationals, Americans in the Philippines, and Filipinos in the United States, the majority of Filipinos live transnational lives whether or not they ever leave the Philippines. On the one hand, these transnational connections led to the hypersexualization of Filipina women and even of men. On the other hand, by according young Filipinos more economic independence and mobility and infusing their imagination with other ways of living and loving, these connections have (re)defined interpretations of premarital sex, virginity, nonmarital pregnancy, and sexual desirability. Although double standards of morality and generational hierarchy remain, my interviews indicate that these social disruptions have enabled at least some women and men to defy or evade social and family rules governing their sexuality and notions of marriageability.

Morality, Sexual Virtuousness, and Compromises: The Second Generation

When recalling their lives in the Philippines, first-generation immigrants reported that they sometimes adopted and at other times rejected the sexual scripts imposed on them by their families and the larger society. In particular, the purported rigid sexual strictures, however powerful and idealized, did not or could not stop Filipinas from dating without chaperons, getting pregnant out of wedlock, or marrying without their parents' permission. Yet, when asked to describe the sexual mores of the Philippines, the majority of interviewees collapsed the multiple sexualities that existed there into a rigid set of sexual prescriptions that elevated Filipina sexual virtuousness. In 1945, 33-year-old Ruth Abad migrated to the United States, intending to "go to school or to travel [and] maybe even join the U.S. Navy." A self-described independent woman, Ruth was not interested in marriage because she did not "want to be stuck at home with the babies." When she did marry in 1946, to a Filipino Navy man whom she met in San Diego through a blind date, Ruth "just wrote to [her] family about it" and did not return to the Philippines until 1964, when her mother died. Her story suggests a life of independent decision making regarding her career and marriage choices, with the full support of her Papa who "trained us to take care of ourselves." Yet, years later, in an effort to discipline her teenage daughter, Ruth would reconstruct a Philippines that was much more conservative than the one she experienced as a young woman:

> In the Philippines, . . . [w]hen we go to dances, we have our uncle, our grandfather, and auntie all behind us to make sure that we behave in the dance hall. Nobody goes necking outside. You don't even let a man put his hand on your shoulders. When you were brought up in a conservative country, it is hard to come here and see that it is all freedom of speech and freedom of action. Sex was never mentioned in our generation. I was 30 already when I learned about sex. But to the younger generation in America, sex is nothing!

The seeming discrepancy in Ruth's narrative suggests that immigrants' retellings of the sexual mores of the "old country" need to be recognized for what they are: narratives that individuals construct and modify over time to suit their intended audiences and changing life circumstances. Other scholars have noted the same phenomenon among other immigrant groups. As Foner (2009) reports, in part as an attempt to keep the traditional culture alive, immigrant parents often hold up an idealized version of traditional values and practices as a model for their children, even when they themselves were not subject to these strictures or when these traditions have changed considerably since they left their home country.

Instead of positioning immigrants' shifting cultural claims in histories, economics, and politics, most scholars have assumed that these claims perfectly correspond to a bounded and static set of practices imported from the home country into the host society. Accordingly, the literature on second-generation sexuality emphasizes and naturalizes the perceived tensions between immigrant parents and their children over (im)proper sexual behaviors. Although details vary, studies of young immigrant women across groups, space, and time—second-generation Chinese women in San Francisco in the 1920s (Yung, 1995), U.S.-born Italian women in East Harlem in the 1930s (Orsi, 1985), young Mexican women in the Southwest during the interwar years (Ruiz, 1992), and daughters of Caribbean and Asian Indian immigrants on the East Coast in the 1990s (Waters, 1996; Dasgupta & Das-Gupta, 1996)—have all identified strict parental control on their activities and movements as the primary source of intergenerational strains. Informed by the tradition-to-modernity paradigm, the literature on the second generation conceptualizes intergenerational strain over sexuality as a product of "cultural clash" between "traditional" immigrant parents and their "modernized" U.S.-born or -raised children, rather than as a social, historical, and transnational affair that exposes multiple and interrelated forms of power relations.

At first glance, my interviews appear to confirm the tradition-to-modernity "cultural clash" account. Filipino immigrant parents seldom allowed their daughters to date, to stay out late, to spend the night at a friend's house, or to take an out-of-town trip. For their part, many of the second-generation women I spoke to railed against their parents' perceived constant surveillance, which they named as a source of frustration and even intense anger toward their parents. Gender greatly affected tensions and conflicts between the generations, as daughters denounced what they saw as gender inequity in their families—the fact that their parents placed far more restrictions on their activities than on their brothers' activities. U.S.-born Maricela Rebaya decried this double standard: "My parents are very strict. . . . I don't go out at all normally. They put a guilt trip on you. It's more like the guys can do anything. Boy, oh boy, they can brag about girls and my parents won't say anything. But wait till we start talking." This is not to say that immigrant parents do not have unreasonable expectations of their sons, but rather that these expectations seldom pivot around the son's sexuality or dating choices. Parental control over the movement and action of daughters begins the moment they are perceived as young adults and sexually vulnerable, and it regularly consists of monitoring their whereabouts and forbidding dating (Espiritu, 2003).

In place of the "cultural clash" paradigm, which defines culture as innate and abstracted from unresolved histories of inequalities, we need to situate parental control over daughters within the larger history of U.S. racialization of Filipinos. Elsewhere, I have shown that gender is a key to immigrant identity and a vehicle for racialized immigrants to assert cultural superiority over the dominant group. In light of the pervasive hypersexualization of Filipina women that emerged from the colonial process, the construction of the "ideal" Filipina—as family-oriented and sexually chaste—can be read as a strategic effort to reclaim the morality of the community, rather than as a depoliticized and static set of Filipino practices brought intact from the "old country" (Espiritu, 2003, p. 215). As the designated "keepers of culture," immigrant women, particularly young daughters, are expected to comply with male-defined criteria for what constitutes "ideal" feminine virtues. While the sexual behavior of adult women is confined to a monogamous, heterosexual context, that of young women is often denied completely. The immigrants' gendered discourse of moral superiority often leads to patriarchal calls for cultural "authenticity," which locate family honor and national integrity in the community's female members and render them emblematic of its cultural survival (Espiritu, 2003). At the same time, it is important to note that this "patriarchal culture" is not indigenous to Filipino immigrant communities but rather is a constantly negotiated strategy deployed to claim through gender the power denied them by racism.

Although intergenerational conflicts over sexual choices are socially recognized occurrences in Filipino communities, there is a wide gap between what parents say they want of their children and their ability to control them. My interviews suggest that parents' ability to monitor second-generation daughters is spotty at best. Faced with parental restrictions, young Filipinas struggle to gain some control over their social lives, particularly dating. Repeatedly, young women report that they simply misinform their parents of their whereabouts or date without their parents' knowledge. Mona Ampon, a 22-year-old U.S.-born Filipina, listed the strategies she used as a teenager to escape her parents' surveillance:

> [In high school], I was very policed by my parents, like I couldn't have a boyfriend. They kept saying, "You can't date. You can't have a boyfriend until you finish college." . . . So I would have to resort to, you know, doing it behind my parents' back. Like, I would sneak out when my parents are away out of town. . . . Like, I would say I am going over to a friend's house to spend the night and then I would go out on a date . . . or I would tell my mom that I was going out with a bunch of girls . . . and then just like after school, just hanging out with my boyfriend until when my parents were supposed to be home and then I would take off for my house. I was bad!

Young women's ability to evade their parents' surveillance says less about their deceitfulness or the parents' gullibility and more about the shifts in generational power caused by the migration process. Many parents I interviewed, like Ofelia Velasco, who migrated to the United States 25 years ago as a nurse, complained about the loss of parental authority in the United States: "It's hard to raise kids when you're here. . . . You can't hit your kid but in the Philippines, you can do whatever you want to do with your kid to discipline. . . . You can't hit them because if you hit them, they will call the police." It is not that calling the police on parents is a rampant activity among young Filipinos; indeed, no one I interviewed resorted to this method. Rather, the phrase "they will call the police" symbolizes a widespread sentiment among immigrant parents that the migration process has recalibrated the balance of power between them and their children, making it difficult if not impossible to control the children's movements and choices. In particular, parents' unfamiliarity with school culture in the United States—with its dances, extracurricular activities, and after-school tutoring sessions—makes it difficult for them to discern between legitimate and illegitimate school activities and thus to monitor their children's whereabouts.

Parents' demanding work schedules also affect their ability to supervise their children. In particular, Navy life, with its mandated absences, fundamentally transforms the balance of power in Filipino American families. Prolonged separation often exacts a toll on the father-child relationship, widening generational distance and decreasing the father's authority to discipline his children. When the father returns home after a long absence, the reintegration process requires adjustments from all family members. Eleanor Ocampo, a 21-year-old U.S.-born Filipina, confided that the only time she was able to date was when her strict father was away from home. When her father returned: "He just said, 'It's over. It's gonna stop.'" Although Eleanor abided by her father's rules, she resented what she characterized as his "intrusion" into her life. Sadly, many Navy fathers remain unable to integrate back into the family. According to Amanda Flores, who grew up as a "latchkey kid," her father remained a marginal member of the family:

> Even after my dad retired, he was still unable to fit into the family easily, because we were already grown and it was hard for us to see him as a father figure who could place restrictions on us and tell us what to do. . . . So he kinda kept his distance. So my mom would place the restrictions on us and enforce them. . . . My dad didn't have a say because I think he just felt so detached.

Although much of the literature on immigrant families emphasizes intergenerational conflicts, relations between immigrant parents and their children are more nuanced and complex, "filled with inconsistencies and contradictions and shift in different contexts over time" (Foner, 2009, p. 8). Mothers, as the designated reproducers of culture, play a key role in "controlling" their children. Where some immigrant mothers replicate their own parents' strictness, others allow their children "to do whatever they wanted"—to enjoy the social and sexual freedom that the mothers themselves never had. Connie Rodriquez, who came to the United States as a nurse in the 1980s, often cited her restrictive upbringing in trying to convince her husband to be more lenient toward their children:

> I'm not very, very strict with my kids as long as I know who they are dating. . . . Sometimes, even if their dad don't want, I will help them by talking to my husband. . . . I tell my husband, "I did not enjoy that when I was a kid. I want them to enjoy it." Like if my husband won't let them go to a party, like, sometimes, I am talking to him, while we are about to sleep. I said, "Don't do that to them, things like that."

This example reminds us that the household is seldom a unified social group.

Even as members of the second generation rebel against their parents' restrictions, most continue to recognize the importance of family and feel deep loyalty and gratitude to their parents. Debra Ragaza intimated that even when she was going through "a rebellious stage," she never wanted her parents to find out that she was dating "behind their back." "I'd do anything to cover up," she recalled. "Any notes that I got I would hide them in a box under my bed, you know, any kind of evidence, just get rid of it so that I would have my parents believing that I was paying attention to them and not disobeying them." Although young Filipinas like Debra conceal their transgressions from parents partly in order to keep the peace, the desire to have "my parents believing that I was paying attention to them" also bespeaks something other than respect for one's elders. I argue that this desire to "pay attention" to their parents must be understood within the larger context of U.S. anti-immigrant racism. Over and over again, those I interviewed recounted the many indignities that their parents have had to face as immigrants in the United States. U.S.-born Luella Barcenas remembered how other Navy men used to heckle her father:

> Part of my father's story is that he worked as a Navy steward and it was a very, very prejudiced time [the 1950s and 1960s]. . . . I can still remember, when

I was a little kid, standing on the pier with my mother waving good-bye to him. . . and seeing that the white sailors, you know, were making fun of him, criticizing him and looking down at us and heckling and that kind of stuff.

Similarly, U.S.-born Jovy Flores recalled how upset she felt as she watched how others mistreated her immigrant mother, who was working at the time as a cashier at a commissary: "[Y]ou have to have a military ID card to shop [at the commissary]. This man, my mom asked him to please show her the card, he put it straight in front of her face and said, 'Can't you read English?' . . . It's very insulting, but my mom had to take it."

These stories suggest that children often witness and brave acts of racism alongside their parents. Relations between immigrant parents and their children are thus not only about conflicts, but also about joint (or linked) lives (Moen, 1996). Although generation, culture, and language often divide immigrant parents and their children, their shared histories bind them. These shared histories cajole the second generation to be respectful of and grateful for their parents, even as they resent and reject what they perceive to be unwanted parental intrusion.

Shared histories—and thus shared lives—also lead to compromises between parents and children. Many immigrant parents who do subscribe to idealized notions of Filipino values and traditions have had to modify their ideas and practices, not only because of their inability to monitor their children, but also because of their desire to forge new ways of life "here in America." For racialized immigrants, forging new ways of life in the United States is never simply about acculturation but about intricate negotiations, both with self and with kin, on how to live and love differently in the "new country." Far from the stereotype of the inflexible and tradition-bound immigrant parents, many parents I interviewed were thoughtful and contemplative about parenting, mindful of the crucial role they play in preparing their children for successful lives in the United States. Repeatedly, parents explained their increasingly relaxed attitudes toward their children's curfews, dating, and marriage choices by exclaiming that "it's the way of life here in America." Read within the context of Filipino racial positioning in the United States, this refrain is less about forsaking the old for the new, and more about adapting to the "country of [their] children" to ensure that the second generation wouldn't be "ignorant of the American ways." Discursively constructed to be outside the U.S. nation, Filipino immigrants understand full well that "to survive here, you have to learn their ways and their language"—thus their earnest attempts to adapt in the new context, for the children's sake. Some parents were sorely tested when their daughters turned up pregnant, despite repeated warnings about the dire consequences of sexual freedom. However disappointed, these parents ended up supporting their daughters and welcoming the babies into the family, thereby expanding notions of normative sexuality and the ideal family unit.

Conclusion

Adopting a life course framework, with an eye toward history and inconsistencies, contradictions, and shifting contexts, this chapter has analyzed the changing sexual practices and standards of sexual morality among Filipino migrants over time. My interviews suggest that Filipino immigrant parents have both constructed idealized notions of female chastity and relaxed rigid expectations for their children's behaviors. They also indicate that sexuality is a malleable and contested process in constant flux, (re)shaped by social, cultural, political, and economic forces. Most popular and scholarly writings on immigrant families tend to naturalize and domesticate intergenerational tension over sexuality, attributing it to the "culture clash" between "traditional" immigrant parents and their more "Americanized" children. Challenging the acculturation and assimilation paradigms, I have examined intergenerational conflicts over sexual matters *not* as a private matter between Filipino immigrant parents and their children, but as a social, historical, and transnational affair that exposes, defies, contradicts, and advances multiple and overlapping forces of power relations. I have argued that the perceived inflexible expectation of Filipina chastity is not only about reinforcing masculinist and patriarchal power but also about bolstering national and ethnic self-respect in light of the pervasive sexualization of Filipinas and other Asian women in the United States. At the same time, I have shown how sexual scripts are always documents in progress because both parents and children constantly negotiate, revise, and sometimes rewrite these scripts as they imagine and build new ways of living with and loving each other.

NOTES

1. The 1965 Immigration Act abolished national origins quotas and permitted entry based primarily on family reunification or occupational characteristics.

2. For the total county population, the median family income was $69,099; about 57% owned their own home; and 8% lived in poverty (U.S. Census Bureau, 2006).

3. All participant names are pseudonyms.

4. The Exchange Visitor Program is designed to promote mutual understanding between the United States and other countries through educational and cultural exchanges. At the conclusion of their program, Exchange Visitors are expected to return to their home countries to utilize the experience and skills they have acquired while in the United States.

9

Starting Over

Dating Risks and Sexual Health among Midlife
Women after Relationship Dissolution

BRONWEN LICHTENSTEIN

Women who begin dating after a long-term relationship face uncertainty and risk, if only because the social terrain is different from what they knew in their youth. How should they "do" sex in a youth-oriented culture? How can they avoid the pitfalls of dating inexperience? The transition from coupledom to singlehood can be like emerging from a time warp; there are new rules to learn as well as concerns about physical attractiveness, the safety of self and children, and susceptibility to sexually transmitted infections (STIs), including HIV/AIDS. A bodily focus is likely to be heightened at this turning point because "the most obvious fact of human existence [is that] human beings have, and to some extent are, bodies" (Turner, 1996, p. 60). Rituals of birth, sexual debut, divorce, and death all involve bodily markers and effects. In the case of middle-aged women who are starting over, rituals of courtship involve redefinitions of sexual selves and new rules for courtship display.

This chapter examines women's sexual embodiment and experiences of dating against a backdrop of risk for STIs. Scholarly attention to this topic is timely because STIs and HIV/AIDS have increased among middle-aged and older U.S. adults, especially women over 50 years old (National Institute on Aging, 2007). Many older women who are widowed, divorced, or separated engage in sexual activity, and, like younger women, they need to be educated about risks in an era when both HIV and Viagra have complicated the dating terrain.

Research on Older Women's Sexuality

The scholarly literature on dating generally addresses the experiences of adolescents and young adults. Indeed, my exhaustive searches of library catalogs and scholarly databases identified only four studies that had a primary focus on dating among midlife and older women. One study of courtship among women aged 60 and older found that the "nurse and purse" issue—referring to men seeking women for caretaking or money—deterred romantic dating or relationships leading to marriage (Dickson, Hughes, & Walker, 2005). In another study of people aged 60 and older, women were more likely than men to gain social prestige through dating, although both genders viewed dating as a hedge against loneliness in their senior years (Bulcroft & O'Connor, 1986). Moorman, Booth, and Fingerman (2006) found that age and depression both played a role in starting over, with younger and unhappier widowed women being more likely than others to form new relationships. A fourth study posited that ageism and sexism impeded 40- to 59-year-old women's ability to form new relationships, insofar as older men were often paired with younger women and/or because older women were considered less desirable than men of similar age (Carpenter, Nathanson, & Kim, 2006). Older women in all four studies sought partners for many of the same reasons as younger women: for fun, companionship, intimacy, and, sometimes, marriage.

The literature on aging helps to locate the sexuality of older women in a biopsychosocial context. Researchers increasingly have addressed older women's sexual behavior (DeLamater & Sill, 2005) and relationship satisfaction (DeLamater & Moorman, 2007; Mansfield, Koch, & Voda, 1998; Winterich, 2003), as well as postmenopausal changes such as declining libido (Birnbaum, Cohen, & Wertheimer, 2007), vaginal atrophy (Gelfand, 2000), and hormonal deficits (Leiblum, 1990). However, Rostosky and Travis (2000) have critiqued the tendency to regard older women's sexual functioning as a "condition" rather than as a lived experience. Similarly, Gibson (1996, p. 434) complained that the "veritable deluge of material [about] the problems of old women" is flawed conceptually and ultimately disempowering. Inquiry into the lived sexual experiences of adult women, the physiological effects of aging (e.g., menopause), and the import of social status markers such as marriage and widowhood is lacking. Furthermore, midlife women are often underrepresented in sexuality research (Avis et al., 2003).

Gibson (1996) has attributed the eclipse of women's lived experiences in academic discourse to the twin discriminations of ageism and sexism. Indeed, the lack of attention to dating and HIV risks among midlife and older women appears to be symptomatic of social anxieties over women's sexuality, especially that of mothers, grandmothers, and widows who are framed as both nurturing and asexual. Researchers marginalize women through their silences over women's lived experiences of sexuality; silence certainly has been implicated in the lack of age-specific information about STI/HIV risk among women over 40 years old (National Institute on Aging, 2007). Yet, HIV cases among women age 50 and older have tripled in the last decade (Fowler, 2009).

By contrast, a considerable body of research has addressed the cultural ethos of marriage, the role of marriage in promoting health and well-being, and the "problem" of divorce. In the United States, cultural beliefs in the value of marriage and family life and ambivalence over divorce are remarkably persistent (Thornton & Young-DeMarco, 2001). This promarriage ethos represents an ideology of exclusion, whereby singlehood is viewed widely as a flawed state that can only be resolved by marriage (Byrne & Carr, 2005). For example, in Reynolds and Wetherell's (2005) qualitative study of "women alone" (i.e., women who never married or who were once married), participants spoke about singledom in terms of deficit and exclusion even if they viewed their own status in positive terms. Furthermore, the benefits of marriage for health and longevity are often contrasted to the poorer health and life expectancy of singles (Rook & Zettel, 2005). The privileging of marriage means that "the single status raises questions about why a person has not attained (or is no longer in) the valued state of marriage" (Koropeckyj-Cox, 2005, p. 93). Such a promarriage ethos not only may motivate newly single women to date again but also may affect their perceptions of self and dating behavior in relation to HIV risk.

Both age and gender norms are likely to complicate life for women who reenter the dating scene after long-term relationships have dissolved. Many women find that they must pursue their quest for sexual renewal within the bounds of social acceptability, especially in relation to norms for aging. Moreover, as noted by Calasanti and Slevin (2006, p. 3), "the body has become central to identity and to aging, and the maintenance of its youthful appearance has become a lifelong project that requires increasing levels of work." The notion of body work is especially salient for midlife women who must wrestle with the belief that women's physical capital declines with age and (for older heterosexual women) that men partners are no longer available because they are married, ill, or have not survived into old age. This chapter examines how newly unattached adult women experience sexuality, perceive bodily risks and emotional harms in the context of dating, and manage their bodies in relation to these perceived risks. My analysis centers on the intersections of gender, age, race/ethnicity, and dating as described in women's own narratives of dating in a promarriage southern state.

Method

Recruitment began with four newspaper advertisements for "midlife women reentering the dating scene" to be interviewed about their dating experiences. I intentionally sought participants aged 35 years or older who had been in relationships for 5 years or longer and who had resumed dating. Twenty women participated, with an additional seven volunteers being ineligible because they were too young, had not been in a relationship for at least 5 years, or did not show up to be interviewed. All participants were residents of a midsized college city in the southeastern United States.

Most of the women were employed, divorced, and college-educated. Fifteen were white and five were African American. The mean age was 45 years (ranging from 35 to 66 years) with prior relationships averaging 10.5 years (ranging from 5 to 25 years). Fourteen of the women had been divorced or separated at least once; six women had been divorced between two to four times. Domestic violence, incarceration, drug and alcohol use, and infidelity by the woman or, more often, her partner were common reasons for relationship dissolution. Fourteen women had children; 10 had dependent children (all of the African Americans had minor children). Women with dependents were younger on average (42) than women whose children had left home (52). The women were occupationally diverse, with one third being business owners or career professionals (mostly white) and one fourth being unemployed or on disability (all African American). The remaining respondents were employed in service or clerical work. Sixteen women reported being exclusively heterosexual. One woman self-identified as bisexual and three women who self-identified as heterosexual reported having sexual experiences with both men and women during adulthood. Seven women (five white, two African American) reported having been diagnosed with STIs such as gonorrhea, herpes, crabs, genital warts, and chlamydia during their lifetime, and two additional women reported undiagnosed vaginal infections. High rates of lifetime abuse were reported, with 18 women recounting experiences of childhood abuse, rape, or domestic violence (see Carbone-Lopez, this volume).

The interviews, which lasted from 1 to 1½ hours, were held at my university office and respondents were compensated $50 for their time. I took a brief inventory of demographic information at the beginning of each interview. The semistructured interview topic sheet contained 7 items and 15 subitems about date-seeking, dating locations and experiences, dating histories, perceptions of dating, and scenarios for sexual risk taking, in addition to concerns over finances, children, and personal safety within the dating context. The interview ended with a discussion of plans or dreams for the future. Most women framed their responses in terms of working through experiences and disappointments. Their responses typically went beyond concrete items on the topic sheet to reveal the women's own interpretations of dating risks after relationship dissolution.

I transcribed the interviews and analyzed them using Glaser and Strauss's (1967) constant comparison method. This method compares text-blocks for particular topics (e.g., dating locations) until a set of themes emerges from the data (e.g., the most likely meeting places are bars or grocery stores; the least likely are churches or the Internet). I used topics from the interview guide to organize and code data during the initial analysis (Miles & Huberman, 1994). This process generated five main themes: where and how to date, transitional dating, dating risks and rules, rationales for unprotected sex, and scripts and strategies for safer dating (see table 9.1).

Results

Definitions of Dating

In response to my request for definitions of dating, the women framed dates either as time-bound events (e.g., a single date) or as meaning-classifications for types of partner (e.g., "the convenience date"). Conceptualizations of dating involved a spectrum of partners and activities. Four typologies emerged when I asked participants to define "risky" and "safe" dating. The category women saw as most problematic was the "risky date," encompassing casual partners, one-night stands, and pickups. These dates occurred mainly on weekends and in the absence of a regular partner. Risky dates were also defined as such because of the location (e.g., bars or nightclubs), because of sexual anonymity, or because of retrospective assessments of flawed partners such as those who turned out to be married, alcoholic, or abusive. The least risky category was the "convenience date," defined as someone who provided occasional, often platonic, company or who was an escort on social occasions. The next safest was the "interview date," which the women described as occurring with someone new (e.g., blind dates) or as the first step toward a second, potentially romantic date. Interview dates usually took place in restaurants and other public spaces and were used to ensure safety when meeting someone for the first time. The fourth and most idealized category was the "romantic date," defined as "someone you might have a relationship with, something deeper." The women did not construct these categories in terms of risk reduction for STIs; rather, this ordering shows how they conceptualized dating in terms of companionship and potential for romantic relationships.

TABLE 9.1

A Summary of Responses to Each of the Five Themes for All Participants (n=20)

Theme	Mentioned	Not mentioned	Reasons/responses
1) Relationship seeking	20	0	Loneliness; companionship; financial security.
2) Risky sex[a]	18	2	Freedom sex; sex-with-the-ex; gap sex; rebound sex; revenge sex; needy sex; one-night stands; drug-and alcohol-enhanced sex; casual partners.
3) Risky dates[b]	20	0	Abusers; losers; cheats/liars; controlling types; drug or alcohol users; pickups from bars, the Internet or newspaper personals; bad with money; emotionally needy.
4) Condom use	17	3	"No" responses: "Not needed because of birth control (tubal ligation or menopause)"; "Nasty"; "You hate to ask"; "It's the men who decide"; "It's not a southern [US] thing"; "Older women don't know how." "Yes" responses: "It's my life"; "I don't want to die over sex"; "I'm too scared not to."
5) Safer-sex scripts	8	12	About condoms: "I say, 'Do you have protection?' If they don't, I take a condom from my purse"; "No condoms, no sex." Other: "I don't have one night stands"; "I find it easy to say, 'Get lost'"; "I ease it into conversations and Google them first"; "I ask them to take a bath with me [to look for sores]"; "If it's through the Internet, I have a no-touching rule for the first three dates"; "I back off and call my friends."

a. Eighteen women reported one or more of these scenarios prior to or after relationship dissolution.
b. All women cited more than one risk factor in defining risky dates, and all women perceived risk in terms of risky partners rather than unprotected sex.

Where Do I Go to Meet Someone and How?

The difficulty of being a single woman in a couples-oriented society was a major theme in the interviews. In a context in which social networks consisted mainly of family-church connections, the newly single woman was socially suspect and suddenly without invitations because she lacked a male partner. Local venues, such as churches, usually catered to married couples and their families, and the change of status from "wife" to "divorcée" might bring unwelcome attention or result in a bad reputation. For example, Jeanne (36, white) said, "It was just awkward to be there. In my [church-based] singles group, I felt like I was fresh meat on the market or something—just a fresh find, let's hit on her." (All participant names are pseudonyms.)

The perceived need to find a new partner for companionship or romance depends on age, personality, and stage of singlehood (Wade & DeLamater, 2002). Four women spoke about wanting to find "someone, anyone" immediately after relationship dissolution, while two widows spoke provisionally about dating after lengthy periods of mourning. However, all of the interviews ultimately segued into discussions of how and where to meet someone new, primarily because of the lack of venues for adult women in a college town. Local bars were popular but were also dismissed as places of last resort because of their risky reputation. Conversely, Wal-Mart, Lowe's, and grocery stores had become default locations in which people could safely seek each other out in covert patterns of "man spotting." Participants spoke about seeking potential dates in produce sections, cosmetics departments in which men suddenly appeared as if they had lost their way, and the electronics and power tool aisles in which women could legitimately ask for help from men whose sparsely stocked shopping carts signified their single status. Suzanna's (48, African American) date-seeking experience was illuminating:

> I have been at the grocery store once or twice, you know, to have a chit-chat with them over the bananas, or you bump a cart into their cart to start up a conversation. And for men, you can meet that poor little helpless woman who knows nothing about electronics at Wal-Mart, because I am clueless when it comes to that stuff and they will come up to you and try to help you.

Such gendered strategies were carefully staged and often artful, especially in terms of timing ("any time after 8:00 pm on a Friday or Saturday"). Laura (55, white) spoke of using her physical capital to attract men in the electronics section at Wal-Mart: "You have to look on the top shelf that you need some help with, and you know, I'm so short, I need help with everything."

Learning how to "be" single after a long-term relationship meant trying to reshape one's identity, learn new dating scripts, and find new friends or activities to offset the loss of a partner. Said Erin (40, white), "[O]ne year ago I had a good circle of friends and since I've become single I'm not part of that circle. I find that married girlfriends truly do not want to socialize with singles because they have one thing on their minds, they think perhaps she is trying to steal my husband." The sudden loss of social status and friends could be so dismaying that usually cautious women sometimes went to local bars where patrons were drunk or were deemed risky or undesirable: "The first place women go to after a relationship is the bar. I mean, straight to a bar. They need someone to make them feel better about themselves, even if it's just for the night" (Karen, 35, white).

Transitional Dating, Cautions, and Concerns

Postrelationship dating could involve risk taking as women worked through inexperience, emotional upheaval, or the excitement of newly found freedom. Eighteen women reported postrelationship sexual activity they later considered to be risky, such as one-night stands after meeting someone in a bar or unprotected sex with multiple partners. The emotional fallout of failed relationships often led to risk taking. Aidene (48, African American) recounted, "I was so starved for attention that I went with the first person who noticed me. It was all about needing someone to validate me."

At this early point in the transition, dating motives mainly included wanting to meet someone "just to have contact with the opposite sex" or in the hope of regaining self-esteem or companionship after failed relationships. The workplace provided some opportunities for meeting potential partners but also raised the issue of being a "woman alone." Gwen (51, white) said, "I kept getting emails from this guy in management. He wouldn't leave me alone but I couldn't say anything because he's a big shot." Similarly, Debra (38, white) recalled, "This guy at work offered to pay my bills if I had sex with him." Women who were mothers found it particularly difficult to meet someone, not only because caregivers could be viewed as undesirable (e.g., "No one wants me now because I've got three kids" [Tiffany, 36, African American]) but also because "I have to work two jobs to pay the bills and there's never any time left over for me" (Erin). Friends, relatives, and acquaintances became a source for dating opportunities regardless of caregiver status.

In Belinda's (42, white) experience, "My brother would set me up with his friends and they were all nice guys but if you had sex with one of them it would get around. You can get a bad reputation that way, so I told my brother that I didn't want to keep dating his friends."

Women who were caregivers reported being torn between being sexually (or emotionally) needy and the responsibilities of motherhood. Strategies to manage these tensions ranged from "I had men over because I couldn't afford a babysitter. But the kids would be asleep and I never let them [men] stay all night. I didn't want the kids to get attached in case they got hurt or disappointed and I didn't want to risk them being abused" (Athena, 35, African American) to "I never had anyone come to my home. My [new] boyfriend has his own place and we meet over there. My kids are older now [in their twenties] so they can stay by themselves" (Aidene). In the worse case, "Loneliness will drive you. I cared more about getting a man into my bed than I did about the kids" (Darlene, 55, white).

Women's reasons for bringing dates home revolved around factors from emotional neediness to lack of options for childcare, the expense of dining out, or the simple convenience of having one's own place. Debra described caregivers' emotional neediness:

> Women with children take bigger risks than women without children. We are usually more desperate. We are afraid of being by ourselves and you are feeling unwanted and cheated if you have kids. Ninety-nine percent of the time you will be cheated because he gets away scot free while you have to raise, pay for, deal with, and have sleepless nights while he basically gets to have his life.

Making ends meet on only one income or, for five participants, while on unemployment benefits or disability benefits, was a major consideration. The prospect of finding someone who was financially secure was especially attractive to low-income caregivers who expressed an eagerness to date despite concerns about risks to self or children. As Wendy (40, white) noted, "There are financial issues. Some of us have children and we struggle to support them on one income, so we seek out a partner who we think can help us." Suzanna was the most explicit on this issue, saying that "there's a moral compromise when you're poor so you look for men who can give you money or something. It's just the thing to do. Where I come from [rural county], it's normal. If some of the women tell you they don't do it then they're not telling you the truth."

Dating generally became less fraught only after a period of adjustment from socially valued coupledom to being a "woman alone" (see also Wade & DeLamater, 2002). Older women tended to reevaluate dating needs or strategies after encountering the nurse-and-purse problem. Irene (53, white) explained how this gendered expectation had affected her peer group: "My friends don't date. They just don't bother because it's not worth it. You date someone a couple of times and they want to come over and have you fix dinner and stay home and watch TV and that doesn't work. The world is full of those men." For younger women, however, the desire for a happily-ever-after-relationship altered their outlook. Tiffany said, "There's that little flurry [of sex] for the first month or so, but it kind of wore off fast because I always wanted to be married. So I started looking at men differently."

Three women who self-defined as naturally cautious spoke about dating in different terms. In particular, they were afraid to repeat past mistakes. "I don't want to date right now. I want to take time off. Take a breather. I have a lot of things going through my mind about dating, like is he a pervert or is he abusive? I don't want to let my guard down" (Judith, 43, white). Reasons for caution were generally framed in terms of fears of rejection or betrayal: "I am just terrified of being rejected after what happened [her husband had an affair]. I've been on a couple of blind dates but that's about it" (Genna, 53, white).

Four older, financially independent women (all white) spoke about dating as an optional activity. For them, transitions to dating were neither emotionally driven nor unduly cautious. (One was a widow, another a business owner, and two had well-paid jobs and owned their own homes.) They each had strong friendships and interests, felt relatively comfortable about being single, and did not express the fears, hurt, or loneliness of other women in the study. Only one of these women had a dependent child. Like Bertha (59, white), who stated, "I can take it or leave it," these women viewed dating in terms of expanded social horizons rather than being driven by emotional, sexual, or financial need.

Dating Risks and Rules in the Postrelationship Context

Women expressed concern about risky partners, whom they defined as abusers, losers, and addicts. Dating risks were perceived in terms of "bad dates" or "going on a little rampage" rather than in terms of unprotected sex. In the "bad date" scenario, a lack of experience made the transition to "safe" (i.e., good) dating tenuous. Initial steps called for protective strategies such as attending local bars with friends, or avoidance strategies such as resisting the urge to respond to newspaper personals or to seek partners through an Internet dating service. All of the women agreed that carefully vetting a potential date's reputation or circumstances was imperative. However, this "bad date/good date" script could not be operationalized until dating had occurred, men's reputations could be established, or a getting-to-know-you period had passed without undue incident.

One element to successful dating was knowing how to look attractive without being deceptively youthful. The six women who admitted to "going on a little rampage" after relationship dissolution did not report being sexually overt during this time, although two of them described how they had "dressed up to the nines" to attract a date. Success or failure was apparent in how potential partners reacted to information about women's actual rather than assumed age. Brenda (52, white) claimed, "Age is a barrier. I tend to look younger and when they find out how old I am they aren't interested." Karen reported that women who "dressed like a 20-year old" faced rejection or worse because "if you don't look your age you risk being seen as a whore." Still, it was possible to resist the explicit ageism of this gender rule despite social pressure. Gwen had rejected advice from friends to tone down her appearance by declaring, "Excuse me, but I am not going to wear dresses down to my ankles and flat shoes if I don't want to. If I am going to wear heels and a dress above my knees every day for the rest of my life, I will do so."

Few participants expressed concerns about unprotected sex, even though seven reported a diagnosis of chlamydia, crabs, genital warts, herpes, or gonorrhea at some point in their lifetime. Women over 50 typically blamed courtship patterns from their adolescence and youth for their lack of interest in STI risk. Irene explained, "Back then, you know, we'd have fun and not worry about it. Of course, life was safer then and basically you were safer because you didn't have to worry about diseases like AIDS. It's not something we had to worry about and most of us haven't changed." In fact, most women resisted my attempts to draw them out on this issue, preferring instead to return to the theme of partners who abused, neglected, or left them for other women. Most women strongly associated STIs with bad partners rather than with sexual activity per se, seeing diagnosis as synonymous with a partner's infidelity or sexual abuse. The conflation of STIs with abusive partners was exemplified by Athena, who had married at age 16. Athena's husband raped and beat her throughout their 9-year marriage; he also infected her with chlamydia, which resulted in an ectopic pregnancy. She associated this experience with female victimization rather than in terms of developing safer-sex strategies for future dating. Like other women, Athena viewed condoms as a male prerogative because "if you ask men to use a condom they lie about not having one or make you feel guilty for asking. They say, 'Don't you trust me?' Or 'I'm allergic to latex.'"

The five women who had been diagnosed with curable STIs all viewed these infections as past history with abusive or unfaithful partners and thus irrelevant to current dating. The exception to this rule involved an incurable infection: herpes. Two women with herpes reported that a series of recurrent outbreaks and the fear of stigma had prompted anxiety over finding a partner (see also Nack, 2008). Genna had been infected with herpes during a 14-year marriage to her third husband and had experienced outbreaks on an occasional basis ever since. Although she invariably disclosed her STI status to sexual partners, she also reported: "I am so terrified of rejection [after her husband left her for another woman and a subsequent partner "couldn't take it"] that I only tell someone about it if I think things are going well." However, Genna's disclosure to sexual partners did not result in condom use because "men do not want to use condoms and it is too embarrassing to ask them to do so." Erin, the only woman to express an interest in HIV prevention strategies, was so fearful of being infected that "most times I just avoid dating and avoid having sex."

Age, Gender, and Unprotected Sex

Seventeen women reported having unprotected sex after relationship dissolution. Most of the participants had encountered resistance to condom use. One woman's older partner accused her of acting like a man when she raised the topic. Condom use was a particularly difficult or unladylike subject to broach with a new date. This resistance was both age- and gender-related. Said Suzanna, "My last one was older and didn't like the idea of me asking him to use one, but he knew he would wear one or not get any. That's just the bottom line and he grumbled but he did it." Judith compared the attitudes of younger and older male partners, saying, "The younger ones are more welcoming when it comes to condoms, but they don't initiate it, I do." Men's resistance resulted in the women deeming a "my-way-or-no-way" attitude with sexual partners to be the only effective strategy for safer sex. However, few women employed this strategy, either because it was not within their sexual repertoire or because it was considered too confrontational, awkward, or sexually aggressive.

Narratives about condom use evoked a context in which gender rules were clear—male partners did not initiate condom use and, in most cases, did not want to discuss safer sex either. Generally, women also did not raise the issue because they were using birth control or were postmenopausal (and associated condom use with pregnancy), or because of male impotence. This last issue was raised by Bertha: "This gentleman was a diabetic so he could not perform sexually. We tried to have sex with a condom once and it just went limp so it was too difficult and depressing for me." Other women cited sexual propriety as playing a primary role in unprotected sex: "It never crossed my mind to ask about condom use. You hate to ask. It's embarrassing" (Laura).

Women also contextualized men's expectations for sex in generational terms. Genna noted: "Men of my age have been married and are used to being in a sexual relationship and when you meet them it hangs in the air. They are expecting it." Men's high expectations for sex, matched by their low interest in condom use and their equally low interest in discussing safer sex in open and gender-neutral dialogue, combined to produce STI risk.

Scripts and Strategies for Safer Dating

Too few of these women had been dating long enough or seriously enough to permit a conclusive analysis of successful transitions. However, there were hints that a successful transition involved de-emphasis on active partner-seeking and emphasis on broader interests and social networking. In fact, women who reported being emotionally needy found themselves being a target for unwanted attention: "[it's] like a flashing light—they seem to know if you're lonely" (Suzanna). By contrast, buffering by social networks of family and friends as well as by hobbies, church, and peer groups helped offset fears of loneliness so that "I'm not by myself at home" (Brenda) and "I've got someone to be with over the holidays" (Jeanne). Rosemary's (66, white) love of motorcycles meant that, after relocating to a new state, "I just called up the club when I came to town and they said, come on. They make sure I'm okay and that I'm included in everything. As for dating someone, you just trust the group to approve so you don't make stupid decisions."

Eight women had formulated safer-sex scripts or strategies to avoid risky dates. These women tended to be over 50, single for long enough to know how to assess risky partners, taking a more measured approach to dating, and/or free from a single-minded focus on finding Mr. Right. They found convenience (platonic) dates useful in providing safe male company and escorts to social events. Irene said, "When there's a wedding in the family or some occasion, I always take [name]. He is not very healthy, but I am comfortable with him. He's nine years older than me and we go to dinner and places and that kind of thing." However, this type of dating was viewed as a backstop rather than in terms of potential romance. Casual partners were similarly viewed but were defined in terms of sexual need rather than platonic friendship. This type of partner could provide enjoyable, even protected, sex despite being perceived as covert or risky. In Darlene's experience, for example, "It's much easier for me to have a casual relationship with [names a 28-year-old man] or use a vibrator and with either one there are no consequences where no one needs to know. No serious commitment there, just bring your condoms and we will take care of business." This age-mixing might relate to the absence of suitable older male partners for heterosexual women but also suggests that condom use is more common when it involves casual sex (Macaluso, Demand, Artz, & Hook, 2000).

Other strategies to avoid risk involved limiting sexual activities, particularly among postmenopausal women. The lack of available partners and the nurse-and-purse problem played a role in these decisions, although women who had been through menopause also reported being less eager for sex than their younger counterparts. These participants voiced resentment at being perceived as matronly caregivers, especially if their own desires involved fun, freedom, and expanded social horizons. But being older also meant that dating or sex could be viewed as optional or safe, particularly if poor health or male impotence was involved. As Rosemary joked, "My libido since my husband died has gone down to nothing. Of course, a lot of men my age are impotent, which would be fine with me. I have a checklist. He has got to be between 60 and 69, he has to have a little money, be healthy, and he must be impotent."

Discussion

Women in this study perceived postrelationship dating in terms of gains or losses and were concerned about midlife dating in relation to sexual desirability, social status, parental status, and health. Regarding sexual desirability, postrelationship dating took place against a backdrop of gender norms for older women's sexuality, that is, within "the traditional notion that women [are] desirable but not desiring" (Turner, 1996, p. 58). Gender norms framed this perception insofar as a woman's character was judged according to her physical appearance and the acceptability (i.e., subtlety) of her goals of partner-seeking. To avoid negative judgments, women often expressed desire through covert date-seeking strategies such as grocery shopping. In all dating settings, women expressed desire in idealized terms, focusing on the pursuit of romantic and sexual fulfillment rather than on protecting sexual health. Notably, these strategies took place in the context of women's pursuit of the normative coupledom that is characteristic of promarriage contexts such as the U.S. South (Byrne & Carr, 2005).

Regarding social status, being excluded from former social networks constituted a risk factor in terms of sexual health and well-being. The crisis of separation from intimate partners, which may be a temporary state or, for the less fortunate, a downward cycle (Amato, 2000), was a catalyst to visiting bars where alcohol and the promise of sex were temporary antidotes to social rejection and vulnerability. Such experiences compromised the protective aspects of women's invisibility, putting gender stereotypes about merry widows or sex-starved divorcées in play. Women thus exposed had to manage sexual visibility and desire while being unfamiliar with dating scripts and coping with changes in financial and parenting status. Statements about "little rampages" and "going crazy for a while" embodied a context of risk that resembled adolescence in its tumultuousness, helping to explain why the National Institute on Aging (2007) considers this stage of life to be risky in terms of women's sexual health.

Regarding parental status, women with dependent children (mostly African American), were more likely than other women to take sexual risks when dating. Explanations centered on beliefs that men did not want to date caregivers (thus creating anxiety about finding partners) and worries about bringing up children without adequate financial support. Risk taking also occurred because the women were lonely, emotionally needy, or angry about having to shoulder parental responsibilities alone. Financial hardship was a recurrent theme for single mothers, as acknowledged by one woman who claimed that "survival sex" (i.e., sex with men who provide gifts or resources) was common among unmarried mothers in her rural Black community. Regardless of parental status, previously partnered women are worse off in financial terms than never-married women and this economic disparity persists over the long term (Arber, 2004). This alarming statistic is exacerbated by single motherhood; 36% of single mothers in the United States live below the poverty line (Bernstein, 2006).

The mothers in this study also feared that they could attract the wrong sort of man—one who might abuse them or their children. These fears did not always mean that women were not eager to date someone in order to explore new possibilities, repair damage to self-image, or gain relief from constant caregiving; nor did it lead to more selective partner-seeking. Despite retrospective regrets, women did not always take their children into consideration when deciding to bring partners home. Women's explanations for the latter phenomenon included their emotional needs, the lack of options for childcare, the expense of dining out, simple convenience, or "not thinking it through" at the time. Colletta (1979) found that low-income divorced mothers who lacked social support suffered unrelieved stress from being caretakers and were emotionally needy and dissatisfied—perhaps a precursor to risk taking as suggested by the participants in this study. Whitbeck, Simons, and Kao (1994, p. 616) report that "new, often confusing dating and courtship norms" may indeed create situations in which newly single women make compromises that they later realize put themselves or their children at risk. By contrast, divorced caretakers who were better off financially had a strong sense of independence and greater satisfaction with life. Similarly, in this study, financially independent women who had a "take-it-or-leave-it" attitude to dating felt more empowered in sexual relationships.

Regarding health status, it is worth employing Turner's (1996) "all illness is social illness" rubric to examine a social context in which the sexual health risks of postrelationship dating are effectively hidden from view. In this terrain, dating is sought for the maintenance of normative (i.e., heterosexually coupled) relationships. The participants prioritized these relationships despite citing social dis-ease(s) such as infidelity, domestic abuse, and addiction to drugs and alcohol as reasons for losing or leaving partners (see also Amato & Previti, 2003). The fragility of normative coupledom was exposed by these troubled breakups and also by relationships that were iterative in nature (e.g., six of the women had two or more marriages). According to Turner (1996), social practices (e.g., heterosexual marriage) are legitimized when they are valued as much for their symbolic as practical worth. Such legitimization was evident in women's desires to reclaim an idealized partnership status through active dating. This quest often obscured awareness or concerns about protected sex, an oversight that was further legitimized in the local context in which nonmarital sex and condom use were associated with immorality (Lichtenstein, 2003).

I would like to reiterate that health, the initial focus of this study, ranked a distant second to women's concerns about partners who could disappoint or harm them. Women viewed health status in terms of emotional and personal safety. Indeed, the study's focus on STI risk in postrelationship dating was reframed, in part, by women's fears about bad dates or sexual predators. Such fears limited certain types of dating such as Internet matching, despite evidence that the Internet can be used to minimize personal risk and to maximize chances for safer sex (Couch & Liamputtong, 2008). (Only one woman used online dating, after being prompted by a family member.) This agenda meant that concerns about "bad partners" were more urgent than the dangers of STIs, a finding that held true even for women who had already been diagnosed with infections that signaled the need for safer sex. Reluctance to engage in safer sex occurred, in part, because the sexual body was perceived as a private space in which sex was practiced—figuratively speaking—with the lights out.

As a final point, the women viewed condoms in terms of birth control, or as irrelevant, embarrassing, inhibiting, or as a threat to the male prerogative. This risk scenario, of course, did not apply to everyone, especially the few women who initiated condom use because they viewed sexuality more pragmatically or because they embraced an assertive approach to sexuality. These women were likely to be white, older, financially independent, and/or more discerning in their choice of partners, especially if they wished to avoid nurse-and-purse scenarios involving older men. Women who were more discerning when it came to dating also tended to be less sexually active than other participants. This outcome suggests that STI messages should be tailored to different groups within the age/gender and race/ethnicity spectrum so that the messages are relevant to the particular circumstances and contexts of midlife and older women.

Conclusion

Scholarly attention to women's dating during the postrelationship transition has the potential to generate useful data for sexual health interventions that are sensitive to age, income levels, social context, parental status, and differences in women's experiences relative to divorce or widowhood. My interview data suggest that anxiety about finding someone, uncertainty about how to date, and risky behavior are common themes among midlife women after relationship dissolution, but that income levels, parental status, and partner availability affect STI/HIV risk as well. A provocative (if tentative) finding was that the African American women cited low incomes, high levels of stress from single parenthood, and the lack of stable male partners in discussions about risky behavior. If these factors promote risk among poor women of color relative to higher-earning white and African American women, as suggested here, then such insights might help to explain why STI/HIV rates are disproportionately higher among blacks than among whites in the United States (Centers for Disease Control and Prevention, 2009a). Future research should investigate intersections between gender, poverty, partner availability, and caregiving status, so that differentials in STI/HIV risk among midlife women are identified more clearly.

The data presented here suggest that health providers need to be aware that newly single women might be unfamiliar with condom use, uncertain about negotiating safer sex, and unwilling to initiate discussions about safer sex with partners or health providers (see Grant & Ragsdale, 2008). Appropriate techniques and technologies for STI prevention should be made available through doctors' offices and other points of contact as a matter of urgency. Providers should also understand that newly single heterosexual women in midlife usually date older men who resist condom use through force of habit, male prerogative, or fears of impotence. It would be useful to determine the extent of this resistance among older men and to assess whether the patterns of sexual behavior I have identified among women also occur among men who begin dating after relationship dissolution. It would also be helpful if newly single women were informed that transitional sex is normative (i.e., they are not alone or socially deviant) and that safer-sex scripts and/or a ready supply of condoms are essential tools for sexual health in the long run. Safer-sex education for older women should de-emphasize the "risky partner" motif in favor of self-protective behaviors that can help to instill or maintain a sense of control in sexual relationships. This final point is a lesson in sexual health over the life span, but might be a point of departure for midlife women whose understandings (and those of their sexual partners) are rooted in dating scripts from their youth.

10

Secrets and Magic Pills

Constructing Masculinity and Sexual
"Normalcy" Following Spinal Cord Injury

ALEXIS A. BENDER

According to a recent population-based survey, approximately 1.275 million people in the United States are currently living with a spinal cord injury (SCI) and a total of 5.5 million have some form of paralysis (The Christopher and Dana Reeve Foundation, 2009). The most common causes of SCI include motor vehicle accidents (42%), falls (27%), and violence (15%). SCI primarily affects people during their adult years, with an average age at injury of 38, and it disproportionately affects men (81%). The majority of people who experience SCI are single at the time of injury (52%). For those who are married (32%) or who eventually marry, the likelihood of divorce is higher than in the general population (National Spinal Cord Injury Statistical Center, 2009). Information about the experiences of people with disabilities who identify as lesbian, gay, bisexual, or transgendered (LGBT) is lacking (Harley, Nowak, Gassaway, & Savage, 2002). Regardless of age or relationship status, people with SCI experience a major turning point and therefore have different life course trajectories than people who do not experience traumatic injury.

Although most people with SCI report engaging in intercourse and sexual relationships after injury, many people with physical disabilities have difficulty establishing sexual relationships (Shuttleworth, 2000; Taleporos & McCabe, 2003). Furthermore, among people with disabilities, men are more likely than women to be single, suggesting that men with physical disabilities face more barriers in forming relationships (Taleporos & McCabe, 2003). Age at onset of disability also influences the sexual lives of people with SCI. Men who acquire SCI later in life are more dissatisfied with their sexual lives than younger men and women of all ages with SCI (Valtonen, Karlsson, Siösteen, Dahlöf, & Viikari-Juntura, 2006).

The intersection of sexuality and SCI was rarely studied before the 1970s, in part because of pervasive myths that people with disabilities are sexless or possible deviants (DiGiulio, 2003; Gerschick & Miller, 1995; Milligan & Neufeldt, 2001). People with disabilities are often presented as genderless and "as freaks of nature, monstrous, the 'Other' to the social norm" (Meekosha, 2006, p. 765). These social images and attitudes can further stigmatize and marginalize people with disabilities. The myth of asexuality can result in a "self-fulfilling prophecy," causing people with disabilities to avoid sexual and intimate relationships (Milligan & Neufeldt, 2001; Zola, 1982). People who acquire their disability later in life might have to alter the physical, psychological, and emotional aspects of their sexual identity. Bringing these parts of the self together following injury is made even more difficult when discussions of sexuality are missing from the rehabilitation process (Hess, Hough, & Tammaro, 2007; Wazakilli, Mpofu, & Devlieger, 2009).

Disability from a Life Course Perspective

This chapter draws on key life course principles—timing, linked lives, location in time and place, and human agency (Giele & Elder, 1998)—to examine the sexual trajectories of men following SCI. First, the *timing* of injury affects how men with SCI conceptualize sexuality following their injury. For example, men who sustain an injury earlier in life might have a less-established sexual identity whereas older men might have more difficulty incorporating their previous sexual identity into a new, disabled identity. Second, the concept of *linked lives* recognizes that men do not experience traumatic injury in a social vacuum; rather they interact with family members, medical professionals, and sexual partners. Third, *location in time and place* refers to the cultural background (in terms of both social and physical context) that people experience. The medical technologies available at the time of men's injury can have a significant impact on how they are able to (re)construct their masculinity. Finally, *human agency* relates to the decisions individuals make and how individuals prioritize different aspects of their life within the structures of society (Giele & Elder, 1998). Although individuals are capable of making their own decisions that can alter their life pathways, sociologists recognize that these choices are constrained or facilitated by the limitations and opportunities of individuals' social location. Although this chapter relies on all four aspects of the life course perspective, the central focus is men's agency following SCI.

The Study

The findings in this chapter come from a larger qualitative study involving in-depth interviews with ten black and ten white heterosexual men who had experienced a traumatic injury. Most of the respondents (n = 18) had SCI. One respondent was a double above-the-knee amputee and one had physical limitations similar to SCI as a result of a neurological disease contracted in his twenties.[1] Of those with SCI, an equal number of respondents had quadriplegia (n = 9) and paraplegia (n = 9).[2] Despite these dichotomous medical designations, there was variation in ability and function within these two groups. The respondents ranged from 24 to 67 years old with an average age of 38. The mean time since injury for this sample was 11 years, with a range of 4 to 21 years. Most respondents (n = 14) were single or divorced. Of the six who were married, three were with the same spouses as at the time of injury. Three of the single men were married at the time of injury and those relationships had since ended. All of my respondents identified as heterosexual, which was not a specific criterion for recruitment but might be a byproduct of the sampling methodology used.

Two-thirds of the participants were recruited from a rehabilitation center in a large southern city with the assistance of a peer support coordinator and the sport teams' director. The remaining third of the respondents were recruited using snowball sampling (Miles & Huberman, 1994). I collected data using in-depth, face-to-face, open-ended interviewing between March 2005 and June 2006. Interviews took place at the rehabilitation center, respondents' homes and places of employment, a local university, and over the telephone. All of the interviews were conducted in private, except one in which a participant's wife was home at the time of my visit, but not present during the formal interview. The interviews loosely followed an interview schedule addressing major topics related to masculinity, sexuality, work, family, and public perceptions. Interviews lasted approximately 2 hours each and were audio-recorded and transcribed verbatim.

Data were analyzed using grounded theory methods (Glaser & Strauss, 1967; LaRossa, 2005; Strauss & Corbin, 1998), which allow the researcher to develop theory inductively from the data collected. Grounded theory uses constant comparative methods, allowing me to identify key themes and concepts that emerged from the data and to examine the ways SCI was experienced by this group of men.

As a white, nondisabled female, I was concerned about my status as an "outsider" during this process. However, I found that my respondents spoke openly about their experiences. My status as a partner to a man with SCI allowed me to gain entry to the group and to identify with some of the experiences they discussed. My "insider-outsider" status (Sherif, 2001) also provided for many in-depth conversations about experiences that we might not have explored had we shared the same vantage point. However, as other women sociologists who study masculinity have noted, my gender may have shaped the interview process (Williams, 1995). Men frequently relied on my status as a partner to a man with SCI to share information about their sexual functioning by saying something like, "You understand this because you have seen it, but I wouldn't tell other women."

Findings

Through the use of grounded theory, two core categories emerged as central to how these men's sexual trajectories shifted following SCI: "Agency" and "Hegemonic Masculine Presentation." Agency identifies perceived control on the part of the respondents in relation to their sexual trajectories. The term "life course agency" refers to ways in which individuals try to control their own life trajectory (Hitlin & Elder, 2007) and how individuals are able to position themselves to achieve long-term goals. For example, did they take control of dating or did they allow others to control their interactions?

The second category, Hegemonic Masculine Presentation, reflects how men individually presented their masculinity. Hegemonic masculinity refers to an idealized and normative view of masculinity that values strength, perfection, potency, and physical activity (Connell, 1995; Shakespeare, 1999). The masculine performance of gender centers on the body and sets up boundaries for the performer to be active and physical and takes away the option for men to be weak, vulnerable, or imperfect. There are varieties of masculine forms and relations, which are often complex and contradictory, especially when intersecting with race, class, and ability. Every form of masculinity has its own history and is manifest based on these histories, but given the importance of the body for masculine performance I focused on ways that men relied on hegemonic masculinity in relationship to sexuality.

Using these concepts, I explored the strategies men used or did not use to display their masculinity and asked questions of the data, such as "How willing are men to show weakness?" and "To what lengths are they willing to go to in order to present a 'perfect' body to women?" This chapter examines the ways these men use life course agency to construct their own sexual trajectories in relation to their reliance on masculine presentation.

Types of Sexual Trajectories: Class, Race, and Postinjury Trajectories

By analyzing the two core categories that emerged from the data—Agency and Hegemonic Masculine Presentation—in relation to one another, I was able to recognize a clear pattern of masculine presentation. The narratives of the men in this study aligned with four sexual trajectories following injury. Two trajectories involved men with high levels of agency: "Adaptation," which included men who were flexible with their masculine presentation, and "Performance," which included men who relied on idealized, normative aspects of masculinity and who worked hard to manage their self-presentation. The other two trajectories were followed by men with lower levels of agency who frequently relied on stereotypes and interactions with others to shape their sexual lives. "Conformity" included men who defined masculinity broadly and "Relinquishment" included men who held on to idealized aspects of masculinity but were constrained from masculine performance by their social location. The men in these latter two categories viewed themselves as having high levels of agency, yet their personal biographies were highly structured by external forces (Shanahan & Macmillan, 2007).

Examining demographic differences is especially important in life course research because transitions and trajectories will have different outcomes depending on one's social location. Age at injury, time since injury, marital status, and social class are key factors in understanding the different experiences of men's sexual trajectories following SCI.[3] Cumulative processes that take place before and after injury further help to make sense of how people experience turning points in their lives (Shanahan & Macmillan, 2007). For example, men who are injured earlier in life will most likely have fewer pre-injury sexual experiences to draw on than men who are injured later in life, which will result in different sexual trajectories. Furthermore, the more time that has passed since injury the greater the accumulation of sexual experiences that will either reinforce or weaken men's sexual confidence.

People also experience cumulative advantages and disadvantages in relation to their class and racial statuses, which will influence how they experience dating and sexuality following injury. In this study, social class[4] greatly affected men's level of sexual interaction with women. Men with more social and financial resources were able to spend time (and money) in typical dating venues, like bars, whereas men without similar resources were limited because they were dependent on family members for housing and transportation. Within this sample, race also influenced cumulative advantages and disadvantages over time, but in ways that surprised me. For some men, especially black men, the turning point of injury resulted in a "knifing off" (Sampson & Laub, 1990) of social ties that existed before injury. For the black men, their injury provided them with opportunities they would not have otherwise had—college education and job placement through vocational rehabilitation programs, a monthly stipend from insurance settlements, or a reason to move out of a public housing project. Although both black and white men had access to the same state programs, more black men in my sample relied on them for support soon after injury, which resulted in greater access to other social and financial resources over time. In short, within this sample, race and class interacted with hegemonic masculinity in clear and distinct ways for a multitude of experiences following injury; however, in terms of sexuality, class appeared to be more salient than race.

High Agency Trajectories
Adaptation

Men who offered Adaptation narratives (i.e., Adapters) demonstrated high levels of agentic control over their sexual trajectories while simultaneously exhibiting less reliance on a traditional masculine presentation. Adapters (n = 7) were mostly men with paraplegia (n = 5), who tended to be younger at the time of injury (mean = 22.8 years) and had been injured for the longest period of time (mean = 15.6 years). Men who used adaptation narratives were primarily black (n = 6), had relatively higher levels of education and household incomes, and were almost equally likely to be married or single. The men in this group described being open with sexual partners about their level of sexual function and used this disclosure to their advantage when meeting women. Adapters also defined their sexual satisfaction in terms of communication and equal pleasure in sexual relationships. Among the groups, they appeared to have the most fulfilling sex lives, in part because of their high level of perceived control and their willingness to seek alternative ways to be intimate.

Control over dating and sexual relationships was central to the narratives of the men in this group. Robert (black, middle-class) was 18 at the time he was injured 22 years earlier.[5] He has never married, lives alone, and employs caregivers for assistance with daily tasks. When asked about his dating history, Robert said he had a girlfriend at the time of his injury, but he had to break it off. He explained:

> She wanted to marry me at the time. But [I was] trying to deal with so much at that time. I broke up with her. She was pressuring me, and it was to the point where she was very, very possessive and obsessive. And that was just too much pressure. . . . So, I broke it up. I just said, "This is

not working; I just can't deal with this like this. I got to focus on myself here. . . . This is a new life, I gotta figure out what I'm gonna do in it."

Robert viewed this relationship as taking away his control over his life. In order to regain control, he ended the relationship. He has since had relationships with other women, but in all of his sexual encounters, he maintained control over the level of commitment and intimacy. He explained:

Of course, I'm a man, I'm going to get horny. Just because I'm in a wheelchair, that doesn't stop my sex drive. Sometimes it goes into overdrive, but I'm just like [any] other man. But I don't allow sex to control me. It doesn't make who I am. I'm still able to make the decision. If I want to go out and have sex, I make the decision to do it. If I don't, I don't.

Although Robert's narrative indicates a desire for independence and control, which are commonly associated with masculine ideals, his desire for independence focuses on self-growth rather than on proving his ability to be independent. This strategy is similar to what Gerschick and Miller (1995) term "reformulation" of masculinity. Like the men in Gerschick and Miller's study, the Adapters I spoke with had high levels of confidence about their sexuality and were able to shape their ideas of masculinity to fit their own needs and desires.

The men in the Adapter group were more flexible in what they considered masculine than men in the other three groups and they allowed people to see them as "imperfect" through the disclosure of their sexual function. Three of the men in this category were married at the time of injury, which made it difficult—if not impossible—to keep levels of sexual function secret from their partners. However, the single men in this group also disclosed their level of sexual function and their use of erection-enhancing drugs. Their location in time when they were injured likely contributed to their level of disclosure. Most of these men's injuries occurred before the introduction of Viagra, Cialis, and other erection-enhancing drugs, thereby requiring them to disclose more often because of a lack of options.

Taylor (black, lower middle-class), who was 20 when he was injured 12 years before our interview, explained:

You can ask me anything you want. . . . I don't get offended by it, because I want you to know. I would rather you know than assume something crazy. If [women] ask me something about sex, I might tell them, "I'll tell you later. If you really want to know, find out."

Like other men in this category, Taylor is open about his level of sexual functioning with friends and potential sexual partners. He also uses his injury as an opportunity to flirt with and tease women, a strategy that is also documented in *Murderball* (Rubin & Shapiro, 2005), a popular film about quadriplegic rugby.

Anthony (black, middle-class) presents another example of how sexual trajectories changed for men in this group. Anthony is married and was 29 when he was injured 12 years ago. He uses a different strategy than the single Adapters. He explained:

> [*How has sex changed for you?*] Uhh . . . there's the substitute for a penis. There are toys, there's oral sex. There's more touching and compassion. It ain't just wham, bam, thank you ma'am. Foreplay. It's a lot of foreplay, so once she reaches the peak, you know. She enjoys it. At least that['s] what she says. You be creative, you have to be creative. You don't do it as much now. You don't do it like rabbits no mo'.

The men in this group express great confidence in their identity and appear to be in control of gaining the things they desire in their lives. Although Adapters value some aspects of masculine performance—such as being able to make their partner reach an orgasm or having a fully erect penis—overall they adapt to situations with open communication and the potential to be seen as sexually vulnerable.

Performance

The second group of men who exhibited high levels of agency were also younger when injured (mean = 24.5 years) but have been injured for a considerably shorter time (mean = 6.5 years) than men with Adaptation narratives. Men in the Performer group (n = 5) had slightly lower household incomes than men in the Adapter group, were mostly high school–educated, and worked in skilled labor positions or were in the military prior to their injury. Men in this group tended to be single (n = 4), white (n = 3), and, like men in the Adapter group, to have paraplegia (n = 3). They also exhibited a greater need for independence, a concept that is central to masculinity in America (Kimmel, 1996), and relied on stereotypical presentations of masculinity and disability to shape their actions. Like Adapters, Performers exhibited control over ending and initiating relationships as well as high rates of sexual experimentation following their injury. Unlike Adapters, however, Performers rarely disclosed their level of sexual function or their use of erection-enhancing drugs. The men in this category are Performers because of their desire to present themselves as strong, virile men who control their own destiny, consistent with idealized notions of hegemonic masculinity.

Like Adapters, Performers ended and pursued relationships on terms that were beneficial to them; however, their motivations were grounded in more hegemonic notions of masculinity—independence and masculine performance. Philly's narrative provides a useful case for understanding this group. Philly (black, middle-class) was 21 when he was injured in a car accident, 5 years before our interview. He was in a relationship that he ended one year following his injury. Philly lives alone and does not need assistance for daily activities. When asked how his relationship ended, he answered:

> About a year after the accident I had to leave [her]. 'Cause, I don't know, the relationship would feel cool, but I felt like we got along so much less, because we were around each other so much because of the injury. . . . I pushed everybody away. And, like now, I'm still, pushing people away. . . . I don't let them in. I got my friends, and that's my buddies, and that's all I need. I got a couple friends here, got a girlfriend here, boom. That's all I need. That's all I want. Everybody else is extra. . . . That's it. When it came to her, I had to push her away, and I pushed my mother away, and let people know, that I'm going to this life thing on my own. I don't need you. I'm glad you're there, and I appreciate the support, but I can't, I can't need you. I don't want to need you. . . . I can't turn into that.

Philly had internalized a primary requirement of an idealized version of masculinity—independence—before his injury and went to great lengths to continue to present it, even at the cost of losing relationships with partners, friends, and family members. This excerpt highlights that although injury is a turning point, one's prior life experiences influence the path one takes after injury.

Another key distinction between Adapters and Performers involved their willingness to share information about their level of sexual function with friends and potential sexual partners. Men in the Performer category aimed to present a self that was "normal" and not weakened or altered by paralysis; however, in reality, SCI frequently results in the decreased ability to achieve and maintain an erection without the use of drugs or pumps. The association of masculinity with sexual performance can create anxiety for many men whose erections do not appear "normal" (Grace, Potts, Gavey, & Vares, 2006). Not surprisingly, men in this category frequently described the use of drugs in order to present a reality that they could still perform in a "normal" way. According to Philly:

It's more of a secret now than anything. Like, my boys, they know nothing about me. What they know is whatever I tell them. And, it's pretty much, everything is just normal. And it's not. . . . All the girls that know me, they think that it's normal just like anybody else. They think it is, but I know it's not. It's just what I want you to believe. I want it to remain secret. I don't know why. Even if I never get with any of them, it does me and my heart right to know that they think I'm normal. And that's the whole point. And that's what I want. That's what I try to maintain.

Chris (white, middle-class) echoes Philly's secrecy about erection-enhancing drugs. As he explains:

I began to anticipate [sex] a little bit with the medication. I don't have to have it every time, but it's a lot better if I do get a little bit of help. And, sometimes I tell her that I'm going to the bathroom and take a pill and drain my bladder before we get down and dirty. And there's sometimes when I don't [tell her].

Whereas Philly uses a strict no-tell policy, Chris will occasionally (but infrequently) disclose his use of drugs. For the men in this group, the presentation of masculinity was an active process, involving constant awareness that others were observing their presentation; in effect they are "doing gender" (West & Zimmerman, 1987). Men created and performed normative masculinity by focusing on particular expectations of manhood: independence and a normative body—especially an erect penis.

Social cues and interactions bolstered the sexual self-esteem of some men in this category, which might explain their higher level of agentic control over dating and sex. As Chris explained:

I'm really still amazed at how many people still don't know that I can date. They never really see me with a date. . . . They smile at me, and it's just "Why are you smiling at me now? Last week I saw you, and you didn't want anything to do with me and now I've got a girl with me and you want to talk." It's amazing how warm and open people are to, to know that. . . . It's like—"Wow, he must be really cool if he's got a girlfriend." And if I didn't have the girl right beside me, they would think, "Ah, poor guy in the wheelchair." Now, it's "Aw man, there's a guy in a wheelchair with a girlfriend." And it's two completely different things, but it's the same guy in the same wheelchair.

Relying on hegemonic masculinity can be a useful coping mechanism for men following SCI, especially in the first few years following injury (Gerschick & Miller, 1995). For Chris and other men in this category, having others view them as complete, successful men with fully functioning masculine bodies was important. They sought control over their relationships in a manner that protected this presentation—independent, strong, desirable, and virile.

Low Agency Trajectories
Conformity
One trajectory associated with lower agency was Conformity. Respondents whose narratives belong in this group were considerably older at the time of injury (mean = 56 years) and had been injured for less time than other groups (mean = 4.5 years). Conformers are still figuring out how this injury is affecting their relationships and frequently conform to stereotypes associated with age and disability that outweigh their desire for masculine presentation. Although only two men's narratives fell into the conformity category, their biographies and transitions are worth exploring because they were markedly different from all other groups. Both men were married at the time of their injuries and interviews, had the highest income of any group, and had injuries that required a lot of assistance for daily activities (both had quadriplegia and used motorized wheelchairs for mobility). Both described their relationships as "in flux" or "freefall." Men in this group do not adhere to hegemonic masculinity as much as men in the other groups, and they perceive a great loss of control over their sexual selves. They have experimented with different sexual aids, including medication, and tried to have sex with their wives but have not (yet) had success. Compared with men in the other categories, they have lower expectations for themselves or their partners in terms of sexual intimacy. Additionally, they have low reliance on ideals of masculine performance and high levels of disclosure to their partners, in part due to their relationship status at the time of injury.

Men in this group frequently gave up control over sexuality to the medical community or to their partners. Allen (white, upper middle-class) was the oldest respondent in this study (64) and was injured for the least amount of time (4 years) at the time of our interview. He expressed that he and his wife were not able to have sex anymore:

[*What about sex and intimacy in your marriage. Is that something that changed?*] Yeah. Absolutely. There is no more. . . . [*Is that something that you miss?*] Mmm, yeah. [*Have the two of you tried, in any way, to bring that back into your marriage?*] Uh, no, not really. I don't know, I always assumed that Viagra is not an option for me, because, they never offered it to me and they offered it to everybody else, at [the hospital]. . . . Everybody in there was young compared to me, most of those guys in there were kids. When I was in there it seemed most of 'em was 22 and down. . . . It's just a young person's injury. [*Did you ever ask anyone at [the hospital]?*] I didn't. I just assumed that it wasn't an option for me . . . because they offered it to everybody else but never talked to me about it.

The medical community appeared to deny Allen's sexuality, and therefore his masculinity, because of his age. He never questioned his doctors' failure to provide information about drugs for impotence following SCI; rather, he complied with the medical community's authority over his sexuality by not asking about medication or for guidance about how to bring sex back into his marriage.

Unlike Allen, Gary (white, upper middle-class) has used medication to achieve an erection; however, he perceives his wife's lack of sexual satisfaction as a reason for not having sex. When I asked him about sex and intimacy with his wife, he answered:

We always have intimacy, we just don't have sex. We haven't figured out how yet. We're still in freefall after we jumped off the bridge, we're still in freefall. We haven't found a place to land yet. . . . We still would like to get back to it, but we haven't figured out how. [*Do you have sexual function?*] No. Well. . . . Those [drugs] all work. But, I'm just laying there, so [my wife] has to do everything, and I wouldn't have any sensation of an orgasm or anything else. So, my pleasure would be zippity-doo-dah, and for her, it would be all the work, the times that we have tried it, it's her having to do all the work which means she's not getting any satisfaction out of it either. . . . Every now and then we really start talking about it and thinking about it, but we can cuddle. But she's gotta get the lift, put me in bed, roll me over . . . well, it's hard for her to think about us with the sex relationship when she's doing all my bodily functions. She doesn't really think of me, much, in any other way.

For Gary, a lack of physical control over his entire body, not just his sexual functioning, has translated into a lack of control over his sex life with his wife. He reports that her assistance with daily activities has resulted in a burden for her, which has caused him to believe that sex is also a burden because it is "work" for his wife. Both Gary and Allen have the financial resources to hire personal-care assistants, but they choose not to because they informed me their wives would "feel uncomfortable" with someone else caring for them.

Because of their age, these men have more life experiences than other men in this study, possibly resulting in a greater loss of self following injury insofar as they had previously achieved a number of personal and professional goals. For example, they had reached a point of financial and social stability, were retired, and had fully grown and independent children who no longer relied on them for care. Perhaps these men did not rely on many aspects of hegemonic masculinity to define who they were as men, before their injuries, in part, due to their maturity. Men in this group allow their partners to see them as weak, dependent, or vulnerable, all of which go against stereotypical notions of masculinity, while at the same time they conform to ageist stereotypes of being a burden or too old to have sex. Although unhappy about needing assistance from their wives, they did not reject the assistance and expressed concern about their partners' needs in terms of caregiving and intimacy.

Relinquishment

For some men, fear of intimacy becomes a barrier to achieving a fulfilling sexual life. Four of the men I interviewed had given up on dating and sex. These Relinquishers were similar to the men in the Performer group in their age at injury (mean = 26.5 years) and time since injury (mean = 9 years); however, they had fewer financial and social resources than any other group. There are a few possible reasons for this difference. First, the men in this group were less likely to have attended college and more likely to have quadriplegia, negatively affecting their earning potential. Second, they were less likely to have worked in stable occupations or to have large peer groups prior to injury; therefore, their social safety net was unstable at the time of their injuries and it failed to support them after their injuries. All of the men in this group were single at the time of our interview and they did not have control over when previous relationships ended. These men were in their mid-twenties at the time of injury and were at about 10 years postinjury, yet they had not achieved steady employment and relied on government or family support to meet their financial needs. This has resulted in a "failure" of masculinity on levels other than the physical. Relinquishers indicate that their own high expectations of masculine performance are at odds with their perceptions of themselves as "less than men." These men struggle with the competing popular culture narratives of "man as strong" and "disabled as weak."

Interactions with strangers and images in popular culture have led these men to view themselves as unable to fulfill their masculine roles. Unlike Performers, who described positive interactions with others when in dating situations, Relinquishers frequently recalled examples of negative social interactions. As one respondent, Kirk (white, working-class), said, "One thing that bothered me [on] a couple of the dates is that we'd be out to eat and [the server] would look to the woman to ask what I wanted." The actions of strangers, and occasionally friends and acquaintances, can strip men's perceptions of themselves as being in control of dating situations. Bobby (white, lower-class) was 22 when he was injured in a fall. He lives at home with his father and has not held a steady job since his accident 13 years ago. He described an interaction with a female friend at a local bar:

> I made a comment toward one of the girls that I used to [sit] around the table and drink with. . . . [I told her] you have some pretty pockets, talking about her blue jeans, she had 'em skin tight, you couldn't help but notice. And, she told me I was acting like a man. [*What did you take from that comment?*] I guess I'm not supposed to be a man anymore, just because I'm paralyzed. That's what I took from that. I guess I'm not a man anymore.

These men's interactions with other people have encouraged them to see themselves as less than men. Over time this perception has influenced how they interact with women and approach dating situations, eventually resulting in a relinquishment of sexual control. When comparing the men in this group to the men in the Adapter group, the patterns of cumulative advantage and disadvantage are noticeable. Over time, Relinquishers' lack of financial resources has made it difficult to engage in typical dating behaviors. First, they lack the money to spend time in bars and clubs. Second, if they do meet women, they might not have a car (to drive to a potential partner's house) or a private place to bring a potential partner since some of them still live with their parents.

The men in this group also express a greater fear of not being able to "perform." This phenomenon is closely tied to masculine expectations of sexual performance. Larry (black, lower-class), who was 34 when he was injured and was 6 years postinjury, described his hesitation to engage in a sexual relationship with a potential partner: "It [lack of sex] didn't bother me 'til my libido started to kick in. And I had met this young lady. . . . And I thought, I wish I could perform. I wish I could perform. It kinda bothers me. It ain't nothing I can do about it." Larry explained that he never had sex with this woman because he was too worried that he would not be able to maintain an erection. Larry and other men whose narratives fell into this category relied heavily on hegemonic sexual performance, specifically penetrative sex. They viewed their inability to engage in penetrative sex as a sexual defeat.

Relinquishers described a lack of control over their bodily functions, which not only affected their outward presentation but also how they approached the dating scene. As Kirk explained, the need to perform "bodily maintenance" to prevent bowel and bladder accidents has limited his ability to go on dates with women:

> A lot of the spontaneity of relationships is gone. There's a lot more planning. . . . It's kind of difficult to explain to a woman you're just meeting that, okay, we have to go out at seven, because I have to be home by eleven, because I have something I have to do every night at a certain hour. But, you don't want to go into it. . . . Not the best for starting a relationship. Especially if you're a proud individual and don't want a pity-type situation. . . . It's kind of hard to go into a relationship, yeah, well . . . the way I have to empty my bowels, I got to shove a finger up my ass and twist it around a few times, and I thought getting fingers stuck in my ass before the injury was supposed to be a sexual turn-on, now it's just maintenance.

Kirk, like other men in this group, perceived the loss of control over his body as an obstacle to dating and sexuality and has given up on trying to meet women or engage in sexual relationships. Men in this group held on to idealized aspects of masculinity and saw their inability to meet them as a "failure" on their part, causing them to relinquish their sexual selves.

Discussion and Conclusion

Men who experience SCI in their adult years are constantly battling with their own and others' expectations of masculine performance. The typology presented in this chapter provides a useful framework for understanding how men's sense of agency and ideals of masculinity intersect to influence their sexual trajectories following injury. Some men exhibit great control over their sexual trajectories while others do not see a way to overcome the myriad of internalized stereotypes—strength, sexual prowess, etc.—and external material circumstances—race, class, level of injury, and age—that shape their lives.

Using the life course perspective as a framework, I suggest that there are at least four paths for men's sexual trajectories following SCI. First, men who used Adaptation strategies appeared to be most successful, and satisfied, in their sex lives. Their high level of agentic control offered ways to overcome some of the negative stereotypes facing people with SCI. The men in this group had been injured the longest of any group, so they have had the most opportunities to accumulate postinjury sexual experiences. Additionally, this group consisted of mostly middle- to upper middle-class men and included more black men than other groups. This intersection of race and class has some bearing on how these men experience life after injury. First, they have social and financial resources that put them in positions to meet women. Second, their narratives suggest an adaptation of masculine presentation, perhaps because black men are frequently portrayed and treated as (hyper) masculine in ways that help lessen the effects of having a disability.

Men in the second group with high agency, Performers, are also able to assert control over their sexual trajectories. However, their narratives reflect a high reliance on hegemonic masculine presentation, with emphasis on independence and the desire to appear normal and sexually perfect. Although the men in this group are successful in meeting women and controlling aspects of their relationships, they appear to engage in a good deal of impression management in order to present themselves as "complete men." Performers have been injured for a relatively short period of time compared with Adapters; therefore, they continue to rely on the sexual scripts they had before their injuries. Over time, the cumulative sexual experiences following an injury might result in a narrative shift, either positive or negative, depending on the types of reinforcement these men receive from sexual partners.

Men in the remaining two groups indicate more feelings of powerlessness in relationships. The Conformers were the oldest men in the sample and therefore faced ageist stereotypes about their inability to have or desire sex. Through their interactions with physicians, they have yielded to these stereotypes and have opted out of having sex with their wives. On the upside, their willingness to be flexible in their ideas of sexuality and intimacy has served them well for maintaining caring relationships. On the downside, they perceive the level of care provided by their spouse to be a burden and obstacle to intimacy. Men in the last group, Relinquishers, have internalized many idealized aspects of masculinity—independence, virility, perfection, and strength—but are prevented from meeting these standards in part because of their lack of social and financial resources. Over time, these class constraints and the cumulative processes these men have experienced have resulted in feelings of failed masculinity and these men have, in turn, left the dating marketplace.

Although this is a useful typology for understanding how these men's sexual trajectories are shaped following SCI, this project is not without limitations. First, this project only included the narratives of 20 heterosexual men.

A larger sample with greater variability by race, class, age, or sexual identity might allow for fuller development of the typology. Specifically, how might this typology be different if gay men's narratives were included? Broader questions about race and class also remain, such as how sexual trajectories are altered if we closely examine issues of race or social class alongside other key life course concepts, such as linked lives? For example, examining how caregiving affects couples' sexual trajectories after injury would allow us to explore how giving and receiving care might or might not alter sexuality for couples. This typology shows that race and class matter when examining the intersection of gender and agency, but also leaves room to further understand the various intersectional experiences of people who have sustained traumatic injury.

Beyond this project's specific focus on SCI, I hope this typology will be useful for understanding other aspects of sexuality and/or health across the life course. In general, why do some men demonstrate a greater ability to overcome the physical, emotional, and financial obstacles before them? What is it that results in high levels of agentic control for some people and not for others? And how does perceived control shape one's life course trajectory following other potentially negative life course events, such as illness or the death of a spouse or child? I hope that this project will serve as a valuable starting point for discussing these questions and for possible future research.

NOTES

1. These latter two men's narratives are not included in this analysis; however, their narratives did not differ appreciably from narratives of men with SCI.

2. When a person sustains an injury above the first thoracic vertebra, the diagnosis is quadriplegia and entails some level of paralysis in all four limbs and chest. Those who sustain an injury below this point are diagnosed with paraplegia and will have full use of their arms, but paralysis of their lower limbs and possibly in the chest or abdomen. However, injuries can also be complete or incomplete. Incomplete injuries result in movement, sensation, or muscle response below the level of injury. So it is possible, for example, for a quadriplegic to walk short distances and for a paraplegic to require assistance with coughing due to weak chest muscles.

3. The reason for the injury did not seem to be important for any men. The men in this study were injured from a wide variety of causes ranging from falls during self-induced alcohol/cocaine binges to violence from others. I initially approached issues of agency with the cause of injury in mind, but that analysis did not yield any meaningful results.

4. Social class was determined based on level of education, previous and current occupation, household income, and additional social and financial resources (i.e., insurance settlements). Although most respondents were not currently employed, their previous occupation might continue to provide them with financial stability (i.e., military benefits or disability insurance).

5. All participant names are pseudonyms.

PART V

Sexualities from Midlife to Later Life

11

Reproductive History as Social Context

Exploring How Women Talk about
Menopause and Sexuality at Midlife

HEATHER E. DILLAWAY

Although we typically characterize sexuality through individuals' behaviors (e.g., intercourse, masturbation) or identities (e.g., heterosexual, homosexual, queer, etc.), sexuality can include a wide range of meanings and experiences for individuals across the life course (Weber, 2001). For instance, women at varying life stages must navigate social norms about the types of intimate relationships they should have, appropriate sexual desires and behaviors, how sexy or sexually available they should be, and whether or not they should become biological mothers (Carpenter, 2005; Lee, 1998; Russo, 1976; Lichtenstein, this volume). Social norms shape women's (and men's) perspectives on sexuality, reproduction, and various life stages.

These norms also vary by race or ethnicity, class, and other social locations. For instance, certain racial or ethnic groups are stereotyped as more or less involved in sexual activity, or they have more or less difficulty negotiating infertility and/or ill health because of varying ideas about and experiences of intimate relationships and biological motherhood (Collins, 1990; Wise, Palmer, Stewart, & Rosenberg, 2005). These norms are also gendered, in that specific prescriptions exist about how women should think and behave across their sexual and reproductive life course, relative to men (Schwartz & Rutter, 1998; Tolman, 1994). Power and privilege are distributed to individuals based on their social locations and their involvement in "acceptable" forms of sexuality and reproduction—usually defined by White, middle-class, heterosexual, male experience—as well (Weber, 2001; Collins, 1990; Rich, 1980/1994).

Additionally, according to dominant ideology and popular assumptions, "sexual" people are primarily teenagers and young adults—especially young men—and younger couples (in their teens, twenties, and thirties). As a result, what individuals, especially women, think and do about sexuality during midlife is only partially understood (see also Lichtenstein, this volume). Brim, Ryff, and Kessler (2004, p. 1) further suggest that midlife is the "last uncharted territory" of the life course, in that we have fewer studies of this life stage than any other; even studies of old age are more numerous. Even feminist scholars have failed to confront their own ageism, in that younger women, youthful reproductive processes (e.g., pregnancy, contraceptive use), and youthful sexual identities and experiences have overwhelmingly been their focus until recently (Calasanti, Slevin, & King, 2006). Scholars of gender, sexuality, reproduction, and the life course are obligated to explore more fully how women's sexuality and reproductive experiences manifest at this important life stage.

Because menopause is an important reproductive transition, any study of women's sexuality at midlife must address the meanings of menopause and how menopause might shape sexuality (or vice versa). Narrowly defined, "menopause" refers to the cessation of menstruation; it is caused by the fluctuation of hormone levels within the ovaries and women's bloodstream (Mansfield, Carey, Andersen, Barsom, & Koch, 2004; Martin, 1987). The average age of cessation is around 48–52 years of age, but women in Western countries may end menstruation anywhere between their early forties and late fifties. Further, hormone fluctuations can occur anywhere from 8 to 10 years prior to cessation and for several years afterward (Mansfield et al., 2004). What women experience, then, is a complex reproductive transition that can span multiple decades. Because of the often long-term nature of menopause, some feminist scholars—myself included—have adopted the term "reproductive aging" as the best conceptualization of this process, illustrating its similarity to other, normal, gradual aging processes as well as its ties to previous, gendered reproductive experiences (Dillaway, 2005). Yet we have not fully defined what reproductive aging means in social terms or, more generally, deciphered what women's experiences of midlife are as they experience menopause.

The Baby Boomer generation, born between 1946 and 1964, is the first to have full access to the birth control pill, legal abortion, and other advances in contraceptive technologies that enable women to avoid biological motherhood (Dillaway, 2005). Because contemporary women may no longer identify menopause with the end of fertility or "womanhood," they may think more positively than women in previous generations about menopause and midlife (Dillaway, 2005; Martin, 1992). Likewise, freed from the triple bur-

dens of the threat of pregnancy, birth control, and menstruation, heterosexual women's ideas and experiences of sexuality may become more positive during menopause than in previous life stages (Dillaway, 2005). We also
know that Baby Boomers have successfully carried "youthful" activities into
midlife (Featherstone & Hepworth, 1991) and that women desire and have
sex at midlife (Dillaway, 2005; Lichtenstein, this volume). Biomedical and
epidemiological literature nonetheless also documents women's sexual "dysfunction" at menopause, in that reproductive aging includes some symptoms
that might affect women's sexual desires and behaviors in a negative way
(e.g., vaginal dryness, changes in sexual desire) (Bancroft, Loftus, & Long,
2003; Dillaway, 2005; Martin, 1992). Most everyday contexts for women's
menopause and sexuality experiences remain unexplored, however—both
for Baby Boomers and the cohorts coming after them (i.e., those born in 1965
or after).[1] For instance, we lack knowledge about how previous reproductive
decisions, difficulties, events, and experiences might influence individual
women's views of menopause and midlife, or how they might affect wom-
en's sexuality at this life stage. In light of the gaps in our knowledge, I use
this chapter to explore women's reproductive histories as a social context for
menopause and sexuality experiences at midlife.

Methods

Between 2001 and 2008, I interviewed 98 midwestern women, aged 38 to
65, with most women in their fifties. Women were interviewed if they self-
identified as "menopausal" or "in menopause." The sample was developed
through snowball and purposive sampling procedures (Babbie, 2007). Eight
women participated in two focus groups at the beginning of the study so that
I could check my interview questions and see how women conversed about
certain topics, and another 90 women were interviewed one on one.

A sample profile is presented in table 11.1. To summarize, half of the sample identified as European American or White (50 women). The vast majority of interviewees were employed in paid work. Almost two-thirds (54 of the
81 women reporting educational information) had earned an undergraduate
degree and many (24 women) held a graduate/professional degree. Thirty-
seven women reported family incomes greater than $70,000 and 25 reported
personal incomes greater than $50,000. Based on income, education, and the
professional nature of most interviewees' paid work, this is a "middle-class"
sample. Most women of color described themselves as African American or
Black (35 women). Eight women of color were Latina, two were Asian Amer-

TABLE 11.1
Demographic Characteristics

Age (N = 98)		Individual Income (N = 78)	
35–39	1 (1.0%)	$0–9,999	11 (14.1%)
40–44	6 (6.1%)	$10,000–19,999	7 (9.0%)
45–49	19 (19.3%)	$20,000–29,999	8 (10.3%)
50–54	41 (41.8%)	$30,000–39,999	13 (16.7%)
55–59	23 (23.5%)	$40,000–49,999	14 (17.9%)
60 and over	8 (8.2%)	$50,000–59,999	9 (11.5%)
		$60,000–69,999	4 (5.1%)
		$70,000 and over	12 (15.4%)

Race (N = 98)		Marital Status (N = 91)	
African American	35 (35.7%)	Never Married	6 (6.6%)
Latina	8 (8.2%)	Married[a]	46 (50.5%)
Asian American[b]	2 (2.0%)	Divorced	27 (29.7%)
European American	50 (51%)	Widowed[c]	6 (6.6%)
Other[d]	3 (3.1%)	Domestic Partner[e]	4 (4.4%)
		Separated	2 (2.2%)

Education (N = 81)		Parental Status (N=98)	
Some High School	2 (2.5%)	Biological Parent	82 (83.6%)
High School Diploma	8 (9.9%)	Adoptive/Foster/Step Parent[f]	10 (10.2%)
Some College	17 (20.9%)	No Children	11 (11.2%)
College Diploma	17 (20.9%)		
Some Graduate Work	13 (16.1%)		
Graduate Degree	24 (29.6%)		

ican, and three identified as multiracial. Finally, 93 of the 98 interviewees identified as heterosexual, four as lesbian, and one as bisexual. Thus, findings primarily represent the thoughts and experiences of European American or African American, middle-class, heterosexual women.

At the time of the interviews, approximately one-half (46) were married. Another 27 were currently divorced from at least one marriage.[2] Thirty-three were self-reportedly "single," often actively looking for a romantic partner and/or casually dating at the time of the interview.[3] Many others (19 women),

TABLE 11.1 *(continued)*

Family Income (N = 73)		Stage of Process, Based on Clinical Definition (N = 98)	
$0–9,999	4 (5.5%)	Perimenopausal	45 (45.9%)
$10,000–19,999	3 (4.1%)	Menopausal	3 (3.1%)
$20,000–29,999	6 (8.2%)	Postmenopausal	22 (22.4%)
$30,000–39,999	6 (8.2%)	Hysterectomy	20 (20.4%)
$40,000–49,999	3 (4.1%)	Unknown[g]	8 (8.2%)
$50,000–59,999	7 (9.6%)		
$60,000–69,999	7 (9.6%)		
$70,000 and over	37 (50.7%)		

a. Includes two women who reported they were in their second marriages. I suspect a few other women were also in their second and third marriages (based on the prevalence of divorce and remarriage in the U. S. population overall), but I did not explore this. Nor did I ask how many times women had been divorced.

b. Both were South Asian in descent.

c. Includes one woman who was also formerly divorced.

d. Includes two multiracial women (both African American and Native American) and one West Indian woman.

e. Includes one woman formerly divorced and one woman formerly widowed.

f. Four women were both adoptive and biological parents.

g. Because some women had been on some form of hormonal therapy (HT) since the beginning of perimenopausal symptoms (or even before), it was impossible to tell which stage of the process they exemplified. For two additional women we were unable to gather enough information about their symptoms to determine which clinical definition they might parallel.

including all four lesbians and one bisexual woman, reported being in long-term, committed, and sometimes cohabiting relationships at the time of the interview.[4] The majority (82 women) had biological children; this included two lesbians. Of the parents, approximately one-half still had children under age 18 living at home. Several were helping to raise grandchildren, and two had partial custody of grandchildren. Twenty had experienced surgical menopause (i.e., partial/full hysterectomies).

Focus groups were conducted on a university campus, and each focus group lasted three hours. Individual interviews occurred in private settings, lasting 90 minutes each on average. The interviews represented a "guided conversation" (Rubin & Rubin, 1995). Women first were asked to describe menopause (e.g., signs/symptoms, length of experience, general feelings). Then they were asked about (1) informational resources (e.g., doctors, friends, family members, mass media); (2) contact with biomedical communities; (3) menopause experiences at home and paid work; (4) the impact of social locations (e.g., gender, race, class, sexuality) on menopause; (5) feelings about aging; (6) body image; and (7) current concerns about menopause and midlife. I used an inductive, phenomenological approach throughout data collection, coding, and analysis, in that, as much as possible, I allowed women to explain their lived experiences of menopause and midlife in their own words. The analysis presented here focuses on how women's reproductive histories form a backdrop for their conversations about sexuality and intimate relationships at menopause. Additional themes related to women's reproductive choices and relationships are reported elsewhere (Dillaway, 2005, 2008).

Findings

Women's reproductive histories operate as a social context for menopause in two ways. First, earlier reproductive experiences—for example, negotiating contraception or getting through a miscarriage—can represent physical and emotional work that eventually affects women's attitudes and experiences of menopause and sexuality at midlife. Second, reproductive histories tell a story about women's decisions about biological motherhood, and these decisions may likewise alter perceptions and experiences of menopause.

Freedom from Reproductive "Burdens"

Feminist scholars have looked at how relief from the reproductive "burdens" of menstruation, contraception, and the threat of pregnancy lead women (especially heterosexual women) to think positively about menopause. In this context, menopause represents "freedom" from a gendered life of reproduction, and it is a time within which women can define themselves as *separate from* reproduction (Dillaway, 2005). Indeed, in about half of my interviews, lengthy and often unprompted discussions of women's excitement over sex at midlife arose. Although the availability of contraceptive technology brought reproductive freedom in theory, menopause brought freedom in practice. Speaking about the threat of pregnancy, two women explained:

[Menopause] was quite freeing to me because, you know, after you've got your children, then there is danger of children. . . . [*laughs*] [European American, middle-class, married, heterosexual, aged 61, six children]

It's like the total opposite from before menopause. Mexicans say that, after age 50, sex gets better because it doesn't make you pregnant. . . . When I got my period, I was glad to know the lady. But I was glad for menopause too. I wanted to be done. [Mexican American, working-class, married, heterosexual, aged 57, three children]

One divorced, heterosexual, middle-class, European American woman, aged 55, with two children, suggested that a new lack of attention to contraception meant that "it's kind of coming to the end of an era. . . . Hell, you can have sex all the time without doing anything! You can do whatever you want to!"[5] A married, heterosexual, middle-class African American woman, aged 54, with two children, also told me that her husband has trouble "keeping up" with her sexual desire: "Not having to [contracept] makes it a lot easier for heaven's sake. . . . He wouldn't have anything to complain about . . . just freedom. [I'm] a wild woman [*laughs*]."

Heterosexual interviewees frequently discussed their sexual selves this way, highlighting that sex after menopause is exciting and more desirable because it is easier and less worrisome. Women of color in my sample were more likely to mention explicitly that they desired sexual activity more upon menopause; but this finding may not represent racial/ethnic differences in sexuality as much as differences in willingness to disclose information. The African Americans I spoke with may have simply been more blunt about sexual desire than the European Americans.

Several interviewees also discussed being relieved to be done with menstruation, without explicitly referring to (yet inferring the continuation of) sex.

I decided that it was safer for me to have a tubal [ligation at age 35]. . . . I would have liked to have either two kids or four kids but I was getting pretty old to have four kids. . . . So, therefore, the bleeding . . . is just a pain in the ass . . . you know, I've been there, got my kids! [*laughs*] And, um, onward. Without the bother. [European American, middle-class, married, heterosexual, aged 48, two children]

Whether or not these interviewees explicitly made reference to sexual activity or sexual desire when talking about the lifting of reproductive burdens, most still clearly contradict equations of menopause and asexuality. They also illustrate how women's perceptions of menopause and sexuality at midlife are linked to their understandings of their own reproductive histories.

Although recent feminist research has begun to document that midlife and older women are interested in and engaged in sexual activity (DeLamater & Moorman, 2007; Dillaway, 2005; Winterich, 2003; Lichtenstein, this volume), the extent to which women's feelings about sex are also intimately connected to their understandings of their previous (and current) reproductive experiences is still a new, fairly unexplored finding. The picture is more complicated still, however, in that women have varied reproductive experiences over their lifetimes that include more than just pregnancy, birth, contraception, and menstruation. These reproductive experiences can be both negative and positive at the same time.

Reproductive Difficulties Create Mixed Feelings

Unprompted by interview questions, about one-third of the women in this study discussed previous reproductive difficulties, such as miscarriage and infertility.[6] In all cases, women cast their stories of reproductive difficulties in a negative light, in order to contextualize their feelings about menopause. Yet, depending on the context surrounding these burdens, menopause itself could be seen positively or negatively. In some cases, women talked about reproductive difficulties right alongside their more "normal" reproductive experiences, in order to stress what they saw as the extremely positive aspects of reproductive aging. For example:

> I've had altogether eight pregnancies, and I've delivered four, miscarried two, and aborted two. I was like a jack rabbit, so . . . I would say, "Don't look at me, or I'll get pregnant." So [menopause] was a relief. [African American, working-class, single, heterosexual, aged 52, four children]

Miscarriage and abortion were additional reproductive burdens that made this woman even more positive about reaching menopause. Other women in the sample, especially African American interviewees, reported that reproductive difficulties like miscarriages just made them "stronger" (tougher) and, therefore, better able to handle the ups and downs of menopause.

> [HD: Why has menopause been positive for you?] Some women are just stronger than others. I'm strong. [HD: Can you tell me more?] Well, I've had five miscarriages. [African American, middle-class, single, heterosexual, aged 50, one child]

Menopause became positive for women in the context of past reproductive difficulties and experiences, illustrating that, although some reproductive experiences (e.g., conception, pregnancy) can or "should" be positive, other reproductive experiences can be quite trying sometimes, especially when women's bodies do not act according to the women's plans. Within the context of previous, difficult reproductive experiences, menopause pales in importance.

Comments about how "easy," "stupid," "no big deal," or "fine" menopause was often arose in conversations with European American women who had experienced infertility, which they described as "hard" or "tough." One woman, who experienced one miscarriage and several years of infertility treatments, was happy to reach menopause because it meant she would soon be done with her reproductive "roller coaster ride":

> I didn't have my son until I was 40. I had gone through about 3 and a half years of just awful fertility work-up stuff, and then tried to have another baby, you know, about a year afterwards and . . . I got pregnant and it lasted all of four weeks. . . . And you finally just say, you know, this was not meant to be . . . [*long sigh*]. . . . I really don't have any negative connotations about going through [menopause], because I'm realizing I've probably been infertile my whole life . . . . I'll just be glad to be done with this, you know, roller coaster ride. [European American, middle-class, divorced, heterosexual, aged 52, one child]

Another woman, a "DES daughter,"[7] scoffed and told me that "menopause is stupid" and "dumb" compared to earlier reproductive trials.

> I was a DES baby . . . that's why I was unable to carry a child to full term. . . . I was able to get pregnant with the doctor and artificial insemination with my husband as the donor, but then I had two miscarriages and two tubal pregnancies. And the first tubal pregnancy was massive, I almost lost my life and I had extensive surgery. [European American, middle-class, married, heterosexual, aged 52, two adopted children]

In light of their difficult reproductive pasts, women were indifferent or positive toward menopause.

Discussions of past reproductive difficulties also arose as women tried to justify negative feelings about menopause. For a handful of interviewees, reproductive difficulties like miscarriages or infertility paralleled the beginning stages of perimenopause. A middle-class, married, heterosexual, 48-year-old European American mother of two exemplifies this group:

Until I had that miscarriage or miscarriage/abortion, um, nothing bad has ever happened to me. . . . Anything I wanted to do, I pretty much did. . . . And when I hit 40 and I lost, you know, this baby . . . things . . . got harder. . . . So . . . I see the negatives [about menopause] too [as well as the positives].

As I discuss more fully below, feelings about current and past reproductive experiences cannot always be separated from decisions that women and their partners make about whether to become parents or how many children they will bear.

The interviewees who were the most open about talking about sexual activity and their "better" sex lives reported the most positive feelings about menopause, as evidenced by the first section of findings above. Nonetheless, women quoted in this second section of findings are telling us about various aspects of their sexuality, even without being explicit. For instance, some are telling us about their choices to continue trying to conceive (and, therefore, about their participation in certain kinds of intimate relationships and behaviors). Tellingly, though, women who reported feeling negatively about menopause, especially in the face of past reproductive difficulties, seemed less comfortable with sexuality as an interview topic. Because I did not ask extremely pointed questions about women's sex lives (because these interviews were really about menopause) and I do not know the effects of my own social locations[8] on interviewees' willingness to converse about sexual topics, I cannot conclude definitively about the reasons for the presence or absence of women's talk about sexuality. Based on my interviews, though, I propose that menopausal women who were dissatisfied or disappointed with their reproductive histories may not have been as ready or willing to talk about sex, because of the associations they make between their sexual activity and their desires for or pursuit of procreation. Future research should explore how women with reproductive difficulties talk about their relationships and sexual lives, so that these possibilities are explored more fully.

"I'm Done Having Kids"

Another major reason why some interviewees might feel purely positive about menopause and feel "free" when reproductive "burdens" are lifted is that they were self-declaredly "done" with childbearing. Thus, discussions about menopause and sexuality at midlife must be put into the context of whether women feel finished with childbearing. A focus group conversation illustrates one of the ways in which women I interviewed talked about being "done." Both of these women were European American, middle-class, and heterosexual, and each had one child. Participant #1 was aged 52 and married and Participant #2 was aged 59 and divorced at the time of the interview.

> PARTICIPANT #1: I find it really interesting that women in their late forties and early fifties are trying to have babies in their second and third marriages. Now, for me, . . . I mean, I decided I wasn't going to have any more children and was still having periods, I mean, it [menstruation] just seemed like a useless thing at that point. . . .
>
> PARTICIPANT #2: You almost wanna say you want to stop it right now. . . .
> [All three focus group participants talk at once, agreeing with Participant #2.]
> PARTICIPANT #1: Well, you look at these women right now who are, in my opinion, trying to . . . deny biology and . . . start second families. And I'm free now [but] my daughter's not. I'm a grandmother and I, I love that experience and . . . why would people my age, 52, . . . wanna start over? No. [Everyone laughs.] And I'm thinking, "What are these women thinking?" [Everyone laughs again.] . . . . I was 19 when I had my daughter, [and my daughter] was 31 when she had her son, so there's a change from my generation to hers. . . . [M]y husband and I [can] come home from work and [decide] that we want to do something stupid like drive to [a city 65 miles away] for dinner. [W]e have the freedom to do that so why would we want to have a baby? [Everyone laughs.] . . .

These focus group participants bore children by their early twenties and had established paid work for themselves only after their children were of school age. Thus, for these women—whose experiences are typical of the older half of the Baby Boomer cohort—the fact that they still menstruated and still could become pregnant in their fifties was burdensome. Neither of these women reported early reproductive difficulties, such as miscarriage or infertility. Menopause was positive because it released them from their "useless" reproductive capacity. Although the above conversation does not explicitly discuss sexual activity, it does illuminate the fact that a husband and wife have more "freedom" to take their relationship in nonprocreative directions after menopause.

Another middle-class, married, heterosexual, European American mother of two, aged 54, simply declared, "Either you're done having a family or you're not done. There's a difference." These women (self-proclaimed Baby Boomers) consciously acknowledge their "difference" from the next cohort of menopausal women (daughters of the Baby Boomers) or from women in their own generation (perhaps the younger half of the Baby Boom) who delayed childbearing.

Other interviewees commented similarly about the end of reproductive capacity, but these feelings were brought on by varied reproductive histories. For instance, the first woman quoted below was concerned about increasing population growth and believed that she was engaging in positive social change by forgoing childbearing. The second woman bore one daughter but did not want to define herself via mothering and promptly finalized her childbearing.

> [If] I still can have kids, this could be a problem. I'm a zero population advocate. As a matter of fact . . . I am in favor of . . . hysterectomies at a certain age as an elective surgery. I would love to stop bleeding. [European American, middle-class, divorced, bisexual, aged 50, no children]

> I was glad to get rid of the periods. . . .I'm really not a mothering person type. . . . I only had one child and I adore her, I didn't have ambition to have more. When she turned 5, my husband had a vasectomy. . . . And it didn't bother me at all. . . . Right now I don't have the desire to have grand-kids even. . . . I don't mind them, but don't force 'em on me [*laughs*]. [European American, middle-class, married, heterosexual, aged 56, one child]

These two women felt positively about menopause and were satisfied with their current intimate relationships because they either had completed their childbearing before reaching menopause or had voluntarily opted out of biological parenthood.

Some women in this sample reported *not* being done with having children, or being ambivalent about the end of reproduction, however, and their comments reveal women's mixed or negative feelings about menopause along similar lines as some women's comments about reproductive difficulties.

Not Done Having Kids?

One of the clear themes that came up among both mothers and nonmothers in this sample is the idea that menopausal women do not always identify themselves as being "done" with childbearing before the onset of menopause. Some interviewees delayed childbearing and only started having children in their thirties and forties. This meant that some were physically "done" at the time of the interview because of the onset of reproductive aging, but they did not really want to be finished (both emotionally and in terms of life goals). A few other women had never actively made the decision to stop having children (even if, in some cases, it was more than 10 or 15 years since their last childbearing experience). For these women, the onset of menopause made it feel like they never got to finalize their decision themselves—the onset of menopause took that final decision out of their hands.

Additionally, some heterosexual women bore one or two children in an earlier life stage and then divorced and remarried, which made them rethink their earlier decisions about being "done" with childbearing. Others—including one lesbian—had never had children but were rethinking their decision at the time of menopause; thus, interview conversations about not being "done" were not confined to those in heterosexual relationships. A few women came to question whether they were truly done when they became pregnant accidentally during perimenopause. At base, decisions to start or stop having kids, or to prioritize careers or other responsibilities over having kids, were not always clear-cut or planned in full. Although the woman quoted below had completed childbearing at the time of the interview because of her menopausal status, her conversation illustrates some initial uncertainty about this status. Her ambivalence about being "done" with childbearing was exacerbated by a miscarriage experience.

> I think menopause is made worse by other things in our lives. . . . [A]t 45, I got pregnant again. . . . I only carried the baby a couple of months and I knew from the beginning that's probably all I would. That was kind of a hard thing to deal with, because I knew my body wasn't functioning like it was supposed to anymore so there probably were not going to be any more children, and here I'd lost the last one I had a chance to have. But I was more excited overall not to have my period anymore and not to have to worry about getting pregnant, and [to be] able to get on with my own life. [European American, middle-class, married, heterosexual, aged 55, six children]

Miscarriage confirmed for this woman that her body was no longer "functioning like it was supposed to anymore," and, therefore, miscarriage and then menopause presented her with a final verdict about whether or not she was finished with childbearing. Although she eventually came to see menopause as positive, she was initially unwilling to think of herself as "done." In the context of indecision about whether or not one is "done" having children, late miscarriages could lead to questioning of earlier decisions and, initially, a more negative perspective on menopause.

Another woman who thought that she and her husband did not want any children began to rethink her decision after she underwent a hysterectomy in her late forties (because of fibroids and heavy bleeding) and then the symptoms of menopause. (Whether her husband also rethought this decision was unclear from our interview.)

[W]e thought briefly about having kids, [but] we were real concerned with the population of the planet . . . and we try to be real responsible people. He . . . is really, um, socially aware and so we decided, well, if we ever want a kid, we'll adopt. . . . I thought about being a foster parent 'cause I really miss having kids around. . . . I don't have to make my own from my own body. . . . I very briefly thought about it not too long ago, that, "Oh, I'll never have my own kid." . . . Oh, well. [European American, middle-class, married, heterosexual, aged 47, no children]

A newly married, perimenopausal woman revealed feelings about her current childlessness:

This is my first time being married and I do think about [having kids]. If I'm going to have some kids [then I have very little time]. . . . [My husband] has two kids already, from his first marriage. . . . My mother was telling me on the phone to go ahead and adopt some kids. . . . My mom had kids when she was almost 40 but . . . she had had [children when she was younger]. . . . [W]omen say they've had kids late, [but] . . . [t]hey weren't just starting out. [African American, middle-class, married, heterosexual, aged 46, no children]

These stories illustrate how a relationship or reproductive change potentially can affect how women perceive reproductive aging and sexuality at midlife.

Many African American women, in particular those who had experienced (or contemplated) hysterectomies, also talked about fearing what men might think of them if they were unable to have children in the future. That is, depending on men's reproductive goals, menopause (surgical or nonsurgical) could be problematic for heterosexual intimate relationships. A working-class, single, heterosexual, African American woman, aged 47, with one adult son, was contemplating a hysterectomy at the time of the interview, and she said, "I just think that . . . there are still men out there [who] want babies . . . and if I was menopausal then they know definitely that I'm not the one [laughs]."

Finally, a few women discussed delaying childbearing until it was "too late" and/or reported that menopause came "earlier" than expected.

[Al]though I was 40 [at the onset of perimenopause] I had still considered with a partner being artificially inseminated. . . . So . . . [that] contributed [to feeling badly about menopause] 'cause I, I didn't do it. . . . My childbearing years are gone . . . a lot earlier [than expected]. . . . [A] lot of women supposedly go through menopause . . . and, lo and behold, they get pregnant. But [after] having ultrasounds done . . . I knew I wasn't ovulating anymore. [European American, middle-class, lesbian, domestic partnership, aged 52, no children]

Reaching perimenopause around age 40 made this woman feel like she had been cheated out of biological motherhood because, in her mind, she had only temporarily delayed childbearing, until she and her partner reached a point when they would decide to have children. Another woman who was diagnosed with "early menopause" after experiencing infertility in her early thirties wondered why she had waited so long to have children. Although she seemed somewhat numb to her reproductive history during the interview, her comments still illuminate how frustrating her reproductive experiences were.

I felt as if my body had deceived me. I felt cheated, like, really it's 10 or 15 years shaved off my reproductive life. I just kind of felt like my body was dying inside. [HD: Do you still feel that way?] No. That was . . . more so when I was faced with the infertility issues. Then I really felt cheated, and kind of like I'd missed my opportunity. I started second guessing, like, "Why did I wait so long to try to have kids?" [European American, middle-class, married, heterosexual, aged 38, two children]

This woman was one of the most negative of all of my interviewees about menopause, because of how "blindsided" she felt by infertility. When her body "deceived" her, she spun into action and spent considerable time, effort, and money in order to conceive two children with the help of new reproductive technologies. She was now raising two preschool-aged children, but she still felt resentful toward her body, infertility, and menopause. In addition, she was dealing with relationship problems because infertility had strained her marriage.

Although most interviewees did not report relationship trouble as a direct result of past or current reproductive difficulties, all of the women quoted in this section hinted at an inability to share their feelings about their reproductive histories and menopause with their current partners. Without mentioning it directly, some also inferred that their attitude about how "done" they were with childbearing differed from that of their partners. In keeping with the concept of "linked lives" (Moen, Robison, & Dempster-McClain, 1995), then, women's feelings about reproductive difficulties and about being "done" or "not done" may be affected by the well-being of intimate relationships and the expectations and experiences of intimate partners, and vice versa. This possibility should be explored in future studies.

Overall, various reproductive trajectories and relationship statuses affected whether or not and how women felt "done" with childbearing. A few women in my sample simply reached menopause and retrospectively rethought their "decisions" to be "done" having kids (e.g., "Did I have the number of kids I wanted?" or "Did I really want to be childfree?"). Others experienced relationship transitions (e.g., divorce, remarriage, newly formed dating relationships, recent singlehood, or recent cohabitation) and rethought whether they desired to be done with biological motherhood. For some women, however, indecision about being "done" was related to delayed childbearing, late miscarriage, or early perimenopause. Some, but by no means all, of the women in my sample explicitly talked about how this affected their sexual lives. Ultimately, these data infer that women (and, at times, their partners) feel that they *should* have children, ideally through biological sexual reproduction, and that satisfying relationships are ones that produce (or at least involve) children; this finding parallels literature about the pressure that all women—even lesbians—feel to pursue motherhood (Russo, 1976; Mamo, 2007; Mezey, 2008).

What were unexpected were the numerous, indefinite, noncommittal, and/or wavering comments made by menopausal women about being "done" with childbearing. Such comments suggest that many women may not make an active decision about being "done"; rather, they simply reach a point in their reproductive or relationship lives that determines their "choice" for them (or at least that makes them rethink whether they made a choice). This may mean that the equation of sexual activity and reproduction is never really severed and that, even upon reaching midlife and menopause, heterosexual women still think about sex as a procreative activity, especially in the face of a new intimate relationship or relationship change, past and present reproductive difficulties, or delayed childbearing. Yet conversations about childbearing arose alongside conversations about menopause and midlife among lesbians in this sample as well, demonstrating that sexual identities and relationship statuses do not determine women's feelings about biological parenthood in simple or straightforward ways. More research on women's decisiveness (or indecisiveness) about the completion of childbearing should be undertaken, especially in light of a "lesbian baby boom" paralleling the trends of delayed childbearing and increasing infertility (Mamo, 2007; Mezey, 2008).

Conclusions

This chapter used unprompted, qualitative interview data to outline a seldom-considered social context—women's reproductive histories—for understanding menopause and sexuality at midlife. I specifically analyzed the ways in which women's attitudes and experiences of menopause and sexuality at midlife are affected by earlier reproductive experiences (both positive and negative), as well as by their decisions (and indecisions) about biological motherhood.

A systematic analysis of interview data allows us to see that women's feelings about sexuality and menopause during midlife stem from the cumulative influence of reproductive and sexual experiences across the life course. Indeed, when asked about menopause, women in this study would first tell me about previous reproductive experiences and only then about menopause. It is almost as though most women think about their reproductive experiences in a cumulative and recursive way, interpreting current reproductive and sexual experience only by going back through past experiences in their minds. Consequently, understanding the reasons why women feel certain ways about sexuality and/or reproduction at menopause and midlife may be hard—if not impossible—to decipher without paying attention to their entire life course.

These data also show that menopause occurs concurrently, or in relation to, other reproductive, relationship, and sexual experiences. Instances in which women have miscarriages during perimenopausal stages indicate that some menopausal/midlife women may not feel finished with childbearing at midlife and that multiple reproductive events/processes coincide or overlap. Not only can contraceptive use, pregnancy, miscarriage, and infertility overlap with the menopausal transition, but also women may have other reproductive "disruptions" during or even after menopause (e.g., fibroids, cancers, hysterectomies, endometriosis).[9] These experiences and their meanings may make women feel more positive, more indifferent, or more negative about menopause and sexuality, depending on the specific situation, and we need to leave room in our future analyses to flush out these variations. Based on my tentative findings, we also know that the meaning and impact, positive or negative, of particular types of past and concurrent reproductive experiences on interviewees' lives might not always wane as completely over time as some of the biomedical literature about psychological distress suggests (Lasker & Toedter, 2000). We do not have long-term, life course studies of women's reproductive experiences and their impacts, negative or positive, and we need to encourage them.

Attention to social location only makes the importance of previous and concurrent reproductive experience more poignant, as certain groups are more likely to report certain reproductive events or difficulties. For instance, African American interviewees reported many more hysterectomies than European American interviewees, as well as increased occurrences of fibroids (the main reason why African American women might have increased rates of hysterectomies [Wise et al., 2005]). Conversely, European Americans in my sample reported more experiences of (diagnosed) infertility than African Americans. European American women were also more likely to report that they were "done" with childbearing, even if they had not had a hysterectomy. Based on mostly unprompted reports, however, European American and African American women in this study seemed to have similar rates of biological motherhood and similar rates of miscarriage. These similarities and differences by race or ethnicity should be confirmed with larger, more heterogeneous samples.

Changes in relationship status and/or specific relationship situations also mattered, in that some women in this sample were in long-term marriages or other committed relationships at midlife whereas others were getting married for the first time, divorcing, remarrying, entering domestic partnerships, dating, or becoming newly single. Based on my analysis, these relationship statuses and relationship changes form a context for how women interpret and live out their menopause experiences and how they think about their reproductive histories. Finally, and closely related, age at first childbearing (if already a biological mother) also mattered, as interviewees who bore children earlier rather than later were more likely to think they were "done" with childbearing and were less likely to report infertility problems. Ultimately, reproductive, sexuality, and relationship experiences intertwine with individuals' social locations across the life course in ways that are quite complex, and relationship and sexuality experiences are as cumulative, recursive, and concurrent as reproductive experiences are.

Barbre (1993) suggests we are experiencing a "Menoboom" with the aging of the Baby Boomers; thus, the study of menopause and sexuality at midlife is extremely relevant. In writing this chapter, however, I realize just how complicated reproductive history is as a social context for women's experiences of menopause, sexuality, or midlife. Much conceptual and empirical work remains to be done on the meanings and experiences of reproduction and sexuality at any one life stage, let alone on how reproduction and sexuality are intertwined across the life course.

NOTES

The author thanks Rita Gallin, Maxine Baca Zinn, Susan Bell, and anonymous reviewers for suggestions on earlier drafts. She additionally thanks the 98 women who were interviewed for this study.

1. Menopause and sexuality experiences at midlife may be different for Baby Boomers than other generations. For instance, rising infertility rates due to delayed childbearing (Greil, 1991) could create unique meanings of menopause for women born in 1965 or after. Cohort comparisons should be explored in future research.

2. The numbers ever experiencing divorce in the sample were higher, however, because a few others reported "marriage" as their current status but did not have a chance to designate a second or third marriage. In addition, two divorced women identified first as lesbians and reported being in domestic partnerships and one other reported being divorced and then widowed. Thus, during interview conversations, women often reported prior marriages and divorces. For many interviewees, both relationship status and sexual identity changed over time (see also Lichtenstein, this volume).

3. This includes most divorced women in the sample (n = 25), as well as some women who were widowed (n = 6) and never married (n = 2).

4. These women also reported other relationship statuses at the same time, however, such as "never married," "divorced," or "widowed," indicating just how complicated a relationship status can be for individuals at any given moment. In addition, I did not ask whether they were currently in a relationship, so this number is undoubtedly underestimated.

5. Whether this woman is inferring participation in risky sexual behaviors (e.g., unprotected sex, multiple partners, and more casual partners than in previous life stages) is unknown. Lichtenstein (this volume) discusses this topic more extensively.

6. Other women also discussed having difficult hysterectomies, fibroids, abortions, endometriosis, ectopic (tubal) pregnancies, breast cancer, and problems with birth control. Here I concentrate on miscarriage and infertility due to space constraints.

7. This woman received prenatal exposure to DES (diethylstilbestrol), "a synthetic estrogen prescribed to pregnant women to prevent miscarriage" (Bell & Apfel, 1995, p. 3). Bell (2009, p. 17) suggests that as many as "five to ten million pregnant women and their fetuses were exposed to DES" in the early 1940s and 1950s. DES daughters have many health problems because of this exposure, including reproductive cancers and infertility.

8. I am European American, middle-class, and heterosexual. I was in my early thirties, unmarried, with no children during earlier interviews, yet during later interviews I was in my mid-thirties and married with children. During my last year of interviews, I was obviously pregnant and this may have affected some conversations as well.

9. Some of these overlaps may be becoming more common than in previous years, as individuals increasingly delay marriage and childbearing and engage in relationship dissolution and re-coupling at midlife.

12

Sexual Expression
over the Life Course

Results from Three Landmark Surveys

ANIRUDDHA DAS, LINDA J. WAITE,
AND EDWARD O. LAUMANN

Although sexuality studies have become increasingly mainstream over the last two decades, large-sample research has only lately picked up steam. Moreover, most social demographic studies still focus on isolated facets of the overall sexual experience, such as sexual precocity, victimization, and dysfunctions and/or on specific segments of the life trajectory. Absent a comprehensive theoretical model of sexuality over the life course, the "global" significance of such isolated findings becomes hard to interpret. In this chapter, we delineate just such a theoretical model, based on observed patterns from three landmark surveys.

Large-sample sexuality studies have typically concentrated on younger ages, with an implicit conception of adolescence as an "entrainment" period. Social and biological events at this juncture are thought to embed a person in a sexual career that—whether due to path dependency or structural pressures—remains relatively fixed thereafter. Analysis of such entrainment processes has been greatly facilitated by nationally representative longitudinal surveys such as the National Longitudinal Study of Adolescent Health. However, these studies offer little guidance on socially triggered branching points later in one's sexual career.[1] Sexual expression and partnership in late life remain underexplored, and comparative studies with other age groups are lacking. Moreover, despite the partnered nature of much of sexuality, the extant literature remains predominantly focused on *individual* behavioral patterns. Finally, the role of social embeddedness in shaping sexual practices and meanings has yet to be fully recognized.

We base our inferences on three landmark surveys, starting with the nationally representative 1992 National Health and Social Life Survey

(NHSLS), the first population-based study of sex among U.S. adults aged 18 to 59 (Laumann, Gagnon, Michael, & Michaels, 1994) and our main data source for the first decades of one's sexual career. Of those sampled, 3,225 people (1,814 women, 1,411 men) completed the interview, yielding a response rate of 78.6%—with large subsamples of both Blacks (317 women, 189 men) and Hispanics (171 women, 127 men). The interview included initial face-to-face responses to an interviewer and later modules on sensitive issues (such as masturbation), in which participants read and answered the questions themselves. Most interviewers were experienced personnel who were given further training by the National Opinion Research Center (NORC) in Chicago.

Sexual patterns in late life are extracted from the 2005–2006 U.S. National Social Life, Health, and Aging Project (NSHAP). The first population-based study of sexuality, health, and social life among older U.S. adults, NSHAP is nationally representative of those aged 57 to 85 (Lindau, Schumm, Laumann, Levinson, O'Muircheartaigh, & Waite, 2007). The sample included 1,550 women and 1,455 men, with an oversampling of Blacks (285 women, 224 men), Hispanics (150 women, 154 men), men, and those aged 75 to 85. In-home interviews of household-dwelling adults in these age ranges were conducted between July 2005 and March 2006 by trained interviewers. The survey had a response rate of 75.5%.

Finally, we use the 29-country Global Study of Sexual Attitudes and Behaviors (GSSAB)—restricted to respondents aged 40 to 80—to cover overlapping NSHAP and NHSLS age groups (Nicolosi, Laumann, Glasser, Moreira, Paik, & Gingell, 2004). Specifically, we base inferences on the GSSAB subsample (1,845 women, 2,205 men) from the English-speaking "Non-European West" (Australia, Canada, New Zealand, South Africa, and the United States). The combination of these three surveys allows us to characterize sexual patterns across the adult life course. Additionally, given the study periods and age ranges, there is substantial overlap between the birth cohorts represented in the NHSLS and in NSHAP. Hence, our exploration resembles a synthetic cohort or quasi-panel analysis. It should be noted, however, that these are distinct cross-sectional surveys and not waves in a single longitudinal study. In other words, they do not represent information on the same individuals over time. Although we use these data to infer life course patterns, they admittedly represent synthetic, and not actual, life trajectories.

Notably, our definitions of "sex" and "sexual activity" are rather broad in order to avoid an overly normative focus on vaginal-penile intercourse (see also Loe, this volume). Instead, the NHSLS defined sex as "any mutually voluntary activity with another person that involves genital contact and sexual excitement or arousal, that is, feeling really turned on, even if intercourse or orgasm did not occur" (Das & Laumann, 2010), with a similar but condensed definition used in NSHAP. This definition covers same-gender as well as heterosexual activity. However, subsample sizes for people with same-gender sexual experiences are too small to allow separate analysis or comparisons with heterosexual activity. For instance, less than 2% of NHSLS participants, and less than 1% of those in NSHAP, report a current same-gender partner. Although we include these partnerships in our analysis, our inferences admittedly apply largely to heterosexual partnerships.

Theoretical Overview

Our theoretical approach centers on three themes: first, a conception of the sexual career as a continuous process of stabilization and change; second, an emphasis on the sexual dyad rather than on individual patterns alone; and third, a network-theoretic model of the role of social "alters" in shaping sexual patterns.

Temporal Structure

As noted, many studies of sexuality imply a channeling or entrainment process. *Stress process* and *social entrainment* models both emphasize the role of early life events as "triggers"—or turning points—that place an individual in a particular type of sexual career. For instance, the literature on pubertal timing suggests that early puberty leads to a more sexualized life trajectory; this may be due to variations in hormone levels or to functioning as a "pull factor" for sexual attention (Moffit, Caspi, Belsky, & Silva, 1992; Udry, 1988). A growing literature also indicates that events such as sexual contact in childhood may channel people into life pathways marked by both greater sexual precocity and subsequent sexual victimization (Browning & Laumann, 1997; Das, 2009; Carbone-Lopez, this volume). This conception of adolescence as a critical "branching point" is also implicit in the general life course literature, with regard to topics like delinquency and substance abuse (Hagan and Foster, 2003; Ramrakha, Bell, Paul, Dickson, Moffitt, & Caspi, 2007).

While not denying the structural relevance of adolescence, we argue that processes later in one's sexual career may also have substantial influence on subsequent trajectories. For instance, roughly 13% of NHSLS women report some form of adult-child sexual contact before puberty (reanalysis of NHSLS raw data; also Browning & Laumann, 1997). Those who do are somewhat more likely than those without such experiences to report low sexual desire (21% vs. 17%) and low levels of happiness (19% vs. 13%). Bigger discrepancies are evident for sexual behavior: 33% of these women (vs. 15% of those non-victimized) report nine or more sexual partners since age 18. The vast majority of victimized women, however, have "normal" sexual careers, suggesting a *progressive* entrainment process, wherein factors later in life channel victimized women differentially into life pathways (Browning & Laumann, 1997, 2003). Therefore, in contrast to the adolescence-centric approach, we advocate a "punctuated equilibrium" model of the sexual career—that is, a sequence of stabilizations and branching points, potentially occurring at any stage of life, and catalyzed by "local" opportunities and constraints (Butts & Pixley, 2004; Gotlib & Wheaton, 1997; see also chapter 1).

Accordingly, we use data from all three surveys to track patterns for a set of key indicators—frequent sexual thoughts, masturbation, and partnered sex—across the life trajectory, and to compare age and cohort interpretations. We also elaborate on some structuring processes that underlie observed patterns, including physical condition, the availability of a partner, beliefs about sex, and one's social network.

The Sexual Dyad

As noted, sexuality research remains predominantly focused on the individual. Lost in this conception is the notion of sex as a transaction, and the role of the dyad—the partnership—in structuring sexual patterns. The most obvious of these influences is through reduced opportunities for partnered sex among those who lose partners, whether through divorce or widowhood (Lindau et al., 2007). Moreover, as we explain below, the acquisition of new partners decreases with age, leading to an increasing tendency toward long-term monogamy. Relationship attributes are a second major influence. Central to our overarching model, therefore, is the conception of sexuality as a jointly produced outcome, dependent on each partner's characteristics and the nature of the partnership itself. Especially with long-term couples, the specific complex of behaviors that defines a sexual act is often the result of an extended negotiation process and of compromises between each partner's expectations and conceptions regarding sex. Such an emergent consensus is also likely to be affected by asymmetries in power within the relationship, as determined not simply by broad gender ideologies (although they certainly matter), but also by "local" factors such as relative physical capacity, income, and social ties. As with individual patterns, dyad-level consensus is subject to change—such as when one partner's age-related sexual incapacities necessitate a renegotiation of mutual responsibilities and practices, or when partners disagree about the necessity or appropriateness of sex with increasing age.

The Stakeholder Network

A key feature of our model is an emphasis on social embeddedness—both of the individual and of the partnership. One consequence of age-related physical incapacities is an increased dependence on close friends and family (Antonucci & Akiyama, 1995; Hurlbert, Haines, & Beggs, 2000). This dynamic, in turn, enhances the monitoring and control capacities of one's network members, who function as "stakeholders" in a person's choices and behaviors (Ellingson, Laumann, Paik, & Mahay, 2004). Social embeddedness, in other words, carries with it normative constraints on permissible behavior. At younger ages, we expect this process to constrain practices such as risky sexual behavior and extramarital sex, and to enhance the likelihood of long-term monogamous relationships (Laumann et al., 1994). Such network influences also may vary across social groups. For instance, studies suggest that kinship ties are closer among Black (Staples & Johnson, 1993; Taylor, Chatters, Tucker, & Lewis, 1991), Hispanic (Lopez et al., 2004; Mulvaney-Day, Alegria, & Sribney, 2007), as well as Asian (Chung, 1991; Ross-Sheriff, 1991) women than among their White counterparts. The degree of stakeholder intervention that is considered acceptable also varies across sociocultural groups. Finally, norms enforced by one's social network tend to be culturally distinctive, such as a greater acceptability of extramarital sex for Hispanic men than women (Ellingson, 2004).

Especially among women, who tend to partner with men several years older than themselves (England & McClintock, 2009; Mahay & Laumann, 2004), increasing age enhances the likelihood of partner loss. As we argue below, this "age hypergamy" also leads to a gender asymmetry in one's opportunities in the partnership market in later life, leaving a large proportion of older women without stable partners. By constraining the search for new partners, fear of disapproval from stakeholders can further enhance this negative dynamic.

In the sections below, we use data from our three surveys—the NHSLS, GSSAB, and NSHAP—to support these theoretical arguments.

Sex over the Life Course
Race Differentials

Our analysis suggests strong race differentials for all three of our key indicators: frequent sexual thoughts, masturbation, and partnered sex (see also Laumann et al., 1994). Sexual thoughts, for instance, are significantly less likely among Black (Odds Ratio[2] [OR] = 0.59, $p < 0.01$) and Hispanic (OR = 0.56, $p < 0.01$) NHSLS women (aged 18 to 59) than among their non-Hispanic White counterparts. Black women in the older NSHAP sample (aged 57 to 85) are also less likely to report sexual ideations than White women (OR = 0.61, $p < 0.05$), but there is no significant difference for Hispanics. Among men, we see no Black-White differentials in sexual thoughts at younger ages (in the NHSLS)—although Hispanic men do report less frequent sexual thoughts (OR = 0.56, $p < 0.05$). At older ages in NSHAP, none of the men's race differentials are statistically significant.

Similarly, both Black (OR = 0.59, $p < 0.01$) and Hispanic (OR = 0.66, $p < 0.05$) NHSLS women are less likely to report any masturbation last year than their White counterparts (see also Das, 2007). Although Black women's lower likelihood remains in the older NSHAP range (OR = 0.66, $p < 0.10$), Hispanic women's masturbation patterns are not statistically different than White women's. Among men, in contrast, Blacks (OR = 0.33, $p < 0.01$) but not Hispanics in the NHSLS are less likely than Whites to masturbate, whereas the NSHAP sample reveals less masturbation among older Black (OR = 0.59, $p < 0.01$) as well as Hispanic men (OR = 0.50, $p < 0.02$).

Finally, NHSLS data also suggest a lower likelihood of any sex in the preceding year among Black (OR = 0.57, $p < 0.05$) but not Hispanic women, compared with their White counterparts. This pattern carries over into the NSHAP age range, with only Black women (OR = 0.69, $p < 0.05$) less likely to report sex than White women. Surprisingly, in contrast to both sexual thoughts and masturbation, men's reports of sexual activity show no significant race differences at any age.

To summarize, relative to their White counterparts, Black women of any age are less likely to report either sexual thoughts or activity, whether unpartnered (masturbation) or partnered—arguably due to strong cultural proscriptions (Laumann & Mahay, 2002; Shulman & Horne, 2003). In contrast, Black men's sexual ideations and partnered sex resemble White men's at any age—although, perhaps due to cultural norms (Das, 2007), both younger (NHSLS) and older (NSHAP) Black men report less masturbation. Patterns for Hispanics are less coherent, although neither Hispanic women nor men report less partnered sex than White women and men at any age.

Life Course Patterns

Frequent sexual thoughts are our purest measure of sexual motivation, and they are arguably most closely linked to physiological or hormonal age trends. Among women, the likelihood of sexual thoughts peaks in the thirties and declines rapidly thereafter (figure 12.1), with the odds almost halved, in our separate analysis, for NHSLS women over 35 (OR = 0.55, $p < 0.01$). Possibly due to hormonal processes, however, men's sexual motivation does not start declining until the early forties. We also note a large gap between women's and men's sexual thoughts at any age. Across the NHSLS age span of 18 to 59, women's odds of frequent sexual thoughts are only about one-fifth that among men (OR = 0.21, $p < 0.01$), a differential that continues into the NSHAP age range of 57 to 85 (OR = 0.16, $p < 0.01$). Within each dataset, this gap is also statistically significant (at $p < 0.01$) for each age segment depicted in figure 12.1. Moreover, the juxtaposition of NSHAP and NHSLS data also reveals a more startling pattern. The youngest NSHAP cohort of women—those in their late fifties, who came of age at the height of the sexual revolution of the 1960s—are no more likely to report more sexual ideations than their NHSLS age peers, who reached sexual maturity in the more conservative late 1940s and early 1950s. Among men, however, we note a divergence of at least ten percentage points between the youngest NSHAP and oldest NHSLS cohorts. It seems, then, that sexual motivation—far from being a purely biologically derived factor—may also have social antecedents. In other words, at least among men, having grown up during the sexual revolution may have led to greater exposure to more liberal "cultural scenarios" of sexuality, the effects of which filter into even purely psychological patterns (Gagnon, 1991).

Age patterns for masturbation partly resemble those for sexual thoughts. As figure 12.2 indicates, the likelihood of reporting any masturbation in the preceding year peaks among women and men in their thirties, although this activity declines somewhat later in the life trajectory than sexual thoughts—in the late thirties and early forties—especially among women. As noted in previous literature (Laumann & Youm, 2001; Waite, Laumann, Das, & Schumm, 2009), masturbation declines steeply among both NHSLS women (OR = 0.44, $p < 0.01$) and men (OR = 0.49, $p < 0.01$) age 50 or older (i.e., the last cohorts to have reached sexual maturity prior to the sexual revolution), again suggesting cohort effects. As with sexual thoughts, across both datasets, we also note a large gender differential in masturbation, significant (at $p < 0.05$) for each age range except the oldest (80 to 85) in NSHAP. Moreover, the juxtaposition of NHSLS and NSHAP data suggests a much stronger

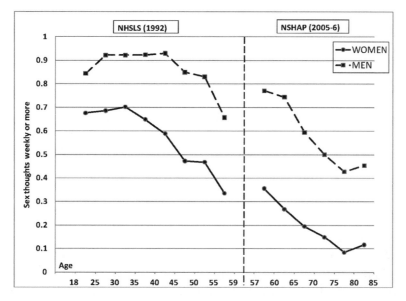

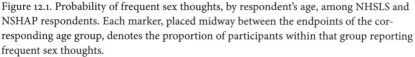

Figure 12.1. Probability of frequent sex thoughts, by respondent's age, among NHSLS and NSHAP respondents. Each marker, placed midway between the endpoints of the corresponding age group, denotes the proportion of participants within that group reporting frequent sex thoughts.

cohort effect for masturbation than for sexual thoughts—one affecting both women and men. Less than 50% of NHSLS men in their late fifties report any masturbation in the preceding year. Among their age peers from the sexual revolution cohort in NSHAP, however, this prevalence is roughly 20 percentage points higher, at nearly 70%. We note an identical pattern for women in this age range, with less than 20% of NHSLS women but about 40% of their NSHAP counterparts reporting masturbation. This sharp rise in masturbation among the generation of the sexual revolution has also been noted for other Western societies (Kontula & Haavio-Mannila, 2002).

As with our other two sexual indicators, partnered sex in the preceding year follows a curvilinear age pattern among both genders, peaking roughly at 95% for respondents in their early thirties (figure 12.3). Unlike masturbation or sexual thoughts, however, women's likelihood of partnered sex stays level with that among men up to the early thirties. A small gender gap, less than five percentage points, appears between the early thirties and late forties. As with masturbation, however, starting with the last pre-sexual revolution cohort (those 50 or older in the NHSLS), there is a steep decline in women's likelihood

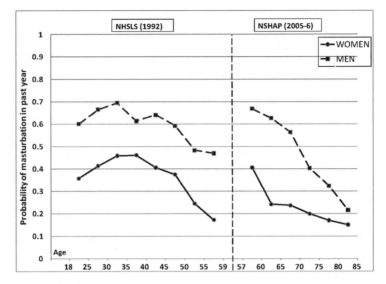

Figure 12.2. Probability of any masturbation in preceding year, by respondent's age, among NHSLS and NSHAP respondents. Each marker, placed midway between the endpoints of the corresponding age group, denotes the proportion of participants within that group reporting masturbation.

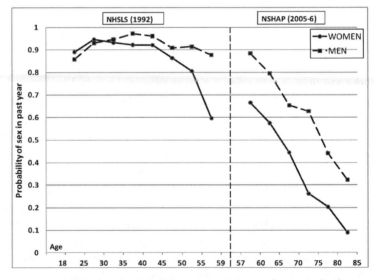

Figure 12.3. Probability of any partnered sex in preceding year, by respondent's age, among NHSLS and NSHAP respondents. Each marker, placed midway between the endpoints of the corresponding age group, denotes the proportion of participants within that group reporting sex.

of sex (OR = 0.32, p < 0.01). By their late fifties, only about 60% of women report having had any sex in the preceding year. In contrast, men's likelihood of sex stays high, above 85%, right into their late fifties, leading to a gender differential in sex of almost 30 percentage points for those 55 to 59 in the NHSLS (OR = 0.32, p < 0.01). In other words, the patterns suggest that having come of age before the sexual revolution may have some effect on older women's but not men's sexuality—perhaps due to the internalization of more conservative and gender-differentiated sexual norms. A second—and perhaps more important—factor behind this growing discrepancy may be gender differentials in partner availability and partners' health, discussed below.

NSHAP data reveal further nuances in these trends. First, women's decline in partnered sex continues apace—dropping to less than 10% among those in their early eighties. Moreover, around age 60, men's sexual activity also hits an inflection point, dropping sharply for those 60 and over (OR = 0.25, p < 0.01). By their early eighties, only about 30% of men report sex. As we discuss below, this turning point is likely due to the onset of age-related sexual dysfunctions.

To summarize, then, patterns for sexual thoughts and masturbation—both roughly indicating sexual motivation—show a large gender gap at any age. In contrast, the likelihood of partnered sex is roughly equal for women and men up through their thirties, although a large and growing gender gap emerges among those in their fifties and older. In other words, consistent with previous conjectures, women of all ages may have lower motivation for sex per se than their male counterparts, and they may be more attuned to the emotional dimensions of intimacy (Basson, 2006). The contrasting lack of a gender gap in partnered sex at younger ages, we speculate, may be due partly to male partners' desire and demand for sex. Finally, juxtaposition of NHSLS and NSHAP data reveals possible cohort patterns—in masturbation (both genders) and in frequent thoughts about sex (among men). In the sections below, we further explicate these trends through a set of underlying determinants—physical health, partnership factors, attitudes and beliefs about sex, and social embeddedness.

Mechanisms

Physical Condition

Changes in physical health with age strongly impact sexual expression. Older women and men are disproportionately prone to health conditions that limit both sexual desire and capacity (Lindau et al., 2007). Declines in sensory function—such as vision and touch—can make one less responsive to sexual cues. Increasing musculoskeletal problems can impair the ability to have partnered sex, as can cardiovascular problems. Diabetes—highly prevalent at older ages—is known to cause men's erectile problems by impairing nerves, blood vessels, and muscle function (Hidalgo-Tamola & Chitaley, 2009). Finally, declines in cognition may lower both sexual desire and capacity. Health issues may also affect sexuality indirectly through poor mental health and by lowering one's attractiveness to a partner.

NSHAP participants were asked about any lifetime diagnoses of a range of medical conditions, of which nine—heart attack, arthritis, ulcers, asthma, stroke, hypertension, diabetes, cancer, and (among men) enlarged prostate—were combined into a single score based on the Charlson comorbidity index (Charlson, Pompei, Ales, & McKenzie, 1987). Seventy-six percent of all respondents report having at least one of these nine conditions, a prevalence slightly higher among women (78%) than men (73%). In our analysis, the likelihood of sex declines sharply among both women (OR = 0.75, p < 0.01) and men (OR = 0.68, p < 0.01) as their comorbidity score increases.

Health may also affect sexual expression more directly, through sexual dysfunctions (Laumann, Das, & Waite, 2008; Laumann, Paik, & Rosen, 1999; Nicolosi et al., 2004). In figures 12.4 and 12.5, we use data from our three samples to present prevalence estimates for some dysfunctions at different ages. We include lack of interest in sex (or hypoactive sexual desire disorder), women's difficulty in lubrication, and men's erectile problems (erectile dysfunction, or ED), because these capture both the psychological/motivational and biological/capacity aspects of sexuality. As figure 12.4 shows, gender patterns for a lack of sexual desire match those for masturbation and sexual thoughts, with women at any age being more likely than their male counterparts to report lower sexual desire. For instance, the odds of reporting a lack of interest in sex are almost three times as high for NHSLS women than men of all ages (OR = 2.66, p < 0.01) and almost twice as high for their NSHAP counterparts (OR = 1.94, p < 0.01). Possibly due to changes in hormonal levels, men's experiences of low desire appear to hit an inflection point around age 60 and increase by 10 to 15 percentage points thereafter. Cohort effects in sensitization to sexual desire may also explain this differential between the oldest NHSLS and youngest NSHAP groups. Coming of age during the sexual revolution—in addition to altering sexual behavior patterns—may also have made people more sensitive to decreases in libido with age, a change that might have been considered more "normal" among previous cohorts. Indeed, among men, the oldest NHSLS group is less likely to report frequent

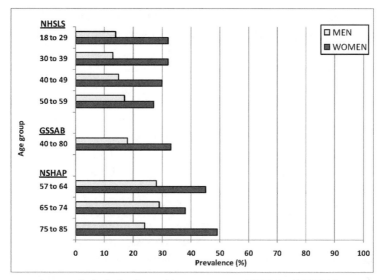

Figure 12.4. Age trends for lack of sexual interest, among NHSLS and NSHAP respondents, and GSSAB subsample from non-European West. (Question only asked if respondent reported any sex in preceding year.)

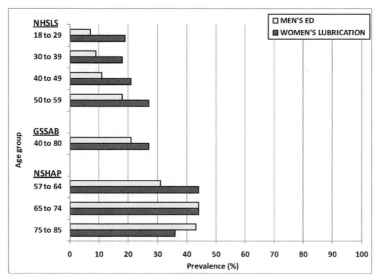

Figure 12.5. Age trends for men's trouble in maintaining or achieving erection, and women's trouble in lubricating, among NSHLS and NSHAP respondents, and GSSAB subsample from non-European West. (Question only asked if respondent reported any sex in preceding year.)

sexual thoughts as well as sexual desire problems than the youngest cohort in NSHAP. Among women, although the differential in sexual thoughts is almost zero, reports of low sexual desire are much higher in the NSHAP group. Comparisons with the age decline in frequent sexual thoughts (figure 12.1) further substantiate this interpretation.

Among older NSHAP age groups, we also note a plateau in sexual desire for both women and men. A first, biological explanation for this pattern is a threshold effect in the impact of age on desire. However, these questions were only asked of respondents who reported any sex in the preceding year—the prevalence of which drops rapidly with age for both genders (figure 12.3). We speculate, therefore, that the leveling off of the decline in sexual desire among older groups may, in part, be due to a selection effect—or, in other words, that it is the more sexually motivated individuals who continue to have sex at older ages. Again, comparisons with age patterns for frequent sexual thoughts (figure 12.1) further validate this conjecture. In both the NHSLS and NSHAP, all respondents, not simply those reporting partnered sex, were queried about the latter. The steep decline in frequent sexual thoughts with age suggests that the lack of a comparable decline in sexual desire may indeed be due to selection effects.

Many of these patterns—especially the increasing likelihood of problems with age—are also evident with more biologically linked dysfunctions, such as men's ED and women's lubrication difficulties (figure 12.5). However, the gender differential in these problems is lower than that for desire, at any age. Among younger participants, as with sexual desire, these biological dysfunctions are more common among women than men (although younger women are less likely to report lubrication issues than low sexual desire). The incidence of ED in men, however, rises more sharply with age than does the incidence of low sexual desire, with the oldest NSHAP men more than four times as likely to report this problem as those below 40 in the NHSLS. As a consequence, among those 65 or older, the prevalence of men's ED draws level with that of women's lubrication problems—and surpasses the latter among the oldest groups (those above 75). In other words, the effect of increasing age may be more biological for men than for women, with the latter possibly more impacted by psychosocial factors. This last conjecture also receives support from previous studies (Laumann et al., 2008) that show strong correlations between men's physical health conditions and their sexual problems, as well as more consistent effects of mental health and relationship factors on women's than men's dysfunctions.

To summarize, sexual activity in late life is strongly affected by the increase in health burdens. Moreover, this factor has a stronger influence among men than women, suggesting that men's sexuality is more influenced by biological issues, with women potentially more responsive to psychosocial factors. As argued above, this pattern is also suggested by gender differences in the effect of age on biologically linked dysfunctions (men's ED and women's lubrication issues), versus gender differences in age's effect on sexual desire. Moreover, as we discuss in the next section, a person's health issues are also linked to our second major structuring process: the availability of a stable partner.

Partnership

As noted, much research on sexuality remains focused on the individual, missing the role of partnership factors in structuring sexual expression. First, increasing age brings with it a growing chance of partner loss through widowhood.[3] Moreover, among those experiencing widowhood, age-related poor health lowers one's chances of (and motivation for) finding a new partner. As a consequence, there is a bifurcation in sexual careers in late life, with long-term monogamy among those with partners and an absence of a (partnered) sex life among those without.

As figure 12.6 makes clear, patterns in the availability of a partner over the life course are gender differentiated. Men's likelihood of having a potential sexual partner (i.e., a marital or cohabiting relationship) remains over 80%, and stable, right into their sixties. Among women, however, partnership prevalence drops sharply after the early fifties. Separate analyses suggest that much of this gender differential is explained by the rise in women's—but not men's—widowhood at these ages. Among NSHAP respondents aged 57 to 60, 8% of women but only 2% of men are widowed. Among those 60 to 70 years old, 15% of women (OR = 2.04, $p < 0.05$), but only 5% of men, are widowed. Comparisons across samples also suggest cohort patterns in this process. Among those aged 55 to 59 in the NHSLS, the prevalence of widowhood among men is slightly higher, at 3%, than in the youngest NSHAP group. Among NHSLS women, however, the prevalence is much higher, at 14%, a differential arguably due to increased male longevity in more recent cohorts. Much of the corresponding differential across samples in the prevalence of partnership among women, illustrated in figure 12.6, stems from this cohort factor.

Gender differentials in late-life widowhood may derive from two processes. First, for as-yet-unexplained reasons, male-female differences in lon-

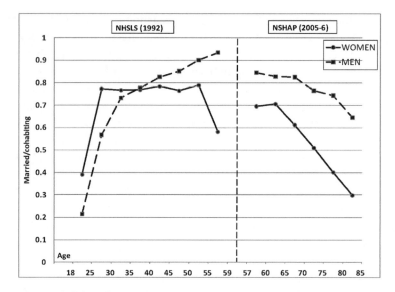

Figure 12.6. Probability of currently having a stable (marital or cohabiting) partner, by respondent's age, among NHSLS and NSHAP respondents. Each marker, placed midway between the endpoints of the corresponding age group, denotes the proportion of participants within that group reporting a partner.

gevity are a well-established fact, with women on average living longer than men (Felder, 2006; Organisation for Economic Co-operation and Development, 2002). Even among couples similar in age, therefore, women are more likely than men to experience partner loss. Moreover, as noted, women on average partner with men several years older than themselves, a phenomenon known as age hypergamy. We use NSHAP and NHSLS data to illustrate this latter pattern in figure 12.7. As is evident from the trendline for men, the oldest men—those arguably at the highest risk of mortality—are especially likely to be partnered with women several years younger. In turn, this increasing age gap may stem from multiple factors. First, there are changes in the sex ratio of the "sexual marketplace" over the life course, with higher male mortality leading to fewer available men at older ages (Mahay & Laumann, 2004). This process gives older heterosexual men entering the marketplace a competitive edge, enhancing their chances of finding the younger and (ostensibly) more desirable women they seek. Gender-differentiated standards of desirability are in themselves a second structuring factor. Whether for evolutionary or cultural reasons, men tend to evaluate desirability in terms of youth and appearance, while women look for a partner with power and socioeconomic status, which tend to be higher among older than younger men (Mahay & Laumann, 2004). Intriguingly, these patterns are becoming less pronounced in younger cohorts, arguably due to enhancements in women's social and economic opportunities. As figure 12.7 shows, NHSLS men below age 30 (who came of age during the 1980s or later) have partners no younger than themselves. Their female age peers also are more likely to report *higher* levels of education than their partners. The gap in education, a rough proxy for socioeconomic status, only swings in favor of male partners for women 35 or older (who came of age in the 1970s or earlier).

Figure 12.8 illustrates the trend toward long-term relationships with age among those with stable (i.e., married or cohabiting) partners. Whether among older NHSLS cohorts or younger NSHAP ones, relationships in late life tend to be long-standing. Fewer than 1% of all NSHAP women and only 3% of NSHAP men aged 57 or above report having more than one partner in the preceding year. This increase in monogamy is likely associated with a lowering of sexual capacity and motivation, due to age and health complications. Moreover, even among partnered individuals, age may hinder sexual expression not simply through one's own but also through a partner's poor

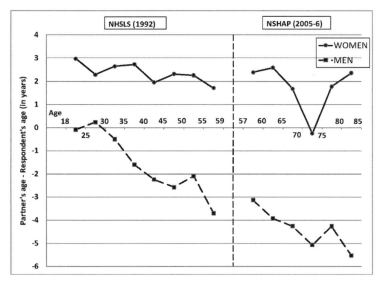

Figure 12.7. Age differentials in partnerships (partner's age – respondent's age) across the life course among NHSLS and NSHAP respondents. Each marker, placed midway between the endpoints of the corresponding age group, denotes the average age differential for that group.

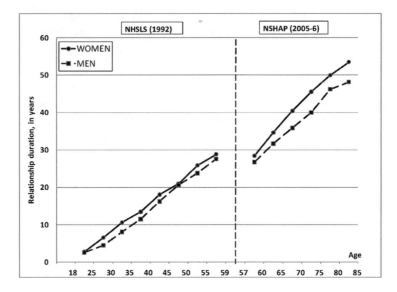

Figure 12.8. Duration of current marital or cohabiting relationship by respondent's age, among NHSLS and NSHAP respondents. Each marker, placed midway between the endpoints of the corresponding age group, denotes the average relationship duration for that group.

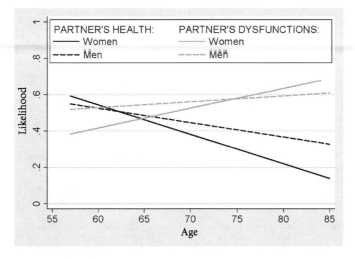

Figure 12.9. Partner's likelihood of being in good or excellent physical health, and of having at least one sexual dysfunction, by respondent's age, among currently married or cohabiting NSHAP respondents.

health and sexual incapacities. As with partner availability, this latter process is also gender differentiated, as figure 12.9 illustrates. Among those with partners, separate Wald tests[4] indicate that the decline with age in the likelihood of reporting that one's partner is in good or excellent health is significantly stronger (at $p < 0.05$) among women (OR = 0.93, $p < 0.01$) than men (OR = 0.97, $p < 0.01$). Although the gender difference in reporting that one's partner has at least one sexual dysfunction is not significant—arguably due to smaller cell sizes—the likelihood of such reports rises significantly with age only among partnered women (OR = 1.05, $p < 0.05$). In other words, whether due to age hypergamy or to gendered biological processes, older women are more likely than older men to have a partner with physical incapacities—which, in turn, lowers their own opportunities for sexual activity.

In summary, then, sexual careers are channeled into two main trajectories in late life: a monogamous relationship with a long-term partner or the disappearance of sexual opportunities through partner loss. With increasing age, heterosexual women are more vulnerable to widowhood, due to sex differences in longevity and/or age hypergamy, although this greater vulnerability seems to be easing in recent cohorts due to enhancements in male longevity. Even among those with stable partners, however, a partner's declining health can constrain sexual activity, with women, again, more vulnerable to this process.

Attitudes

Social and cultural factors also structure sex and partnership patterns. Attitudes and beliefs, for instance, can profoundly influence sexual behaviors. The wide range of cohort patterns discussed above demonstrates that reaching sexual maturity in more permissive times can influence sexual expression—and perceptions of sexual dysfunctions—well into late life.

However, as with other structuring factors, sexual beliefs may also shift over time, adaptively, in response to life-cycle and physiological changes. We use NSHAP data to illustrate some of these shifts in figure 12.10. Increases in physical problems as one transitions into older age groups, it seems, lead to modest changes in both women's (OR = 1.40, $p < 0.01$) and men's (OR = 1.88, $p < 0.01$) perceptions of the impact of age on sexual capacity.[5] Although this pattern holds for both genders, it is slightly stronger among men ($p < 0.05$ in separate Wald test), consistent with our arguments above about the greater impact of age-related biological problems on men's than women's sexuality. In contrast, generalized beliefs about the importance of sex to the maintenance of a healthy relationship[6] are age-independent. Although men are somewhat more likely to hold such beliefs (for all ages, OR = 1.28, $p < 0.05$), the prevalence of these attitudes remains moderately high well into old age among both genders. In other words, if changing attitudes affect sex at all, they do so through perceptions of one's own physical incapacities, not through shifts in one's basic beliefs about sexuality. Figure 12.11, based on NSHAP data, lends additional support to this argument. Although men of all ages are more likely than women to report that sex is an important part of life (OR = 2.62, $p < 0.01$), these reports decline with age among both genders. Moreover, the decline is especially sharp among men (OR = 0.97, $p < 0.01$), from around 50% among those aged 57 to roughly 25% among the oldest men.

In contrast to men's vulnerability to age-related physiological problems, the potentially greater role of psychosocial factors in women's sexuality may stem from a lifetime of socialization into less permissive sexual values and/ or the more negative practical consequences of permissive behavior among women (e.g., whereas women are typically socially sanctioned for having multiple partners, men may be praised). For instance, among NSHAP respondents of all ages, women are much more likely than men to state that love is necessary for sex (OR = 3.31, $p < 0.01$) and that their religious beliefs

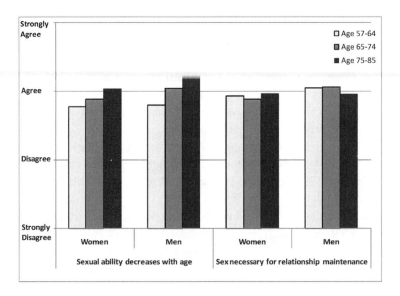

Figure 12.10. Attitudes and beliefs regarding sex, by respondent's age, among NSHAP respondents.

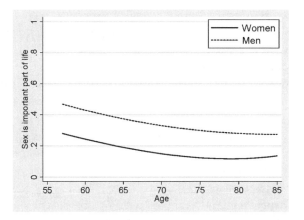

Figure 12.11. Probability of reporting that sex is "very" or "extremely" important part of life, by respondent's age, among NSHAP respondents.

shape their sexual behavior (OR = 2.11). Similarly, among currently unmarried NSHAP respondents who report no sex in the past 3 months, women are more likely than men to cite religious beliefs prohibiting sex outside marriage as the reason (OR = 1.84, p < 0.05).

Social Constraints

A final process structuring age-related sexual trends is network embeddedness. As noted, increases in health burdens with age may induce closer ties to friends, and especially family, as reliable sources of social support (Antonucci & Akiyama, 1995; Hurlbert et al., 2000). A growing literature suggests that the social networks of older adults become more kin-centered with age (Cornwell, Laumann, & Schumm, 2008; McPherson, Miller, Smith-Lovin, & Brashears, 2006). In turn, this increased reliance may heighten the monitoring-and-control capacities of these network members, many of whom may not approve of certain sexual behaviors or relationships for an older person.

NSHAP data provide strong support for these conjectures. For instance, among not-currently-married women and men of all ages, 22% (43% of men; 13% of women) report any partnered sex in the preceding year, with these prevalences varying by reliance on family. Among those who rely on family members "hardly ever (or never)" or "some of the time," about 27% report sex. For those who report "often" having to rely on family, however, the prevalence of sex is lower, just under 20% (OR = 0.65, p < 0.05). Almost all of this discrepancy is due to patterns among women, consistent with a patriarchal double-standard regarding older women's, as opposed to older men's, sexuality. Specifically, the prevalence of sex is roughly equal among unmarried men with and without strong family dependencies (45% and 44%, respectively). In contrast, 18% of unmarried women without strong dependencies on the family report sex in the preceding year, compared with only 10% among those with such ties (OR = 0.52, p < 0.05).

Figure 12.12 graphs these differentials by age group. Among unmarried women, the constraining effects of family reliance become strong only beyond age 65. Among those 65 to 74 years old, for instance, women with strong family dependencies are half as likely to be having sex as women without such dependencies (OR = 0.35, p < 0.05), consistent with the argument that women's nonmarital sex becomes increasingly contrary to social norms with age. Separate analysis, conducted solely among those reporting good or better overall physical health, yields the same patterns, suggesting that they are not driven by health differentials among those women with and without family dependencies. Unmarried men's differentials, in contrast, are both weak and inconsistent. Even among men, however, family ties function as constraints, as suggested by figure 12.13, which graphs unmarried women's (OR = 0.48, p < 0.05) and men's (OR = 0.38, p < 0.01) probabilities of having a cohabiting or other informal partner by the proportion of consanguineal (or blood) kin in their core discussion network.[7] The pattern for men's informal partnership is especially striking; about 50% of unmarried men with few or no blood relatives in their network report a current partner, compared with less than 25% among those with the highest proportions of kin.

Conclusion

We began this chapter by presenting a model of the adult sexual career as a punctuated equilibrium of stable spells broken by branching points that are catalyzed by life processes. Although the sociological literature includes an abundance of studies on sexual behaviors and dispositions at specific, bounded junctures in the life course, it lacks accounts spanning the life trajectory. We juxtaposed data from the 1992 NHSLS and the 2005–2006 NSHAP to track trends for frequent sexual thoughts, masturbation, and partnered sex across the life trajectory. In addition, we introduced two other theoretical themes: sexual expression as a dyadic, rather than simply indi-

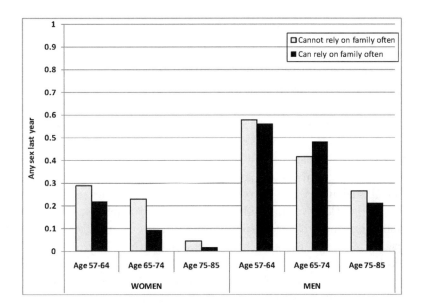

Figure 12.12. Probability of any partnered sex in preceding year, by reliance on family and by age group, among currently unmarried NSHAP respondents.

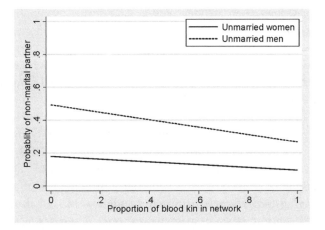

Figure 12.13. Probability of having a non-marital (cohabiting or other informal) partner, by proportion consanguineal kin in core discussion network, among currently unmarried NSHAP respondents.

vidual, phenomenon, and the role of social networks in shaping sexual patterns. Along the way, we noted a range of patterns by gender and race, and we offered substantively based age versus cohort interpretations.

The results of our analyses suggest that adult sexual careers indeed resemble a tree-like "global" structure, with key "local" structuring factors—physical health and sexual dysfunctions, partner availability and a partner's health, attitudes and beliefs regarding sex, and social embeddedness—entraining individuals along specific pathways. Apart from biological age, coming of age in more permissive times has a strong and enduring impact on one's sexuality, arguably due to the internalization of specific sexual templates or scripts. For partnered sex and masturbation alike, and even for internal psychic patterns such as thoughts about sex, our use of data from multiple samples suggests strong cohort effects. Moreover, internalized attitudes do not remain stable over time but rather respond to changes in physical capacity and other factors over the life course. Or in other words, such changes are socially driven "switching points"—branching points in the tree of life—that begin early and continue into old age.

Next, our dyadic focus is strongly validated. We note a bifurcation of sexual careers into two main trajectories in late life: monogamous partnership with a long-term partner and the disappearance of sexual opportunities with partner loss. Due largely to age hypergamy, older women are more at risk than older men of partner loss. Moreover, even among those in stable relationships, a partner's increasing ill health constrains sexual opportunities more for women than for men. Patterns for sexual dysfunctions drawn from all three of our samples suggest that men's sexuality is more responsive to age-related physiological shifts, whereas psychosocial factors may play a larger role for women. Finally, reliance on family members, which may increase with age and health conditions, also leads to social constraints on one's sexual expression, especially for older women.

These patterns yield a picture not of stabilization in particular sexual careers from adolescence onward but of spells of stability and change throughout the entire life course. Moreover, individual-level change is embedded within broader social and demographic shifts, as suggested by the range of cohort effects we identified. The continuing evolution of these great underlying forces—social, cultural, technological, and medical—will likely lead to continuing shifts in sexual expression and sexual careers. In particular, improvements in physical health and capacities in late life, and concomitant changes in mores about sexuality, may enhance possibilities for sexual expression among older adults. Large-sample data will remain critical in unearthing and interpreting such shifts in sexuality over the life course.

The preparation of this chapter was funded by Grant No. R01AG021487 from the Office of Behavioral and Social Sciences Research, National Institute on Aging.

1. We distinguish our conception of "branching points" from the more common notion of "turning points." We define a branching point as a particular juncture or period during which life trajectories are channeled in *multiple* directions—whether positive, negative, or stabilized in the current course—with differential probabilities attached to these inflections. This is a population-level perspective. From the individual's standpoint, the event is experienced as a turning point—a distinction insufficiently clear in existing literature. The idea of a turning point, although potentially open to this multidirectionality, has largely been used in academic literature as indicating change in a particular direction (Elder, 1995; Sampson & Laub, 1993), making our distinction conceptually and analytically useful.

2. An odds ratio is the ratio of the odds of an event occurring in one group over the odds of the event occurring in another (reference) group.

3. Patterns of partner loss due to death are quite different for lesbians and gay men, compared with each other and to heterosexuals. However, we do not have enough data on these women and men to analyze their experiences separately.

4. Wald tests assess the hypothesis that the associations of interest (here, gender-specific effects) are equal to each other.

5. The exact question wording was "The ability to have sex decreases as a person grows older."

6. The exact question wording was "Satisfactory sexual relations are essential to the maintenance of a relationship."

7. NSHAP respondents were asked to nominate their alters—their core discussion networks—through a network-roster method during the face-to-face interview (Cornwell et al., 2008). The exact question wording was "From time to time, most people discuss things that are important to them with others. For example, these may include good or bad things that happen to you, problems you are having, or important concerns you may have. Looking back over the last 12 months, who are the people with whom you most often discussed things that were important to you?"

13

Exploring Embodied Aging and Ageism among Old Lesbians and Gay Men

KATHLEEN F. SLEVIN AND
CHRISTINE E. MOWERY

The sexuality of old women and men is an issue that has seen an upsurge in scholarly attention over the past decade and a half (e.g., Cruikshank, 2009; DeLamater & Moorman, 2007; Levy, 1994).[1] These investigations disprove ageist notions about sexuality in later life, demonstrating that old people continue to desire and have the capacity for sexual intimacy. Although an examination of the sexuality of aging lesbians and gay men is often absent from this research, a nascent attention to the sexuality of old homosexuals has been building over the past 5 years (e.g., Heaphy, 2007, 2009; Herdt & de Vries, 2004; Rosenfeld, 2003). This scholarship needs to maintain a focus on the body, because it is through the body that we experience desire, sexual pleasure, and sexual practices. Additionally, because the body is a critical marker of age, it provides a key site through which to explore how aging and ageism shape the lived experiences of individuals, including sexuality.

This chapter explores the bodily experience of aging, as well as sexual activity and desire, through the narratives of a group of old (ranging in age from 60 to 85), mostly white, economically privileged lesbians and gay men. A focus on old lesbians and gay men allows exploration of how social class, gender, and sexual orientation intersect with age to influence notions of sexuality, femininity/masculinity, and embodied aging. A feminist perspective guides this analysis, highlighting ways that lives are shaped by power relations within and across social statuses. Additional attention is given to life course processes to more fully grasp respondents' understandings of both embodied aging and certain aspects of their sexuality.

Aging, Ageism, and the Body

Feminist scholars have been on the forefront of interdisciplinary attention to the body in recent decades. Although this scholarship investigates connections between gender, race, class, and sexual orientation, it often ignores aging bodies, and lesbian and gay aging bodies in particular (Katz, 2005; Faircloth, 2003; Calasanti & Slevin, 2001). When researchers do focus on old bodies, they primarily emphasize people's loss of function, illness, and disease and engage in a "narrative of decline" (Cruikshank, 2009; Gullette, 1997). Consequently, mundane physical experiences with aging bodies go unstudied, so old people experience their bodies in the context of "profound cultural silence" (Twigg, 2000, p. 115).

Ageist assessments of the body are shaped by various social locations, including gender, race and ethnicity, social class, and sexual orientation. Gender plays an overarching and critical role in shaping how the body is assessed. Regardless of age, physical appearance, including issues of weight and body shape, is of greater concern for women than men (Cash, 2000). In a society where women's cultural capital is tied to appearance, and specifically to attractive, *youthful* bodies, aging presents a heavier burden on women than men. Women, moreover, are subjected to the "double standard of aging," whereby old men's bodies are seen as distinguished and old women's bodies are seen as failing to live up to feminine ideals. Ageist stereotypes that emerge from this culture are therefore especially negative and demeaning to women (Arber & Ginn, 1991; Hurd, 2000).

Race and class also mediate how old people experience their aging bodies. Some scholars argue that racial minorities and people of lower socioeconomic classes hold more accepting and positive attitudes toward aging, which in turn may lead to a more accepting view of old bodies. Although not specifically studying old bodies, Parker and colleagues (1995) found that African American perceptions of beauty are flexible and that Black Americans, especially women, are more likely than European Americans to assess body image in multidimensional terms, rather than in terms of purely physical characteristics (see also Schuler et al., 2008). When one also considers how social class intersects with race and ethnicity, however, the issue of how racial/ethnic minority women view their bodies becomes more nuanced. For example, in a study of old (ages 53–87), middle- and upper middle-class African American women, Slevin and Wingrove (1998) found that, although more positive about being old women than a similar sample of white women, some of their respondents were just as concerned about their weight and body shape in old age as their white counterparts, suggesting that class status may at times override racial/ethnic status in terms of accepting one's body and issues of body image.

Previous research has found that sexual orientation, the focus of this chapter, also contributes to differing approaches to the aging body, although the empirical data are contradictory (Jones & Pugh, 2005; Calasanti & Slevin, 2001). For example, some scholars (e.g., Wolf, 1991) argue that lesbians are more accepting of their bodies, given that they supposedly are not concerned with the approval of the "male gaze," while other researchers find no such difference, arguing that gender is a more significant predictor of body acceptance than sexual orientation (Slevin, 2006; Brand, Rothblum, & Soloman, 1992). Consideration of race, class, and cohort differences further complicates the discussion of lesbians and embodied aging (Slevin, 2006). The narratives of our lesbian interviewees greatly enhance the field of aging studies because little is actually known about women's perceptions of growing old and looking old, or about their strategies for dealing with ageism, be they lesbian or heterosexual.[2]

Similar to old lesbians, old gay men must struggle with the pervasive ageism of U.S. society. A common theme discussed in the literature on old gay men (but not old lesbians) is "accelerated aging" (Wahler & Gabbay, 1997). As Bennett and Thompson (1991, p. 66) note, "Because of the gay community's emphasis on youth, homosexual men are considered middle-aged and elderly by other homosexual men at an earlier age than heterosexual men in the general community." Some scholars thus suggest that gay men, like heterosexual women, have a more difficult time accepting aging bodies because of the dominant role that youth plays in gay urban culture (Jones & Pugh, 2005). However, empirical data regarding how real gay men experience the aging phenomenon are both scarce and contradictory (Jones & Pugh, 2005).

Our interviews allow us to explore these mostly theoretical assertions regarding homosexual individuals' own perspectives on aging and the aging body. Our study adds to the literature on aging and old bodies by exploring the ways that ageism is manifested in the daily embodied lives of this group. Through intensive interviews, we come to see how old women and men understand, articulate, and negotiate the *corporeal* aspects of growing old, which in turn allows us to appreciate how embodiment is critical to making sense of age and aging (Laz, 2003). Analysis of respondents' narratives allows us to uncover whether this group of old lesbians and gay men accepts, rejects, or attempts to modify their old bodies (Laws, 1995). Thus, we consider the ways that they respond to the aging process by ignoring, accepting, or adjusting to it, as well as the ways that they negotiate, resist, or contest ageism. Because they are old and homosexual, we also see how age intersects with sexual orientation and gender to influence individuals' ongoing corporeal understandings and negotiations.

Methods

This study explores the narrative accounts of how nine lesbians, aged 60 to 78, and ten gay men, aged 60 to 85, conceive of aging in general and embodied aging specifically. The intensive interviews from which these narrative accounts are drawn are part of a larger study in which the lead author interviewed 26 men (16 heterosexual, 10 homosexual) and 31 women (22 heterosexual, 9 lesbian) in their sixties, seventies, and eighties to learn how they experienced their bodies in old age. Between 2002 and 2004, the researcher used a snowball sampling method to obtain interviewees from different social backgrounds. The sample size is small in part due to the difficulty of finding openly gay respondents in this age cohort who are willing to discuss issues such as embodied aging and physical and sexual attractiveness. Although the findings cannot be generalized to a larger population, they do help illuminate the importance and influence of bodies as a focus of aging. The intensive, exploratory interviews addressed a variety of topics related to aging and the body, including preventing the aging process, sexuality/ageism/attractiveness issues, and body image.

None of the nine women interviewed took the exact same path to lesbian identity. Five women were previously married to heterosexual men; four of the five had children during those marriages, and all five divorced and came out as lesbians in their forties. Three women were "lifetime" lesbians and one, a 73-year-old who was recommended by a previous partner, did not self-identify during the interview as being lesbian at all. With the exception of the latter woman, all of the lesbian interviewees had current partners; six of the eight partnered women were with women who were 10–19 years younger than themselves. Seven of the lesbians in the sample were white and two were Hispanic. All were highly educated: two had bachelor's degrees, four had at least a master's degree, and three had a Ph.D. Six of the women were formally retired from the workforce and the remaining three were still employed. Seven were or had been professionals in education and two were or had been administrators for nongovernmental organizations (NGOs). All of the women were financially secure, and their professional jobs provided them with financial and health benefits that ensured secure retirements; all were also generally in good health. Finally, all the interviewees were committed to general feminist principles of equality for women and several were intermittently involved in feminist and lesbian political activities.

Two of the ten gay male interviewees were previously married to heterosexual women and one had children during his marriage; both divorced and came out in their forties. The remaining eight were "lifetime" gay men. Three had partners at the time of the interviews; of these three, two were with younger men, one of them younger by 24 years. All of the male interviewees were white and very well educated: all had bachelor's degrees and seven also had earned graduate degrees. Eight of the men were formally retired from the workforce, one was employed full-time, and one was working part-time. Six were or had been employed in the field of education, one had spent his working life as a religious pastor, and the remaining three were or had been executives in various organizations. Similar to the lesbian interviewees, these gay men were also financially secure.

Findings

Sexuality in Old Age

Our interviews focusing on embodied aging allow us to explore certain elements of our respondents' sexuality, including sexual partners, desire, and activity. A life course perspective is especially critical to our exploration of the sexuality of old lesbians and gay men. For instance, the majority (five) of the lesbians interviewed were initially married to heterosexual men and did not come out as lesbians until they were in their forties. Although the majority (eight) of the gay men interviewed were "lifetime" gay men, because of pervasive societal stigma toward homosexuals in earlier decades, they struggled with sexuality issues also. The struggles of both groups reveal the importance of placing biographies within historical time periods. They also reinforce the importance of examining the intersections of historical moments with gender and age in order to uncover more fully how sexuality is experienced in old age.

Miriam's (61 years old) story demonstrates how sexuality is shaped by a personal biography that reveals a shifting sexual orientation over time.[3] Married at 19 to her "high school sweetheart," and then later to a man 17 years her senior, she had her first lesbian sexual experience at age 42. As a result she experienced a new model for her own sexuality: "Once I'd slept with a woman it was so physical I thought 'How in the world did I not get this before?' . . . I don't think I ever really got it with men which was the only model I had." Eliza, who had also been married to a heterosexual man and came out as a lesbian in her forties, describes a similar awakening: "Responding to a woman. . . . You know what makes them feel good, they know what makes you feel good, and my personal opinion is that when you have sex with a man you're focused on satisfying the man."

With the exception of the one lesbian who did not self-identify as lesbian during her interview, the remainder talked openly about their sexuality and about their sex lives as old lesbians. Although there is no one model of sexuality in old age, we heard some common themes in their narratives. For example, Becca (68) echoes others when she talks in very positive terms about her sex life as an old lesbian. Indeed, she claims that her sex life is much better nowadays than it was in earlier decades because she does not "have to go through all that discovery stuff." Rita (78), who sees herself as highly sexually attractive, says about her sex life with her partner: "I love intimacy. I think it's great. The energy is great . . . it's very healthy." But Rita's conversation about how sexuality changes with age reveals how contradictory attitudes coexist. Although she claims to be sexually attractive at one point, she later reveals an important detail that illuminates the internalized stigma of old bodies: "I am very careful about exposing myself to [partner's name]."

Another theme touched upon by some of the lesbian interviewees is the relationship between sexual activity and length of relationship. Deborah (60) summarizes this theme: "It seems to be fairly common [that] long-term female couples are often very celibate for long periods of time and that's not all that unusual." Deborah describes her own sexual relationship with her partner: "Although we have a very intimate relationship, we don't have one that is physically sexual a lot of times." In the case of Miriam, the most important factor in explaining her diminished sex life in recent years is menopause. "Sex went right out the window," once she hit menopause in her fifties. Disturbed and depressed by her lack of libido, Miriam turned to hormone replacement therapy, including a stint with testosterone, in her endeavor to regain the active sex life she had come to enjoy as a lesbian. Attempts to reclaim her active sex life did not succeed and Miriam "finally . . . came to terms with it being over." Nevertheless, Miriam's description of her current relationship hints at a different style of physical intimacy: "We are still very close. We both say we really miss the sex we had. We both talk about how we miss the way it used to be but also about how happy we are and how much we love our physical closeness. . . . We [still] find our joys and pleasures."

Understanding the gay men interviewees' sexuality also requires a life course lens. As with old lesbians, such a perspective allows us to deepen our understanding of how gay men's sexualities were shaped by external forces that shift over time. Interview after interview dwelt on the notion that gay men are sexually promiscuous. Not surprisingly, we uncovered a complicated picture of the multiple forces that influence these men's sexuality and sexual activity. Glen (85) provides a powerful historical description of earlier decades when most of these gay men were coming out:

> When we were younger we [went overboard]. In other words, in a day when we were hostile and our families were very hostile, we just craved . . . being free of that and when we would discover a bar or a little collection of gay men we would not use judgment because of the reaction to the negativity of our individual situations. [So], we just went hog wild.

Glen's words provide historical context and force us to recognize the importance of milieu in understanding the sexual lives of men who are stigmatized for their sexual orientation.

Whether through the passage of time, concern for contracting HIV/AIDS, or the development of relationships with partners, most of the interviewees nowadays have a different perspective on their sexual activities. Glen captures the importance of time with this observation: "Most mature men have become smarter and more thoughtful in their habits—and that includes sex." Jake's story illuminates the importance of developing long-term relationships. At 78, he too claims to have been very promiscuous as a young man. Later he went on to have three long-term partners—the first for 11 years, the second for 30 years; his current relationship is in its tenth year. His words highlight a key aspect of long-term monogamous relationships in the gay world: "I think it is beneficial to me. Especially with this AIDS business, it's better to stick to one person, which is pretty much what I did."

Victor (71), who is currently with a partner, is also open about his past sexual activities. He describes himself: "I have always been a very, very highly sexual person." Yet Victor's biography reminds us how complicated the stories of these old gay men are. He too talks about a younger life of sexual promiscuity and what it was like to be a young gay man in New York in the 1960s: "Yes, I am not proud of it but I was [promiscuous]. And I wasn't proud of it when I was doing it but I did it. I would wake up the next morning after a wild night out and be thoroughly ashamed of myself. A week later [I'd] go right back to the same thing." Victor is happily partnered today and he observes: "I had to settle in the past for casual sex which I never wanted" (see Green, this volume).

Aspects of our respondents' sexuality, including physical intimacy and sexual activity, are influenced by their age as well as their age cohort. The findings regarding the shifting sexual orientation of many of the lesbians and the transition from self-described promiscuity to long-term, monogamous relationships of some of the gay men also uncover struggles related to sexual orientation and highlight the need to understand these struggles in terms of the intersection of biography and history.

Aging and Acceptance of Self/Body

Another related struggle that these respondents have is accepting (or attempting to accept) stigmatized aging bodies in a youth-obsessed society. The narratives of both the lesbians and gay men reveal ambivalence and contradictions in responses to embodied aging. But when comparing the comments of the lesbian and gay male interviewees, it does appear that our female respondents perceive that being lesbian and largely in the company of other lesbians impacts their aging experiences in a positive way, as opposed to our male respondents.

Some of the women's comments underscore a consciousness about how coping with the stigma of being lesbian has helped them accept being old women. As younger women they had to deal with coming out—a process that for most entailed some level of pain and suffering—so their biographies as lesbian women influence their responses to being old women. Aged 71, Eliza captures this well: "Lesbians had to learn to cope with being different so [being old] is not such a shock. . . . You've developed coping mechanisms [and] one is to accept your situation." Beth (67), a lifetime lesbian who consciously fights heterosexual ideals for women and especially old women's embodiment, reinforces this notion that learning to deal with the stigma of being lesbian helps one deal with old age: "I guess whatever got me through knowing . . . that it was not good to be lesbian has gotten me past [the notion that] it's not good to be old." Certainly, Beth directly connects lesbianism to less obsessive attention to bodily appearance when she suggests that "physical appearance is not as big an issue in the lesbian world as it is in the heterosexual world." This comment gives an indication of how sexual orientation might impact an individual's perceptions of aging and the aging body. Finally, Eliza suggests that she is quite conscious about how being lesbian frees her from unrealistic expectations about maintaining a youthful appearance: "Lesbians worry less about aging, about how they look."

In contrast, the old gay male interviewees attest to a long-standing assumption about gay culture: ageism is prominent, and much of this ageism is related to the body. A theme that interviewees cited repeatedly was the youth obsession of gay culture and its consequences for themselves and others. As a political activist for gay issues, Glen (85) has thought a lot about these concerns. Extremely well networked and well known in the gay communities of his city and beyond, Glenn bluntly states that "gays are much more ageist than straights." Eric (60) sees this ageism as having to do with how gay culture "really accentuates youth and body and physical conditions." Ironically, this emphasis on youthful looks may actually help some gay men accept the aging process or at least be more accepting of the way their aging bodies look. Peter (62) argues that homosexual men his age "have not gone to pot, to seed," in comparison to heterosexual men his age. Noting the importance that homosexual men place on physical appearance, Peter nonetheless claims that "the gay people I know are content with their ages." Thus, while part of the portrait that emerges from the narratives of these old, privileged lesbians and gay men includes certain positive advantages in their aging experiences, which appear linked to their sexual orientation, the larger picture that emerges is much more complicated.

Coping with an Aging Body

Analysis of our interviewees' narratives exposes contradictions and tensions regarding embodied aging. We learn that certain positive aging experiences and attitudes coexist with internalized oppressive habits and attitudes toward aging, toward being old women and men, and toward others who are old. Additionally, we come to appreciate the pervasiveness and insidiousness of our youth-obsessed culture. The narratives reveal a multitude of ways, both mental and physical, our old interviewees cope with experiencing an aging body in a society where being old is something to fight against and fear.

One way that our interviewees deal with living in an old body in an ageist society is by "distancing" themselves from their actual chronological age, as well as disassociating themselves from other old people. In these ways, the old lesbians and gay men employ strategies of separation in order to establish that they are not, in fact, "old." But this is a complicated story. Although the topic was not explored specifically in the interviews, it is worth noting that six of the eight partnered lesbians interviewed are with women 10–19 years younger than themselves. This is also the case for the two partnered gay men. A number of our interviewees noted spending time with younger people. At least implicitly, this hints at the role sexual orientation plays in their choice of younger companions and, as such, underscores that the distancing engaged in by these old gay men and women is multifaceted.

Nevertheless, these old gays and lesbians also share some distancing strategies with their heterosexual age cohorts. Like Minichiello, Browne, and Kendig (2000) and Hurd's (1999) old heterosexual respondents, our respondents also negotiate their aging bodies by "distancing" themselves from negative ideas associated with being old and creating alternative examples of what it means to age. This active approach to aging supports Laz's (2003) argument that age is something we accomplish or perform—we "do age," just as we "do gender" (West & Zimmerman, 1987). Within the structures and institutions that frame our worlds, we work to give meaning to our own age and to age in general.

Like Hurd's (1999) interviewees, for example, all the women in this study took great pleasure in their belief that they look and feel younger than their chronological ages. Indeed, the further the distance between their chronological ages and their appearances as judged by others, the greater the satisfaction expressed. Becca (68) mentions how young it makes her feel when people comment: "You don't look your age, I thought you were 58." Covering or passively "passing" as younger than one's real age is also a strategy sometimes used by old gay interviewees, a strategy that seems to be an accommodation to the ageism that old people encounter in their daily lives. Peter (62) attempts to distance himself from his chronological age by asserting, "I do not feel old, so when I hear the word 'old' I can't relate to it." Or, as Bart (67) explains, "I don't like the term 'old.' . . . I hate [the term] 'senior citizens.'"

Another distancing technique employed by our respondents involves differentiating between *feeling* old and *being* old. Consistent with previous research (Hurd, 2000; Minichiello et al., 2000), our respondents define the markers of being "not old" as keeping busy and being intellectually engaged, active, fit, and "productive." For example, Rita's explanation for being seen as younger than her chronological age has to do with "my energy and the vitality with which I . . . live my life." Being energetic and active is critical to the distancing tactics to which other lesbians and gay men also allude. Eliza (71), for instance, explains why she has aged "very well": "A lot has to do with [the fact] that I'm still interested in things and still active and I enjoy life." Our gay male respondents likewise reveal the ambivalence associated with embodied aging in our society. Victor (71), refusing to see himself as "old," claims that "I do not see myself as an older person. I do not feel like an older person. I don't feel much different than I can remember feeling 40 to 50 years ago. I am thrilled with that. I'm so glad that is the case." In a similar vein, Gary (64) states: "I do not admit that my body has slowed down."

When juxtaposed against the previous section on accepting an aging body, particularly within the lesbian community, the above comments illuminate the extent to which our interviewees have internalized negative notions about old age found in the broader culture. The comments also underscore how attractiveness—sexual and otherwise—is based on youthful standards that emphasize being active and involved while also implying negative stereotypes of old people as being inactive and dull. Thus, age relations, regardless of sexual orientation, it seems, dictate that we uphold and value youth and that we recognize nothing positive in being old. Acceptance of these youthful standards by our interviewees reproduces ageism by reinforcing the idea that to be old is bad and that to be seen as more youthful than one's chronological age is good.

Disciplining the Old Body

Whereas the above strategies involve respondents mentally separating themselves from their chronological age and socially separating themselves from other old people, our interviewees also work on their actual physical bodies as a way to negotiate in an ageist society. Exercising, dieting, and having cosmetic surgery are all discussed by our respondents as ways to resist growing or looking old and to remain sexually attractive. Exploring the ways that these old lesbians and gay men deal with and fight against the inevitable corporeal changes that accompany growing old allows us to examine how multiple social locations, including gender, class, and sexual orientation, shape conceptions of the body and highlights the necessity of considering age relations and ageism in order to understand embodied self concepts fully.

Before examining the actual physical ways our respondents discipline their bodies, it is important to briefly consider how these old men and women assess their embodied gender. For the most part, the literature emphasizes women's complicated relationships with their bodies and demonstrates that women experience high levels of dissatisfaction with their bodies in general, and body weight in particular (Abell & Richards, 1996; Cash, 2000). This is not surprising, given that women, but not men, are socialized to view their self-worth in terms of physical appearance. Our interviews lend support to previous studies (e.g., Brand et al., 1992; Copper, 1988; Herzog, Newman, Yeh, & Warshaw, 1992) that show little difference between lesbians and heterosexual women. Overall, our female respondents are not content with their bodies and feel pressure to continue to actively discipline their bodies to obtain the youthful standard of an attractive body. Our male interviewees, although much more body-conscious than the heterosexual men in our larger study, share with their heterosexual counterparts gendered advantages when it comes to body satisfaction. Despite being less effusive about the positive aspects of their aging bodies, they are still much less negative than our female respondents, including our lesbian respondents (see Lakkis et al., 1999; Russell & Keel, 2002; Wood, 2004). James (64) asserts: "I feel okay about [my body]. I'm obviously not totally satisfied with it." Or, as Eric states, he feels "good, not wonderful but good" about his body at this stage of his life. Thus, at least in our study, gender appears to be a better predictor of overall body satisfaction than sexual orientation.

The lesbians in our study, however, do reflect a complicated relationship with their bodies. We hear their ambivalence toward being old in their narratives and how they waver between positive and negative bodily assessments. Although unhappy with the way her body looks, Sara (65) says that "at the end of the day when you come home from the gym [your body] still may not look like what you want it to look like and that's the point at which we have to start learning how to love ourselves as we are." Underscoring the need to consider personal biography and life course issues, others posit that women who were beautiful when young find it more painful to deal with the loss of their youthful looks. Certainly this observation resonates with the experiences of Miriam (61). A former homecoming queen, she is, of all the women interviewed, the most invested in her appearance and the most unhappy with how she looks at this stage of her life. She alleges that "I don't feel quite as much pressure about [my body] now. I'm more accepting of it in a way than I was even when I was young. I was more critical of it back then; now I am more accepting. I'm not happy about it but I am more accepting." Interestingly, while these women *appear* to accept their no longer youthful, thin bodies, they are still dissatisfied and still physically work at achieving an ever elusive younger, thinner, more sexually attractive body.

Although body dissatisfaction appears more tied to gender than sexual orientation, at least based on our interviews, both the old lesbians and gay men in our study engage in dieting, fitness activities, and body maintenance techniques that emphasize youthful appearances. In a society where the ideal body is one that is young and slender it makes sense that these women and men would have a hard time accepting a body that is no longer youthful, or necessarily thin, and would fight looking old in a variety of ways. Disciplining the body in order to strive to meet youthful standards of attractive bodies thus emerges as a strategy of accommodation to ageist notions of what acceptable female and male bodies look like.

Diet

A dominant body image issue for both the women and men we interviewed is weight, and one way to discipline the body is through dieting. Women especially are concerned with weight. Our old lesbians resemble Hurd's (1999) heterosexual interviewees who are uniformly dissatisfied with their weight and who express a sense of failure or defeat in their attempts to discipline their aging bodies. For all of the nine women interviewed, weight emerged as a nagging, problematic concern in our conversations. That these women are lesbian provides them little, if any, relief from the never-ending obsession with weight issues. Eliza (71) states that she is "not very happy right now. I guess I weigh too much. I don't like the fact that I have gained weight." Only one, Gail (73), talked little about weight concerns during the interview because, as she proudly pointed out early in our conversation, she had lost 35 pounds in the last year and felt no need to lose more weight.

Only one gay man claimed to be at his ideal weight while the remaining nine judged themselves to be between 5 to 75 pounds overweight. Four of the ten gay men spoke of actively dieting, four claimed that they did not diet, and two spoke of watching carefully what they ate. In general, they were less critical of their bodies than their lesbian counterparts. For instance, Peter (62), who did not diet, claims that he "could lose 10 pounds and be happy" but is not willing to diet to achieve a slimmer body.

Exercise

In addition to dieting, most of our interviewees engage in some type of physical exercise to accommodate yet again the ageist notion of what an acceptable body should look like. Although many of our respondents justify their exercising as a way to stay healthy and fit (which certainly is an important objective of their working out), their comments make clear that their physical activity is also an attempt to meet the youthful standards of physically and sexually attractive, thin bodies in our culture. Beth, who at 67 goes to the gym three times a week and does strength training with a personal trainer once a week, remarks, "I want to continue to get stronger, to develop some muscles.

I want to get about 10 pounds off. I kind of got stuck. I'd like to get some off this abdomen. I don't know that it will ever happen [*laughs*]." Becca (68) adds, "At this point I'm a little concerned about myself because . . . 4 years ago I was eight pounds lighter and a lot stronger and that stresses me some. I am working on that. I want to get to 4 days a week [in the gym] and then 5 maybe." The women, even as they head into their seventies and beyond, feel obligated to exercise in order to approximate the youthful body standards that our culture requires of women. In addition to showing how women discipline the body through exercise, these quotes also point out the agelessness of many women's (particularly white, affluent women's) weight obsession.

The gay men in our study also work at disciplining their bodies via exercise. As discussed earlier, our male respondents appear to adhere to the importance of looking attractive (i.e., young and thin) because of the emphasis gay culture places on youthful, fit bodies. Several interviewees assert that gay men age better than heterosexual men because they pay more attention to keeping youthful bodies through disciplining them in a variety of ways, including exercise. Raymond (67), for example, is quite explicit about the ageism that underscores this obligatory dictate of keeping up appearances: "Old gay men feel compelled to do everything they can to hide the ravages of their body. They dye their hair, they have facelifts, they wear clothing that they think makes them look younger . . . they do a lot of exercise."

The Impact of Class

As our interviewees talk in different ways about the obligation they feel to discipline their bodies, including by restricting their eating and by exercising regularly, they are able to perform "active" aging. Being well educated, healthy, and health-conscious provides them with a language that justifies their disciplinary activities. As discussed earlier, they frequently emphasize health and not physical attractiveness as the motivator for staying active. What is not acknowledged, however, is the role that social class plays in their disciplinary activities. Social class privilege reinforces the need to engage in body discipline because the means are available and not to avail oneself of what these means can purchase signals "moral failure or laxity" (Hurd, 2000, p. 91). Having the economic resources to work on their bodies on a regular basis links these adults' disciplinary activities to their class privilege—a privilege that allows certain women and men to resist being old (and looking old) longer than those who do not have such resources. Their class position also affords them a final way of disciplining their body via cosmetic surgery.

Cosmetic Surgery

For affluent old women and men, regardless of sexual orientation, cosmetic surgery offers a way to regain or sustain a more youthful appearance and to pass as younger than one's chronological age. Both the old lesbians and gay men in our study discuss this strategy to maintain a youthful look in an ageist society. The assumption that old lesbians might reject such surgery as being the domain of heterosexual women who strive to create an embodied self that is young and attractive to men is not borne out from our interviews. Instead, we find mixed, complicated responses to the issue of cosmetic surgery, lending support to arguments that male approval is not the only reason to have such surgery (Gagné & McGaughey, 2002; Davis, 1995). The majority of our female respondents (six) took the position that lesbians must decide for themselves whether or not to have cosmetic surgery. As Barbara (68) put it: "If it makes you feel better, do it!" One woman in our sample had already had cosmetic surgery, two were actively planning to have some form of surgery in the next few years, and two were very open to the idea but had not yet made up their minds. Miriam (61), who has undergone a modified face lift and "eye job," expressly states that the motivation behind the surgery is to look younger, knowing that to be younger is more valued in our society: "Oh, God, yes it makes me feel better. I look at pictures of myself before [the surgery] and I feel I look younger now than I looked when I was 50." Determined to manage away the outward signs of looking old, Miriam is keenly aware of the cultural obsession with youth and the equation of youth with beauty and sexual attractiveness (Oberg & Tornstam, 2001; Laws, 1995).

Only three women in our sample are opposed to cosmetic surgery. One of these women opposes surgery because she worked in a medical setting and witnessed some very negative outcomes from such surgery. The other two are opposed on the grounds that women in general, and old lesbians in particular, who elect to have such surgeries are adhering to hegemonic cultural norms—especially those that emphasize youthfulness. Beth (67), for example, claims not to know any lesbians who have had cosmetic surgery and she assumes that this is because "it is rejection of that male-identified female stereotype about how you should look." Rita, who knows a number of old lesbians who have had cosmetic surgery or who plan to have it soon, expresses her resistance: "It's more painful to see someone that is older trying to do surgery to look young. I think they lose the dignity and the wisdom of aging. I think there is a beauty in getting old." These two old lesbians, however, are a minority in our sample when it comes to acceptance of surgery as a way to accommodate an aging body in ageist society.

Seeking to maintain a youthful appearance through cosmetic surgery is something that four of the old gay male interviewees are also willing to consider. For instance, James (64) claims, "If I had lots of money, I guess I would. I'd have a body makeover." Considering both a facelift and liposuction, Eric (60) admits that he has been "seriously considering it for a year or two" and has even gone so far as to get the name of a local cosmetic surgeon. Gary (64) said: "You've got to deal with what you've got . . . next time I go to Brazil I'm going to have some face work done." Gary is interested in removing liver spots—an outward sign of aging. Similar to our lesbian respondents, however, some of the gay men in our study are against cosmetic surgery, thus revealing diverse responses to the aging body. Peter (62), who admits to dyeing his hair, insists he would not consider the more extreme body-altering technique of cosmetic surgery: "Never in a thousand years!" Raymond (67) also claims he would never alter his body through surgery.

Complete or even qualified acceptance of cosmetic surgery underscores the pervasiveness of youthful standards of attractiveness in our ageist society. The acceptance of, or at least a laissez-faire attitude toward, cosmetic surgery by the majority of our interviewees appears to reflect an internalized ageism that glorifies youthfulness by obligating privileged old women and men to engage in invasive, expensive body work to avoid looking old.

Conclusion

Our findings illustrate the complexity of the embodied aging experience and provide us a glimpse of how sexuality and aging are experienced by these gay men and lesbians. Additionally, our data underscore how critical a life course perspective is for understanding the complex lives of these populations. Furthermore, while different views on aging and different approaches to growing and being old are evident, our interviews also lend support to previous studies that posit a pervasive ageism in our society (Cruikshank, 2009; Hurd, 2000; Markson & Taylor, 2000). Thus, although not all of the lesbians and gay men interviewed use the same strategies as they negotiate aging, most actively work to acquire a preferred embodied identity of being not old—or at least not looking as old as they are. Their bodies are vehicles for creating meaning about aging and about old age, and their comments and actions reveal an internalized ageism about aging bodies that leads them to distance themselves from and to fight corporeal evidence of aging.

The power of the male gaze in enforcing youthful standards of feminine beauty in our culture may lead one to assume that lesbians, unconcerned with the male gaze, are more accepting of the aging female body. The lesbians in our study, however, provide a more complex view. Although many of the women's comments indicate a relatively accepting view of the aging female body within the lesbian community at large, most of our respondents' personal evaluations of their own bodies reveal some contradictory and negative feelings. These less positive feelings align with the work of Copper (1988), who argues that gender trumps sexual orientation in matters such as body image and body satisfaction. It appears that the hegemonic male gaze sets a standard that women, regardless of sexual orientation, internalize and exercise on themselves (Gagné & McGaughey, 2002). Thus, lesbians, although not dependent on male approval to feel sexually attractive, do ascribe to broader cultural standards of youthful beauty.

Gay men in our study also display a broad range of feelings about aging and the aging body. Overall, however, the narratives of the gay men reveal the coercive nature of the norms of youthfulness and their accompanying emphasis on actively fighting aging bodies. Through the voices of these men, we learn how deeply age matters and how ageist notions of aging prevail. The men's narratives attest to a long-standing assumption about gay culture: ageism is prominent, and much of this ageism is related to the body. Given the emphasis on youth within gay male culture, this ageism is not surprising. But, as with our lesbian interviewees, the men's responses revealed contradictory personal feelings about embodied aging and the stigma involved with aging in a youth-obsessed culture.

The narratives of these lesbians and gay men lend credence to Laws's (1995) claim that ageism is an embodied form of oppression. Like all old people, these lesbians and gay men live in a society where the "cultural imperialism of youthfulness" is pervasive and where ageism plays a central role in identity (Laws, 1995). Lesbians and gay men engage in a variety of ageist coping strategies, including distancing themselves from old age by "age passing," avoiding others who are seen to be old, and disciplining their bodies through diet, exercise, and even cosmetic surgery. Based on the voices of our interviewees, the hegemonic standards of youthfulness that stigmatize old age and old bodies appear to apply to both women and men, regardless of sexual orientation. As stated at the beginning of our chapter, it is through the body that we experience desire, sexual pleasure, and sexual practices, and one has to wonder if our respondents, as well as other old gays and lesbians, would experience these aspects of sexuality differently in a culture that did not denigrate their old bodies.

NOTES

1. Due to the devaluation of the term "old" in our youth-obsessed culture, we want to reclaim its positive connotations, to naturalize and neutralize it. We use it here—rather than "older"—in an activist manner. See Calasanti and Slevin (2001).

2. The little research available in this area includes Furman's (1997) study finding that many of the old (55 to 86) heterosexual white women she interviewed felt both shame and stigma as they experienced the decrease of the male gaze at the same time that they were subjected to a gaze of youth. Hurd's (2000) study of 50- to 90-year-olds confirms the notion that many old women see their bodies negatively.

3. All respondent names are pseudonyms.

14

Pleasure in Old Age

MEIKA LOE

How many of us associate pleasure, joy, or satisfaction with turning 90? It is usually the opposite—we are taught to brace ourselves, preparing for pain and discomfort in the last years of our lives. And yet old age does not necessarily negate pleasure, intimacy, or personal growth. I argue here that the very old, those aged 85 and beyond, actively accomplish both familiar and new forms of sensuality and pleasure, sometimes in spite of themselves.

This chapter takes a close look at 30 of the oldest old, the major transitions and guiding themes across each of their lives, and the ways in which their accumulated experiences contribute to how they currently constitute pleasure. A life course perspective helps to reveal both continuity and change in meanings and experiences of pleasure across one's life (see chapter 1). A "linked lives" perspective also helps to expose how lives, while seeming independent, are very much interdependent, such that the experience of pleasure is always a social and relational process (Moen, 1996; Elder, 1995). Although this chapter incorporates sexualities, life satisfaction and intimacy are much broader. To approach this topic with a traditional sexuality research frame would not do this (or any) age group and their experiences justice. Instead, an approach that focuses on pleasure, broadly construed, can perhaps counter the resounding silence about satisfaction and intimacy in old age.

As Levy (1994) points out, the old are writing new sexual scripts, and researchers interested in sexuality and aging must take into account how sexuality is and has been constructed by elders themselves, now and in the past.[1] Gender inequalities shape approaches to pleasure and common definitions of "normal" sexuality (Calasanti & Slevin, 2001). In other words, gender relations structure how elders experience sex. The majority of contemporary elders, particularly the "oldest old" in the United States (those age 85 and over), are primarily women. Women elders in particular may view their own sexuality in the context of marital and family obligations, health concerns, and male pleasure, and less in terms of individual pleasure (Loe, 2004). Thus, pleasure and sexuality could be antithetical, particularly for some women in this age group. Conversely, male elders have likely been taught to equate masculinity with sexual potency and performance, and therefore they have a vested interest in penile performance throughout life. Ironically, this investment may obscure or reduce pleasure, particularly in the context of health concerns in late life (Loe, 2004).

Few individuals in the age cohort I studied (born between 1910 and 1925) are currently involved in intimate sexual relationships; many have been widowed or single for many years, and they may not remember or care to discuss their past intimate relationships. Additionally, most are living solitary lives. Despite this profile, this heterogeneous group of old women and men desire and experience a range of pleasures in their day-to-day lives, including sexual and/or sensory pleasures and gratifying interpersonal relationships. In fact, social capital, shorthand for what social scientists see as the value associated with social networks and connectedness, may be increasingly salient in old age, in the context of potentially increased isolation and loss (Klinenberg, 2002; Putnam & Feldstein, 2003).

Centering the life experiences of the oldest old, I frame this analysis in broad terms related to pleasure, inclusive of but not limited to intimacy or sexuality, to address the diverse ways that nonagenarians and centenarians subjectively experience delight in late life. This analysis is divided into four nondistinct categories of pleasure. *Sexual relationships* involve sexual intimacy, generally in the context of marriage or dating. *Nonsexual intimacies* are gratifying social and physical connections with others including social groups, family members, strangers, caregivers, pets, and extended kin. *Caretaking* involves tending to the self and others in a multiplicity of ways. *Intellectual stimulation* encompasses personal satisfaction associated with thinking and problem solving in individual and group settings. As we will see, each of these arenas of life may or may not be associated with pleasure for any particular elder. Moreover, these pleasures can be achieved separately or in combination, as when caretaking involves intellectual problem solving and social and physical connectedness. Finally, each of these forms of pleasure is deeply integrated into these elders' everyday lives, so much so that they may seem unremarkable. Remarkable or not, I argue that these everyday pleasures can contribute to health and longevity and can teach us general lessons about the importance of social capital across the life course. I will return to those lessons in the conclusion.

Methods

For three years, I followed 30 individuals, age 85 and older, living in the upstate region of New York. Each person participated in at least one life history interview including open-ended questions about the course of their lives, focusing on family, educational, and work backgrounds as well as current daily routines and approaches to aging and self-care. Interviews took place in their homes (apartment, condo, house, or group home) located in rural, urban, and suburban areas. All interviews were audio recorded, transcribed, and coded thematically.[2]

In addition, I employed ethnographic methods to collect data about lived day-to-day experiences. Beyond regular visits to homes, I participated in these elders' lives and daily routines outside of their homes, including intermittent doctor visits, grocery shopping trips, social club meetings, exercise classes, neighborhood meals, funeral services, birthday parties, and religious rituals. I communicated regularly by phone and email with those who were willing. I also logged approximately 150 hours observing a combination of regional aging-related meetings and conferences, touring institutions dedicated to elder care, and conducting interviews with professionals in elder support and care.

To find study participants, I became a fixture at several senior centers. In an age-segregated, stratified society, elder-oriented organizations are some of the only places to meet old people, particularly those living independently. I met many study participants in fitness classes, over meals, and in discussion groups. Ultimately, I described my research to the leaders of these community organizations, who agreed to contact their elder members and ask if they would be willing to participate in my study. Most of the elders I contacted wondered why anyone was interested in their lives, but in the end many agreed to be interviewed. I also met study participants in intergenerational neighborhoods and in women's organizations. Some were visible anomalies in their organizations and communities, celebrated for their age. One was highlighted in a local newspaper article. Others were introduced to me by people they knew.

Importantly, very few of the oldest old knew others in their age group; most felt alone in their old age.[3] But they were not alone. Combinations of intergenerational networks, family connections, and membership in at least one organization constituted advantages that accumulated over time for these 30 study participants, all of whom were somewhat visible and "known" in their communities. These accumulated social advantages (O'Rand, 2002), I argue, contribute to their health and longevity. More vulnerable and neglected old individuals living independently were difficult to locate; most are rendered further invisible in their poverty and social isolation (Klinenberg, 2002).

This sample is largely representative of the national population in this age group. According to the U.S. Census (He, Sengupta, Velkoff, & DeBarros, 2005), over 90% of those over 85 years old are white. Likewise, this sample includes 26 individuals who identify as white with Polish, Danish, Irish, Italian, and Jewish ethnic backgrounds; three who identify as African American; and one who is Puerto Rican. All would consider themselves to be middle-class, but their late-life realities place them in a range of poor to affluent contexts. Of the 30, 23 are women and 7 are men. This is slightly higher than the national average, with a women-to-men ratio of 2.6:1.

The cohort effect is crucial in understanding these study participants' views and experiences with sexuality (Maddox, 1979; Riley, 1987). All participants in this study belong to the cohort sometimes referred to as the "Greatest Generation" or the "GI Generation." They have likely been exposed to similar social messages and silences regarding sexuality. We can expect this group of mostly nonagenarians to be more modest and guarded about sex than Baby Boomers, who came of age in a more sexually permissive era.[4] That said, those coming of age in the period just after World War I did so against the backdrop of Freudianism, eugenics, a contraceptive revolution led by Margaret Sanger, the growth of coeducational institutions that provided for new sexual freedoms, and the growing middle-class ideal of "companionate marriage" (D'Emilio & Freedman, 1997). This history—in combination with individual characteristics, including one's socioeconomic status, race, ethnicity, gender, sexual orientation, physical ability, and age—has shaped options and opportunities across the life course (Calasanti & Slevin, 2001). As a result, despite some similarities, the ways in which the oldest old have actively accomplished intimacy across their lives differ from one person to the next, largely structured by these varying social relations, locations, and life experiences.

Pleasure across the Life Course

In *The Ageless Self,* Kaufman (1994) reminds us that we all work at continuity across the life course, using guiding themes to ground us, to help us construct meaning, and to transcend changes that result from the physical and mental manifestations of old age. Consequently, how one actively "does" pleasure today may be very much linked to how one has done pleasure in the past. That is not to say that we are all static beings, experiencing pleasure in the same ways over the course of life. My data reveal both continuity and change—and this is where a life course perspective helps to illuminate the ways in which life events push individuals in new and varied directions.

The "oldest old" are rarely if ever included in sexuality research, reinforcing the invisibility of sexuality, intimacy, and pleasure in late life (Laumann, 1995). However, some feminist researchers have been helpful in conceptualizing how pleasure is socially constituted, embodied, and contextualized in the context of aging. Recent empirical studies by Connidis (2006) and Gott (2005), theoretical work by Calasanti and Slevin (2001), and surveys including the National Social Life, Health, and Aging Project (Das et al., this volume) provide important starting places for thinking through pleasure across the life course. These works find a narrow intercourse-centered approach to researching aging and sexuality too limiting. At the same time, most of these studies remain limited in their focus on sexuality rather than a broad conception of pleasure (sexual and nonsexual gratification).

Connidis's (2006) approach is broader than most. To understand intimacy over the life course, she takes the vantage point of accumulated experience, exploring cumulative advantages and disadvantages over one's life. Such a framework can be helpful for understanding how experience shapes intimacy (see chapter 1, this volume). Specifically, Connidis defines intimate relationships as involving commitment, deep feelings and expressions of caring and compassion, thinking about another and sharing values and goals, physical intimacy, and interdependence. However, while Connidis takes into account marriage, remarriage, and other forms of relationships, her model is not broad enough to include close friendship and other nonsexual relationships. Notably, a focus on intimacy may or may not correlate with pleasure and happiness.

Calasanti and Slevin's (2001) work on age relations helps us to see how experience, in this case embodied pleasure, is shaped by one's context—by structural relations and social inequalities—as well as by history and generational cohort. As they point out, sexuality has been historically defined as male; sexual language emphasizes intercourse, penetration, and male pleasure. As a result, women may derive more pleasure outside of traditional sexual scripts, and they may construct intimacy elsewhere. Sex and pleasure may be antithetical for women across the generational spectrum.[5] Beyond gender, the interdisciplinary scholars Kaschak and Tiefer (2001) remind us that subjective experiences of sexual satisfaction are rooted in overlapping relational, cultural, psychological, and generational contexts, and are closely linked to social location. I offer here that the life stage can also be salient; a wide range of social connections and intimate relationships can offer new and important benefits in the last years of life.

The 2005–2006 National Social Life, Health, and Aging Project (NSHAP), a national probability survey of 3,005 men and women between the ages of 57 and 85, focused on intimate social relationships, including marriage, family, social ties, and sexuality. It may be the first national sexuality study to include sexual and nonsexual intimacy in its measures (including nonsexual intimacies with grandchildren, pets, and others). The study authors (Waite et al., 2009) report strong evidence of both sexual and nonsexual intimacies in late life, with a general decline in both with age (see also Das et al., this volume.) Despite its path-breaking understanding of aging in the context of relationships, NSHAP's quantitative design and methodology limit its ability to account for complex and shifting interpersonal meanings and processes. A qualitative retrospective approach has enabled me to further probe the diverse ways in which elders subjectively experience and process pleasure within and outside of traditional sexuality and intimacy frameworks over time.

Sexuality in Old Age

Lillian, Seymour, and Dorothy all talk about sexuality as a part of who they are as ninetysomethings, but each defines and "does" sexuality quite differently, based on accumulated experiences, health, and social locations. Whereas Lillian tells stories of pleasure associated with romantic rituals and "a little bit of sex" with her second husband, Seymour tells of a need for sensuality in the context of physical impairment, and Dorothy derives satisfaction in healing from childhood sexual abuse.

If Lillian, a white, Jewish, hearing-impaired elder, age 90, were to write her autobiography, it would be about how opera brought her pleasure and romance, two wonderful husbands, and a lifelong passion. Lillian shares how, in the 1930s, a fellow student at NYU took her to *Madame Butterfly*. She says, "That day, [my first husband] detected my interest in opera and the way I responded to the music." They went to many shows together and eventually fell in love and married. Lillian went on to teach classes on how to appreciate opera, and she continues to think about her life as a kind of romantic fantasy.

Today Lillian is enjoying sexual intimacy and romance with her second husband, Bernie. Of this guiding theme throughout her life, she says:

We enjoy spending time together and [we enjoy] a little bit of sex. It is very satisfactory, by the way. It always has been for me. Bernie said I can't offer you much in the way of physical things but a lot of hugs and kisses, and I thought okay. . . . Well the first night I felt like I was back to being a virgin again in his bedroom wondering what's coming on your wedding night and he comes in and it was just lovely and I said to him, Bernie, you sold yourself short! . . . I wish I felt better now, but Bernie and I love each other very much. We watch romance movies every night on cable. . . .

Lillian exemplifies how past enjoyment of sexuality shapes one's sexuality late in life (Minichiello et al., 1996). In her case, the accumulation of healthy, satisfying sexual relationships has reinforced the importance of sexual intimacy over her life. However, health status and medical side effects also shape the potential for sexual intimacy (Clements, 1996). In Lillian's case, being constantly connected to an oxygen tank, experiencing problems with hearing, and "not feeling so hot" may limit options for sexual expression; but she makes sure these difficulties do not get in the way of romantic traditions, including physical proximity and togetherness rituals. Lillian's quote also reveals how gender relations play into definitions of sexuality. Whereas Bernie seems to apologize for not being able to perform sexually, Lillian focuses on stroking his ego and emphasizing romance and intimacy for herself. At the same time, Lillian goes against stereotypes of the sexless old in stating that she desires and derives pleasure in sex, and always has.

In contrast to Lillian, Seymour, a short, balding Jewish nonagenarian who has been deaf since his teenage years, has a different vested interest in emphasizing his continuing interest in sexuality and women. In doing this he can continue to accomplish masculinity and youthfulness, even in the context of old age and disability. Seymour suggests that his need for intimacy and sexual touch has intensified in the context of his changing health and physical impairment. Communication is now accomplished through touch with his second wife:

I wouldn't be here if it weren't for her, but don't tell her. [He points to his second wife of 36 years.]. . . Touch is very desirous to me, if for no other reason than it brings the other person closer to me than if it was a conversation, which for all intents and purposes is very difficult because of my severe hearing impairment. This, of course, may not be true for others in my age group who do not have this handicap. . . . Generally speaking I am still very much "aware" of the opposite sex; that feeling has never lessened although there is not much I can do about it!

Here Seymour makes clear that although his ability to be sexually aroused and to communicate have shifted with age and time, he still desires women and feels like a (heterosexual) man. Lillian and Seymour defy the stereotype of the sexless old, actively "doing" sexuality and intimacy through romance and through touch and humor, respectively. Both have been married twice, and they both rave about how satisfying their marriages have been.

Dorothy, a tall, stately 96-year-old with Scottish ancestry, tells a different story about sexual intimacy. Like the others, she had a happy marriage—and many happy years of dating prior to meeting her husband. She described herself as "boy crazy" in college, looking for the perfect mate and dating three men at a time. It was intellect that dazzled her and led her to marry an academic. She recalls romantic moments involving watching sunsets together, and she loved listening to her husband deliver lectures at the university.

Dorothy was widowed in 1988 (at the age of 78), and in the mid-1990s she became close with a man she met on an Elder Hostel excursion.[6] She said, "I would have liked to hug this man, but I didn't. I didn't feel anything. I loved—loved from my head, but didn't feel anything." So she started to think back on her marriage and her relationships prior to that, and how familiar this felt—"not *feeling* anything" other than from her head. At the age of 87, she sought a therapist to help her piece things together.

Dorothy's therapist helped her to realize that she was sexually abused as a child by an uncle who would masturbate and sexually experiment on her. Dorothy remembered that she imitated what she saw her uncle doing and was severely reprimanded as a child. Later, she was warned not to let men make a fool out of her. "I was a preacher's daughter studying theology, after all," she says. These accumulated experiences, she came to understand, led her to be "repressed down there" for many years. Her husband never knew that Dorothy had been sexually abused, and neither did she. At age 87 Dorothy started the healing process, and opened up to her friends about her past in an intimate healing ceremony. (Dorothy borrowed this idea from a friend who held a healing ceremony for something else; she realized that a ritual process based on honesty about her past, coupled with support from close friends and family, and music, could help her to heal.)

Being a victim of childhood sexual abuse by a family member shaped the ensuing nine decades of Dorothy's sexual opportunities (see Carbone-Lopez, this volume). Today, Dorothy's healing work continues with her therapist and on her own. One therapist suggested that she walk back through life events with her child-self, whom she calls Dorothia, to understand how she, as a child, responded to sexual abuse. This therapeutic memory work is both difficult and joyful. For example, Dorothy says, "I was there when Dorothia experienced her first shower. And when she came out of the shower and was giggling she really opened up to me!" Meanwhile, the elder Dorothy continues her lifelong passion for reading, writing, and thinking, daily pleasures that were encouraged by her academic family from an early age and that continued throughout her life married to a professor.

Lillian, Seymour, and Dorothy have experienced intimacy differently throughout their lives in ways that were reinforced through social location, relationship contexts, and accumulated advantages and disadvantages. Today, each is doing and expressing sexuality in new ways in late life. Against adversity, Dorothy is now rediscovering her sexual self in new ways, as are Lillian and Seymour in the context of new partners, health constraints, and loss. All three are actively engaging with intimacy in memory and in material life. As such, they are sexual agents in late life, despite stereotypes to the contrary.

Nonsexual Intimacies: "Adopted" Family and Dinner Dates

Contrary to popular assumptions, social networks do not disappear as one ages. Later life transitions, such as retirement and bereavement, may even prompt greater connectedness (Cornwell et al., 2008). Nonsexual intimacies define most nonagenarians' daily lives. Social connections, including weak and strong social ties with friends, pets, strangers, caregivers, and newly adopted family members, can be crucial to quality of life, social support, visibility, and countering loneliness.[7] Many of the oldest old work at building and maintaining these ties. As Alice, Julia, and Rose describe, connecting with others, making friends, socializing, and creating and reconfiguring social families can be crucial activities in a context of social isolation.

Whereas Lillian, Seymour, and Dorothy spent the majority of their adult lives in spousal relationships, Alice, a tall, slender 92-year-old with British ancestry, bobbed white hair, and waning eyesight, has spent most of her life in close friendship with women. Alice's life exemplifies the multiple worlds of intimacy one can occupy across the life course (Connidis, 2006). In large part because of the gender-segregated nature of her schooling and occupational life, most of her mentors and peers were women. She tells stories of strong friendships with girls and women from her "days of freedom" growing up in a tight-knit, diverse, urban neighborhood and spending endless time with fellow girlfriends and her beloved nursemaid; to passing around illicit lesbian poetry in her all-girl schools; to her years as an "independent woman" and feminist working in a number of occupations and being inspired by the suffragettes of her mother's and grandmothers' generations. Alice's adult life was about self-sufficiency. She supported herself economically through a series of university librarian positions and lived alone, devoting her free time to philanthropic work caring for destitute elder women. In her seventies, Alice had a short marriage to a childhood friend and widower, and she took care of him in his last years of life. After her husband's death, Alice again found solace in close relationships with women. She joined a women's research club, took care of poor women in an elder home, and traveled to Europe with girlfriends into her seventies. Alice speaks of the joy of staying in touch with one close friend of many years, describing what sustains the friendship. "We think very similarly. Although we cannot see each other anymore, we talk [by phone] quite regularly." Although Alice has lost most of her close friends to death, she continues to make new ones, as evidenced by the 100 individuals who attended her ninetieth birthday party.

Alice says her relationships with women have never been intimate in a sexual sense, but they have helped her to grow emotionally, politically, and intellectually. In this way, Alice's life suggests that a spectrum of intimacy can include close friendships along what Adrienne Rich (1980/1994) would call a "lesbian continuum," starting with intimate relationships with one's mother (or, in Alice's case, her nursemaid) and then other women (aunts, friends, teachers, coworkers, peers), providing continuity throughout one's life.

Whenever possible, Alice takes advantage of opportunities to make new connections and construct new friendships, using humor and body language. She says, "I try to understand people and support where they are. To treat them as I would like to be treated." She jokes around in an attempt to make her stern doctor laugh, and she tries a variety of tactics to connect with young people, even when they don't return her eye contact. Alice also insists on certain forms of physical touch with friends, loved ones, and pets. She says, "Hugs are good for people, especially old people. . . . It is a need—almost involuntary." And even though her 13-year-old pet cat Bart has gotten more rebellious with age, sometimes biting her and others, she cannot bring herself to say goodbye to him. (On the importance of physical closeness with pets, particularly for those leading mostly sedentary lives, see Thomas, 2004.)

Physical proximity to others can be so important for those living alone that they may take great risks to achieve this. While Alice insists on hugs from friends and pets (even after being bitten by her cat) and goes out of her comfort zone to make new friends, Julia risked her life driving at night to be in close proximity with others. Before her death in 2008, Julia, a medium-sized former softball player, talked about the importance of "getting with people." Fittingly, Julia was surrounded by people during a church service when she died at the age of 95.

Julia grew up white and middle-class in a small town with a hardworking father and no mother. When her sister, who was her best friend, died young, Julia took it hard. Socializing and physical closeness with others became important to ease loneliness and to stay healthy. She stated:

> [Socializing] keeps my brain from getting scrambled. . . . It is important to get with people. I do the library book group and the bible study at church and read and watch TV. I sometimes go to dinner or lunch although I shouldn't drive at night. Mo comes every night except Sundays. She is good for me.

Julia paid Mo, a homeless woman who was sleeping in various garages in her residential neighborhood, to vacuum her home, rake leaves, and set up holiday decorations. Julia knew that Mo had schizophrenia but still delighted in her company. Julia explained, "Most nights Mo would bring a frozen meal she recovered from the grocery store dumpster, and I would eat a can of soup." This regular dinner date was something Julia looked forward to. At her funeral, family members were eager to meet Mo, Julia's closest friend.

The creation of a social family is nothing new for Rose, a bubbly African American elder with bright blue eyes who adopted three children as an adult and has more recently "adopted" a close friend who checks in on her regularly. Rose says she practically grew up in the church, which she describes as her second family. There, everyone shares their troubles and feels loved:

> I take them all as children—they call me Mother—I'm the oldest in the church, although another lady is creeping up on me. So Eve is just like a daughter—we adopted each other—at this late stage of life! She's 70 and I'm 90. She lost her husband around the same time. So Eve calls me every evening before bed. Every night. And if I need anything, if Peggy [my daughter] can't get something for me . . . can't get to it, she'll do it. She will take me to see a dress shop [clothing store], for example. Eve has more time for me now.

In the absence of spouses, sisters, and daughters, women like Alice, Julia, and Rose capitalize on friendship and regular connections to create and nurture social families. In these cases, gender, race, socioeconomic status, and age all contribute to innovation in friendship and family. As an African American elder of limited means who relies for social support on an extended kin network as well as the church, Rose is not alone (Shirey & Summer, 2000). Widening support networks beyond biological bonds has been crucial for Black survival in America.[8] Alice and Julia, on the other hand, grew up with housekeepers and friends cycling through their White middle-class homes. In the absence of a spouse, they have defined family in the context of shared home space and lifelong sources of support. Without proximal kin, Alice and Julia convert close friends and housekeepers into quasi-kin (Mac Rae, 1992), revealing that "friendship families" are not only limited to ethnic minorities and gays and lesbians (Dorfman et al., 1995). Scholars of aging must now consider this reality for nonagenarians, like Julia and Alice, and for future generations of elders who fashion intimate ties outside of biological family and marriage.

A life course perspective illuminates how social location in combination with life events (e.g., spousal or familial deaths and gender-segregated lives) led each of these women to prioritize close affective ties with women. Alice, Julia, and Rose broaden understandings of intimate relationships across the life course and exemplify the importance of close ties in late life. Intimate friendships can also double as caretaking relationships, as discussed in the next section.

Satisfaction in Caretaking

Nonagenarians and centenarians are expected to be the recipients of care, rarely if ever the caregivers (except caring for the young as grandparents), and almost never in the context of pleasure. And yet many nonagenarians speak of everyday caretaking for loved ones, including spouses, friends, pets, plants, and even themselves. Glenn, Juana, and Ann all emphasize carework as a guiding theme across their lives and as a constant source of satisfaction.[9] However, their objects of care vary dramatically.

Glenn, who was raised by a single mother in Denmark, delights in making others happy. He has great respect for his single mother who was "straitlaced and a good mom," and his mother-in-law, who was "the sweetest lady you'll ever meet." Today, he tends to his four children and numerous grandchildren (none of whom live locally), staying up late into the night to make calls and send emails around the world. He makes daily calls to his son with Parkinson's to try and cheer him up. When asked about his life, Glenn speaks fondly of his two wives, both of whom he took care of for many years. He says of his first wife, "Would you believe our fondness for each other increased in those 3 years she was sick? It was because I knew I would lose her." This case exemplifies how physical infirmities and sickness can shift degrees of closeness and interdependence in a relationship, sometimes in positive ways. Glenn learned from central mother figures in his life that caretaking is both an obligation and an expression of love, and his own experiences have only reinforced his identity and role as a caretaker. Glenn says his wife's doctor complimented him on his care ethic after his second wife died. "I was stunned to learn that there are many husbands who do not care for their wives. I have never imagined any other way."

Today, Glenn takes no relationship for granted, including those in a friendship group he has created for himself. This includes individuals in his exercise classes and his neighbors, a good portion of whom are decades younger. Recently, Glenn invited this group to his home for lunch. He prepared strawberry shortcake for dessert as well as a short speech expressing his gratitude for friendship. This is just one example of the caretaking regimen that continues to give Glenn's life meaning.

Like Glenn, Juana also continues to care for family and community through food preparation and nurturing activities. Juana spent most of her life as a single mother raising her children in a small village in central Puerto Rico. Today, at age 91, she still prepares rice and beans for her children; one lives downstairs from her and another lives in the neighboring town. She also takes pride in baking cakes and flan for her Catholic community. She smiles broadly when she shares that, like Rose, the deacons in her parish call her "Mama," as do community members from diverse ethnic backgrounds. "Here I have children from all over the world," she gloats. Remaining a mother figure in her family and community, and receiving respect for this, is central to Juana's personal satisfaction and well-being. This personal gratification is inextricably linked to her cultural heritage and reinforced by her close relationship with her own mother and experiences as an adult supporting a family on her own.

In contrast to Glenn's and Juana's caretaking for others, Ann, a slender, Irish 94-year-old with reddish brown hair, derives the most pleasure in taking care of herself. Staying healthy, fit, and active and looking good have been lifelong themes for Ann. Like many economically comfortable women, Ann has come to believe that her appearance is central to her self-worth and her value in society and that thinness is an important ideal (Calasanti & Slevin, 2001; Slevin & Mowery, this volume). Ann says, "You have to understand that my mother and sister were slim, and I was not fat, but I was robust. So

I was always watching my food. When my husband died, I lost quite a bit of weight, and I have been trying to stay thin ever since. I am a diet freak, I attend exercise classes, and I walk everywhere."

The death of Ann's husband in 2003 marked a crucial turning point in her life. She began to focus on bodywork and self-care and to derive pride and pleasure from shedding the negative labels she associates with her youth. Today Ann proudly tells of winning a trophy for swimming the most laps at the YMCA, being the oldest person in her water aerobics class, and being the only one who walks to class from the bus stop. Ann does have her concerns. She bemoans that she is getting shorter with age, but she is thrilled that capri pants are in style and wears them daily. As a woman, it is not surprising that Ann's sense of self-worth resides in her body. And although self-care can seem entirely individualistic, it is accomplished in a social context of daily interaction and perception.

In contrast to what we might expect, these nonagenarians are not solely the objects of care; they accomplish self-care and continue with lifelong familial and community-based caretaking rituals that bring personal satisfaction. At the same time, Ann reminds us that self-care can be gratifying in and of itself and that being physically alone does not necessarily equate with unhappiness.

Pleasure in Puzzles

Another form of self-care and personal gratification involves pleasure via intellectual stimulation. Researchers have found that regular participation in "cognitively stimulating leisure activities" may help to prevent Alzheimer's disease and other declines in mental functioning. (See, for example, the now famous "nun study" published by Wilson et al. in 2002.) However, this body of scholarship does not discuss how pleasure and continuity across the life course might drive and reinforce participation in such activities, and it does not acknowledge how such activities can go beyond "leisure" to include required cognitive problem solving and memory work for day-to-day living.

Dorothy, Hyman, and Johanna have spent a lifetime enjoying analytical exercises, and aspects of this still bring satisfaction. Notably, all three are college-educated and Jewish, reflecting how lifelong continuity, as well as overlapping social locational factors such as ethnicity, socioeconomic status, and educational background can contribute to cognitive pleasure and well-being.

As a child, Dorothy, the stately nonagenarian whom we met earlier, loved to read and write. Today she continues with these loves as an active member of a women's research club, where for 40 years she has delighted in the process of researching and writing papers. (Each year she and the other members conduct research on a common theme, culminating in a 20-minute paper to present to the group.) Dorothy decided to stop writing research papers at the age of 92 because she wanted to free up some time for writing her kids' biographies and doing Danish translation work. Yet she still attends meetings, listens to presentations, and remembers the thrill of writing her own work.

Hyman, a tall, athletic emeritus professor of history, likewise takes pleasure in intellectual community and the research process. Hyman describes himself as a typical child of Russian Jewish immigrants whose father "never saw first grade." Hyman had always been the reader in the family and academia was a natural for him. After years of associating satisfaction with campus life, Hyman and his retired colleagues helped to create an "emeritus center" at his university, where retired researchers can make presentations and access ongoing research in their fields. Today, at age 92, Hyman takes the time to read several daily papers and continues to monitor his field of study, marking great continuity throughout his life.

Johanna, a diminutive Jewish centenarian with long white hair tied back in a ponytail, also claims that intellectual stimulation brings her great pleasure. She lives for puzzles. A former elementary school teacher, Johanna still derives great satisfaction through working with words. She says, "When I wake up I am eager to get to the puzzles in the morning paper. To see if my brain is working. This makes me happy." Every Tuesday four friends come to Johanna's house to play Scrabble for 5 hours. They eat snacks and chat, but their primary focus is constructing a high-point word and winning the game. On the day that I observed Johanna's Scrabble group in action, Johanna won the first round and declared, "Well, I'm done for the day!" She then played for another 4 hours. She explained that this mix of intellectual and social stimulation constitutes the highlight of her week.

Conclusion

Opportunities for intimacy, pleasure, and stimulation do not disappear in late life—they can be found in new and familiar manifestations, be it taking care of others, oneself, or one's garden; challenging oneself creatively; connecting with others; or engaging in physical intimacy. Echoing contemporary feminist theorists, these informants remind us that when studying old age and intimacy (particularly in women's lives), it is important to conceive of pleasure as broadly as possible, to include multiple and varied forms of stimulation. Specifically, their experiences remind us of the inappropriately narrow cultural emphasis on penile-vaginal intercourse and the importance of shifting the emphasis to "outercourse" as well as nonsexual forms of pleasure.

Health, social location, and past experiences all contribute to how the oldest old accomplish pleasure in their day-to-day lives. Romance and sexuality have been key sources of pleasure for Lillian across the life course. While partially mitigated by recent health issues, her "romantic life" has been reinforced by her gender socialization, her love of opera, a series of willing boyfriends and husbands, and her access to cable television. For Alice, hugs and companionship with friends and pets have been sources of personal gratification throughout her single life, and particularly now, in the context of limited mobility and ageism. Cognitive memory work has been both painful and liberating for Dorothy, who, in the context of dating, was forced to come to terms with her childhood sexual abuse. In sum, biography, history, and social location are all crucial to understanding how these elders navigate aging, pleasure, and intimacy.

Socioeconomic privileges as well as social networks constitute lifelong benefits, and they contribute to the accomplishment of pleasure for many of these elders. For example, college-educated study participants may be more likely to crave personal challenge and intellectual fulfillment into late life. Education may constitute a social privilege that accrues value over time, as it is positively associated with overall health, well-being, and longevity.[10] That said, social scientists have shown how social oppression can correlate with personal isolation (Klinenberg, 2002) or with personal resilience (Elder, 1974/1999; Newman, 2006) and the construction of strong support networks and interdependency (Stack, 1974). The latter can be tremendously beneficial across the life course, particularly in old age, as we can see in the tightly networked lives of Juana, Rose, Glenn, and others.

Studying the oldest old can be helpful in understanding links among social life, health, pleasure, and longevity.[11] For most, pleasure is rooted in social networks and connective activities that transform across one's life. Family relationships, friendships, and social rituals involving intimacy, exercise, research, games, care, community, and neighbors can be central to quality of life and personal satisfaction. Examples include Johanna's Scrabble club, Glenn's care for his wife and friends, Juana's continuing maternal role with family and community, Rose's faith-based routines with "adoptive" family members, Dorothy's healing ceremony, and even Ann's self-care routine that exists in the context of networks and social perception. Thus, it is not only the activity but also the associated social capital that can bring value and meaning to a life, as well as enhanced health. Most study participants have learned the benefits of connection, or "linked lives," and strive to create social safety nets for themselves, actively reaching out for intergenerational connections, reconfiguring families socially in the absence of biological kin. Although women may be more skilled at fostering friendship and doing carework (having fulfilled related social expectations throughout their lives), this study reveals how men like Glenn have adopted these skill sets and gender repertoires.

These life histories moreover remind us that the oldest old are fluid, embodied subjects engaged in a range of sensory pleasures, some of which shift and intensify with age. In the context of physical impairment (hearing, sight, and/or mobility loss), elders like Seymour, Alice, and Lillian rely increasingly on a range of tactile activities to experience their worlds, to achieve pleasure and intimacy (e.g., with pets, partners, and friends), and to continue their life work. As such, a focus on embodiment reveals continuity and change across a life.

Two recent memoirs take up this theme of lifelong sensuality (continuous and adaptive, and mostly outside of marriage) for nonagenarian single women. Diana Athill, in her prize-winning memoir, *Somewhere Towards the End* (2009), discusses the disappearance of what used to be the most important thing in her life—being a sexual being in her seventies—and how a host of sensory pleasures, including reading, writing, gardening, and friendships with young people, have filled this void into her nineties. Another recent book, Lily Koppel's *Red Leather Diary* (2007), features the sexy, exploratory teenage diaries that nonagenarian Florence Howitt wrote while coming of age in New York City in the 1930s. This book concludes with a discussion of Florence's everyday life living independently in Florida into her nineties. Throughout her life, Florence delighted in the beauty of bodies, seeking out sexual companionship with women and men, and creative self-expression through theater and the arts. In sum, far from passively watching time pass, elder women and men are actively embracing life and creating pleasure in their lives, primarily outside of marital contexts.

Researchers interested in aging and sexuality would do well to expand their research agendas following these nonagenarians' lead. Paying attention to pleasure across the life course and related social and embodied contexts is crucial as individuals live longer lives, and doing so may offer clues to longevity, health, happiness, and overall quality of life.

This chapter is adapted from a paper presented at the British Sociology Association's Aging, Body, and Society Conference in July 2009. I would especially like to thank the elders who made this project possible.

1. Like Slevin and Mowery (this volume), I intentionally use language that positions people as both agentic *and* old. I use the term "old" to defy social stigma, to naturalize and neutralize aging, and to emphasize social stratification related to age. I also use language emphasizing "elderhood," following Thomas's (2004) research emphasizing three key developmental stages in life: childhood, adulthood, and elderhood. Language is always charged with social meaning; even the use of terms like "nonagenarian" can be problematic as it reinforces a focus on chronological age.

2. All interview subjects were given the opportunity to choose pseudonyms for themselves.

3. This lack of connection with age peers may have partly evolved out of social distancing, or age contagion, as discussed by Slevin and Mowery (this volume).

4. For privacy-related reasons, I did not ask study participants directly about sexual orientation.

5. Laumann et al. (1994) found that women aged 18–59 are five times more likely than men to report having been forced to do something sexual they did not want to do. Das et al. (this volume) find that roughly 13% of women aged 18–59 in the NHSLS report some form of adult-child sexual contact before puberty. Although it is tempting to expect that high statistics revealing women's sexual victimization are associated with older generations, Abma, Driscoll, and Moore (1998) find that 9% of girls aged 15–24 report rape and 25% report voluntary but unwanted sexual intercourse.

6. Elder Hostel is a nonprofit educational travel organization for adults aged 55 and over. The organization has recently been renamed Road Scholar.

7. Social scientists make a distinction between strong and weak ties, both of which are central to social capital and personal well-being (Granovetter, 1973). Weak ties are associated with low intensity and emotional distance while strong ties are associated with frequency, loyalty, and trust.

8. The life experiences of Emma, another African American participant, also reflect the historical legacy of looking beyond biological kin for support. Emma has 10 children and countless grandchildren, but she rarely sees any of them. Instead, she depends on the staff at her subsidized senior housing complex for day-to-day support.

9. For more on carework and its gendered, racialized, emotional, familial, and commodified aspects, see England (2005).

10. Cultural value placed on education and higher than average socioeconomic status may offer clues as to why many Jews live into old age. Although the links between education, socioeconomics, and longevity are relatively well established, I was unable to locate any research that explores the relationship between cultural heritage or religious background and life expectancy.

11. Hundreds of social science studies have revealed the importance of social capital (networks) across the life course using empirical evidence to show how mortality risk (a mix of psychological health, physiological health, and health behaviors) can be reduced with advantageous social ties. At the same time, it is important to remember that damaging social ties can undermine health.

PART VI

Conclusion

15

Toward an Interdisciplinary Science of Lifelong Sexualities for the Twenty-First Century

JOHN DELAMATER AND LAURA M. CARPENTER

How do sexual and social experiences at one point in a person's life affect their sexual beliefs and behaviors later on? How are individuals' sexual biographies shaped by broader cultural and historical changes? In what ways do intersections among gender, race, ethnicity, social class, and sexual identity influence these life course processes, even as life course processes influence those intersecting social statuses in turn? These are the questions with which we introduced this volume.

The life course perspective provides a uniquely fruitful approach for answering these questions. It improves over other approaches by allowing for serious exploration of how events at one stage in life affect sexual attitudes, behavior, and relationships at other later stages. It also recognizes that sexual expression is shaped by biological, psychological, social, cultural, and historical forces. Furthermore, the life course perspective meshes well with contemporary theories positing social statuses like gender, sexual orientation, race, ethnicity, and social class not as merely static and acquired at birth but as mutable, ongoing accomplishments.

Life course analyses of human sexuality have come a long way since the first edited collection applying a life course approach to sexuality (Rossi, 1994). Many of the studies in this present volume illustrate how specific aspects of sexuality unfold across multiple stages of the life course. Almost all of them address at least three of the major forces—biology, psychology, society, culture, and history—shaping sexual expression. Moreover, whereas earlier work often examined race, ethnicity, gender, social class, and sexual identity in isolation, complex analyses of social location are incorporated in almost every chapter in this book.

The "second generation" studies collected here also improve on their "first generation" predecessors through their explicit use of life course concepts.

Although previous publications pointed the way toward a conceptual framework for studying sexuality over the life course, chapter 1 in this volume represents one of the first articulations of a general, transferable model that can be applied to myriad sexuality-related issues. A chief goal of *Sex for Life* has been to show, through concrete empirical studies, how such a framework can help to shed new light on sexual beliefs, behaviors, and identities at every stage of life. Taken together, our contributors' studies push the limits of the framework and point to places where it can be further developed and refined.

Another goal of this volume has been to showcase the wide range of substantive topics that can benefit from analysis through a life course lens. We selected the chapters with an eye toward addressing key sexual phenomena from childhood to old age. However, as noted in the introduction, our choices were limited by the limits of the research conducted to date. We hope this book spurs more scholars to recognize how much can be gained from wedding a life course perspective to sexuality studies.

This concluding essay aims to provide a "state-of-the-art" assessment of the study of sexualities over the life course, circa 2012, as represented by our contributors' research. We begin by summarizing how the empirical chapters have employed—and helped to advance—a general conceptual framework for studying sexualities over the life course. This discussion is structured in terms of the gendered sexuality over the life course (GSLC) framework presented in chapter 1. After outlining an agenda for future research on sexualities over the life course, including sites for theory-building and substantive areas that demand further study, we conclude by enumerating some of the practical and policy implications that emanate from this line of inquiry.

Honing a Framework for Studying Gendered Sexualities over the Life Course

The study of sexualities over the life course has developed considerably since the field's inception. The first calls to juxtapose the two areas of inquiry were followed by a progression of publications employing specific life course concepts, like turning points and the life-stage principle, to illuminate different aspects of sexuality at various junctures in life (see the introduction). These efforts have culminated in the articulation of a general conceptual framework that brings the nuts-and-bolts of the life course approach—transitions, trajectories, and turning points; cumulative (dis)advantage dynamics; agency; physiological processes; sociohistorical context; and generation—into conversation with sophisticated understandings of gender and sexual identity as they intersect with race, ethnicity, and social class, and with the influential scripting approach to sexual conduct (see chapter 1; see also Carpenter, 2010). Every chapter in this volume draws on multiple elements of this framework, showing just how advantageous its use can be. Taken together, these chapters also point toward several dimensions along which the conceptual model can be refined and developed further.

Transitions, Trajectories, and Turning Points

Life course scholars conceptualize human lives as being composed of multiple, simultaneous trajectories through different dimensions of life—such as health, residence, and employment—extending from birth until death. This book focuses on the sexuality trajectory, and many chapters explore how the sexuality trajectory intersects with other life trajectories. For example, Carbone-Lopez demonstrates how assault early in one's sexuality trajectory affects one's romantic relationship trajectory. Wade and Heldman show how educational trajectories provide new contexts for the unfolding of sexual trajectories, while Dillaway examines the recursive, intertwined relationship among family/fertility, developmental biology, and sexuality trajectories.

Charting how individuals move—or transition—from one social status or life stage to another (e.g., from married to divorced [Lichtenstein]; from midlife to old age [Slevin and Mowery]), within specific life trajectories is fundamental to understanding sexualities over the life course. Yet, as Carbone-Lopez points out, we still know relatively little about what happens in the periods between transitions. For instance, through what processes or chain of events do women and men who were sexually assaulted as children wind up more likely to marry someone who physically abuses them? Collecting more and different kinds of data can help sexuality researchers to delineate better the events and experiences that transpire in the "black boxes" between social transitions.

The timing and sequence of transitions, especially in relation to widely shared social expectations, is of particular importance. As Green shows, heterosexual men who have been socialized to expect marriage begin, at a "socially appropriate" age, to shift from a free-wheeling bachelor script to one emphasizing heterosexual family formation. Men who make the transition "early" may feel that they are "missing out" on sexual experimentation whereas men who transition "late" (or never) may be looked upon with suspicion. Dillaway's research highlights the importance of the order in which transitions occur. Women who have consciously achieved their fertility goals when they reach menopause interpret that biological transition, including its sexual aspects, quite differently than women who still wish to have more (or any) children.

How old people are when they make a transition (i.e., the life stage principle) also matters; for example, women who reach menopause at relatively young ages are more likely not to be "done" with childbearing. The duration of particular life stages or statuses also carries important consequences. As Russell, Van Campen, and Muraco and Jeynes point out, the lengthening period between puberty and the transition to marriage/long-term partnership produces an ever-wider window in which "premarital" sexual activity can occur. The durations of transitions themselves may also affect sexuality. For example, a divorce that takes many years to resolve may impact the sexual and relationship trajectories of the erstwhile couple and their children more intensely than a divorce that takes only months, due to the longer period of animosity and uncertainty.

Certain transitions—such as marriage and childbearing, for heterosexuals—are anticipated and indicate (indeed, constitute) continuity within life trajectories. Other transitions represent dramatic breaks, or turning points, in the expected life course. For example, Espiritu shows how migration can alter the speed and nature of courtship and require people to negotiate new sets of sexual mores. Likewise, Green posits coming out as gay as a turning point that necessitates "a reconceptualization of the sexual life path and a reconfiguration of sexual scripts, norms, and practices."

Beyond demonstrating the importance of the timing, sequencing, and duration of transitions and turning points, the research assembled here highlights the utility of thinking more systematically about the salience of particular transitions—both to individuals and to the societies in which they live. Green cogently argues that marriage powerfully shapes gay and straight men's sexual lives precisely because it has historically been viewed as one of life's most important transitions. Bender's research indicates that men are affected, often negatively, by their own and others' assumptions that spinal cord injury (SCI) inevitably represents a watershed in one's sexual history. The salience of these and many other transitions (e.g., immigration, divorce) seems to stem from social constructions and structural factors, although, as Dillaway shows, biological markers matter, too. One might reasonably hypothesize that the more salient the transition, the more intense its effects; however, the exact nature of this relationship remains an important empirical question. It is worth noting, for example, that the women in Lichtenstein's study experienced divorce as a far more salient turning point than contracting an STI (perhaps regardless of the relative objective impact on their lives).

The effects of the *desirability* of certain transitions likewise remain an important empirical question. Studies like Carbone-Lopez's offer a window onto transitions that are almost universally considered undesirable (being sexually assaulted and entering abusive adult relationships), while Jeynes's research considers transitions that may be positive in some cases, negative in others (parental divorce and sexual initiation in adolescence).

The Dynamics of Cumulative (Dis)advantages

Evaluating how multiple transitions compose trajectories follows from establishing those transitions' order, timing, and duration. Clearly, experiences at one life stage give shape to later desires and opportunities, in ever-lengthening chains. These cumulative processes do not necessarily unfold in simple, inevitable, or obvious ways. That many different "plays" can issue from "stages" set in adolescence—sometimes defying all expectations—is adeptly demonstrated by Loe. As Das, Waite, and Laumann observe, multiple trajectories of sexual conduct and thoughts emerge over time, through many "branching points" and events that may not be under individuals' control. Older men and women who lose their long-term romantic/sexual partners may or may not acquire new partners, who may or may not remain healthy enough to engage in sexual activity, and their children may or may not approve.

One of the key tasks for the researcher lies in tracking how positive, neutral, and negative experiences accumulate into advantageous, disadvantageous, and mixed trajectories. Which transitions are positive, which negative, and which neutral may appear "obvious" but is often an empirical question. For example, one might assume—and numerous studies demonstrate (see Jeynes's meta-analysis)—that the transition of parental divorce heightens a child's chances of experiencing putatively negative sexual outcomes such as unintended pregnancy, but not every child with divorced parents experiences those outcomes. For example, research indicates that children show little change in measures of well-being when divorce ends a high-conflict marriage, whereas well-being often declines for a child when divorce ends a low-conflict marriage (Amato, 2010).

Members of different social groups frequently experience different transitions in different sequences and durations, as evidenced throughout this book. Thigpen's research, for example, suggests how gendered socialization and sex differences in the visibility and configuration of genitalia lead to gender differences in masturbation in childhood, which in turn may launch distinctive trajectories that incrementally culminate in gender differences in sexual desire and conduct in adulthood. Green considers how individual men, gay and straight, accumulate sexual and romantic experiences and expectations from childhood onward—in ways powerfully shaped by their positions in social structures—such that "same-sex married couples today arrive at the doorstep of marriage having travelled along a very different pathway from their heterosexual counterparts." Analyses of trajectories that attend to the complex intersections of gender, sexual orientation, race, ethnicity, and social class can help to illuminate how trajectories may start in similar places but wind up in altogether different territories.

Our contributors also adeptly reveal the cumulative sexual dynamics that unfold across different stages of the life course. Carbone-Lopez connects reports of events in childhood, adolescence, and adulthood to show how experiencing (or not experiencing) sexual and physical violence at different life stages sets distinctive relationship (and sexual) trajectories into motion. Bender traces how "the cumulative sexual experiences following injury" can result in positive or negative "narrative shift[s] . . . depending on the types of reinforcement [men] receive from sexual partners." However, tracking how specific aspects of sexuality unfold across multiple stages of the life course is exceedingly difficult, because of the lack of longitudinal (or even sufficiently retrospective) data, as many of our contributors note.

Physiological Processes

Historically, social scientists who study sexuality have tended to neglect physiological processes, whereas scholars in biomedicine have tended to neglect the social. Social scientists are increasingly aware that age-related and other physiological changes, illnesses, and treatments for those illnesses affect sexuality, but they have too often declined to address these factors directly in their research.

The chapters collected here, on the whole, represent an exception to this tendency. Many of our contributors show how physical and mental health trajectories and physiological processes interact with social factors at every stage of the life course. Thigpen and Russell and colleagues consider how biological maturation, specifically pubertal development, interacts with developmental maturity (psychology) to affect sexual desire and behavior. Dillaway highlights the importance of biological maturation later in the life course, analyzing menopause, as well as the physiological phenomenon of infertility. How aging alters bodies' appearances and physical abilities, and how those alterations may affect life course sexuality processes, lies at the heart of Slevin and Mowery's and Loe's analyses. Other authors focus on illnesses and injuries that could occur at any point in the life course. Bender explores the sexual impact of traumatic injury, noting how it differs depending on age at injury, while Das and colleagues show how one's own and one's partners' health problems limit sexual activity, especially (but not only) at older ages.

Taken together, the preceding chapters show how much bodies matter to social and sexual life. Bodies set limits and open possibilities. Theories of embodiment—such as those employed by Lichtenstein and by Slevin and Mowery—can provide direction and lend nuance to future research on sexualities over the life course. Several contributors also highlight the importance of considering developmental (i.e., psychological) maturity; we encourage further exploration of this closely related phenomenon at all ages, not just among children and adolescents, as has been the tendency thus far. The more scholars can communicate—and truly understand—across disciplines, the better they can situate the biological and psychological in its social context and vice versa, for every aspect of sexuality at every stage of the life course.

Human Agency

Comprehending the ongoing tension between agency and social structures (or choice and constraint) lies at the heart of the sociological enterprise. The life course perspective is especially well suited to evaluate this tension as it impinges on sexuality. How people exercise agency within social-structural constraints is a central topic in many chapters in this volume. (Biology also constrains agency, of course, as discussed above.)

Among our contributors, Bender offers the most explicit analysis of agency, showing how different groups of men exercise different degrees— and qualitatively different kinds—of agency after SCI, given the constraints of socioeconomic status and age at time of injury. Lichtenstein's research likewise demonstrates social class's impact on agency. The most recently single and most economically constrained women in her study typically made choices with short-term goals (e.g., paying this month's grocery bills) in mind, whereas women who had been single for longer or who were financially better off tended to focus on longer-term issues like relationship quality. Disentangling the temporal dimensions of agency helps to produce a nuanced analysis of sexuality over the life course.

How adolescents can be encouraged—and given space—to make choices that enhance their sexual well-being, both in the short and long term, is one of Russell and colleagues' key concerns. Espiritu shows how decisions—about when and how often to migrate, how to court and whom to marry, and how to rear and monitor one's children—are made and play out in the differently constraining and enabling contexts of the Philippines and United States. The importance of *feeling* able to exercise agency is highlighted in Dillaway's chapter; many women's responses to menopause and midlife sexuality were contingent on whether they felt they had chosen to complete (or never begin) childbearing.

It is more difficult, but not impossible, to see agency operating in studies that rely on survey data. Certainly, the children in Thigpen's chapter made choices about whether or not to touch themselves or others, and the youth in the studies Jeynes analyzes have decided whether or not to initiate sex, and with whom; but in neither case do the data indicate how conscious those choices were or how effectively they were constrained. Likewise, the participants in Das and colleagues' study have chosen to pursue (or not) new partners or novel sexual practices, but their data shed little light on the subjective aspects of these dynamics. Designing future surveys with an eye toward gathering data that would permit analyzing agency and decision making would be a tremendous boon to scholars of sexualities over the life course.

Sociohistorical Context and Generation

Arguably the greatest insights of the life course perspective are the recognition that major historical changes affect individual lives and that, consequently, members of different generations have distinctive experiences. Our contributors expertly capture the interplay between individual lives and the ever-changing sociohistorical context. Green's chapter illuminates how major historical changes in the United States and Canada—including the development of urban gay subcultures and the possibility of gay marriage—have shaped gay and straight men's approaches to partnership and sexual practices. Lichtenstein shows us how women who first dated and became sexually active in a era when unintended pregnancy represented the "worst" outcome must, as new "women alone," learn to navigate an era where STIs are more widespread (and potentially deadly) and sexual activity outside of committed relationships is not only widely accepted but also expected.

Dillaway's research demonstrates the importance of distinguishing between age and generation. Although her respondents reached menopause at about the same chronological ages as their mothers and grandmothers, the meanings attached to that transition have changed dramatically due to historical and cultural shifts. The sexual impacts of broad social changes and generation are also evident in the work of Bender (men who experienced SCI before and after the advent of Viagra and Cialis), Slevin and Mowery (gay men and lesbians' changing responses to aging as access to cosmetic surgery expands), and Loe (nonagenarians bearing the imprint of the sexually less-permissive era in which they came of age).

Social Location and Sexual Expression

In the past two decades, scholars have increasingly recognized that social statuses like gender, race, ethnicity, and social class have intersecting rather than additive effects (Collins, 1990). Our contributors demonstrate not only how individuals' social locations guide them to certain sexual attitudes and conduct, but also how they use sexual expression to construct and negotiate particular versions of social identities.

Gender, race, ethnicity, social class, and sexual orientation are indicators or markers of social location. They identify dimensions on which people differentiate themselves, and are differentiated by others, into groups. Membership in these groups often shapes people's past experiences and present circumstances in ways that impact their sexuality. One's location on these dimensions, such as middle-class Latina lesbian or working-class White heterosexual man, is often visible to others and determines how one is enabled and constrained in interaction. To appreciate the nuances of sexual relationships and lifestyles, scholars need continually to take intersecting social locations into consideration.

Social location affects people in several ways. One's gender, race, ethnicity, and social class may be associated with distinctive patterns of socialization, starting very early in childhood. Reflecting culture (the beliefs, values, and skills of one's social groups), socialization teaches specific norms regarding sexual relationships and behavior, ideal sexual scripts, and skills that may facilitate or inhibit the development of stable intimate relationships. Early experiences facilitate specific trajectories or paths in adolescence and into adulthood. At the same time, social statuses are not fixed but are continually (re)constructed by individuals through social interaction. As the chapters in this book have shown, intersections among social statuses do not shape people's life courses in simple or deterministic ways.

Although the following discussion focuses in turn on gender, race and ethnicity, social class, and sexual orientation, it does so largely for analytic convenience—that is, in order to highlight patterns of shared experience among people who share a social status. It is important to bear in mind that, in particular groups, each of these aspects of identity/status intersects with the others, shaping sexual expression (and other life course trajectories) in distinctive ways.

Gender

That gender is associated with differences in socialization, experience, and lifestyles that impact the sexual life course is amply demonstrated in virtually every chapter in this volume. For example, Thigpen notes significant gender differences in the frequency with which caregivers observe sexual conduct among 7- to 12-year-olds. Girls were less likely than boys to engage in the majority of the 22 behaviors assessed by the Child Sexual Behavior Inventory. This may reflect differences in socialization, with girls taught to be demure and passive and boys to be sexually aggressive, or it could reflect the ongoing performance of gender and efforts to avoid sanctions for doing gender in "inappropriate" ways. Self-stimulation and masturbatory behaviors were more common among boys, perhaps reflecting anatomical sex differences. These gender differences varied by race, however, with self-stimulatory behaviors more common among White girls and boys, behaviors reflecting sexual interest among African American boys, trying to look at nude pictures among White girls, and trying to watch movies or TV programs showing nudity or sex among African American girls.

Russell, Van Campen, and Muraco detail gender differences in adolescent sexuality. Boys are encouraged to develop agency over their sexuality, whereas girls typically are not. Consequently, many girls reach womanhood without becoming skilled in techniques for preserving sexual safety. As Lichtenstein demonstrates, this gendered training, coupled with fear of sanctions for seeming too "loose," contributes to risk taking among women who are reentering the dating scene at midlife, in ways mediated by social class. In both generations of the Filipino families that Espiritu studied, parents exercised greater control over daughters' behavior than sons', likely inhibiting girls' development of agency; however, many girls found ways to resist their parents' control, especially in the U.S. cultural context.

In later life, males and females experience aging differently, because of the differential emphasis on physical appearance by gender. In Slevin and Mowery's research, gender was strongly associated with satisfaction with one's body and with participation in activities designed to "discipline" the body. In this middle-class sample, women experienced the aging body more negatively because of the cultural emphasis on beauty as women's chief source of social capital, whereas men could rely on other resources, including greater income on average, for continuing reinforcement of their masculinity.

Race and Ethnicity

Race and ethnicity also represent important influences on sexuality, as illustrated in multiple chapters. Russell and colleagues state that sexual risk taking is more common among racial-ethnic minority adolescents than White adolescents, with the consequence that African American, Native American, and Hispanic teens are disproportionately likely to become pregnant and to contract HIV. In 2007, pregnancy rates for female Hispanic and non-Hispanic Black adolescents were much higher (132.8 and 128.0 per 1,000 people) than for non-Hispanic Whites (45.2 per 1,000). Black female adolescents were more likely to be living with AIDS (49.6 per 100,000) than Hispanic (12.2 per 100,000) or non-Hispanic White (2.5 per 100,000) adolescents (Gavin et al., 2009). The intersection of race with social class complicates this picture, however; today these outcomes are more common among lower-class Whites as well (Furstenburg, 2009).

In adulthood, race is associated with relationship patterns. As Carbone-Lopez's research shows, African American men and women were more likely than White men and women to experience multiple committed relationships during their lives and to be separated or divorced at the time her data were collected. Espiritu recounts how women and men raised in the Philippines are exposed to stereotypes of Filipino and White sexuality, which are rooted in the U.S. colonization of the Philippines. Before and after migration to the United States, these stereotypes influenced adults' sexual attitudes and behavior, and their socialization of their children.

Dillaway suggests that racial differences in experience and life course timing influence women's reactions to reproductive aging. African American heterosexual women were more likely than their White counterparts to be concerned about how their male partners would react to the women's loss of reproductive ability. White women's reactions to that loss depended more on whether they felt "done" with having children. These patterns suggest a social class dynamic as well, insofar as women are increasingly delaying childbearing for reasons of educational and career accomplishment (notably, Dillaway's sample was largely middle-class).

Social Class

Social class indexes the resources available to a person. Class status is associated with education (knowledge), income and wealth, and the nature of the social networks to which one belongs. The greater one's resources, the more readily (not necessarily easily) one can cope with life events and stressors.

As noted in the chapter by Russell and colleagues, social class influences sexual socialization and experience in childhood and adolescence, in ways that intersect with race and ethnicity. Young people in families with fewer resources are more likely to experience unintended pregnancy as teenagers, a transition associated with a lower probability of enrolling in and finishing college; college attendance in turn affects employment opportunities and income—an illustration of cumulative disadvantage. The desire for economic mobility motivated many of Espiritu's participants to migrate from the Philippines to the United States; that migration in turn (re)shaped sexual beliefs and conduct across two generations.

Social class and material resources also influence adjustment, including opportunities for dating and sexual intimacy, following SCI. As Bender explains, greater economic resources provide men with access to quality health care and rehabilitation, as well as mobility-enhancing devices. They also improve men's chances of attracting or keeping a romantic partner. These factors, moreover, contribute to men's ability to demonstrate their masculinity to themselves and others. The presence of network resources associated with class also may enhance quality of life.

Slevin and Mowery discuss ways that social class mediates individuals' ability to adjust to their aging bodies, typically in gendered ways. Well-educated, professional men and women can call upon greater knowledge and economic resources to resist bodily aging. The old gay men and lesbians Slevin and Mowery interviewed used economic resources to pay for exercise programs and cosmetic surgery in attempts to maintain youthful bodies. Some women and men also spoke of using economic resources to help attract substantially younger partners.

Sexual Orientation

North American culture is heteronormative, as Green and Russell and colleagues note, and most children and adolescents are taught that the ideal intimate relationship is a heterosexual one and that the ideal, satisfying adult life involves having children (i.e., taking a parental role). Numerous scholars have documented the stress experienced by youth who sense that they are not moving easily into the heterosexual script. As Green explains, the young man who seriously considers acknowledging that he is gay has to let go of the desire to be a partner in a civil marriage and may believe he has to give up being a parent, too. Green analyzes how lack of access to these valued adult roles, stemming from historical events and contemporary social arrangements, has shaped recent gay culture in the United States and Canada. He also traces this impact across the adult life course of gay men.

People who fit comfortably into heterosexual roles experience considerable social support for entry into certain trajectories. Socialization in childhood leads to differences in presexual behaviors between boys and girls, as observed by Thigpen, which are consistent with becoming heterosexual adults. Jeynes documents how being raised in an intact, heterosexual family has positive consequences on children's transition to adulthood, given a social context in which such families are widely deemed the only "normal" option. Dillaway charts the consequences of the emphasis on reproduction in U.S. society, insofar as it can cause distress for the heterosexual woman who enters menopause without fulfilling her fertility desires, or for the heterosexual partner of such a woman. The value placed on physical attractiveness in North America, reflected in the multibillion-dollar cosmetics and cosmetic surgery industries, may lead to stress for heterosexual women as they age, as Lichtenstein and Loe note. Declining attractiveness by conventional standards erodes women's cultural capital in a heterosexual "marketplace" and may raise their fears of losing mates; some gay men experience a similar situation, as Slevin and Mowery note, given the emphasis on the youthful male body in gay culture.

This collection, as a whole, does a much better job than previous work in addressing how social location—the intersections of gender, race, ethnicity, class, and sexual orientation—affects sexual expression over the life course. Researchers have only begun to plumb the complex ways that sexuality is shaped by, and shapes, intersecting social statuses. More socially diverse samples and more interactionist analyses (in the mode of Bender's and Slevin and Mowery's work) will greatly enhance future studies of sexualities over the life course.

Sexual Scripts

The last, but by no means the least, element in the GSLC framework is sexual scripting at the cultural, interpersonal, and intrapsychic levels. Our contributors expertly demonstrate how the life course dynamics outlined above contribute to individuals' adoption (or rejection) of specific scripts, even as choices among available scripts influence individuals' life course processes in turn. Lichtenstein shows how women who become single at midlife must unlearn the dating and sexuality scripts they adopted, decades before, as teenagers and young adults and find new scripts more appropriate to their age and social circumstances (e.g., as mothers) and to the contemporary context (i.e., the HIV era). The dyadic nature of mainstream cultural scenarios is a main theme in Das, Waite, and Laumann's chapter; they show how midlife and older adults' scripting choices are limited by the presence or absence of a partner, as well as by their own and their partner's health.

Several chapters draw our attention to the coexistence of divergent cultural scenarios and to potential tensions and discrepancies between levels of scripts. Green, for example, shows how heterosexual and gay men's personal choices and partnered practices (i.e., their interpersonal scripts) unfold. Each turning point in a man's life—such as coming out or falling in or out of love—"involves a reconceptualization of the sexual life path and a reconfiguration of sexual scripts, norms, and practices." By showing the discrepancies between sexual ideals (cultural scenarios) and actual practices (interpersonal scripts), Espiritu eloquently underlines the need for more subtle ways of thinking about the multiple sexual scripts that coexist in specific social locations (such as in Manila and San Diego).

Another important issue concerns the relationship between scripting processes and social structures and institutions. This is especially evident in Wade and Heldman's analysis of the ways that first-year college students grapple with the difference between the prevailing cultural scenarios at their high schools and on their new campus.

Directions for Future Theorizing and Research

The foregoing discussion points to a number of ways in which the GSLC framework can be usefully extended. In addition to these, numerous chapters indicate the vital importance of attending to *linked lives* and *intergenerational dynamics* when examining sexualities over the life course. Das, Waite, and Laumann, for example, show how both phenomena affect the sexual lives of older men and women through their analysis of social embeddedness. Loe expertly demonstrates how past and present intimate ties within and across generations not only shape nonagenarians' sexual selves, but also provide them with important sources of pleasure and intimacy. The powerful effects of lives linked across generations can also be seen in the work of Jeynes, Carbone-Lopez, and Espiritu.

Frameworks for studying sexuality over the life course might also be enhanced by more explicitly incorporating the institutions that structure social life. Green's analysis of the legal institution of marriage, Wade and Heldman's discussion of the organizational features of an institution of higher learning, and Espiritu's treatment of the U.S. military as a transnational institution provide excellent examples. Future research should develop these insights more systematically.

Finally, our understanding of sexuality over the life course can be enriched with greater attention to meaning-making and the symbolic dimensions of life. Possibilities for this sort of analysis can be found in chapters by Green, Loe, Slevin and Mowery, Dillaway, and Thigpen.

Taken together, this book's chapters suggest that one of the most critical tasks now facing life course sexuality scholars is the systematic charting of the different pathways that lives can take from childhood through old age. Every sexual and social transition has multiple potential outcomes, every one of which leads to further possible transitions with multiple potential outcomes, and so on. Dillaway's research, for example, reveals multiple possible reproductive trajectories—each of which stems from a particular accumulation of previous decisions and experiences—which contribute to different sorts of postmenopause sexual trajectories. Similarly, Das, Waite, and Laumann observed two major trajectories among older heterosexual adults, depending on the presence or absence of a long-term partner at midlife; within these broad trajectories, various distinctive pathways unfold.

Empirical demonstrations of the ways in which specific aspects of sexuality—such as sexual satisfaction or sexual agency—unfold across multiple stages of the life course remain rare, even here. We look forward to future research that will fulfill this great promise of the life course perspective. How wonderful it would be if we could follow a single individual from Thigpen's childhood survey to Wade and Heldman's first-year college course to the structurally constrained decisions about life-partnering studied by Green to starting over in the dating scene (Lichtenstein) and/or experiencing menopause (Dillaway) or andropause to the branching, embodied trajectories of late midlife and early old age (Das et al.; Slevin and Mowery) to life in one's nineties in Loe's senior centers.

Achieving this and other promises of the life course perspective on sexualities will require new approaches to data collection. To better understand the processes that have unfolding, long-term effects, we badly need high-quality longitudinal data. Retrospective accounts such as those collected by Dillaway, Loe, and Carbone-Lopez and quasi-panel analyses such as that undertaken by

Das, Waite, and Laumann can illuminate many life course processes. But retrospective accounts are subject to the vagaries of memory and reflect people's present interpretations of past experiences; there is no substitute for following the same individuals over time. True longitudinal data can also help unpack the complicated relationship between age and generation.

Collecting more detailed quantitative data can also help to address many questions of interest. Most large-scale surveys include only a few, limited items related to sexuality. Consequently, scholars are restricted in the questions they may ask and answer with those data. The National Social Life, Health, and Aging Project (NSHAP) survey is a rare exception. We hope its example will not only prompt more sexuality-related surveys but also inspire scholars to include within general and other surveys more items that tap into important sexuality-related issues.

Expanding qualitative inquiries is no less crucial. Qualitative data are especially valuable for making sense of subjective understandings and unfolding processes in social life. Data that will enable us to get inside of the "black boxes" between social transitions are greatly needed, as Carbone-Lopez notes. Qualitative—or quantitative—data that would help us say more about the timing, sequencing, and duration of sexuality-related transitions are also much desired.

In the years to come, we also hope to see more studies combining qualitative and quantitative approaches to life course sexualities. This volume sheds new light on a number of aspects of sexuality by juxtaposing studies based on both kinds of data. For example, the works of Dillaway, Das and colleagues, Slevin and Mowery, and Loe give us an unusually rounded and nuanced picture of sexuality in midlife and early old age. How much more leverage and insight could be provided, then, by bringing both types of data to bear in a single study? We also hope to see more studies using expansive definitions of sexual activity and pleasure, as do Loe, Bender, and Das and colleagues.

Samples also matter. As is apparent from the preceding discussion, more diverse samples—especially in terms of race, ethnicity, and social class—are badly needed, especially in order to increase our understanding of the ways that intersecting identities influence sexuality (and vice versa). For a variety of reasons, many studies still focus on a single racial-ethnic group (typically White) or compare Whites and African Americans. A number of chapters here include racially diverse samples but cannot analyze them by race/ethnicity because of small sample size or concerns about confidentiality (Wade and Heldman, Lichtenstein, Green, and Loe). Including enough people from the full range of racial and ethnic backgrounds in the locale studied is absolutely critical.

Finally, we would like to draw attention to *substantive areas* of sexual life that demand further study. Children's sexuality, including its normative aspects, is woefully understudied (as Thigpen notes). So are the life course dynamics of people who do not fit the gender binary: transgender women and men. Numerous transitions and turning points need careful study. How does becoming a parent affect sexual life? How does relationship dissolution (differentially) affect the sexual lives of the "left" and the "leaver"? What (if any) impact do transitions in economic status—such as getting one's first full-time job, receiving a substantial raise, becoming unemployed, or retiring—have on sexual functioning and relationships? The impact of engaging in different varieties of sex work over the life course merits more study as well (for an outstanding example, see Barton, 2006).

Practical and Policy Implications

The breadth of topics and ages covered by our contributors make it clear that there is a sexual component to every life at every age. Recognizing this reality and incorporating it into our thinking will hopefully make us more sensitive to the sexual realities that our family members, friends, and coworkers face. It would be beneficial if sexuality were to be brought "out of the closet." We do not mean that daily life should become more sexual; some critics think it is already too much so. We mean that we should recognize that those around us are sexual individuals, that their sexualities are a source of both pleasure and problems, and that we contribute, knowingly or not, to both. We contribute to the problems if we make jokes about, bully, harass or abuse someone because of age, gender, or choice of sexual lifestyle. We contribute to the pleasure if we are open to other's expressions of sexual health and relationship concerns and if we help them to find resolution for their problems.

The chapters in this volume reflect an engagement with the sexual lives of people in many circumstances. We have already noted the need for more qualitative and quantitative, as well as longitudinal, research. The results of such research can have important practical effects, by helping actual people make sense of their lives and by addressing actual—social and individual— problems. Examples based on themes in our contributors' chapters include the transition to college, relationship dissolution, major physical trauma, and menopause. Better understanding of these phenomena and of the factors that influence them, and communication of that understanding to the public at large, can help individuals cope with their changing circumstances. Once an adequate research base is established, we can imagine the development of programs designed to facilitate a transition (e.g., to life with SCI) that incorporates sexuality as an important dimension and concern.

The recognition that there is a sexual component to every life at every age has important implications for public policy. Many policies that deal with people's lives focus narrowly on one trajectory, such as work or family or physical health. And many focus on only one aspect of one trajectory, such as unemployment or access to health care. The life course perspective and the chapters in this book remind us that these trajectories are inextricably intertwined. Thus, policies created by educational institutions influence the sexual trajectories of students (and faculty and staff). Policies created by agencies and institutions serving the aging should take into account the sexual lifestyles and needs of their clients. Policies and practices designed to deal with immigration into the United States have a tremendous impact on romantic relationship formation, childrearing, and adolescent and young adult sexuality.

It is our hope that this volume will raise the collective consciousness about the interrelations of sexualities with other aspects of daily life and with public policy.

Bibliography

Abell, S. C., & Richards, M. H. (1996). The relationship between body shape and satisfaction and self esteem: An investigation of gender and class differences. *Journal of Youth and Adolescence, 25,* 691–703.

Abma, J., Driscoll, A., & Moore, K. (1998). Young women's degree of control over first intercourse: An exploratory analysis. *Family Planning Perspectives, 30,* 12–18.

Adam, B. (1987). *The rise of a gay and lesbian movement.* Boston: Twayne.

Adam, B. (2006). Relationship innovation in male relationships. *Sexualities, 9,* 5–26.

Ageton, S. S. (1983). *Sexual assault among adolescents.* Toronto: Lexington Books.

Alexander, J. M. (1991). Redrafting morality: The postcolonial state and the sexual offences bill of Trinidad and Tobago. In C. T. Mohanty, A. Russo, & L. Torres (Eds.), *Third world women and the politics of feminism* (pp. 133–152). Bloomington: Indiana University Press.

Allers, R. (1998). *What's wrong with Freud: A critical study of Freud's psychoanalysis.* Ft. Collins, CO: Roman Catholic Press.

Allgood-Merten, B., & Stockard, J. (1991). Sex role identity and self-esteem: A comparison of children and adolescents. *Sex Roles, 25,* 129–140.

Amaro, H., Navarro, A., Conron, K., & Raj, A. (2002). Cultural influences on women's sexual health. In G. Wingood & R. DiClemente (Eds.), *Handbook of women's sexual and reproductive health* (pp. 71–92). New York: Kluwer Academic/Plenum.

Amato, P. R. (2010). Research on divorce: Continuing trends and new developments. *Journal of Marriage and Family, 72,* 650–666.

Amato, P. R. (2000). The consequences of divorce for adults and children. *Journal of Marriage and Family, 4,* 1269–1287.

Amato, P. R., & Previti, D. (2003). People's reasons for divorcing. *Journal of Family Issues, 24,* 602–626.

Amato, P. R., & Sobolewski, J. M. (2001). The effects of divorce and marital discord on adult children's psychological well-being. *American Sociological Review, 66,* 900–921.

American Social Health Association (2006). *STD/STI statistics—Fast facts.* Retrieved from http://www.ashastd.org/learn/learn_statistics.cfm

Antonucci, T. C., & Akiyama, H. (1995). Convoys of social relations: Family and friendships within a life span context. In R. Blieszner & V. H. Bedford (Eds.), *Handbook of aging and the family* (pp. 355–371). Westport, CT: Greenwood.

Araji, S. K. (1997). *Sexually aggressive children: Coming to understand them.* Thousand Oaks, CA: Sage.

Araujo, A., Mohr, B., & McKinlay, J. (2004). Changes in sexual function in middle-aged and older men: Longitudinal data from the Massachusetts Male Aging Study. *Journal of the American Geriatrics Society, 52,* 1502–1509.

Arber, S. (2004). Gender, marital status and ageing: Linking material, health and social resources. *Journal of Aging Studies, 18*, 91–108.

Arber, S., & Ginn, J. (1991). The invisibility of age: Gender and class in later life. *Sociological Review, 39*, 260–291.

Armstrong, E., England, P., & Fogarty, A. (2009). Orgasm in college hookups and relationships. In B. Risman (Ed.), *Families as they really are* (pp. 362–377). New York: Norton.

Armstrong, E., & Hamilton, L. (2009). Nonrelational sex in young adulthood: Neither feminist victory nor intensified sexism. Paper presented at the annual meeting of the Pacific Sociological Association, San Diego, CA.

Asencio, M. (Ed.). (2009). *Latino/a sexualities: Probing powers, passions, practices, and policies*. New Brunswick: Rutgers University Press.

Athill, D. (2009). *Somewhere towards the end: A memoir*. New York: Norton.

Attwood, F. (2007). Sluts and riot grrrls: Female identity and sexual agency. *Journal of Gender Studies, 16*, 233–247.

Avis, N. E., Cain, V. S., Johannes, C. B., Mohr, B., Ory, M., Shocken, M., & Skurnik, J. (2003). Sexual functioning and practices in a multi-ethnic study of midlife women: Baseline results from SWAN. *The Journal of Sex Research, 40*, 266–276.

Avis, N. E., Stellato, R., Crawford, S. et al. (2000). Is there an association between menopausal status and sexual functioning? *Menopause, 7*, 297–309.

Babbie, E. (2007). *The basics of social research* (4th ed.). Belmont, CA: Wadsworth.

Bancroft, J. (Ed.) (2003). *Sexual development in childhood*. Bloomington: Indiana University Press.

Bancroft, J., Loftus, J., & Long, J. S. (2003). Distress about sex: A national survey of women in heterosexual relationships. *Archives of Sexual Behavior, 32*, 193–208.

Bandura, A. (2006). Adolescent development from an agentic perspective. In F. Pajares & T. Urdan (Eds.), *Self-efficacy beliefs of adolescents* (pp. 1–43). Greenwich, CT: Information Age Publishing.

Barbre, J. W. (1993). Menopause and moral guardians: An exploration of the cultural construction of menopause. In J. Callahan (Ed.), *Menopause: A midlife passage* (pp. 23–35). Bloomington: Indiana University Press.

Barton, B. (2006). *Stripped: Inside the lives of exotic dancers*. New York: NYU Press.

Basson, R. (2006). The complexities of women's sexuality and the menopause transition. *Menopause, 13*, 853–855.

Basson, R., Brotto, L. A., Laan, E., Redmond, G., & Utian, W. H. (2005). Assessment and management of women's sexual dysfunctions: Problematic desire and arousal. *Journal of Sexual Medicine, 2*, 291–300.

Battle, J., & Barnes, S. L. (Eds.). (2010). *Black sexualities: Probing powers, passions, practices, and policies*. New Brunswick: Rutgers University Press.

Battle, J., Bennett, M., & Lemelle, A. (Eds.). (2006). *Free at last? Black America in the twenty-first century*. New Brunswick, NJ: Transaction.

Bech, H. (1997). *When men meet*. Chicago: University of Chicago Press.

Beitchman, J. H., Zucker, K. J., Hood, J. E., daCosta, G. A., Akman, D., & Cassavia, E. (1992). A review of the long-term effects of child sexual abuse. *Child Abuse and Neglect, 16*, 101–118.

Bell, S. (2009). *DES daughters: Embodied knowledge and the transformation of women's health politics*. Philadelphia: Temple University Press.

Bell, S., & Apfel, R. (1995). Looking at bodies: Insights and inquiries about DES-related cancers. *Qualitative Sociology, 18*, 3–19.

Belsky, J., Steinberg, L., & Draper, P. (1991). Childhood experience, interpersonal development, and reproductive strategy: An evolutionary theory of socialization. *Child Development, 62*, 647–670.

Bennett, K. C., & Thompson, N. L. (1991). Accelerated aging and male homosexuality: Australian evidence in a continuing debate. *Journal of Homosexuality, 20*, 65–75.

Bennett, W. J. (2001). *The broken hearth*. New York: Doubleday.

Berger, P., & Luckmann, T. (1966). *The social construction of reality*. Garden City, NY: Doubleday.

Bernstein, J. (2006). Work, poverty, and single-mother families. *Economic Policy Institute*. Retrieved from http://www.epi.org/economic_snapshots/entry/webfeatures_snapshots_20060809

Birnbaum, G. E., Cohen, O., & Wertheimer, V. (2007). Is it all about intimacy? Age, menopausal status, and women's sexuality. *Personal Relationships, 14*, 167–185.

Blumberg, E. (2003). The lives and voices of highly sexual women. *The Journal of Sex Research, 40*, 146–157.

Blumstein, P., & Schwartz, P. (1983). *American couples: Money, work, sex*. New York: William Morrow.

Boat, B., & Everson, M. (1992). Exploration of anatomical dolls by nonreferred preschool-aged children: Comparisons by age, gender, race, and socioeconomic status. *Child Abuse and Neglect, 18*, 139–153.

Bogaert, A. (2004). Asexuality: Prevalence and associated factors in a national probability sample. *The Journal of Sex Research, 41*, 279–287.

Bogle, K. (2008). *Hooking up: Sex, dating, and relationships on campus*. New York: NYU Press.

Bolen, R. M., & Scannapieco, M. (1999). Prevalence of child sexual abuse: A corrective meta-analysis. *Social Service Review, 73*, 281–313.

Bordo, S. (1999). *The male body*. New York: Farrar, Straus & Giroux.

Bohrnstedt, G. W., & Knoke, D. (1994). *Statistics for social data analysis* (3rd ed.). Itasca, IL: F. E. Peacock.

Borneman, E. (1990). Progress in empirical research on children's sexuality. In M. E. Perry (Ed.), *Childhood and adolescent sexology: Handbook of sexology* (pp. 201–210). Amsterdam: Elsevier.

Brand, P., Rothblum, E., & Soloman, L. (1992). A comparison of lesbians, gay men, and heterosexuals on weight and restricted eating. *International Journal of Eating Disorders, 11*, 253–259.

Briere, J. N., & Elliott, D. M. (1994). Immediate and long-term impacts of child sexual abuse. *The Future of Children, 4*, 54–69.

Brim, O. G., Ryff, C. D., & Kessler, R. C. (Eds.). (2004). *How healthy are we? A national study of well-being at midlife*. Chicago: University of Chicago Press.

Brooks-Gunn, J., & Furstenberg, Jr., F. F. (1989). Adolescent sexual behavior. *American Psychologist, 44*, 249–257.

Browne, A., & Finkelhor, D. (1986). Impact of child sexual abuse: A review of the research. *Psychological Bulletin, 99,* 66–77.

Browning, C. R., & Laumann, E. O. (1997). Sexual contact between children and adults: A life course perspective. *American Sociological Review, 62,* 540–560.

Browning, C. R., & Laumann, E. O. (2003). The social context of adaptation to childhood sexual maltreatment. In J. Bancroft (Ed.), *Sexual development in childhood* (pp. 383–403). Bloomington: Indiana University Press.

Brumberg, J. J. (1995). *The body project: An intimate history of American girls.* New York: Random House.

Bulcroft, K., & O'Connor, M. (1986). The importance of dating relationships on quality of life for older persons. *Family Relations, 35,* 397–401.

Bullough, V. L. (2004). Children and adolescents as sexual beings: A historical overview. *Child and Adolescent Psychiatric Clinics of North America, 13,* 447–459.

Bulosan, C. (1946). *America is in the heart.* Seattle: University of Washington Press.

Burton, D. (2000). Were adolescent sexual offenders children with sexual behavior problems? *Sexual Abuse: Journal of Research and Treatment, 12,* 37–48.

Butts, C. T., & Pixley, J. E. (2004). A structural approach to the representation of life history data. *Journal of Mathematical Sociology, 28,* 81–124.

Byrne, A., & Carr, D. (2005). Caught in the cultural lag: The stigma of singlehood. *Psychological Inquiry, 16,* 84–141.

Calasanti, T. M., & Slevin, K. F. (2001). *Gender, social inequalities, and aging.* Walnut Creek, CA: Altamira.

Calasanti, T. M., & Slevin, K. F. (Eds.). (2006). *Age matters: Realigning feminist thinking.* New York: Routledge.

Calasanti, T. M., Slevin, K. F., & King, N. (2006). Ageism and feminism: From "et cetera" to center. *National Women's Studies Association Journal, 18,* 13–30.

Call, V., Sprecher, S., & Schwartz, P. (1995). The incidence and frequency of marital sex in a national sample. *Journal of Marriage and Family, 57,* 639–652.

Cantu, L., Jr. (2009) *The sexuality of migration: Border crossings and Mexican immigrant men.* New York: NYU Press.

Carpenter, L. M. (2001). The first time/das erstes mal: Approaches to virginity loss in U.S and German teen magazines. *Youth & Society, 33,* 31–61.

Carpenter, L. M. (2002). Gender and the social construction of virginity loss in the contemporary United States. *Gender & Society, 16,* 345–65.

Carpenter, L. M. (2005). *Virginity lost: An intimate portrait of first sexual experiences.* New York: NYU Press.

Carpenter, L. M. (2007). Sexual health. In *Encyclopedia of sociology* (Vol. IX, pp. 4234–4238). Oxford: Blackwell.

Carpenter, L. M. (2010). Gendered sexuality over the life course: A conceptual framework. *Sociological Perspectives, 53,* 155–178.

Carpenter, L. M., Nathanson, C. A., & Kim, Y. J. (2006). Sex after 40? Gender, ageism, and sexual partnering in midlife. *Journal of Aging Studies, 20,* 93–106.

Carpentier, M., Silovsky, J., & Chaffin, J. (2006). Randomized trial of treatment for children with sexual behavior problems: Ten-year follow-up. *Journal of Consulting and Clinical Psychology, 74,* 482–488.

Carrington, C. (1999). *No place like home: Relationships and family life among lesbians and gay men*. Chicago: University of Chicago Press.

Cash, T. F. (2000). *Women's body images: For better or for worse*. Unpublished manuscript.

Casper, M. J., & Moore, L. J. (2009). *Missing bodies: The politics of visibility*. New York: NYU Press.

Caspi, A., Bem, D. J., & Elder, Jr., G. H. (1989). Continuities and consequences of interactional styles across the life course. *Journal of Personality, 57*, 375–406.

Caspi, A., & Moffitt, T. E. (1993). When do individual differences matter? A paradoxical theory of personality coherence. *Psychological Inquiry, 4*, 247–271.

Cass, V. (1979). Homosexual identity formation: A theoretical model. *Journal of Homosexuality, 4*, 219–235.

Centers for Disease Control and Prevention. (2008). Trends in HIV-and STD-related risk behaviors among high school students—United States, 1991–2007. *Morbidity and Mortality Weekly Reports, 57*, 817–822.

Centers for Disease Control and Prevention. (2009a). *HIV/AIDS among African Americans*. Fact sheet. Retrieved from http://www.cdc.gov/hiv/topics/aa/resources/factsheets/aa.htm

Centers for Disease Control and Prevention. (2009b). Sexual and reproductive health of persons aged 10–24 years. United States, 2002–2007. *Morbidity and Mortality Weekly Reports 58*(SS06), 1–58. Retrieved from http://www.cdc.gov/mmwr/preview/mmwrhtml/ss5806a1.htm?s_cid=ss5806a1_e

Charlson, M. E., Pompei, P., Ales, K. L., & McKenzie, C. R. (1987). A new method of classifying prognostic comorbidity in longitudinal studies: Development and validation. *Journal of Chronic Diseases, 40*, 373–383.

Cherlin, A. (2002). *Public and private families* (3rd ed.). New York: McGraw Hill.

Cherlin, A., Burton, L., Hurt, T., & Purvin, D. (2004). The influence of physical and sexual abuse on marriage and cohabitation. *American Sociological Review, 69*, 768–789.

Cherlin, A. J., Kiernan, K., & Chase-Lansdale, P. L. (1995). *Parental divorce in childhood and demographic outcomes in young adulthood*. Baltimore, MD: Johns Hopkins University Press.

Choy, C. (2003). *Empire of care: Nursing and migration in Filipino American history*. Durham: Duke University Press.

The Christopher and Dana Reeve Foundation (2009). *One degree of separation: Paralysis and spinal cord injury in the United States*. Retrieved from http://www.christopherreeve.org/site/c.ddJFKRNoFiG/b.4427055/k.F3F9/Brochures.htm

Chu, J. A. (1992). The revictimization of adult women with histories of childhood abuse. *Journal of Psychotherapy Practice and Research, 1*, 259–269.

Chung, D. (1991). Asian cultural commonalities: A comparison with mainstream American culture. In S. Furuto, R. Biswas, D. Chung, K. Murase, & F. Ross-Sheriff (Eds.), *Social work practice with Asian Americans* (pp. 27–44). Newbury Park, CA: Sage.

Clausen, J. A. (1995). Gender, contexts, and turning points in adults' lives. In P. Moen, G. H. Elder, Jr., & K. Lüscher (Eds.), *Examining lives in context: Perspectives on the ecology of human development* (pp. 365–389). Washington, DC: American Psychological Association.

Clements, M. (1996, March 17). Sex after 65. *Parade Magazine*, 4–6.

Cohen, J. (1988). *Statistical power analysis for the behavioral sciences* (2nd ed.). Hillsdale, NJ: Lawrence Erlbaum.

Coleman, M., Ganong, L., & Fine, M. (2000). Reinvestigating remarriage: Another decade of progress. *Journal of Marriage and Family, 62*, 1288–1307.

Colletta, N. D. (1979). Support systems after divorce: Incidence and impact. *Journal of Marriage and Family, 41*, 837–846.

Collins, P. H. (1990). *Black feminist thought: Knowledge, consciousness, and the politics of empowerment*. Boston: Unwin Hyman.

Collins, P. H. (2005). *Black sexual politics: African Americans, gender, and the new racism*. New York: Routledge.

Connell, R. W. (1987). *Gender and power*. Stanford, CA: Stanford University Press.

Connell, R. W. (1995). *Masculinities*. Berkeley: University of California Press.

Connidis, I. A. (2006). Intimate relationships: Learning from later life experience. In T. Calasanti & K. Slevin (Eds.), *Age matters* (pp. 123–153). New York: Routledge.

Cooley, C. H. (1908). A study of the early use of self-words by a child. *Psychological Review, 15*, 339–357.

Coontz, S. (1997). *The way we really are: Coming to terms with America's changing families*. New York: Basic Books.

Copper, B. (1988). *Over the hill: Reflections on ageism between women*. Freedom, CA: Crossing Press.

Cornwell, B., Laumann, E. O., & Schumm, L. P. (2008). The social connectedness of older adults: A national profile. *American Sociological Review, 73*, 185–203.

Corsaro, W. (2005). *Sociology of childhood (2nd ed.)*. Thousand Oaks, CA: Pine Forge Press.

Couch, D., & Liamputtong, P. (2008). On-line dating and mating: The use of the internet to meet sexual partners. *Qualitative Health Research, 18*, 268–279.

Cruikshank, M. (2009). *Learning to be old: Gender, culture, and aging* (2nd ed.). Lanham, MD: Rowman & Littlefield.

Das, A. (2007). Masturbation in the United States. *Journal of Sex and Marital Therapy, 33*, 301–317.

Das, A. (2009). Sexual harassment at work in the United States. *Archives of Sexual Behavior, 38*, 909 921

Das, A., & Laumann, E. O. (2010). How to get valid answers from survey questions: What we learned from asking about sexual behavior and the measurement of sexuality. In G. Walford, M. Viswanathan, & E. Tucker (Eds.), *The SAGE handbook of measurement*. Thousand Oaks, CA: Sage.

Dasgupta, S. D., & DasGupta, S. (1996). Public face, private face: Asian Indian women and sexuality. In N. B. Maglin & D. Perry, *"Bad girls"/"good girls": Women, sex, and power in the nineties*. New Brunswick: Rutgers University Press.

Dash, L. (2003). *When children want children: The urban crisis of teenage childbearing*. Urbana: University of Illinois Press.

Davis, K. (1995). *Reshaping the female body: The dilemma of cosmetic surgery*. New York: Routledge.

Deeks, A. A., & McCabe, M. (2001). Sexual function and the menopausal woman: The importance of age and partner's sexual functioning. *The Journal of Sex Research, 38*, 219–225.

DeLamater, J., & Hasday, M. (2007). The sociology of sexuality. In C. D. Bryant & D. L. Peck (Eds.), *21st century sociology: A reference handbook* (pp. 254–264). Thousand Oaks, CA: Sage.

DeLamater, J., Hyde, J., & Fong, M. (2008). Sexual satisfaction in the seventh decade of life. *Journal of Sex & Marital Therapy, 34,* 439–454.

DeLamater, J., & Karraker, A. (2009). Sexual functioning in older adults. *Current Psychiatry Reports, 6,* 6–11.

DeLamater, J., & Moorman, S. (2007). Sexual behavior in later life. *Journal of Aging and Health, 19,* 921–945.

DeLamater, J., & Sill, M. (2005). Sexual desire in later life. *The Journal of Sex Research, 42,* 138–149.

DeMaris, A. (2000). Till discord do us part: The role of physical and verbal conflict in union disruption. *Journal of Marriage and Family, 62,* 683–692.

D'Emilio, J., & Freedman, E. (1997). *Intimate matters: A history of sexuality in America* (2nd ed.). Chicago: University of Chicago Press. (Original work published 1988.)

Dennerstein, L., Dudley, E., & Burger, H. (2001). Are changes in sexual functioning during midlife due to aging or menopause? *Fertility and Sterility, 76,* 456–460.

DeVault, M. (1999). *Liberating method: Feminism and social research.* Philadelphia: Temple University Press.

DeWilde, C., & Uunk, W. (2008). Remarriage as a way to overcome the financial consequences of divorce. *European Sociological Review, 24,* 393–407.

Diamond, L. (2003). Was it a phase? Young women's relinquishment of lesbian/bisexual identities over a 5-year period. *Journal of Personality and Social Psychology, 84,* 352–364.

Diamond, L. (2008a). Female bisexuality from adolescence to adulthood: Results from a 10-year longitudinal study. *Developmental Psychology, 44,* 5–14.

Diamond, L. M. (2008b). *Sexual fluidity: Understanding women's love and desire.* Cambridge: Harvard University Press.

Dickson, F. C., Hughes, P. C., & Walker, K. L. (2005). An exploratory investigation into dating among later-life women. *Western Journal of Communication, 69,* 67–82.

DiGiulio, G. (2003). Sexuality and people living with physical or developmental disabilities: A review of key issues. *Canadian Journal of Human Sexuality, 12,* 53–68.

DiLillo, D., Giuffre, D., Tremblay, G. C., & Peterson, L. (2001). A closer look at the nature of intimate partner violence reported by women with a history of child sexual abuse. *Journal of Interpersonal Violence, 16,* 116–132.

Dillaway, H. E. (2008). "Why can't you control this?" Women's characterizations of intimate partner interactions about menopause. *Journal of Women & Aging, 20,* 47–64.

Dillaway, H. E. (2005). Menopause is the "good old": Women's thoughts about reproductive aging. *Gender & Society, 19,* 398–417.

Donnelly, D., Burgess, E., Anderson, S., Davis, R., & Dillard, J. (2001). Involuntary celibacy: A life course analysis. *The Journal of Sex Research, 38,* 159–169.

Dorfman, R., Walters, K., Burke, P., Hardin, L., Karanik, T., Raphael, J., & Silverstein, E. (1995). Old, sad and alone: The myth of the aging homosexual. *Journal of Gerontological Social Work, 24,* 29–44.

Dornbusch, S. M., Carlsmith, J. M., Duncan, P. D., Gross, R. T., Martin, J. A., Ritter, P. L., & Siegel-Gorelick, B. (1984). Sexual maturation, social class, and the desire to be thin among adolescent females. *Journal of Developmental and Behavioral Pediatrics, 5,* 308–314.

DuBois, L. Z. (2009). Shifting identities within the binary of sex: Identity management, stress, and resilience among transgender men. Paper presented at the annual meeting of the American Anthropological Association, Philadelphia, PA.

Dunne, E. F., Unger, E. R., Sternberg, M., McQuillan, G., Swan, D. C., Panel, S. S., & Markowitz, L. E. (2007). Prevalence of HPV infection among females in the United States. *Journal of the American Medical Association, 29*, 813–819.

Dunne, G. A. (1997). *Lesbian lifestyles: Women's work and the politics of sexuality.* Toronto: University of Toronto Press.

Dworkin, S., & O'Sullivan, L. (2005). Actual versus desired initiation patterns among a sample of college men: Tapping disjunctures within traditional male sexual scripts. *The Journal of Sex Research, 42*, 150–158.

Edin, K., & Kefalas, M. (2005). *Promises I can keep: Why poor women put motherhood before marriage.* Berkeley: University of California Press.

Egan, T. (1996, May 26). Mail-order marriage, immigrant dreams, and death. *New York Times*, p. 12.

Elder, G. H., Jr. (1999). *Children of the Great Depression.* Boulder, CO: Westview Press. (Original work published 1974.)

Elder, G. H., Jr. (1985). Perspectives on the life course. In G. H. Elder, Jr. (Ed.), *Life course dynamics: Trajectories and transitions* (pp. 23–49). Ithaca, NY: Cornell University Press.

Elder, G. H., Jr. (1994). Time, human agency, and social change: Perspectives on the life course. *Social Psychology Quarterly, 57*, 4–15.

Elder, G. H., Jr. (1995). The life course paradigm: Social change and individual development. In P. Moen, G. H. Elder, Jr., & K. Lüscher (Eds.), *Examining lives in context: Perspectives on the ecology of human development* (pp. 101–139). Washington, DC: American Psychological Association.

Elder, G. H., Jr., & Giele, J. (Eds.). (2009). *The craft of life course research.* New York: Guilford Press.

Ellingson, S. (2004). Constructing causal stories and moral boundaries: Institutional approaches to sexual problems. In E. O. Laumann, S. Ellingson, J. Mahay, A. Paik, & Y. Youm (Eds.), *The sexual organization of the city* (pp. 283–308). Chicago: University of Chicago Press.

Ellingson, S., Laumann, E. O., Paik, A., & Mahay, J. (2004). The theory of sex markets. In E. O. Laumann, S. Ellingson, J. Mahay, A. Paik, & Y. Youm (Eds.), *The sexual organization of the city* (pp. 3–39). Chicago: University of Chicago Press.

Elliott, G. C., Avery, R., Fishman, E., & Hoshiko, B. (2002). The encounter with family violence and risky sexual activity among young adolescent females. *Violence and Victims, 17*, 569–592.

England, P. (2005). Emerging theories of carework. *Annual Review of Sociology, 31*, 381–399.

England, P. (2009). Is there a gender war over relational versus casual sex? Paper presented at the annual meeting of the Pacific Sociological Association, San Diego, CA.

England, P., & McClintock, E. A. (2009). The gendered double standard of aging in US marriage markets. *Population and Development Review, 35*, 797–816.

England, P., Shafer, E., & Fogarty, A. (2008). Hooking up and forming relationships on today's college campuses. In M. Kimmel & A. Aronson (Eds.), *The gendered society reader* (3rd ed.) (pp. 531–547). New York: Oxford University Press.

Espin, O. (1999). *Women crossing boundaries: The psychology of immigration and the transformations of sexuality.* New York: Routledge.

Espiritu, Y. L. (2003). *Home bound: Filipino American lives across cultures, communities, and countries*. Berkeley: University of California Press.

Espiritu, Y. L. (2008). *Asian American women and men: Labor, laws, and love* (2nd ed.). Lanham, MD: Rowman & Littlefield.

Faircloth, C. A. (Ed.). (2003). *Aging bodies: Images and everyday experience*. Walnut Creek, CA: Altamira.

Featherstone, M., & Hepworth, M. (1991). The mask of ageing and the postmodern life course. In M. Featherstone, M. Hepworth, & B. Turner (Eds.), *The body: Social process and cultural theory* (pp. 371–389). London: Sage.

Felder, S. (2006). The gender longevity gap: Explaining the difference between singles and couples. *Journal of Population Economics, 19*, 543–557.

Fergusson, D. M., Horwood, J., & Beautrais, A. L. (1999). Is sexual orientation related to mental health problems and suicidality in young people? *Archives of General Psychiatry, 56*, 876–880.

Fergusson, D. M., Lynskey, M. T., & Horwood, L. J. (1996). Childhood sexual abuse and psychiatric disorder in young adulthood: Prevalence of sexual abuse and factors associated with sexual abuse. *Journal of the American Academy of Child and Adolescent Psychiatry, 34*, 1355–1364.

Fields, J. (2003). America's families and living arrangements: 2003. *Current Population Reports*, P20–553. Washington, DC: U.S. Census Bureau.

Fine, M. (1988). Sexuality, schooling and adolescent females: The missing discourse of desire. *Harvard Educational Review, 58*, 29–53.

Fine, M., & McClelland, S. I. (2006). Sexuality education and desire: Still missing after all these years. *Harvard Educational Review, 76*, 297–338.

Finkelhor, D. (1994). Current information on the scope and nature of child sexual abuse. *The Future of Children, 4*, 31–53.

Finkelhor, D., & Browne, A. (1985). The traumatic impact of child sexual abuse: A conceptualization. *American Journal of Orthopsychiatry, 55*, 530–541.

Finkelhor, D., Hotaling, G., Lewis, I. A., & Smith, C. (1989). Sexual abuse and its relationship to later sexual satisfaction, marital status, religion, and attitudes. *Journal of Interpersonal Violence, 4*, 279–399.

Finkelhor, D., Hotaling, G., Lewis, I. A., & Smith, C. (1990). Sexual abuse in a national survey of adult men and women: Prevalence, characteristics, and risk factors. *Child Abuse and Neglect, 14*, 19–28.

Finkelhor, D., Ormrod, R. K., & Turner, H. A. (2007). Polyvictimization and trauma in a national longitudinal cohort. *Development and Psychopathology, 19*, 149–166.

Fischer, C. S. (1980). Theories of urbanism. In G. Gmelch & W. Zenner (Eds.), *Urban life*. New York: St. Martin's Press.

Fisher, T. D. (2004). Family foundations of sexuality. In J. H. Harvey, A. Wenzel, & S. Sprecher (Eds.), *The handbook of sexuality in close relationships* (pp. 385–409). Mahwah, NJ: Lawrence Erlbaum.

Fitzgerald, F. (1987). *Cities on a hill*. New York: Simon and Shuster.

Flack, W., Daubman, K., Caron, M., Asadorian, J. D'Aureli, N., Gigliotti, S., Hall, A., Kiser, S., & Stine, E. (2007). Risk factors and consequences of unwanted sex among university students. *Journal of Interpersonal Violence, 22*, 139–157.

Fletcher, J. M. (2007). Social multipliers in sexual initiation decisions among U.S. high school students. *Demography, 44,* 373–388.

Foner, N. (2009). Introduction: Intergenerational relations in immigrant families. In N. Foner (Ed.), *Across generations: Immigrant families in America* (pp. 1–20). New York: NYU Press.

Ford, C., & Beach, F. (1951). *Patterns of sexual behaviors.* New York: Harper & Row.

Foucault, M. (1978). *The history of sexuality,* Volume 1. New York: Pantheon.

Fowler, J. (2009). Things you should know about HIV and older women. HIV wisdom for older women. Retrieved from http://www.hivwisdom.org/facts.html

Frayser, S. (1994). Defining normal childhood sexuality: An anthropological approach. *Annual Review of Sex Research, 5,* 173–217.

Freedman, D., Pisani, R., & Purves, R. (1998). *Statistics* (3rd ed.). New York: Norton.

Freedman, D., Thornton, A., Camburn, D., Alwin, D., & Young-DeMarco, L. (1988). The life history calendar: A technique for collecting retrospective data. *Sociological Methodology, 18,* 37–68.

Freitas, D. (2008). *Sex and the soul: Juggling sexuality, spirituality, romance, and religion on America's college campuses.* New York: Oxford University Press.

Friedrich, W. (1997a). Foreword. In S. Araji (Ed.), *Sexually aggressive children: Coming to understand them* (pp. xiii–xix). Thousand Oaks, CA: Sage.

Friedrich, W. (1997b). *CSBI Child sexual behavior inventory: Professional manual.* Odessa, FL: Psychological Assessment Resources.

Friedrich, W. (2007). *Children with sexual behavior problems: Family-based, attachment-focused therapy.* New York: Norton.

Friedrich, W., Fisher, J., Broughton, D., Houston, M., & Shafran, C. (1998). Normative sexual behavior in children: A contemporary sample. *Pediatrics,* 101:e9. Retrieved from www.pediatrics.org/cgi/content/full/101/4/e9

Friedrich, W., Grambsch, P., Broughton, D., Kuiper, J., & Beilke, R. (1991). Normative sexual behavior in children. *Pediatrics, 88,* 456–464.

Friedrich, W., Sandfort, T., Oostveen, J., & Cohen-Kettenis, P. (2000). Cultural differences in sexual behavior: 2–6 year-old Dutch and American children. *Journal of Psychology and Human Sexuality, 12,* 117–129.

Furman, F. K. (1997). *Facing the mirror: Older women and beauty shop culture.* New York: Routledge.

Furstenburg, F. F., Jr. (2009). If Moynihan had only known: Race, class, and family change in the late twentieth century. *Annals of the American Academy of Political and Social Science, 621,* 94–110.

Gagné, P., & McGaughey, D. (2002). Designing women: Cultural hegemony and the exercise of power among women who have undergone elective mammoplasty. *Gender & Society, 16,* 814–838.

Gagnon, J. (1985). Attitudes and responses of parents to pre-adolescent masturbation. *Archives of Sexual Behavior, 14,* 451–466.

Gagnon, J. (1991). The implicit and explicit use of scripts in sex research. *Annual Review of Sex Research, 1,* 1–41.

Gagnon, J., Giami, A., Michaels, S., & de Colomby, P. (2001). A comparative study of the couple in the social organization of sexuality in France and the United States. *The Journal of Sex Research, 38,* 24–34.

Gagnon, J., & Simon, W. (1973). *Sexual conduct: The social origins of human sexuality.* Chicago: Aldine.

Galambos, N. L., Almeida, D. M., & Petersen, A. C. (1990). Masculinity, femininity, and sex role attitudes in early adolescence: Exploring gender intensification. *Child Development, 61*, 1905–1914.

Ganong, L. H., & Coleman, M. (2004). *Stepfamily relationships: Developments, dynamics, and interventions.* New York: Kluwer.

Gaona, E. (2005, October 2). Thousands of Filipino-Americans celebrate with festival, fiesta. *San Diego Union-Tribune.*

Garcia, L. (2009). Love at first sex: Latina girls' meanings of virginity loss and relationships. *Identities: Global Studies in Culture and Power, 36*, 601–621.

Garland-Thomson, R. (2005). Feminist disability studies. *Signs, 30*, 1557–1588.

Gates, G., & Sonenstein, F. (2000). Heterosexual genital sexual activity among adolescent males: 1988 and 1995. *Family Planning Perspectives, 32*, 295–297, 304.

Gavin, L., MacKay, A., Brown, K., et al. (2009). Sexual and reproductive health of persons aged 10–24 years—United States, 2002–2007. *Morbidity and Mortality Weekly Reports, 58*, SS-6.

Gelfand, M. M. (2000). Sexuality among older women. *Journal of Women's Health & Gender-Based Medicine, 9*, 15–20.

Genazzani, A., Gambacciani, M., & Simoncini, T. (2007). Menopause and aging, quality of life, and sexuality. *Climacteric, 10*, 88–96.

Gergen, K. (1985). The social constructionist movement in modern psychology. *American Psychologist, 40*, 266–275.

Gerschick, T. J., & Miller, A. S. (1995). Coming to terms: Masculinity and disability. In D. Sabo (Ed.), *Masculinity and health and illness* (pp. 183–204). Thousand Oaks, CA: Sage.

Gibson, D. (1996). Broken down by gender: "The problem of old women" redefined. *Gender & Society, 10*, 433–448.

Giele, J. Z., & Elder, G. H., Jr. (1998). Life course research: Development of a field. In J. Z. Giele & G. H. Elder, Jr. (Eds.), *Methods of life course research: Qualitative and quantitative approaches* (pp. 5–27). Thousand Oaks, CA: Sage.

Gilmartin, S. (2006). Changes in college women's attitudes toward sexual intimacy. *Journal of Research on Adolescence, 16*, 429–454.

Gindi, R., Ghanem, K., & Erbelding, E. (2008). Increases in oral and anal exposure among youth attending STD clinics in Baltimore, Maryland. *Journal of Adolescent Health, 42*, 307–308.

Giordano, P. C., Manning, W. D., & Longmore, M. A. (2005). The romantic relationships of African-American and White adolescents. *Sociological Quarterly, 46*, 545–468.

Glaser, B. G., & Strauss, A. L. (1967). *The discovery of grounded theory: Strategies for qualitative research.* Chicago: Aldine.

Glass, G. V., McGaw, B., & Smith, M. L. (1981). *Meta-analysis in social research.* Beverly Hills, CA: Sage.

Goldman, R., & Goldman, J. (1982). *Children's sexual thinking: A comparative study of children aged 5 to 15 years in Australia, North America, Britain and Sweden.* New York: Academic Press.

Gomez, C. A., & Marin, B. V. (1996). Gender, culture, and power: Barriers to HIV prevention strategies for women. *The Journal of Sex Research, 33*, 355–362.

González-López, G. (2005). *Erotic journeys: Mexican immigrants and their sex lives*. Berkeley: University of California Press.

Gordon, B., & Schroeder, C. (1995). *Sexuality: A developmental approach to problems*. New York: Plenum.

Gordon, B., Schroeder, C., & Abrams, J. (1990a). Children's knowledge of sexuality: A comparison of sexually abused and nonabused children. *American Journal of Orthopsychiatry, 60*, 250–257.

Gordon, B., Schroeder, C., & Abrams, J. (1990b). Age and social-class differences in children's knowledge of sexuality. *Journal of Clinical Child Psychology, 1*, 33–43.

Gotlib, I. H., & Wheaton, B. (1997). *Stress and adversity over the life course: Trajectories and turning points*. Cambridge: Cambridge University Press.

Gott, M. (2005). *Sexuality, sexual health and ageing*. Berkshire, UK: Open University Press.

Grace, V., Potts, A., Gavey, N., & Vares, T. (2006). The discursive condition of Viagra. *Sexualities, 9*, 295–314.

Granovetter, M. (1973). The strength of weak ties. *American Journal of Sociology, 78*, 1360–1380.

Grant, K., & Ragsdale, K. (2008). Sex and the "recently single": Perceptions of sexuality and HIV risk among mature women and primary care physicians. *Culture, Health, & Sexuality, 10*, 495–511.

Green, A. I. (2006). "Until death do us part?" The impact of differential access to marriage on a sample of urban men. *Sociological Perspectives, 49*, 163–189.

Green, A. I. (2008). The social organization of desire: The sexual fields approach. *Sociological Theory, 26*, 25–50.

Green, A. I. (2010). Queer unions: Lesbian and gay male spouses marrying tradition and innovation. *Canadian Journal of Sociology, 35*, 399–436.

Greil, A. L. (1991). *Not yet pregnant: Infertile couples in contemporary America*. New Brunswick: Rutgers University Press.

Grocke, M., Smith, M., & Graham, P. (1995). Sexually abused and nonabused mothers' discussions about sex and their children's sexual knowledge. *Child Abuse and Neglect, 19*, 985–996.

Gross, N. (2005). The detraditionalization of intimacy reconsidered. *Sociological Theory, 23*, 286–311.

Gudykunst, W. B. (2004). *Bridging differences: Effective intergroup communication* (4th ed.). Thousand Oaks, CA: Sage.

Gullette, M. M. (1997). *Declining to decline: Cultural combat and the politics of the midlife*. Charlottesville: University of Virginia Press.

Gullette, M. M. (2004). *Aged by culture*. Chicago: University of Chicago Press.

Hagan, J., & Foster, H. (2003). S/he's a rebel: Toward a sequential stress theory of delinquency and gendered pathways to disadvantage in emerging adulthood. *Social Forces, 82*, 53–86.

Halpern, C. T., Udry, J. R., Campbell, B., & Suchindran, C. (1999). Effects of body fat on weight concerns, dating, and sexual activity: A longitudinal analysis of Black and White adolescent girls. *Developmental Psychology, 35*, 721–736.

Halpern-Felsher, B., Cornell, J., Kropp, R., & Tschann, J. (2005). Oral versus vaginal sex among adolescents: Perceptions, attitudes, and behavior. *Pediatrics, 115*, 845–851.

Halualani, R. T. (1995). The intersecting hegemonic discourses of an Asian mail-order bride catalog: Pilipina "oriental butterfly" dolls for sale. *Women's Studies in Communication, 17*, 45–64.

Hamilton, L., & Armstrong, E. (2009). Gendered sexuality in young adulthood: Double binds and flawed options. *Gender & Society, 23*, 589–616.

Hanson, T. L. (1999). Does parental conflict explain why divorce is negatively associated with child welfare? *Social Forces, 77*, 1283–1315.

Harley, D. A., Nowak, T. M., Gassaway, L. J., & Savage, T. A. (2002). Lesbian, gay, bisexual, and transgender college students with disabilities: A look at multiple cultural minorities. *Psychology in the Schools, 39*, 525–538.

Hartup, W. W. (1985). Relationships and their significance in cognitive development. In R. A. Hinde, A. N. Perret-Clermont, & J. Stevenson-Hinde (Eds.), *Social relationships and cognitive development* (pp. 66–82). New York: Oxford University Press.

He, W., Sengupta, M., Velkoff, V., & DeBarros, K. (2005). 65+ in the United States: 2005. *Current Population Reports*, P23–209. Washington, DC: U.S. Census Bureau.

Heaphy, B. (2007). Sexualities, gender and ageing: Resources and social change. *Current Sociology, 55*, 193–210.

Heaphy, B. (2009). The storied, complex lives of older GLBT adults: Choice and its limits in older lesbian and gay narratives of relational life. *Journal of GLBT Family Studies, 5*, 119–138.

Heatherington, L., & Lavner, J. A. (2008). Coming to terms with coming out: Review and recommendations for family systems-focused research. *Journal of Family Psychology, 22*, 329–343.

Hedges, L. V., & Vevea, J. L. (1998). Fixed and random effects models in meta-analysis. *Psychological Method, 3*, 486–504.

Heins, M. (2007). *Not in front of the children: "Indecency," censorship, and the innocence of youth.* New Brunswick: Rutgers University Press.

Heldman, C., & Wade, L. (2010). Hook up culture: Setting a new research agenda. *Sexuality Research & Social Policy.* Retrieved from http://lisawadedotcom.files.wordpress.com/2011/02/heldman-wade-2010-hook-up-culture-setting-a-new-research-agenda.pdf

Helms, J. (1994). The conceptualization of racial identity and other "racial" constructs. In E. Trickett, R. Watts, & D. Birman (Eds.), *Human diversity: Perspectives on people in context* (pp. 285–311). San Francisco: Jossey-Bass.

Herdt, G. (Ed.). (1992). *Gay culture in America: Essays from the field.* Boston: Beacon Press.

Herdt, G., & Boxer, A. (1992). Introduction: Culture, history, and the life course of gay men. In G. Herdt (Ed.), *Gay culture in America: Essays from the field* (pp. 1–28). Boston: Beacon Press.

Herdt, G., & de Vries, B. (Eds.) (2004). *Gay and lesbian aging: Research and future directions.* New York: Springer.

Herdt, G., & McClintock, M. (2000). The magical age of 10. *Archives of Sexual Behavior, 29*, 587–606.

Herdt, G., Russell, S. T., Sweat, J., & Marzullo, M. (2007). Sexual inequality, youth empowerment, and the GSA: A community study in California. In N. Teunis & G. Herdt (Eds.), *Sexual inequalities* (pp. 233–252). Berkeley: University of California Press.

Herzog, D. B., Newman, K. L., Yeh, C. J., & Warshaw, M. (1992). Body image satisfaction in homosexual and heterosexual women. *International Journal of Eating Disorders*, 11, 391–396.

Hess, M. J., Hough, S., & Tammaro, E. (2007). The experience of four individuals with paraplegia enrolled in an outpatient interdisciplinary sexuality program. *Sexuality and Disability*, 25, 189–195.

Hetherington, E. M. (2003). Social support and adjustment in children from divorced and remarried families. *Childhood*, 10, 217–236.

Hetherington, E. M., Henderson, S. H., Reiss, D., & Anderson, E. R. (1999). *Adolescent siblings in stepfamilies*. Malden, MA: Blackwell.

Hidalgo-Tamola, J., & Chitaley, K. (2009). Type 2 diabetes mellitus and erectile dysfunction. *Journal of Sexual Medicine*, 6, 916–926.

Higgins, J. A., & Hirsch, J. S. (2007). The pleasure deficit: Revisiting the "sexuality connection" in reproductive health. *Perspectives on Sexual and Reproductive Health*, 39, 240–247.

Hirsch, J. (2003). *A courtship after marriage: Sexuality and love in Mexican transnational families*. Berkeley: University of California Press.

Hitlin, S., & Elder, G. H., Jr. (2007). Time, self, and the curiously abstract concept of agency. *Sociological Theory*, 25, 170–191.

Hoganson, K. (1998). *Fighting for American manhood: How gender politics provoked the Spanish-American and Philippine-American wars*. New Haven: Yale University Press.

Holland, J., Ramazanoglu, C., & Thomson, R. (1996). In the same boat? The gendered (in) experience of first heterosex. In D. Richardson (Ed.), *Theorising heterosexuality* (pp. 143–160). Bristol, UK: Open University Press.

Hondagneu-Sotelo, P. (1994). *Gendered transitions: Mexican experiences of immigration*. Berkeley: University of California Press.

Hong, S. K., Han, B. K., Jeong, S. J., et al. (2007). Effect of statin therapy on early return to potency after nerve sparing radical retropubic prostatectomy. *Journal of Urology*, 178, 613–616.

Horne, S., & Zimmer-Gembeck, M. J. (2005). Female sexual subjectivity and well-being: Comparing late adolescents with different sexual experiences. *Sexuality Research & Social Policy*, 2, 25–40.

Howe, J. (2003). *Older people and their caregivers across the spectrum of care*. New York: Haworth.

Huerta, R., Mena, A., Malacara, J., & Diaz de Leon, J. (1995). Symptoms at perimenopausal period: Its association with attitudes toward sexuality, life-style, family function, and FSH levels. *Psychoneuroendocrinology*, 20, 135–148.

Human Rights Watch. (2001). *Hatred in the hallways: Violence and discrimination against lesbian, gay, bisexual, transgender students in U.S. schools*. New York: Author.

Huntemann, N. (2000). *Game over: Gender, race, and violence in video games*. Northampton, MA: Media Education Foundation.

Hurd, L. C. (1999). "We're not old!" Older women's negotiation of aging and oldness. *Journal of Aging Studies*, 13, 419–439.

Hurd, L. C. (2000). Older women's body image and embodied experience: An exploration. *Journal of Women and Aging*, 12, 77–97.

Hurlbert, J. S., Haines, V. A., & Beggs, J. J. (2000). Core networks and tie activation: What kinds of routine networks allocate resources in nonroutine situations? *American Sociological Review*, 65, 598–618.

Hyde, J. S., et al. (1996). Sexuality during pregnancy and the year postpartum. *The Journal of Sex Research, 33*, 143–151.

Hyde, J. S., & DeLamater, J. (2011). *Understanding human sexuality* (11th ed.). Boston: McGraw-Hill.

Impett, E. A., Schooler, D., & Tolman, D. L. (2006). To be seen and not heard: Femininity ideology and adolescent girls' sexual health. *Archives of Sexual Behavior, 35*, 131–144.

Ingraham, C. (1996). The heterosexual imaginary: Feminist sociology and theories of gender. In S. Seidman (Ed.), *Queer theory/sociology* (pp. 168–93). Oxford: Blackwell.

Jeynes, W. (1999). The effects of religious commitment on the academic achievement of black and Hispanic children. *Urban Education, 34*, 458–479.

Jeynes, W. (2000). The effects of several of the most common family structures on the academic achievement of eighth graders. *Marriage and Family Review, 30*, 73–97.

Jeynes, W. (2002a). *Divorce, family structure, and the academic success of children.* Binghamton, NY: Haworth.

Jeynes, W. (2003a). A meta-analysis: The effects of parental involvement on minority children's academic achievement. *Education & Urban Society, 35*, 202–218.

Jeynes, W. (2003b). The effects of black and Hispanic twelfth graders living in intact families and being religious on their academic achievement. *Urban Education, 38*, 35–57.

Jeynes, W. (2005). A meta-analysis of the relation of parental involvement to urban elementary school student academic achievement. *Urban Education, 40*, 237–269.

Jeynes, W. (2006a). Standardized tests and the true meaning of kindergarten and preschool. *Teachers College Record, 108*, 1937–1959.

Jeynes, W. (2006b). The impact of parental remarriage on children: A meta-analysis. *Marriage and Family Review, 40*, 75–102.

Jeynes, W. (2007a). *American educational history: School, society, and the common good.* Thousand Oaks, CA: Sage.

Jeynes, W. (2007b). The relationship between parental involvement and urban secondary school student academic achievement: A meta-analysis. *Urban Education, 42*, 82–110.

Jeynes, W. (2010). *Parental involvement and children's academic achievement.* New York: Taylor & Francis.

Jhally, S. (2007). *Dreamworlds 3: Desire, sex, & power in music videos.* Northampton, MA: Media Education Foundation.

Jones, J., & Pugh, S. (2005). Aging gay men. *Men and Masculinities, 7*, 248–260.

Kahn, J. R., & Pearlin, L. I. (2006). Financial strain over the life course and health among older adults. *Journal of Health and Social Behavior, 47*, 17–31.

Kaiser Family Foundation. (2006, September). *Sexual health statistics for teenagers and young adults in the United States.* Menlo Park, CA: Kaiser Family Foundation Publications.

Kandel, D. B., Yamaguchi, K., & Chen, K. (1992). Stages of progression in drug involvement from adolescence to adulthood: Further evidence for the gateway theory. *Journal of Studies in Alcohol, 53*, 447–457.

Karjane, H., Fisher, B., & Cullen, F. (2002). *Sexual assault on campus: What colleges and universities are doing about it.* Washington, DC: U.S. Department of Justice.

Karlberg, J. (2002). Secular trends in pubertal development. *Hormone Research, 57*, 19–30.

Kaschak, E., & Tiefer, L. (Eds.). (2001). *A new view of women's sexual problems.* New York: Haworth.

Katz, S. (2005). *Cultural aging: Life course, lifestyle, and senior worlds.* Peterborough, Canada: Broadview Press.

Kaufman, S. (1994). *The ageless self: Sources of meaning in late life.* Madison: University of Wisconsin Press.

Kendall-Tackett, K., Williams, L., & Finkelhor, D. (1993). The impact of sexual abuse on children: A review and synthesis of recent empirical studies. *Psychological Bulletin, 113,* 164–180.

Kenny, J. A. (1973). Sexuality of pregnant and breastfeeding women. *Archives of Sexual Behavior, 2,* 215–229.

Kerrigan, D., Andrinopoulos, K., Johnson, R., Parham, P., Thomas, T., & Ellen, J. M. (2007). Staying strong: Gender ideologies among African-American adolescents and the implications for HIV/STI prevention. *The Journal of Sex Research, 44,* 172–180.

Kim, J. K. (2009). Asian American women's retrospective reports of their sexual socialization. *Psychology of Women Quarterly, 33,* 334–350.

Kimmel, M. (1996). *Manhood in America: A cultural history.* New York: Free Press.

Kimmel, M. (2008). *Guyland: The perilous world where boys become men.* New York: HarperCollins.

Kingsberg, S. (2002). The impact of aging on sexual function in women and their partners. *Archives of Sexual Behavior, 31,* 431–437.

Kinsey, A., Pomeroy, W., & Gebhard, P. (1953). *Sexual behavior in the human female.* Philadelphia: W. B. Saunders.

Kinsey, A., Pomeroy, W., & Martin, C. (1948). *Sexual behavior in the human male.* Philadelphia: W. B. Saunders.

Klinenberg, E. (2002). *Heat wave: A social autopsy of disaster in Chicago.* Chicago: University of Chicago Press.

Koch, P. B., Mansfield, P. K., Thurau, D., & Carey, M. (2005). "Feeling frumpy": The relationship between body image and sexual response changes in midlife women. *The Journal of Sex Research, 42,* 215–223.

Kontula, O., & Haavio-Mannila, E. (2002). Masturbation in a generational perspective. In W. O. Bockting & E. Coleman (Eds.), *Masturbation as a means of achieving sexual health* (pp. 49–83). Binghamton, NY: Haworth.

Koppel, L. (2007). *The red leather diary: Reclaiming a life through the pages of a lost journal.* New York: Harper Perennial.

Koropeckyj-Cox, T. (2005). Singles, society, and science: Sociological perspectives. *Psychological Inquiry, 16,* 91–97.

Kruttschnitt, C., & Macmillan, R. (2006). The violent victimization of women: A life course perspective. In C. Kruttschnitt & K. Heimer (Eds.), *Gender and crime: Patterns in victimization and offending* (pp. 139–170). New York: NYU Press.

Kumar, R., Brant, H. A., & Robson, K. M. (1981). Childbearing and maternal sexuality: A prospective survey of 119 primiperae. *Journal of Psychosomatic Research, 25,* 373–383.

Kunzel, R. (2008). *Criminal intimacy: Prison and the uneven history of modern American sexuality.* Chicago: University of Chicago Press.

Kurz, D. (1996). Separation, divorce, and woman abuse. *Violence Against Women, 2,* 63–81.

Laan, E., & Janssen, E. (2007). How do men and women feel? Determinants of subjective experience of sexual arousal. In E. Janssen (Ed.), *The psychophysiology of sex* (pp. 278–290). Bloomington: Indiana University Press.

Lakkis, J., Ricciardelli, L. A., & Williams, R. J. (1999). Role of sexual orientation and gender-related traits in disordered eating. *Sex Roles, 41,* 1–16.

Lam, A. G., Russell, S. T., & Leong, S. J. (2008). Maternal correlates of noncoital sexual behavior: Examining a nationally representative sample of Asian and White American adolescents who have not had sex. *Journal of Youth and Adolescence, 37,* 62–73.

Lamb, S., & Coakley, M. (1993). Normal childhood sexual play and games: Differentiating play from abuse. *Child Abuse and Neglect, 17,* 515–526.

Lantz, J., Keyes, J., & Schultz, M. (1975). Occurrence of the romantic-love ideal in major American magazines, 1741–1865. *American Sociological Review, 40,* 21–36.

LaRossa, R. (2005). Grounded theory methods and qualitative family research. *Journal of Marriage and Family, 67,* 837–857.

Larsson, I., Svedin, C., & Friedrich, W. (2000). Differences and similarities in sexual behavior among pre-schoolers in Sweden and USA. *Nordic Journal of Psychiatry, 54,* 251–257.

Lasker, J. N., & Toedter, L. J. (2000). Predicting outcomes after pregnancy loss: Results from studies using the Perinatal Grief Scale. *Illness, Crisis and Loss, 8,* 350–372.

Laub, C., Somera, D. M., Gowen, L. K., & Diaz, R. M. (1999). Targeting "risky" gender ideologies: Constructing a community-driven, theory-based HIV prevention intervention for youth. *Health Education & Behavior, 26,* 185–199.

Laumann, E. O. (1995). Sex, politics, and science: A case history of the National Health and Social Life Survey. Paper presented at the annual meeting of the American Sociological Association, Washington, DC.

Laumann, E. O., Das, A., & Waite, L. J. (2008). Sexual dysfunction among older adults: Prevalence and risk factors from a nationally representative U.S. probability sample of men and women 57 to 85 years of age. *Journal of Sexual Medicine, 5,* 2300–2311.

Laumann, E. O., Ellingson, S., & Mahay, J. (Eds.). (2004). *The sexual organization of the city.* Chicago: University of Chicago Press.

Laumann, E. O., Gagnon, J., Michael, R., & Michaels, S. (1992). *National health and social life survey.* Health and Medical Care Archive, Robert Wood Johnson Foundation.

Laumann, E. O., Gagnon, J., Michael, R., & Michaels, S. (1994). *The social organization of sexuality: Sexual practices in the United States.* Chicago: University of Chicago Press.

Laumann, E. O., & Mahay, J. (2002). The social organization of women's sexuality. In G. M. Wingood & R. J. DiClemente (Eds.), *Handbook of women's sexual and reproductive health* (pp. 43–70). New York: Kluwer Academic/Plenum.

Laumann, E. O., Nicolosi, A., Glasser, D. B., Paik, A., Gingell, C., Moreira, E., et al. (2005). Sexual problems among women and men aged 40–80 y: Prevalence and correlates identified in the Global Study of Sexual Attitudes and Behaviors. *International Journal of Impotence Research, 17,* 39–57.

Laumann, E. O., Paik, A., & Rosen, R. C. (1999). Sexual dysfunction in the United States: Prevalence and predictors. *Journal of the American Medical Association, 281,* 537–544.

Laumann, E. O., West, S., Glasser, D., et al. (2007). Prevalence and correlates of erectile dysfunction by race and ethnicity among men aged 40 or older in the United States: From the Male Attitudes Regarding Sexual Health Survey. *Journal of Sexual Medicine, 4,* 57–65.

Laumann, E. O., & Youm, Y. (2001). Sexual expression in America. In E. O. Laumann & R. T. Michael (Eds.), *Sex, love, and health in America* (pp. 109–148). Chicago: University of Chicago Press.

Lauritsen, J. L., & Davis Quinet, K. F. (1995). Repeat victimization among adolescents and young adults. *Journal of Quantitative Criminology, 11,* 143–166.

Laws, G. (1995). Understanding ageism: Lessons from feminism and postmodernism. *The Gerontologist, 35,* 112–118.

Laz, C. (2003). Age embodied. *Journal of Aging Studies, 17,* 503–519.

Lee, J. (1998). Menarche and the (hetero)sexualization of the female body. In R. Weitz (Ed.), *The politics of women's bodies* (pp. 82–99). New York: Oxford University Press.

Lefkowitz, E. S., Romo, L. F., Corona, R., Au, T. K., & Sigman, M. (2000). How Latino American and European American adolescents discuss conflicts, sexuality, and AIDS with their mothers. *Developmental Psychology, 36,* 315–325.

Lehr, V. D. (2008). Developing sexual agency: Rethinking late nineteenth and early twentieth century theories for the twenty-first century. *Sexuality & Culture, 12,* 204–220.

Leiblum, S. R. (1990). Sexuality and the midlife woman. *Psychology of Women Quarterly, 14,* 495–508.

Leitenberg, H., Greenwald, E., & Tarran, M. (1989). The relation between sexual activity among children during preadolescence and/or early adolescence and sexual behavior and sexual adjustment in young adulthood. *Archives of Sexual Behavior, 18,* 299–313.

Lerdau, M., & Avery, C. (2007). The utility of standardized tests. *Science, 316*(5832), 1694.

Levine, M. (1998). *Gay macho.* New York: NYU Press.

Levy, J. A. (1994). Sex and sexuality in later life stages. In A. S. Rossi (Ed.), *Sexuality across the life course* (pp. 287–309). Chicago: University of Chicago Press.

Lewis, R., & Janda, L. (1988). The relationship between adult sexual adjustment and childhood experiences regarding exposure to nudity, sleeping in the parental bed, and parental attitudes toward sexuality. *Archives of Sexual Behavior, 17,* 349–362.

Lichtenstein, B. (2003). Stigma as a barrier to treatment of sexually transmitted infection in the American Deep South. *Social Science & Medicine, 57,* 2435–2445.

Lindau, S. T., Laumann, E. O., Levinson, W., & Waite, L. J. (2003). Synthesis of scientific disciplines in pursuit of health: The interactive biopsychosocial model. *Perspectives in Biology and Medicine, 46,* S74–S86.

Lindau, S. T., Schumm, L. P., Laumann, E. O., Levinson, W., O'Muircheartaigh, C. A., & Waite, L. J. (2007). A study of sexuality and health among older adults in the United States. *New England Journal of Medicine, 357,* 762–774.

Lindberg, L., Jones, R., & Santelli, J. (2008). Noncoital sexual activities among adolescents. *Journal of Adolescent Health, 43,* 231–238.

Littleton, H., Tabernik, H., Canales, E., & Backstrom, T. (2009). Risky situation or harmless fun? A qualitative examination of college women's bad hook-up and rape scripts. *Sex Roles, 60,* 793–804.

Liu, C. (2003). Does quality of marital sex decline with duration? *Archives of Sexual Behavior, 32,* 55–60.

Lock, M. L. (1993). *Encounters with aging: Mythologies of menopause in Japan and North America.* Berkeley: University of California Press.

Loe, M. (2004). *The rise of Viagra: How the little blue pill changed sex in America.* New York: NYU Press.

Long, J. S. (1997). *Regression models for categorical and limited dependent variables.* Thousand Oaks, CA: Sage.

Lopata, H. Z. (1973). *Widowhood in an American city.* Cambridge, MA: Schenkman.

Lopez, S., Nelson, H., Polo, A., Jenkins, J., Karno, M., Vaughn, C., et al. (2004). Ethnicity, expressed emotion, attributions, and course of schizophrenia: Family warmth matters. *Journal of Abnormal Psychology, 113*, 428–439.

Lorber, J., & Moore, L. J. (2002). *Gender and the social construction of illness* (2nd ed.). Walnut Creek, CA: Altamira.

Lucal, B. (1999). What it means to be gendered me: Life on the boundaries of a dichotomous gender system. *Gender & Society, 13*, 781–797.

Lund, K. (2008). Menopause and the menopausal transition. *Medical Clinics of North America, 92*, 1253–1271.

Macaluso, M., Demand, M. J., Artz, L. M., & Hook, E. W. III. (2000). Partner type and condom use. *AIDS, 14*, 537–546.

MacKinnon, C. (1989). Sexuality, pornography and method: Pleasure under patriarchy. *Ethics, 99*, 314–346.

Mac Rae, H. (1992). Fictive kin as a component of the social networks of older people. *Research on Aging, 14*, 226–247.

Maddox, G. L. (1979). Sociology of later life. *Annual Review of Sociology, 5*, 113–135.

Mahay, J., & Laumann, E. O. (2004). Meeting and mating over the life course. In E. O. Laumann, S. Ellingson, J. Mahay, A. Paik, & Y. Youm (Eds.), *The sexual organization of the city* (pp. 127–164). Chicago: University of Chicago Press.

Mahay, J., Laumann, E. O., & Michaels, S. (2001). Race, gender, and class in sexual scripts. In E. O. Laumann & R. Michael (Eds.), *Sex, love, and health in America: Private choices and public policies* (pp. 197–238). Chicago: University of Chicago Press.

Malavige, L. S., & Levy, J. C. (2009). Erectile dysfunction in diabetes mellitus. *Journal of Sexual Medicine, 6*, 1232–1247.

Mamo, L. (2007). *Queering reproduction: Achieving pregnancy in the age of technoscience.* Durham: Duke University Press.

Manalansan, M. F. (2003). *Global divas: Filipino gay men in the diaspora.* Durham: Duke University Press.

Mansfield, P. K., Carey, M., Anderson, A., Barsom, S. H., & Koch, P. B. (2004). Staging the menopausal transition: Data from the Tremin research program on women's health. *Women's Health Issues, 14*, 220–226.

Mansfield, P. K., Koch, P. B., & Voda, A. M. (1998). Qualities midlife women desire in their sexual relationships and their changing sexual response. *Psychology of Women Quarterly, 22*, 285–303.

Marin, B. V., Gomez, C. A., & Hearst, N. (1993). Multiple heterosexual partners and condom use among Hispanics and non-Hispanic whites. *Family Planning Perspectives, 26*, 170–174.

Markson, E. W., & Taylor, C. A. (2000). The mirror has two faces. *Ageing and Society, 20*, 137–160.

Marsden, P. V. (1987). Core discussion networks of Americans. *American Sociological Review, 52*, 122–131.

Marsiglio, W., & Greer, R. A. (1994). A gender analysis of older men's sexuality. In J. Edward, H. Thompson, & M. S. Kimmel (Eds.), *Older men's lives* (pp. 122–140). Thousand Oaks, CA: Sage.

Martin, A. D., & Hetrick, E. S. (1988). The stigmatization of the gay and lesbian adolescent. *Journal of Homosexuality, 15*, 163–184.

Martin, E. (1992). *The woman in the body: A cultural analysis of reproduction.* Boston: Beacon Press.

Martin, K. (2009). Normalizing heterosexuality: Mothers' assumptions, talk, and strategies with young children. *American Sociological Review, 74,* 190–207.

Martin, K., & Luke, K. (2010). Gender differences in the ABC's of the birds and the bees: What mothers teach young children about sexuality and reproduction. *Sex Roles, 62,* 278–291.

Mastro, D., & Behm-Morowitz, E. (2005). Latino representation on primetime television. *Journalism and Mass Communication Quarterly, 8,* 110–130.

Maxwell, S. (2008). *The talk: What your kids need to hear from you about sex.* New York: Avery.

Maynard, R. A. (1997). *Kids having kids: Economic costs and social consequences of teen pregnancy.* Washington, DC: Urban Institute Press.

McCall, L. (2005). The complexity of intersectionality. *Signs, 30,* 1771–1800.

McLanahan, S., & Sandefur, G. (1994). *Growing up with a single parent: What hurts, what helps.* Cambridge: Harvard University Press.

McPherson, J. M., Miller, J., Smith-Lovin, L., & Brashears, M. E. (2006). Social isolation in America: Changes in core discussion networks over two decades. *American Sociological Review, 71,* 353–375.

Meadows, M. (1997). Exploring the invisible: Listening to mid-life women about heterosexual sex. *Women's Studies International Forum, 20,* 145–152.

Meekosha, H. (2006). Gender, international. In *Encyclopedia of disability* (Vol. 2, pp. 764–769). Thousand Oaks, CA: Sage.

Messman-Moore, T. L., & Long, P. J. (2003). The role of childhood sexual abuse sequelae in the sexual revictimization of women: An empirical review and theoretical reformulation. *Clinical Psychology Review, 23,* 537–571.

Meyer, I. H. (2001). Why lesbian, gay, bisexual, and transgender public health? *American Journal of Public Health, 91,* 856–859.

Mezey, N. (2008). *New choices, new families: How lesbians decide about motherhood.* Baltimore, MD: Johns Hopkins University Press.

Miles, M. B., & Huberman, A. M. (1994). *Qualitative data analysis: An expanded sourcebook.* Thousand Oaks, CA: Sage.

Milligan, M. S., & Neufeldt, A. H. (2001). The myth of asexuality: A survey of social and empirical evidence. *Sexuality and Disability, 19,* 91–109.

Mills, C. W. (1959). *The sociological imagination.* Oxford: Oxford University Press.

Minichiello, V., Browne, J., & Kendig, H. (2000). Perceptions and consequences of ageism: Views of older people. *Ageing and Society, 20,* 253–278.

Minichiello, V., Plummer, D., & Seal, A. (1996). The asexual older person: Australian evidence. *Venereology, 9,* 180–188.

Modell, J. (1989). *Into one's own: From youth to adulthood in the United States, 1920–1975.* Berkeley: University of California Press.

Moen, P. (1996). Gender, age, and the life course. In R. H. Binstock & L. K. George (Eds.), *Handbook of aging and the social sciences* (pp. 171–187). San Diego, CA: Academic Press.

Moen, P., Elder, G. H., Jr., & Lüscher, K. (Eds.). (1995). *Examining lives in context: Perspectives on the ecology of human development.* Washington, DC: American Psychological Association.

Moen, P., Robison, J., & Dempster-McClain, D. (1995). Caregiving and women's wellbeing: A life course approach. *Journal of Health & Social Behavior, 36,* 259–273.

Moffit, T. E., Caspi, A., Belsky, J., & Silva, P. A. (1992). Childhood experience and the onset of menarche: A test of a sociobiological model. *Child Development, 63,* 47–58.

Money, J., & Ehrhardt, A. (1996). *Man & woman, boy & girl: Gender identity from conception to maturity.* Northvale, NJ: Jason Aronson.

Montemurro, B. (2006). *Something old, something bold: Bridal showers and bachelorette parties.* New Brunswick: Rutgers University Press.

Moorman, S. M., Booth, A., & Fingerman, K. L. (2006). Women's romantic relationships after widowhood. *Journal of Family Issues, 27,* 1281–1305.

Morell, C. M. (1994). *Unwomanly conduct: The challenges of intentional childlessness.* New York: Routledge.

Morrison, D. R., & Coiro, M. R. (1999). Parental conflict and marital disruption: Do children benefit when high conflict marriages are resolved? *Journal of Marriage and Family, 61,* 626–637.

Mulvaney-Day, N. E., Alegría, M., & Sribney, W. (2007). Social cohesion, social support, and health among Latinos in the United States. *Social Science and Medicine, 64,* 477–495.

Murray, S. (1996). *American gay.* Chicago: University of Chicago Press.

Nack, A. (2008). *Damaged goods: Women living with incurable sexually transmitted diseases.* Philadelphia: Temple University Press.

Nathanson, C. A. (1991). *Dangerous passage: The social control of sexuality in women's adolescence.* Philadelphia: Temple University Press.

National Institute on Aging. (2007). *HIV, AIDS, and older people.* U.S. Department of Health and Human Services, Public Health Service, National Institutes of Health. Retrieved from www.nia.nih.gov/HealthInformation/Publications/hiv-aids.htm

National Spinal Cord Injury Statistical Center. (2009). *Spinal cord injury: Facts and figures at a glance.* Birmingham: University of Alabama.

Newman, K. (2006). *A different shade of gray: Midlife and beyond in the city.* New York: New Press.

Nicolosi, A., Laumann, E. O., Glasser, D. B., Moreira, E. D., Jr., Paik, A., & Gingell, C. (2004). Sexual behavior and sexual dysfunctions after age 40: The global study of sexual attitudes and behaviors. *Urology, 64,* 991–997.

Nonoyama, H. (2000). The family and family sociology in Japan. *American Sociologist, 31,* 27–41.

Oberg, P., & Tornstam, L. (2001). Youthfulness and fitness—Identity ideals for all ages? *Journal of Aging and Identity, 6,* 15–29.

Okami, P., Olmstead, R., & Abramson, P. (1997). Sexual experiences in early childhood: 18-year longitudinal data from the UCLA Family Lifestyles project. *The Journal of Sex Research, 34,* 339–347.

Okami, P., Olmstead, R., Abramson, P., & Pendleton, L. (1998). Early childhood exposure to parental nudity and scenes of parental sexuality ("Primal Scenes"): An 18-year longitudinal study of outcomes. *Archives of Sexual Behavior, 27,* 361–384.

O'Muircheartaigh, C., & Smith, S. (2007). *NSHAP (National Social Life, Health, and Aging Project) wave 1 methodology report.* Chicago: National Opinion Research Center.

O'Rand, A. (1996). The cumulative stratification of the life course. In R. H. Binstock & L. K. George (Eds.), *Handbook of aging and the social sciences* (pp. 188–207). San Diego, CA: Academic Press.

O'Rand, A. (2002). Cumulative advantage theory in life course research. *Annual Review of Gerontology and Geriatrics*, *22*, 14–20.

O'Rand, A. (2003). The future of the life course: Late modernity and life course risks. In J. T. Mortimer & M. J. Shanahan (Eds.), *Handbook of the life course* (pp. 693–701). New York: Kluwer Academic/Plenum.

Oransky, M., & Marecek, J. (2009). "I'm not going to be a girl": Masculinity and emotions in boys' friendships and peer groups. *Journal of Adolescent Research*, *24*, 218–241.

Organisation for Economic Co-operation and Development (OECD). (2002). *OECD health data* (4th ed.). Paris: Author.

Orsi, R. A. (1985). *The Madonna of 115th street: Faith and community in Italian Harlem, 1880–1950*. New Haven: Yale University Press.

O'Sullivan, L. F., & Meyer-Bahlburg, H. F. L. (2003). African-American and Latina inner-city girls' reports of romantic and sexual development. *Journal of Social and Personal Relationships*, *20*, 221–238.

Owen, J., Rhoades, G., Stanley, S., & Fincham, F. (2010). "Hooking up" among college students: Demographic and psychosocial correlates. *Archives of Sexual Behavior*, *39*, 653–663.

Park, S. Y., Bae, D-S., Nam, J. H., et al. (2007). Quality of life and sexual problems in disease-free survivors of cervical cancer compared with the general population. *Cancer*, *110*, 2716–2725.

Parker, S., Nichter, M., Vuckovic, N., Sims, C., & Rittenbaugh, C. (1995). Body and weight concerns among African-American and White adolescent females: Differences that make a difference. *Human Organization*, *54*, 103–114.

Pascoe, C. J. (2007). *Dude, you're a fag: Masculinity and sexuality in high school*. Berkeley: University of California Press.

Paternoster, R., Brame, R., Mazerolle, P., & Piquero. A. (1998). Using the correct statistical test for the equality of regression coefficients. *Criminology*, *36*, 859–866.

Paul, E. (2006). Beer goggles, catching feelings, and the walk of shame: Myths and realities of the hook up experience. In D. C. Kirkpatrick, S. Duck, & M. K. Foley (Eds.), *Relating difficulty: The processes of constructing and managing difficult interaction* (pp. 141–160). New York. Routledge.

Paul, E., & Hayes, K. (2002). The casualties of "casual" sex; A qualitative exploration of the phenomenology of college students' hookups. *Journal of Social and Personal Relationships*, *19*, 639–661.

Paul, E., McManus, B., & Hayes, A. (2000). "Hookups": Characteristics and correlates of college students' spontaneous and anonymous sexual experiences. *The Journal of Sex Research*, *37*, 76–88.

Pitts, M., & Rahman, Q. (2001). Which behaviors constitute "having sex" among university students in the UK? *Archives of Sexual Behavior*, *30*, 169-176.

Pleck, J. H., Sonenstein, F. L., & Ku, L. (2004). Adolescent boys' heterosexual behavior. In N. Way & J. Y. Chu (Eds.), *Adolescent boys: Exploring diverse cultures of boyhood* (pp. 256–270). New York: NYU Press.

Pong, S., Dronkers, J., & Hampden-Thompson, G. (2003). Family policies and children's school achievement in single- versus two-parent families. *Journal of Marriage and Family*, *65*, 681–699.

Presser, H. B. (1975). Age differences between spouses. *American Behavioral Scientist*, *19*, 190–205.

Prinstein, M., Meade, C., & Cohen, G. (2003). Adolescent oral sex, peer popularity, and perceptions of best friends' sexual behavior. *Journal of Pediatric Psychology, 28,* 243–249.

Putnam, R., & Feldstein, L. M. (2003). *Better together: Restoring the American community.* New York: Simon and Schuster.

Raffaelli, M., & Green, S. (2003). Parent-adolescent communication about sex: Retrospective reports by Latino college students. *Journal of Marriage and Family, 65,* 474–481.

Raffaelli, M., & Ontai, L. L. (2004). Gender socialization in Latino/a families: Results from two retrospective studies. *Sex Roles, 50,* 287–299.

Raley, R. K., & Bumpass, L. L. (2003). The topography of the plateau in divorce: Levels and trends in union stability after 1980. *Demographic Research, 8,* 246–258.

Ramrakha, S., Bell, M. L., Paul, C., Dickson, N., Moffitt, T. E., & Caspi, A. (2007). Childhood behavior problems linked to sexual risk taking in young adulthood: A birth cohort study. *Journal of the American Academy of Child and Adolescent Psychiatry, 46,* 1272–1279.

Rangel, M. C., Gavin, L., Reed, C., Fowler, M. G., & Lee, L. M. (2006). Epidemiology of HIV and AIDS among adolescents and young adults in the United States. *Journal of Adolescent Health, 39,* 156–163.

Reis, H. T., Collins, W. A., & Berscheid, E. (2000). Relationships in human behavior and development. *Psychological Bulletin, 126,* 844–872.

Reynolds, J., & Wetherell, M. (2005). The discursive climate of singleness: The consequences for women's negotiation of a single identity. *Feminism & Psychology, 13,* 489–510.

Rich, A. (1994). Compulsory heterosexuality and lesbian existence. In *Blood, bread, and poetry* (p. 23–75). New York: Norton. (Original work published 1980.)

Riley, M. W. (1987). On the significance of age in sociology. *American Sociological Review, 52,* 1–14.

Rind, B., & Tromovitch, P. (1997). A meta-analytic review of findings from national samples on psychological correlates of child sexual abuse. *The Journal of Sex Research, 34,* 237–255.

Risman, B., & Schwartz, P. (2002). After the sexual revolution: Gender politics in teen dating. *Contexts, 1,* 16–24.

Roberts, D. (1997). *Killing the black body: Race, reproduction, and the meaning of liberty.* New York: Pantheon.

Robinson, G. (1996). Cross-cultural perspectives on menopause. *Journal of Nervous and Mental Disease, 184,* 453–458.

Rodgers, K. B., & Rose, H. A. (2002). Risk and resiliency factors among adolescents who experience marital transitions. *Journal of Marriage and Family, 64,* 1024–1037.

Rook, K. S., & Zettel, L. A. (2005). The purported benefits of marriage viewed through the lens of physical health. *Psychological Inquiry, 16,* 116–121.

Rose, S., & Frieze, I. H. (1993). Young singles' contemporary dating scripts. *Sex Roles, 28,* 499–509.

Rosenfeld, A., Bailey, R., Siegel, B., & Bailey, G. (1986). Determining incestuous contact between parent and child: Frequency of children touching parents' genitals in a non-clinical population. *Journal of the American Academy of Child Psychiatry, 25,* 481–484.

Rosenfeld, D. (2003). Homosexual bodies in time and space: The homosexual body as a sexual signifier in lesbian and gay elders' narratives. In C. Faircloth (Ed.), *Aging bodies: Meanings and perspectives* (pp. 171–203). Walnut Creek, CA: Altamira.

Ross-Sheriff, F. (1991). Adaptation and integration into American society: Major issues affecting Asian Americans. In S. Furuto, R. Biswas, D. Chung, K. Murase, & F. Ross-Sheriff (Eds.), *Social work practice with Asian Americans* (pp. 45–64). Newbury Park, CA: Sage.

Rossi, A. S. (Ed.). (1994). *Sexuality across the life course*. Chicago: University of Chicago Press.

Rostosky, S. S., Riggle, E. D. B., Horne, S. G., & Miller, A. D. (2009). Marriage amendments and psychological distress in lesbian, gay, and bisexual (LGB) adults. *Journal of Counseling Psychology, 56*, 56–66.

Rostosky, S. S., & Travis, S. B. (2000). Menopause and sexuality: Ageism and sexism unite. In S. Travis & J. White (Eds.), *Sexuality, society, and feminism: Psychology of women* (pp. 181–209). Washington, DC: American Sociological Association.

Rubin, G. (1975). Traffic in women: Notes on the political economy of sex. In R. Reiter (Ed.), *Toward an anthropology of women* (pp. 157–210). New York: Monthly Review.

Rubin, G. (1984). Thinking sex: Notes for a radical theory of the politics of sexuality. In C. S. Vance (Ed.), *Pleasure and danger* (pp. 267–319). Boston: Routledge.

Rubin, H., & Rubin, I. (1995). *Qualitative interviewing: The art of hearing data*. London: Sage.

Rubin, H. A., & Shapiro, D. A. (Directors). (2005). *Murderball* [DVD]. New York: ThinkFilm.

Ruiz, V. (1992). The flapper and the chaperone: Historical memory among Mexican-American women. In D. Gabbaci (Ed.), *Seeking common ground: Multidisciplinary studies* (pp. 141–158). Westport, CT: Greenwood.

Russell, C. J., & Keel, P. K. (2002). Homosexuality as a specific risk factor for eating disorders in men. *International Journal of Eating Disorders, 31*, 300–306.

Russell, D. E. H. (1986). *The secret trauma: Incest in the lives of girls and women*. New York: Basic Books.

Russell, S. T. (2002). Queer in America: Sexual minority youth and citizenship. *Applied Developmental Science, 6*, 258–263.

Russell, S. T. (2005). Conceptualizing positive adolescent sexuality development. *Sexuality Research & Social Policy, 2*, 4–12.

Russell, S. T., Clarke, T. J., & Clary, J. (2009). Are teens "post-gay"? Contemporary adolescents' sexual identity labels. *Journal of Youth and Adolescence, 38*, 884–890.

Russell, S. T., & Consolacion, T. B. (2003). Adolescent romance and emotional health in the United States: Beyond binaries. *Journal of Clinical Child and Adolescent Psychology, 32*, 499–508.

Russell, S. T., Muraco, A., Subramaniam, A., & Laub, C. (2009). Youth empowerment and high school gay-straight alliances. *Journal of Youth and Adolescence, 38*, 891–903.

Russo, N. F. (1976). The motherhood mandate. *Journal of Social Issues, 32*, 143–154.

Rust, P. C. (1996). Sexual identity and bisexual identities: The struggle for self-description in a changing sexual landscape. In B. Beemyn & M. Eliason (Eds.), *Queer studies* (pp. 64–86). New York: NYU Press.

Rutter, M. (1971). Normal psychosexual development. *Journal of Psychological Psychiatry, 11*, 259–283.

Ryan, C., & Futterman, D. (1998). *Lesbian and gay youth: Care and counseling*. New York: Columbia University Press.

Ryan, C., Huebner, D., Diaz, R. M., & Sanchez, J. (2009). Family rejection as a predictor of negative health outcomes in White and Latino lesbian, gay, and bisexual young adults. *Pediatrics, 123,* 346–352.

Salonia, A., Briganti, A., Deho, F., Naspro, R., Scapaticci, E., Scattoni, V., Rigatti, P., & Montorsi, F. (2003). Pathophysiology of erectile dysfunction. *International Journal of Andrology, 26,* 129–136.

Sampson, R. J., & Laub, J. H. (1990). Crime and deviance over the life course: The salience of adult social bonds. *American Sociological Review, 55,* 609–627.

Sampson, R. J., & Laub, J. H. (1993). *Crime in the making: Pathways and turning points through life.* Cambridge: Harvard University Press.

Sanders, S., & Reinisch, J. (1999). Would you say you "had sex" if…? *Journal of the American Medical Association, 281,* 275–277.

San Juan, E. J. (1991). Mapping the boundaries: The Filipino writer in the U.S. *Journal of Ethnic Studies, 19,* 117–131.

Savin-Williams, R. C. (1994). Dating those you can't love and loving those you can't date. In R. Montemayor, G. R. Adams, & T. P. Gullotta (Eds.), *Personal relationships during adolescence* (pp. 196–215). Newbury Park, CA: Sage.

Savin-Williams, R. C. (1995). Lesbian, gay male, and bisexual adolescents. In A. R. D'Augelli & C. J. Patterson (Eds.), *Lesbian, gay, and bisexual identities over the lifespan* (pp. 165–189). New York: Oxford University Press.

Savin-Williams, R. C. (2005). *The new gay teenager.* Cambridge: Harvard University Press.

Savin-Williams, R. C., & Diamond, L. M. (2000). Sexual identity trajectories among sexual-minority youths: Gender comparisons. *Archives of Sexual Behavior, 29,* 419–440.

Schalet, A. (2004). Must we fear adolescent sexuality? *Medscape General Medicine, 6,* 1–23.

Schalet, A., Hunt, G., & Joe-Laidler, K. (2003). Respectability and autonomy: The articulation and meaning of sexuality among the girls in the gang. *Journal of Contemporary Ethnography, 21,* 108–143.

Schiavi, R. C. (1994). Effect of chronic disease and medication on sexual functioning. In A. S. Rossi (Ed.), *Sexuality across the life course* (pp. 313–339). Chicago: University of Chicago Press.

Schlesinger, L. (1996). Chronic pain, intimacy, and sexuality: A qualitative study of women who live with pain. *The Journal of Sex Research, 33,* 249–256.

Schuler, P., Vinci, D., Isosaari, R., Philipp, S., Todorovich, J., Roy, J., et al. (2008). Body-shape perceptions and body mass index of older African American and European American women. *Journal of Cross-Cultural Gerontology, 23,* 255–264.

Schwartz, D., Dodge, K., & Coie, J. (1993). The emergence of chronic peer victimization in boys' play groups. *Child Development, 64,* 1755–1772.

Schwartz, P., & Rutter, V. (1998). *The gender of sexuality.* Thousand Oaks, CA: Pine Forge.

Seidman, S. (1991). *Romantic longings: Love in America, 1830–1980.* New York: Routledge.

Settersten, R. A., Jr. (2003). Age structuring and the rhythm of the life course. In J. T. Mortimer & M. J. Shanahan (Eds.), *Handbook of the life course* (pp. 81–98). New York: Kluwer Academic/Plenum.

Shaffer, L. S. (1977). The golden fleece: Anti-intellectualism and social science. *American Psychologist, 32,* 814–823.

Shafran, C. (1995). *Normal sexual behavior of young children: Contextual and family influences* (unpublished doctoral dissertation). Santa Barbara, CA: Fielding Institute.

Shakespeare, T. (1999). The sexual politics of disabled masculinity. *Sexuality and Disability, 17*, 53–64.

Shanahan, M. J., & Macmillan, R. (2007). *Biography and the sociological imagination.* New York: Norton.

Sheff, E. (2005). Polyamorous women, sexual subjectivity, and power. *Journal of Contemporary Ethnography, 34*, 251–283.

Shek, D. T. (2007). A longitudinal study of perceived parental psychological control and psychological well-being in Chinese adolescents in Hong Kong. *Journal of Clinical Psychology, 63*, 1–22.

Sherif, B. (2001). The ambiguity of boundaries in the fieldwork experience: Establishing rapport and negotiating insider/outsider status. *Qualitative Inquiry, 7*, 436–447.

Shirey, L., & Summer, L. (2000). *Caregiving: Helping the elderly with activity limitations. Challenges for the twenty-first century: Chronic and disabling conditions.* Washington, DC: National Academy on Aging in Society.

Shulman, J. L., & Horne, S. G. (2003). The use of self-pleasure: Masturbation and body image among African American and European American women. *Psychology of Women Quarterly, 27*, 262–269.

Shuttleworth, R. P. (2000). The search for sexual intimacy for men with cerebral palsy. *Sexuality and Disability, 18*, 263–282.

Simon, W., & Gagnon, J. H. (1986). Sexual scripts: Permanence and change. *Archives of Sexual Behavior, 15*, 97–120.

Slevin, K. F. (2006). The embodied experiences of old lesbians. In T. Calasanti & K. F. Slevin (Eds.), *Age matters* (pp. 247–268). New York: Routledge.

Slevin, K. F., & Wingrove, C. W. (1998). *From stumbling blocks to stepping stones: The life experiences of fifty professional African American women.* New York: NYU Press.

Smetana, J. G., & Gettman, D. C. (2006). Autonomy and relatedness with parents and romantic development in African American adolescents. *Developmental Psychology, 42*, 1347–1351.

Smiler, A. P., Ward, L. M., Caruthers, A., & Merriwether, A. (2005). Pleasure, empowerment, and love: Factors associated with a positive first coitus. *Sexuality Research & Social Policy, 2*, 41–55.

Smith, P. H., White, J. W., & Holland, L. J. (2003). A longitudinal perspective on dating violence among adolescent and college-age women. *American Journal of Public Health, 93*, 1104–1109.

Stack, C. (1974). *All our kin: Strategies for survival in a Black community.* New York: Basic Books.

Staples, R. (1972). The sexuality of black women. *Sexual Behavior, 2*, 4–15.

Staples, R. (1973). *The black woman in America: Sex, marriage, and the family.* New York: Harper & Row.

Staples, R., & Johnson, L. B. (1993). *Black families at the crossroads: Challenges and prospects.* San Francisco, CA: Jossey-Bass.

Stein, E. (1999). *The mismeasure of desire.* New York: Oxford University Press.

Sterk-Elifson, C. (1994). Sexuality among African American women. In A. S. Rossi (Ed.), *Sexuality across the life course* (pp. 99–126). Chicago: University of Chicago Press.

Stets, J. E., & Straus, M. A. (1989). The marriage license as a hitting license: A comparison of assaults in dating, cohabiting, and married couples. *Journal of Family Violence, 4*, 161–180.

Stoler, A. L. (1995). *Race and the education of desire: Foucault's history of sexuality and the colonial order of things*. Durham: Duke University Press.

Storr, A. (1996). *Freud*. Oxford: Oxford University Press.

Strachey, J. (1962). *Sigmund Freud: Three essays on the theory of sexuality*. London: Hogarth Press.

Straus, M. A. (1979). Measuring intrafamily conflict and violence: The conflict tactics (CT) scales. *Journal of Marriage and Family, 41*, 75–88.

Straus, M. A. (1990). Social stress and marital violence in a national sample of American families. In M. A. Straus & R. J. Gelles (Eds.), *Physical violence in American families* (pp. 473–487). New Brunswick, NJ: Transaction.

Strauss, A. L., & Corbin, J. (1998). *Basics of qualitative research: Techniques and procedures for developing grounded theory* (2nd ed.). Thousand Oaks, CA: Sage.

Sun, S., Schubert, C., Chumlea, W., Roche, A., Kulin, H., Lee, P., et al. (2002). National estimates of the timing of sexual maturation and racial differences among US children. *Pediatrics, 110*, 911–919.

Sussman, M. B., Steinmetz, S. K., & Peterson, G. W. (1999). *Handbook of marriage and the family*. New York: Springer.

Taleporos, G., & McCabe, M. P. (2003). Relationships, sexuality and adjustment among people with physical disability. *Sexual and Relationship Therapy, 18*, 25–43.

Taylor, C. A., Boris, N. W., Heller, S. S., Clum, G. A., Rice, J. C., & Zeanah, C. H. (2008). Cumulative experiences of violence among high-risk urban youth. *Journal of Interpersonal Violence, 23*, 1618–1635.

Taylor, R. J., Chatters, L. M., Tucker, M. B., & Lewis, E. (1991). Developments in research on Black families: A decade review. *Journal of Marriage and Family, 52*, 993–1014.

Teti, D. M., & Lamb, M. E. (1989). Socioeconomic and marital outcomes of adolescent marriage, adolescent childbirth, and their co-occurrence. *Journal of Marriage and Family, 51*, 203–212.

Teti, D. M., Lamb, M. E., & Elster, A. (1987). Long-range socioeconomic and marital consequences of adolescent marriage in three cohorts of adult males. *Journal of Marriage and Family, 49*, 499–506.

Tharyan, P., & Gopalakrishanan, G. (2009). Erectile dysfunction: Clinical evidence. *British Medical Journal*. Retrieved from www.clinicalevidence.bmj.com

Thigpen, J. W. (2009). Early sexual behavior in a sample of low-income, African American children. *The Journal of Sex Research, 46*, 67–79.

Thigpen, J. W., & Fortenberry J. (2010). Toward a theoretical and empirical understanding of variation in normative childhood sexual behavior: The significance of family context. *Social Service Review, 83*, 611–631.

Thigpen, J., Pinkston, E., & Mayefsky, J. (2003). Normative sexual behavior of African-American children: Preliminary findings. In J. Bancroft (Ed.), *Sexual development in childhood* (pp. 241–254). Bloomington: Indiana University Press.

Thirlaway, K., Fallowfield, L., & Cuzick, J. (1996). The sexual activity questionnaire: A measure of women's sexual functioning. *Quality of Life Research, 5*, 81–90.

Thomas, W. H. (2004). *What are old people for? How elders will save the world*. Acton, MA: VanderWyck and Burnham.

Thompson, S. (1995). *Going all the way: Teenage girls' tales of sex, romance, and pregnancy*. New York: Hill and Wang.

Thornton, A., & Young-DeMarco, L. (2001). Four decades of trends in attitudes toward family issues in the United States: The 1960s through the 1990s. *Journal of Marriage and Family, 63,* 1009-1037.

Tjaden, P., & Thoennes, N. (2000). *Full report of the prevalence, incidence, and consequences of violence against women.* Washington, DC: U.S. Department of Justice.

Tjaden, P., Thoennes, N., & Allison, C. J. (1999). Comparing violence over the life span in samples of same-sex and opposite-sex cohabitants. *Violence and Victims, 14,* 413–425.

Tolman, D. L. (1994). Doing desire: Adolescent girls' struggles for/with sexuality. *Gender & Society, 8,* 324–342.

Tolman, D. L. (1996). Adolescent girls' sexuality: Debunking the myth of The Urban Girl. In B. J. Leadbetter & N. Way (Eds.), *Urban girls: Resisting stereotypes, creating identities* (pp. 255–271). New York: NYU Press.

Tolman, D. L. (2002). *Dilemmas of desire: Teenage girls talk about sexuality.* Cambridge: Harvard University Press.

Tolman, D. L., Spencer, R., Harmon, T., Rosen-Reynoso, & Striepe, M. (2004). Getting close, staying cool: Early adolescent boys' experiences with romantic relationships. In N. Way & J. Y. Chu (Eds.), *Adolescent boys: Exploring diverse cultures of boyhood* (pp. 235–255). New York: NYU Press.

Tolman, D. L., Striepe, M. I., & Harmon, T. (2003). Gender matters: Constructing a model of adolescent sexual health. *The Journal of Sex Research, 40,* 4–12.

Tomlinson, B. (1999). Intensification and the discourse of decline: A rhetoric of medical anthropology. *Medical Anthropology Quarterly, 13,* 7–31.

Tosh, A. K., & Simmons, P. S. (2007). Sexual activity and other risk-taking behaviors among Asian-American adolescents. *Journal of Pediatric and Adolescent Gynecology, 20,* 29–34.

Trudel, G., Turgeon, L., & Piché, L. (2000). Marital and sexual aspects of old age. *Sexual and Relationship Therapy, 15,* 381-406.

Turner, B. S. (1996). *The body and society.* London: Sage.

Twigg, J. (2000). *Bathing, the body and community care.* New York: Routledge.

Udry, J. R. (1988). Biological predispositions and social control in adolescent sexual behavior. *American Sociological Review, 53,* 709–722.

Udry, J. R., & Campbell, B. C. (1994). Getting started on sexual behavior. In A. S. Rossi (Ed.), *Sexuality across the life course* (pp. 187–207). Chicago: University of Chicago Press.

U.S. Census Bureau. (n.d.). *American community survey: S0201, Selected population profile in the United States: Filipinos alone.* Retrieved from http://factfinder.census.gov

U.S. Census Bureau. (2006). *Income, poverty, and health insurance coverage in the United States.* Retrieved from http://www.census.gov

U.S. Department of Education. (2005). *Digest of education statistics.* Washington, DC: Author.

Valentine, D. (2004). The categories themselves. *GLQ, 10,* 215–220.

Valtonen, K., Karlsson, A.-K., Siösteen, A., Dahlöf, L.-G., & Viikari-Juntura, E. (2006). Satisfaction with sexual life among persons with traumatic spinal cord injury and meningomyelocele. *Disability & Rehabilitation, 28,* 965–976.

Vance, C. S. (Ed.). (1993). *Pleasure and danger: Exploring female sexuality.* New York: HarperCollins.

VanLaningham, J., Johnson, D., & Amato, P. (2001). Marital happiness, marital duration, and the U-shaped curve: Evidence from a five-wave panel study. *Social Forces, 79*, 1313–1341.

Vaughan, D. (1986). *Uncoupling: Turning points in intimate relationships.* New York: Oxford University Press.

Villarreuel, F., & Walker, N. (2003, March/April). "Invisible" Latino youth find injustice in the justice system. *Focus*, 1–4.

Vinokur, A. D., Price, R. H., & Caplan, R. D. (1996). Hard times and hurtful partners: How financial strain affects depression and relationship satisfaction of unemployed persons and their spouses. *Journal of Personality and Social Psychology, 71*, 166–169.

Wade, L., & DeLamater, J. (2002). Relationship dissolution as a life stage transition: Effects on sexual attitudes and behaviors. *Journal of Marriage and Family, 64*, 898–891.

Wade, L., Kremer, E., & Brown, J. (2005). The incidental orgasm: The presence of clitoral knowledge and the absence of orgasm for women. *Women and Health, 42*, 117–138.

Wahler, J., & Gabbay, S. G. (1997). Gay male aging: A review of the literature. *Journal of Gay and Lesbian Social Services, 6*, 1–20.

Waite, L. J., Laumann, E. O., Das, A., & Schumm, L. P. (2009). Sexuality: Measures of partnerships, practices, attitudes, and problems in the National Social Life, Health and Aging Study. *Journals of Gerontology: Social Sciences, 64B*, i56–i66.

Wallerstein, J. S., & Blakeslee, S. (2003). *What about the kids?* New York: Hyperion.

Wallerstein, J. S., & Lewis, J. (1998). The long-term impact of divorce on children: A first report from a 25-year study. *Family and Conciliation Courts Review, 36*, 368–383.

Ward, L. M. (2004). Wading through the stereotypes: Positive and negative associations between media use and black adolescents' conceptions of self. *Developmental Psychology, 40*, 284–294.

Warner, M. (1991). Introduction: Fear of a queer planet. *Social Text, 29*, 3–17.

Waters, M. C. (1996). The intersection of gender, race, and ethnicity in identity development of Caribbean American teens. In B. J. Leadbeater & N. Way (Eds.), *Urban girls: Resisting stereotypes, creating identities* (pp. 65–81). New York: NYU Press.

Wazakilli, M., Mpofu, R., & Devlieger, P. (2009). Should issues of sexuality and HIV and AIDS be a rehabilitation concern? The voices of young South Africans with physical disabilities. *Disability & Rehabilitation, 31*, 32–41.

Weber, L. (2001). *Understanding race, class, gender and sexuality: A conceptual framework.* New York: McGraw-Hill.

Weber, M. (1958). The social psychology of the world religions. In H. H. Gerth & C. W. Mills (Eds.), *From Max Weber: Essays in sociology* (pp. 267–301). New York: Oxford University Press. (Original work published 1915.)

Weeks, J., Heaphy, B., & Donovan, C. (2001). *Same sex intimacies: Families of choice and other life experiments.* New York: Routledge.

Weinberg, M., & Williams, C. (1988). Black sexuality: A test of two theories. *The Journal of Sex Research, 25*, 197–218.

Welsh, D. P., Haugen, P. T., Widman, L., Darling, N., & Grello, C. M. (2005). Kissing is good: A developmental investigation of sexuality in adolescent romantic couples. *Sexuality Research & Social Policy, 2*, 32–41.

Wertlieb, D. (1996). Children whose parents divorce. Life trajectories and turning points. In I. Gotlib & B. Wheaton (Eds.), *Stress and adversity over the life course: Trajectories and turning points* (pp. 179–196). Cambridge: Cambridge University Press.

West, C. (2001). *Race matters*. New York: Vintage.

West, C., & Zimmerman, D. H. (1987). Doing gender. *Gender & Society, 1*, 125–151.

Whitbeck, L. B., & Simons, R. L. (1990). Life on the streets: The victimization of runaway and homeless adolescents. *Youth and Society, 22*, 108–125.

Whitbeck, L. B., Simons, R. L., & Kao, M-Y. (1994). The effects of divorced mothers' dating behaviors and sexual attitudes on the sexual attitudes and behaviors of their adolescent children. *Journal of Marriage and Family, 56*, 615–621.

White, E. F. (2001). *Dark continent of our bodies: Black feminism and the politics of respectability*. Philadelphia: Temple University Press.

White, S., Halpin, B., Strom, G., & Santilli, G. (1988). Behavioral comparisons of young sexually abused, neglected, and nonreferred children. *Journal of Clinical Child Psychology, 17*, 53–61.

Wilkins, A. C. (2008). *Wannabes, goths, and Christians: The boundaries of sex, style, and status*. Chicago: University of Chicago Press.

Williams, C. (1995). *Still a man's world: Men who do women's work*. Berkeley: University of California Press.

Williams, L. S. (2002). Trying on gender, gender regimes, and the process of becoming women. *Gender & Society, 16*, 29–52.

Williams, S. R., Pham-Kanter, G., & Leitsch, S. A. (2009). Measures of chronic conditions and diseases associated with aging in the National Social Life, Health, and Aging Project (NSHAP). *Journals of Gerontology: Social Sciences, 64B*, i67–i75.

Wilson, R. S., Mendes de Leon, C. F., Barnes, L. L. Schneider, J. A., Bienias, J. L., Evans, D. A., & Bennett, D.A. (2002). Participation in cognitively stimulating activities and risk of incident Alzheimer disease. *Journal of the American Medical Association, 287*, 742–748.

Wilson, W. J. (1987). *The truly disadvantaged: The inner city, the underclass, and public policy*. Chicago: University of Chicago Press.

Winterich, J. A. (2003). Sex, menopause, and culture: Sexual orientation and the meaning of menopause for women's sex lives. *Gender & Society, 17*, 627–642.

Wirtz, W. (1977). *On further examination*. New York: College Entrance Examination Board.

Wise, L. A., Palmer, J. R., Stewart, E. A., & Rosenberg, L. (2005). Age-specific incidence rates for self-reported uterine leiomyomata in the Black Women's Health Study. *Obstetrics & Gynecology, 105*, 563–568.

Wittberg, R. A., Northrup, K. L., & Cottrel, L. (2009). Children's physical fitness and academic achievement. *American Journal of Health Education, 40*, 30–36.

Witten, T. M. (2003). Life course analysis: Middle adulthood issues in the transgender and intersex community. *Journal of Human Behavior in the Social Environment, 8*, 189–224.

Wolf, N. (1991). *The beauty myth*. New York: Anchor.

Wood, M. (2004). The gay male gaze: Body image disturbance and gender oppression among gay men. *Journal of Gay & Lesbian Social Services, 17*, 43–62.

Woolwine, D., & McCarthy, D. (2005). Gay moral discourse: Talking about identity, sex, and commitment. *Studies in Symbolic Interaction, 28*, 379–480.

Working Group on a New View of Women's Sexual Problems. (2001). A new view of women's sexual problems. In E. Kaschak & L. Tiefer (Eds.), *A new view of women's sexual problems* (pp. 1–8). New York: Haworth.

Wu, L. L. (2003). Event history models for life course analysis. In J. T. Mortimer & M. J. Shanahan (Eds.), *Handbook of the life course* (pp. 477–502). New York: Kluwer Academic/Plenum.

Wu, Z., & Schimmele, C. (2005). Repartnering after first union disruption. *Journal of Marriage and Family, 67*, 27–30.

Wysocki, D. (1998). Let your fingers do the talking: Sex on an adult chat-line. *Sexualities, 1*, 425–452.

Yung, J. (1995). *Unbound feet: A social history of Chinese women in San Francisco*. Berkeley: University of California Press.

Zayas, L., Lester, R., Cabassa, L., & Fortuna, L. (2005). Why do so many Latina teens attempt suicide? A conceptual model for research. *American Journal of Orthopsychiatry, 75*, 275–287.

Zola, I. K. (1982). *Missing pieces: A chronicle of living with disability*. Philadelphia: Temple University Press.

About the Contributors

ALEXIS A. BENDER is a doctoral candidate in sociology and working toward a graduate certificate in gerontology at Georgia State University. Her scholarship focuses on medicine, sexuality, gender, and social relationships across the life course. Her dissertation is a longitudinal study of marital relations following spinal cord injury.

KRISTIN CARBONE-LOPEZ received her Ph.D. in sociology from the University of Minnesota. She is Assistant Professor in the Department of Criminology and Criminal Justice at the University of Missouri, St. Louis. Her research examines the intersections among gender, victimization, and offending across the life course.

LAURA M. CARPENTER, Ph.D., is Associate Professor of Sociology at Vanderbilt University and the author of *Virginity Lost: An Intimate Portrait of First Sexual Experiences*. Her research focuses on sexual beliefs and behavior across the life course, the politics of sexual health, and mass media depictions of sexuality and romance. In 2007, she was named an Emerging Professional by the Society for the Scientific Study of Sexuality.

ANIRUDDHA DAS, Ph.D., is a postdoctoral fellow at the National Opinion Research Center (NORC), University of Chicago. He has published research on masturbation, sexual harassment, and sexual practices and problems among older adults. His other interests include the life course, biodemography, social networks, and semantic analysis.

JOHN DELAMATER, Ph.D., is Conway-Bascom Professor of Sociology at the University of Wisconsin-Madison. His recent research focuses on sexuality through the life course, using a biopsychosocial perspective. He was awarded the 2002 Alfred E. Kinsey Award for distinguished contributions by the Society for the Scientific Study of Sexuality, and he served as editor of *The Journal of Sex Research* from 1998 to 2009.

HEATHER E. DILLAWAY, Ph.D., is Associate Professor and Director of Graduate Studies in Sociology at Wayne State University. Her work on menopause is published in the *Women's Studies Review, Journal of Women & Aging, Healthcare for Women International, Women & Health*, the *NWSA Journal, Sex Roles*, and *Gender & Society*.

YEN LE ESPIRITU, Ph.D., is Professor of Ethnic Studies at the University of California, San Diego. She has authored three award-winning books: *Asian American Panethnicity: Bridging Institutions and Identities*; *Asian American Women and Men: Labor, Laws, and Love*; and *Home Bound: Filipino American Lives Across Cultures, Communities, and Countries*.

ADAM ISAIAH GREEN, Ph.D., is Assistant Professor of Sociology at the University of Toronto. His research sits at the intersection of the sociology of sexuality, theory, and health. His work is published in *Sociological Theory, Theory and Society, Journal of Health and Social Behavior, Social Problems*, and *Social Psychology Quarterly*.

CAROLINE HELDMAN, Ph.D., is Assistant Professor of Politics at Occidental College, Los Angeles. She is a featured media personality on FOX News and Al-Jazeera, and her work has appeared in the top journals in her field. She coedited the popular book *Rethinking Madame President: Is the US Really Ready for a Woman in the White House?*

WILLIAM JEYNES, Ph.D., is Professor of Education at California State University, Long Beach. He has spoken before the White House, G. W. Bush and Obama administrations, and the acting president of South Korea. He has authored more than 100 publications, including 10 books, many of which involve conducting meta-analyses.

EDWARD O. LAUMANN, Ph.D., is George Herbert Mead Distinguished Service Professor of Sociology at the University of Chicago. He was a director of the National Health and Social Life Survey, the principal investigator of the Chicago Health and Social Life Survey, and the co-principal investigator of the National Survey of Chinese Sexual Practices. He is currently a co-investigator on the National Social Life, Health, and Aging Project, sponsored by the National Institute of Aging.

BRONWEN LICHTENSTEIN, Ph.D., is Associate Professor in the Department of Criminal Justice at the University of Alabama and is the author of the forthcoming book *Colonizing Stigma: Race, Gender, and Social Power in the Sexual Epidemics*. She received the 2007 Distinguished Contribution to Scholarship Article Award from the American Sociological Association's Race, Gender, and Class section and the 2010 Career Award for Contributions in the Sociology of HIV/AIDS.

MEIKA LOE, Ph.D., is Associate Professor of Sociology and Women's Studies at Colgate University. She is the author of *The Rise of Viagra: How the Little Blue Pill Changed Sex in America*. She just published her second book, an ethnography on aging, community, and social capital, titled *Aging Our Way: Lessons for Living from 85 and Beyond*.

CHRISTINE E. MOWERY, Ph.D., is Visiting Professor of Sociology at the University of Richmond. Her research interests include gender, social movements, aging, and sexuality. She recently coauthored a chapter titled "How *USA Today* Constructs the Problem of Mercury Pollution" in an interdisciplinary edited book on mercury poisoning.

JOEL A. MURACO is a student in the doctoral program in Family Studies and Human Development at the University of Arizona. His research interests include sexual orientation and adult partner relations, as well as resilience among sexual minority youth.

STEPHEN T. RUSSELL, Ph.D., is Professor and Fitch Nesbitt Endowed Chair in Family and Consumer Sciences in the John and Doris Norton School of Family and Consumer Sciences at the University of Arizona. He studies adolescent pregnancy and parenting, parent-adolescent relationships, and the health and development of sexual minority youth. He is the president-elect of the Society for Research on Adolescence.

KATHLEEN F. SLEVIN, Ph.D., is Chancellor Professor of Sociology at the College of William and Mary. She is the coeditor of *Age Matters: Realigning Feminist Thinking* and the coauthor of a Gender Lens book, *Gender, Inequalities, and Aging*, as well as *From Stumbling Blocks to Stepping Stones: The Life Experiences of Fifty Professional African American Women*.

JEFFRY W. THIGPEN, M.S.W., Ph.D., is Assistant Professor in the School of Social Work at Indiana University. His research interests include childhood sexual behavior, sexual development, sexual culture within families, and sexual health. His most recent work examined the sexual behavior of preadolescent African American children.

KALI S. VAN CAMPEN is a graduate research and teaching associate in the Family Studies and Human Development program in the John and Doris Norton School of Family and Consumer Sciences at the University of Arizona. She conducts research on adolescent sexuality and sexual health, with a focus on sexual socialization and sexual self-efficacy.

LISA WADE holds a Ph.D. in sociology from the University of Wisconsin-Madison and an M.A. in human sexuality from New York University. She is Assistant Professor of Sociology at Occidental College, Los Angeles. She received the 2010 Pacific Sociological Association Early Career Teaching Award for her website Sociological Images (www.thesocietypages.org/socimages).

LINDA J. WAITE, Ph.D., is Lucy Flower Professor in Urban Sociology at the University of Chicago, and Director of the Chicago Center on Aging. She is a principal investigator on the National Social Life, Health, and Aging Project, sponsored by the National Institute of Aging. Her research interests include social demography, aging, families, health, and the links among biology, psychology, and the social world.

Index

Abortion, 73–74, 218, 224, 226, 235n6

Abstinence, 70, 73, 76. *See also* Celibacy; Virginity

Abuse, sexual, 12, 24, 27, 40, 45–46, 88, 106n1, 183, 190–191, 238–239, 285–286, 293. *See also* Assault; Victimization; Violence in intimate relationships

Abusive partners, 131, 188–190, 194–195, 303. *See also* Violence in intimate relationships

Academic achievement, 109, 112–113. *See also* Educational trajectories

Accentuation effect, 91. *See also* Cumulative advantages and disadvantages

Adolescence, 17, 71–87, 149–150, 180–181, 236, 238–239, 303, 306–307, 310. *See also* Puberty; Teenagers

Affection, 128–129, 142–143, 155

African Americans, 11, 16, 19, 33, 45–68, 69n10, 81, 83–85, 104, 130, 196–197, 202–203, 213, 224, 230, 234, 240, 261–263, 288–289, 295n8, 308–309, 314. *See also* Ethnicity; Race

Age, 31, 47, 74–75, 88, 99–101, 105, 132, 151, 182, 189, 191, 196–198, 202, 205, 227, 234, 239, 242–246, 248–249, 253–255, 257–258, 302, 307

Age difference between partners. *See* Age hypergamy

Age hypergamy, 81, 181, 240, 250–251, 253, 258, 268–269

Ageism, 6, 181, 190, 208–210, 260–262, 268–270, 273–275, 277, 293

The Ageless Self (book), 281

Agency, 15, 29–31, 36–37, 71, 74–76, 78, 84–86, 138, 199, 201–205, 208–214, 286, 295n1, 305–306, 308, 313

Aggression, sexual, 45–46, 308. *See also* Assault; Victimization; Violence

Aging, 6, 14, 17, 28, 40, 181, 190, 218, 260–263, 267–269, 272–273, 310

AIDS. *See* HIV/AIDS

Alcohol use, 103, 128–129, 131, 134, 136–139, 144, 150, 189, 194–195. *See also* Drug use

American Sociological Association, 4, 16–17

Americanization, 164, 169, 178–179. *See also* Modernization

Anal sex, 65

Andropause, 8–9, 313. *See also* Climacteric; Menopause

Appearance, physical, 15–16, 72, 139, 180, 182, 190, 193, 246, 265, 269–273, 276, 290–291, 305, 308–309. *See also* Body image; Cosmetic surgery

Armstrong, Elizabeth A., 130–131

Arousal. *See* Desire

Asexuality, 34, 36, 80, 157, 199, 223

Asian Americans, 82–83, 163, 165, 174, 240. *See also* Ethnicity; Filipino Americans; Race

Assault, sexual, 34, 88–105, 106n1, 128, 131, 301, 303. *See also* Aggression; Coerced sex; Violence

Athill, Diana, 294

Attitudes, sexual, 7, 10, 111, 123–124, 135–136, 172–179, 253–255

Attractiveness. *See* Appearance; Body image

Australia, 74

Conflict Tactics Scale (CTS), 94, 106n4
Connidis, Ingrid, 282
Constant comparison method, 184, 200.
    See also Grounded theory
Continuity and discontinuity, across life
    course, 13, 68, 91, 238, 258, 281–282, 302
Contraception, 30, 37, 73, 81, 84, 123–124,
    222–223, 225, 233, 281. See also Birth
    control; Condom use; Safer sex
Control groups, 114
Coping mechanisms, 208, 267
Copper, Baba, 276
Cosmetic surgery, 273–275, 307, 310–311.
    See also Appearance; Body image
Couples, 10, 16, 186, 194–195, 238–240, 256–
    258. See also Partners and Partnering
Courtship, 169–170, 181, 195, 302, 306. See
    also Dating; Relationship formation
Creativity, 16, 205, 286, 292, 294, 306. See
    also Experimentation, sexual
Cultural capital, 261, 311
Culture, 45, 48–50, 78, 174–175, 179, 153, 307
Cumulative advantages and disadvan-
    tages, 8, 24–27, 30, 36, 39–40, 202, 211,
    303–304, 310
Cumulative processes, 7, 10, 12–16, 23,
    33, 81, 89–91, 233–234, 278, 280–282,
    284–286, 293, 300, 313

Dating, 80–81, 129, 132, 144, 171, 180–197,
    202–203, 211–213, 310, 312–313. See also
    Courtship; Relationship formation
DeLamater, John, 13–14, 63
Delinquency, 84, 89
DES (Diethylstilbestrol) daughters, 225,
    235n7
Desirability, 172, 193, 250. See also Appear-
    ance, physical
Desire, 14, 28, 33–39, 74, 76–78, 143, 181, 193,
    204, 219, 223–224, 238–239, 245–248, 260,
    276, 284, 304. See also Interest in sex
Development. See Cognitive development;
    Psychological development
Diamond, Lisa, 12–13
Disability, 198–214, 283–285, 294, 302,
    304–305, 307, 310

Disciplinary background of contributors,
    17–18
Disciplining the body, 270, 309
Distancing, from age peers, 268–270,
    275–276, 295n3
Diversity within cohorts, 27–28
Divorce, 26, 30, 90, 102, 112, 125, 149,
    182–183, 198, 232, 234, 239, 302, 309;
    effects on children, 109–126, 303. See also
    Relationship dissolution; Separation
Domestic violence. See Violence in inti-
    mate relationships
Donnelly, Denise, 13, 16
Double standard, sexual, 76, 83, 172, 174,
    256, 261
Drug use (illicit), 103, 131, 134, 150, 189, 195.
    See also Alcohol use
DuBois, L. Zachary, 20
Dyads. See Couples; Partners and
    partnering
Dysfunction, sexual, 27, 103, 105, 219, 236,
    246, 248, 252–253. See also Erectile dif-
    ficulties; Lubrication

Eating disorders, 84. See also Body image
Edin, Kathryn, 131
Educational trajectories, 26–27, 30, 84, 301,
    310. See also Academic achievement;
    School culture
Ehrhardt, Anke, 64
Elder, Glen Jr., 9–10, 25
Elder Hostel, 285, 295n6
Elderhood, 295n1. See also Later life; Old
    age
Elopement, 170
Embodiment. See Bodies
Emotional intimacy, 130, 140, 156–157, 188,
    245
Employment trajectories, 25–27, 30, 36, 130,
    167, 173, 187, 229, 292, 316
"Empty nest syndrome," 6–7
Entrainment model, 238, 258
Erectile difficulties, 8–9, 37, 193, 209, 211,
    246–248. See also Dysfunction, sexual
Erection-enhancing medications, 9, 180,
    204–207, 209, 307

Gender theory, 8, 31–32, 64, 201, 207

"Gendered sexuality over the life course" framework, 24–25, 35, 300, 312–315

Genealogical analysis, 3, 22n1

Generation, 172–179, 192, 287, 300, 306–307, 310. *See also* Cohort effects; *specific generations*

Generation X, 30, 227

Geographic variation, in sexuality, 15, 19, 23, 67, 79, 185, 194. *See also* Immigration; *specific countries*

Germany, 73

Gerschick, Thomas, 204

"GI" Generation, 29, 279, 281

Gibson, Diane, 181

Giele, Janet, 10

Glaser, Barney, 184

Global Study of Sexual Attitudes and Behaviors (GSSAB), 237

Gonzalez-Lopez, Gloria, 15–16, 163

Gordon, Betty, 47

Gott, Merryn, 282

Grandmothers, sexuality of, 181

Great Depression, 9

Green, Adam, 22n1

Greer, Richard, 12

Grounded theory, 200. *See also* Constant comparative method

Hamilton, Laura, 130–131

Harassment, sexual, 187, 315. *See also* Aggression, sexual

Health, physical, 11, 14–16, 27–28, 36–37, 40, 73, 79–81, 146, 182, 193, 195, 217, 240, 245–253, 255–256, 272, 279, 284, 286, 288, 290, 294, 295n11, 310, 312, 316. *See also* Illness

Health providers, 197, 208–209, 213

Helms, Janet, 49

Heteronormativity, 67, 76, 79–80, 85, 125, 149–150, 155, 157–158, 160n1, 310

Heterosexism, 78

Heterosexuality, 31–32, 80, 135, 267, 277n2, 311. *See also* Sexual identity; Sexual orientation

Higgins, Jenny, 21

High school, 139, 312. *See also* Educational trajectories; School culture

Hirsch, Jennifer, 21

Hispanic Americans. *See* Latino/as; Mexican Americans

Historical context, 23, 29–30, 72, 159, 171, 173–174, 264, 266, 299–300, 306–307

HIV/AIDS, 30, 81, 84, 86, 180–182, 190–191, 266, 312

Homophobia, 32, 78–79, 81

Homosexuality, 79, 139, 238. *See also* Gay men; Lesbians; LGBTQ youth; Queer sexualities; Sexual identity; Sexual orientation

Hondegneu-Sotelo, Pierrette, 163

Hooking up, 128–145, 151. *See also* Casual sex

Hormone replacement therapy, 5, 265

Human subject review, 21. *See also* Research methods

Hurd, Laura, 269, 277n2

Hyde, Janet, 14, 63

"Hypersexuality," 67, 165–168, 172, 175

Hysterectomy, 228–230, 233–234, 235n6

Identities, intersecting, 11, 19–20, 32, 299, 301, 304, 307–308, 311

Identity, social, 13, 150, 205, 275, 290

Illness, 7, 15–16, 19, 28–29, 37, 195, 233, 235n6, 246, 304–305. *See also* Health, physical

Immigration, 15, 19, 40, 83–84, 163–165, 169–179, 292, 302, 306, 316

Impairment, physical. *See* Disability

Impotence. *See* Erectile difficulties

Independence, 170–173, 205–206

Individual models of sexual expression, 236, 249

Inequality, 26–27, 131. *See also specific forms of inequality*

Infertility, 224–225, 227, 230–231, 233–234, 305

Infidelity, 160n4, 190–191, 195, 240

Ingraham, Chrys, 31

Initiation, sexual, 28–29, 33–34, 46, 74, 81, 89, 303, 306. *See also* Virginity loss

Innocence, 45, 48–49, 67, 83. *See also* Virginity

Institutions, social, 37, 152–153, 155, 312–313. *See also specific institutions*

Intellectual stimulation, 279, 291–292

Interactional continuity. *See* Cumulative processes

Interactionist theories, 31–32, 311

Intercourse-centered approach, critique of, 282, 293

Interdisciplinary approaches to sexuality research, 4, 18, 72

Interest in sex, 5, 7, 58–59, 62–63, 70, 241, 243, 245–246, 248, 258. *See also* Desire

Intergenerational dynamics, 179, 280, 294, 312

Internet, 79, 190, 195–196. *See also* Technology

Intersectionality. *See* Identities, intersecting

Interview data, 148–149, 165, 183–184, 200, 219–222, 233, 263, 280. *See also* Research methods

Intimacy, 90, 130, 132, 140, 203, 208–212, 279, 281–284, 286–289, 292

Isolation, in old age, 281, 293

Jewish Americans, 283–284, 291, 295n10. *See also* Ethnicity; European Americans

Kaschak, Ellyn, 282

Kaufman, Sharon, 281

Kefalas, Maria, 131

Kimmel, Michael, 130, 139

Kinsey, Alfred, 21

Kinship. *See* Families; Fictive kin

Kissing, 74, 137, 284

Koch, Patricia, 16–17

Koppel, Lily, 294

Later life, 236–258, 308. *See also* Old age

Latinos/as, 49, 82–83, 85, 130, 240–241, 290, 309. *See also* Ethnicity; Mexican Americans

Laub, Carolyn, 86

Laumann, Edward, 12, 16, 27, 46, 65, 90, 103, 295n5

Lauritsen, Janet, 91

Laws, Glenda, 276

Learning theory, 90

Lesbians, 79, 130, 229, 232–233, 260–276, 287, 310. *See also* LGBTQ youth; Queer sexualities; Sexual identity; Sexual orientation

Levy, Judith, 278

LGBTQ youth, 79, 85, 125. *See also* Gay men; Homosexuality; Lesbians; Queer sexualities

Liberation, sexual, 155

Libido. *See* Desire; Interest in sex

Life course perspective, 3–4, 9–17, 24–29, 41n3, 90, 109–110, 129, 179, 199, 264–265, 275, 282, 289, 299–301

Life History Calendar, 36

Life stages, 217, 283, 299. *See also specific life stages*

Life-stage principle, 9, 12, 20, 38, 91, 300, 302

Life-stage transitions, 34, 37, 39, 129, 301

Linked lives, 178, 199, 214, 232, 278, 294, 312, *See also* Social networks

Longevity, 182, 249–250, 253, 294–295. *See also* Health, physical

Longitudinal research, 13, 104, 236, 304, 313–315. *See also* Research methods

Looking-glass self, 156

Love, 10, 140, 254–255, 312. *See also* Affection; Romance

Lubrication, 28, 246–248. *See also* Dysfunction, sexual

Lucal, Betsy, 31

Mahay, Jenna, 65

Male gaze, 262, 276

Manalansan, Martin, 164

Marginalization. *See specific marginalized groups*

Marin, Barbara, 64

Marriage, 26, 99, 105, 119, 131, 146, 149, 163, 173, 182, 195, 231–232, 235n2, 235n4, 302, 304, 313; same-sex, 29, 79, 125, 147, 150, 154–160, 304, 306. *See also* Relationship status

Relationship formation, 12–13, 25–26, 36–37, 92, 94, 98, 129–130, 144, 153, 198, 316. *See also* Cohabitation; Marriage; Partner seeking

Relationship status, 34, 200, 202, 220, 235n2, 235n4, 255. *See also specific statuses*

Relationships, 12, 90, 92, 94, 131, 151, 153–154, 170, 208–209, 232, 251–253, 265–266, 309, 315. *See also* Partners and partnering; *specific types of relationships*

Religion and religious institutions, 23, 38–39, 65, 130–131, 186, 254–255, 288, 290, 293, 295n10

Remarriage, 111, 113, 123–124, 149, 229, 232, 234, 285. *See also* Relationship formation

Reproduction, 5–6, 147, 217–234, 313. *See also* Childbearing; Pregnancy

Reproductive aging, 218, 228–229, 309. *See also* Andropause; Climacteric; Menopause

Reputation, sexual, 186, 188. *See also* Respectability

Research methods, 10–13, 19, 27, 67, 93, 104, 116, 132–134, 148–149, 165, 183–184, 200–201, 219–222, 226, 235n8, 263–264, 280–281, 313–314. *See also specific methods*

Resistance, 39, 75–76, 85–86, 175–176, 262–263, 274–275

Respectability, 167–168. *See also* Reputation

Retirement, 286. *See also* Employment trajectories

Reynolds, Margaret, 182

Rich, Adrienne, 287

Riley, Matilda White, 28

Rind, Bruce, 102, 106n2

Riot Grrrl movement, 85

"Risk" approach to adolescent sexuality, 71–73, 84

Risk taking, 27, 46, 78, 81, 83–84, 89, 103, 144, 184–185, 187, 189–190, 235n5, 240, 287–288, 308–309

Rites of passage, 32, 150–151

Road Scholar, 295n6. *See also* Elder Hostel

Romance, 10, 74, 80, 83, 86, 184, 193, 283–285, 293. *See also* Love

Rossi, Alice, 3, 10–11, 20, 299

Rostosky, Sharon, 181

Rubin, Gayle, 31

Russell, Stephen, 80

Rutter, Michael, 63

Safer sex, 123–124, 185, 191–192, 196. *See also* Birth control; Condom use; Contraception

Sampling methods, 165, 200, 214, 219, 236, 263, 311, 314. *See also* Research methods

San Diego, 164, 312

Sanger, Margaret, 281

Satisfaction: relationship, 6, 15–16, 36, 74, 90, 102–103; sexual, 6, 16, 129, 141–142, 154, 198, 203, 209, 282–284, 313. *See also* Orgasm; Pleasure

Savin-Williams, Ritch, 12–13, 79

Schalet, Amy, 73

Schlesinger, Lynn, 15–16

Scholastic Aptitude Test (SAT), 112

School culture, 135, 167, 176. *See also* College; Educational trajectories; High school

Scripts, sexual. *See* Sexual scripts

Self-esteem, 27, 78, 143, 187, 207, 270, 290–291

Self-fulfilling prophecy, 91, 199

Self-image, 7, 91, 194–195

Sensory pleasure, 278–279, 294

Separation, 92, 309. *See also* Divorce; Relationship dissolution

Sequencing, of life transitions, 13, 301–302, 314

Sex, definitions of, 237–238

Sex drive. *See* Desire; Interest in sex

Sex education, 17, 49, 70, 72, 197, 199

Sex ratios, 171, 278–279, 281

Sex work, 89, 166, 315

Sexism, 75, 181

Sexual health, 41n4, 71, 82, 194, 196–197, 315

Sexual identity, 12–13, 24, 30–34, 39–40, 41n1, 77–78, 160, 164, 198, 235n2, 300. *See also* Sexual orientation; *specific identities*

Sexual orientation, 11, 71, 75, 130, 154, 159, 198, 238, 250, 259n3, 262, 264–268, 271, 276, 304, 310–311. *See also* Sexual identity; *specific orientations*

Valentine, David, 31
Vance, Carole, 21
Viagra. *See* Erection-enhancing
  medications
Victimization, 45, 84, 88, 95, 101–103, 236,
  238, 295n5; serial, 89, 91–92, 101–103,
  105. *See also* Abuse; Assault; Trauma;
  Violence
Violence, 101, 106n6, 131, 304; in intimate
  relationships, 89, 91, 94–95, 98, 183,
  195. *See also* Abuse; Abusive partners;
  Assault; Coerced sex; Victimization
Virginity, 16, 30, 130, 143, 172–174, 179, 284.
  See also Abstinence; Innocence
Virginity loss, 28–29, 34, 73, 134, 137, 143.
  See also Initiation
Volunteering, 287, 292
Voyeuristic behavior, 58–59, 62–63
Vulnerability, sexual, 174

Wade, Lisa, 13
Waite, Linda, 16–17
Walster, Elaine (Hatfield), 21

Warner, Michael, 160n1
Weber, Lynn, 32
Weber, Max, 150
Wertlieb, Donald, 109
West, Candace, 66
Whitbeck, Les, 195
White Americans. *See* European
  Americans
Widowhood, 29, 36, 113, 181, 186, 193, 239,
  249, 279, 285, 288, 291. *See also* Relation-
  ship dissolution
Wilkins, Amy, 131
Witten, Tarynn, 20–21
Wolf, Diane, 165
Women's movement, 30, 73, 141
Woolwine, David, 158
World Health Organization, 41n4
World Values Survey, 160n4
World War II, 29

Youth, cultural valuation of, 180, 261, 267–
  268, 270, 274–275. *See also* Adolescence;
  Ageism; Childhood; Teenagers